SALES COMPENSATION ALMANAC 2020

DAVID J. CICHELLI

About the Alexander Group, Inc.

The Alexander Group (www.alexandergroup.com) provides revenue growth consulting services to the world's leading go-to-customer organizations, serving Global 2000 companies from across all industries. Founded in 1985, Alexander Group combines deep experience, a proven methodology and data-driven insights to help revenue acquisition leaders anticipate change, align their customer contact force with company goals and make better informed decisions with one goal in mind–to grow sales. The Alexander Group has offices in Atlanta, Chicago, San Francisco, Scottsdale, Stamford and London.

Our Sales Compensation Consulting Services

As the leading firm in sales compensation design, we help our clients create incentive plans that align selling resources with corporate objectives. The Alexander Group is the recognized thought leader in sales compensation solutions, as widely acknowledged by clients and professional associations.

We have helped thousands of clients, including worldwide sales organizations, realize the full benefits of effective sales compensation programs to reward and recognize high-performing sales resources.

From strategic alignment to design, market pricing and program implementation, we can help with all elements of your sales compensation program.

AGI Press

2020 Sales Compensation Almanac

ISBN: 978-0-9899480-8-1

For information about this title or to order other books, contact us at www.alexandergroup.com.

TABLE OF CONTENTS

ACKNOWLEDGMENTS

The Alexander Group's *Sales Compensation Almanac* is now in its seventh edition. The *2020 Sales Compensation Almanac* provides contemporary reference information, research findings and case studies reflecting the Alexander Group's sales compensation consulting practice leadership.

I would like to extend my gratitude to those who have contributed to this resource book.

A high-value feature of the Almanac is the market survey trends and practices reports. Thank you to the hundreds of sales compensation professionals, who carefully and thoroughly complete the survey questionnaires. Your submissions provide the basis for leading-edge reports on contemporary sales compensation practices.

I would like to acknowledge OpenSymmetry for generously providing the *Sales Compensation Automation Solutions Vendor Guide* for reprint.

Thank you to the many companies who develop and provide market pay surveys. These companies have completed and submitted their product profiles featured here. I would like to recognize Emily Schur in the Scottsdale office for compiling the *Reference Guide to Sales Compensation Surveys.*

The Almanac features the work of several Alexander Group consultants, who have prepared case studies and insightful whitepapers for this edition. They are Dashon Catlett and Devan Cortland of the Atlanta office; Mason Ginsberg and Yang Liu of the Chicago office; Arshad Carim of the San Francisco office; and Mike Burnett, Mick Cannon and Tim Meuschke of the Stamford, Conn., office.

Thanks to Lori Feuer, editor-in-chief, who has edited and managed the production and distribution of this edition.

Finally, to my wife, Kathleen, thanks for your loving support.

INTRODUCTION

INTRODUCTION

Welcome to the seventh edition of the *Sales Compensation Almanac!*

The *2020 Sales Compensation Almanac* provides the latest trends, resources and insights into sales compensation solutions. Look for a new edition as we update select topics, findings and resources to reflect current content. The *2020 Sales Compensation Almanac* features a new survey, *Careers in Sales Compensation Survey,* which provides an up-close look at people working in the sales compensation field and advice for those seeking to enter the field.

What is the *Sales Compensation Almanac?*

For many sales entities, sales compensation is an important management tool, yet needs constant attention. Excellent designs one year may give way to necessary updates and revisions the following year. Sales compensation stakeholders, including executive management, sales leaders, finance and HR professionals, are often looking for specific resources, survey findings and publications to address sales compensation design and administration challenges. The *Sales Compensation Almanac* provides the latest research and resources in this space.

2020 Edition Sections

This year's edition contains the following sections:

Sales Compensation Trends Survey. Conducted each December and published in January of the following year, the *Sales Compensation Trends Survey* provides a look back at the previous year and a look forward to the next fiscal year on key sales compensation metrics, such as budgets, costs, turnover, program changes and program effectiveness. The survey also presents the results of select topics regarding specific and topical sales compensation challenges. The full survey results are available to survey participants exclusively for six months.

Sales Compensation Hot Topics Survey. Each year, the sales compensation "hot topics" survey provides in-depth insight into select sales compensation practices. The *Sales Compensation Hot Topics Survey* examined recent and popular topics in sales compensation practices, including sales personnel—new hires, equity incentives, specialty customer contact jobs, new FASB regulations, performance measure categories used in the primary sales job and sales compensation practices for the first-line sales manager.

NEW: Careers in Sales Compensation Survey. The *Careers in Sales Compensation Survey* is a new survey conducted by the Alexander Group. The survey provides an in-depth profile of sales compensation professionals and advice for those interested in entering the field.

Multiyear Research Findings–Trends and Practices Surveys. Our many years of sales compensation research offer compelling multiyear observations.

Sales Compensation Market Pay Surveys. Need to locate a sales compensation market pay survey? The *Reference Guide to Sales Compensation Surveys* catalogs many of the available surveys on sales compensation pay levels. Use these vendor products to price and manage your sales compensation costs.

Sales Compensation Administration Vendors. Sales compensation administration software and service providers use powerful administration tools to track, report and model sales compensation transactions. Use this list of vendors to locate and assess the right administration software to help manage your pay program.

Educational and Publication Resources. Use these resources to help gain leading-edge knowledge about sales compensation concepts and principles.

Sales Compensation Case Studies. Learn how other companies examine and update their sales compensation practices with case studies from the Alexander Group's client engagements. The case studies include the following industries:

- Financial Services
- Hospitality
- Manufacturing (2)
- Media (2)
- Pharmaceutical Distribution

Whitepapers. Explore select topics authored by the Alexander Group's consultants. This book features whitepapers on the following topics:

- Key Considerations for Transitioning Between Sales Compensation Plans
- Sales Compensation: Are Corporate Measures Wrong?

- Sales Compensation Options for Sales Force Integration
- Sales Compensation Plans: Should Payouts Have A Performance Threshold?

Recent Articles of Interest. Finally, view our listing of the latest published sales compensation articles.

SALES COMPENSATION SERVICES

WORLD-CLASS SALES COMPENSATION SOLUTIONS

Assessment. The Alexander Group's program assessment incorporates a review of your current practices and objectives. The assessment report encompasses a checklist of action items and suggestions for further consideration. Our assessment report answers your most pressing question: "How well is the current plan working?" Our team can determine if your current practices are effective, need minor modification or a major redesign.

Design. During our design engagements, the Alexander Group reviews the results of the fact-finding efforts, provides alternative designs for evaluation and helps with the selection of preferred plans. Once your management team selects the plan, the focus shifts to the development phase to estimate costs and document the new plans. Finally, implementation includes the creation of all supporting materials to train managers and communicate the new plan to staff.

Depending on your firm's needs and circumstances, the Alexander Group can help reconfigure your support programs, including quota allocation, sales crediting, account management and plan automation.

Implementation. We provide hands-on implementation support, including creating program collateral, training managers and ensuring program adoption. Additional services ensure that your administration team has all of the plan elements fully defined in order to automate the new pay program.

Program Management. Need sales compensation program management protocols? We can create design principles, plan parameters, platform jobs, and governance and program accountabilities. Use these program management solutions to keep widely dispersed stakeholders aligned with best practices and sanctioned corporate policies.

The Alexander Group's consultants have helped nearly half of the Fortune 1000 increase sales and profits through the effective design and implementation of sales strategies and solutions. Our incentive compensation solutions leverage the best ideas and adapt them to your organization's needs and circumstances.

OFFICES

Atlanta 404.249.1338

Chicago 312.357.0500

San Francisco 415.391.3900

Scottsdale 480.998.9644

Stamford 203.975.9344

London +44.2037.249417

SALES COMPENSATION TRENDS SURVEY

2019 SALES COMPENSATION TRENDS SURVEY

Conducted each December and published in January of the following year, the *Sales Compensation Trends Survey* provides a look back at the previous year and a look forward to the next fiscal year on key sales compensation metrics, such as budgets, costs, turnover, program changes and program effectiveness. The survey also presents the results of select topics regarding specific and topical sales compensation challenges. The full survey results are available to survey participants exclusively for six months.

IN THIS SECTION

- Executive Summary
- Multiyear Trends
- Sales Department Trends
- Sales Compensation–What Happened in 2018?
- Sales Compensation–What Will Happen in 2019?
- Sales Compensation Changes Planned for the Primary Sales Job in 2019
- Quotas
- Most Asked Questions
- Demographics

EXECUTIVE SUMMARY

Overall Observations

Sales departments increased sales volume 6% in 2018. This was equal to the estimated growth of 6% projected at the end of December 2017 for 2018 performance. Meanwhile, sales leaders expect sales revenue to grow 6% in 2019.

3% was the median increase in incentive payments to sales personnel in 2018, exceeding the planned 2% increase anticipated at the beginning of the year. 3% is the projected increase in incentive payments for 2019.

Noteworthy Change: Headcount expansion jumped from 49.6% of companies planning headcount increases in 2018 to 59% planning headcount expansion in 2019. There is no evidence of significant wage or incentive inflation occurring in 2019.

Introduction

80 sales departments participated in this year's 17th annual *2019 Sales Compensation Trends Survey©*. Participants provided data in November and December 2018 on what occurred in 2018 and what they plan for 2019.

2019 KEY METRICS

2019 Revenue Expectations

10th Perc	25th Perc	50th Perc	75th Perc	90th Perc	Average
2	4	6	10	26.8	10.1

2018 Increase in Incentive Pay Compared to 2017

10th Perc	25th Perc	50th Perc	75th Perc	90th Perc	Average
−5	0	3	9.5	17.6	4.7

2019 Average Change in Base Pay

10th Perc	25th Perc	50th Perc	75th Perc	90th Perc	Average
2	3	3	3	4	3.3

2019 Increase in Total Earnings for Primary Sales Job

10th Perc	25th Perc	50th Perc	75th Perc	90th Perc	Average
0	0	3	4	9.1	2.8

MULTIYEAR TRENDS

2014 to 2019 Sales Revenue Trends

2018 sales growth was 6%. Survey participants are projecting 6% growth for 2019. Sales projection and actual sales outcomes were 6% (median) for 2018.

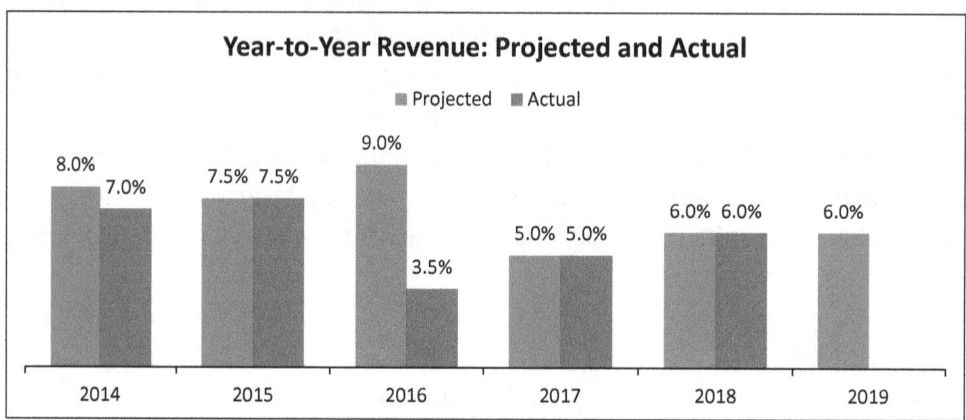

2015 to 2019 Staffing Changes

59% of the respondents plan to increase staffing in 2019. While 49.6% *projected* staffing growth for 2018, 66.3% reported *actual* staffing growth in 2018.

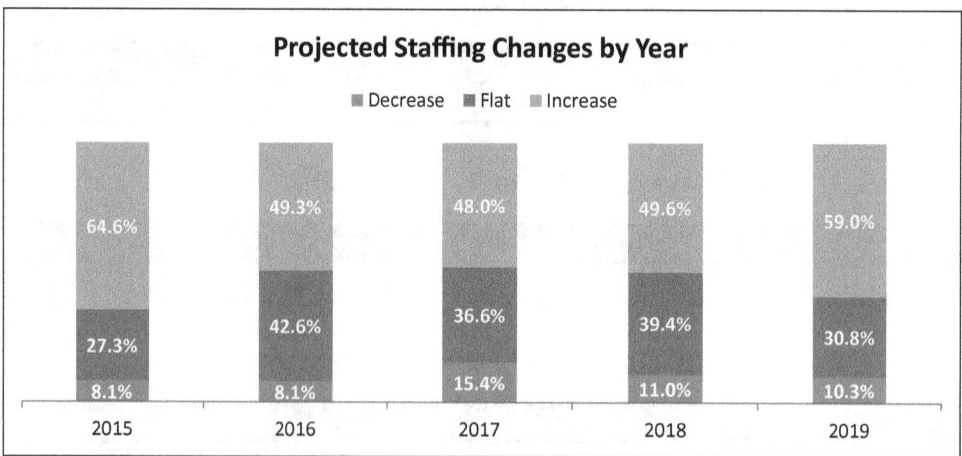

2014 to 2019 Sales Compensation Incentive Payouts

The 2018 3% actual incentive payouts exceed the 2% median estimate made at the end of 2017. Sales leadership projects 3% increase in payouts for 2019.

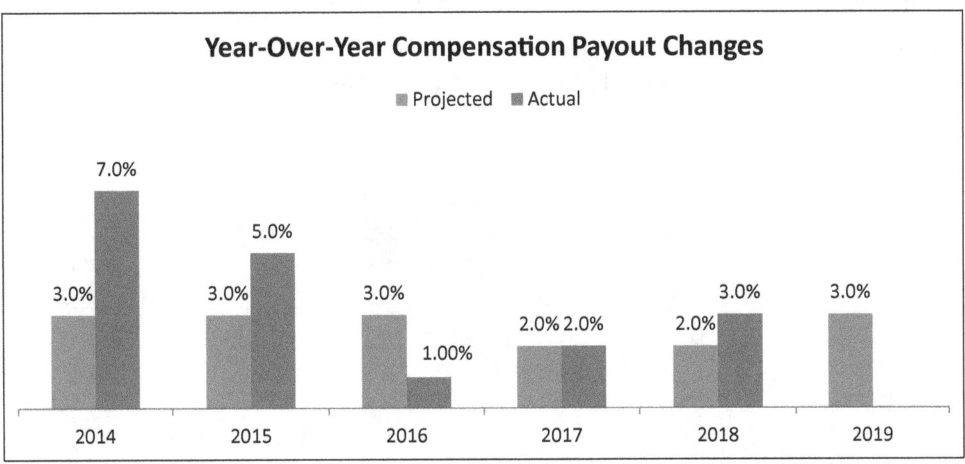

2014 to 2018 Sales Compensation Plan Effectiveness

67.9% of the reporting companies rated their 2018 sales compensation plans as effective.

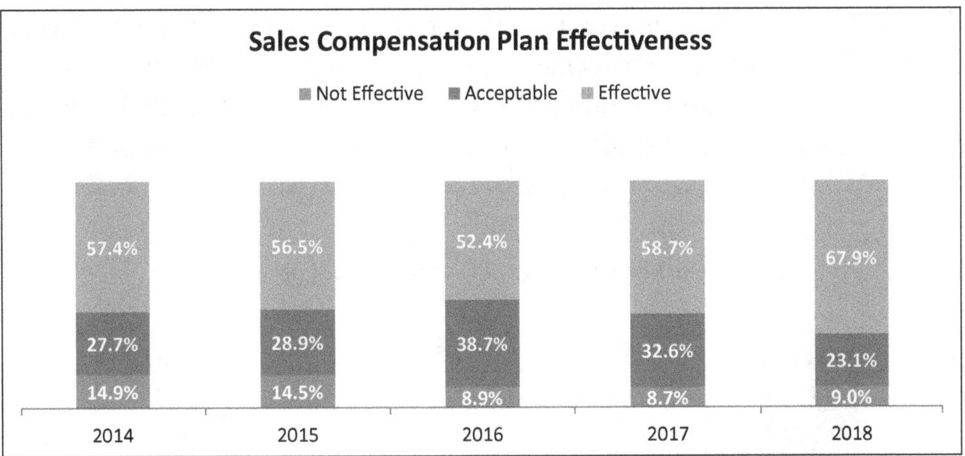

2015 to 2019 Planned Program Changes

Each year, approximately 90% of the reporting companies make sales compensation plan changes. 96.2% will make changes to their 2019 sales compensation plans. This is an increase from historical norms.

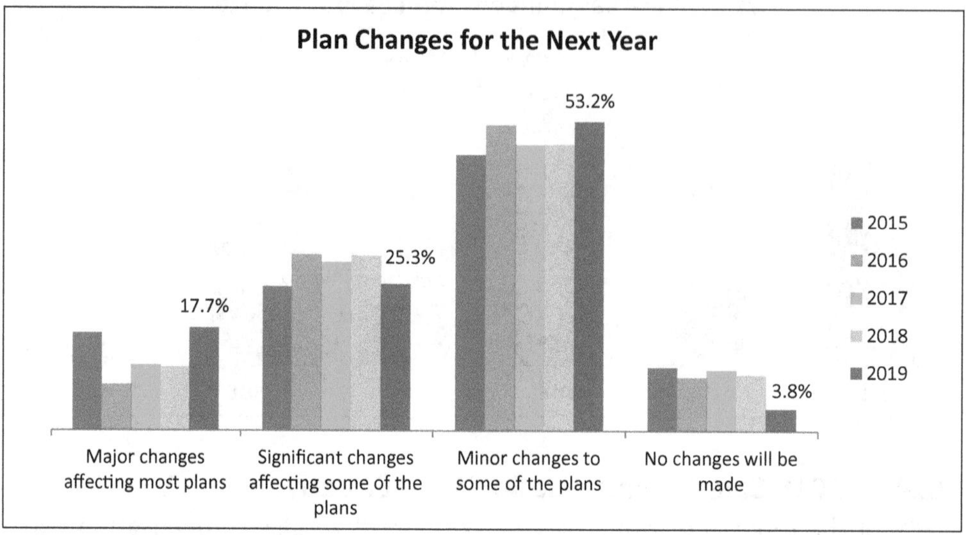

2016 to 2019 Next Year's Sales Compensation Challenges

At 58.8% of the reporting companies, correct goal/quota setting retains its unrivaled position as the most challenging part of sales compensation program effectiveness. Joining the traditional top five sales compensation challenges are the following important challenges for 2019: timely quota distribution (25%); sales data for compensation purposes (22.5%) and fixing the pay mix (21.3%).

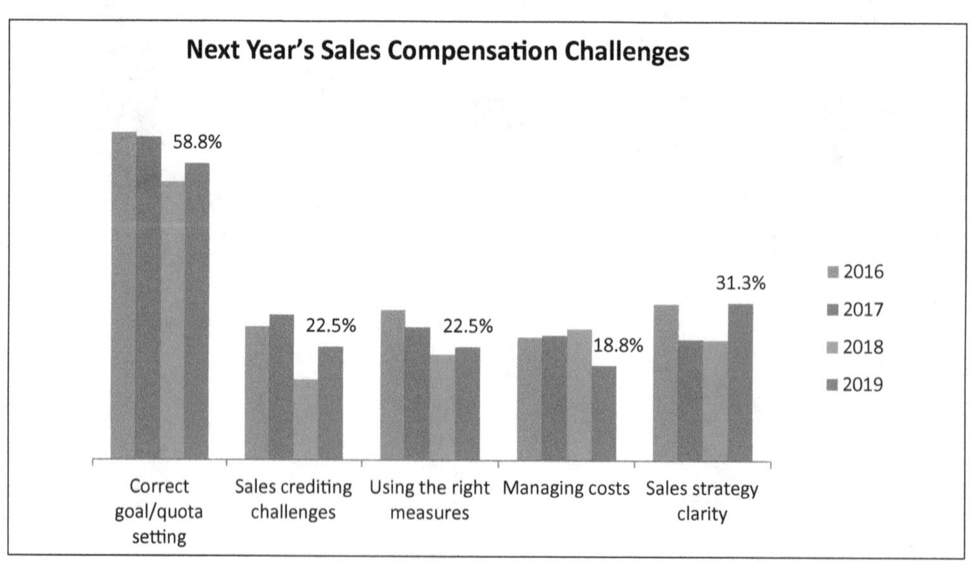

2015 to 2019 Most Common Plan Changes

43.6% identified changing performance measures as the most common program change for the primary sales job for 2019. New to the top five common plan changes is component weighting (35.9%).

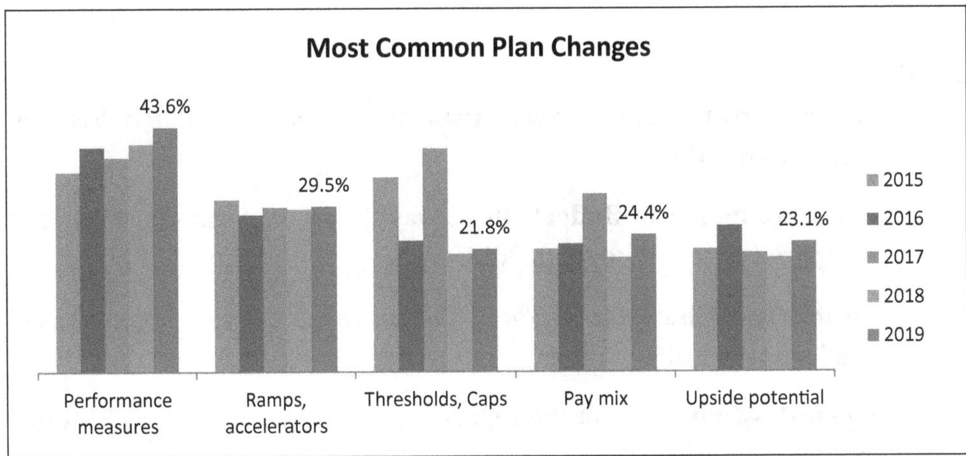

2016 to 2019 Most Common Performance Measures

79.5% of the reporting companies use sales revenue as the primary performance measure in the 2019 incentive plan. 34.6% rate units/orders as the second most important measure. Both measures reflect a focus on volume production. Joining the top five performance measures list in 2019 is renewals (21.8%).

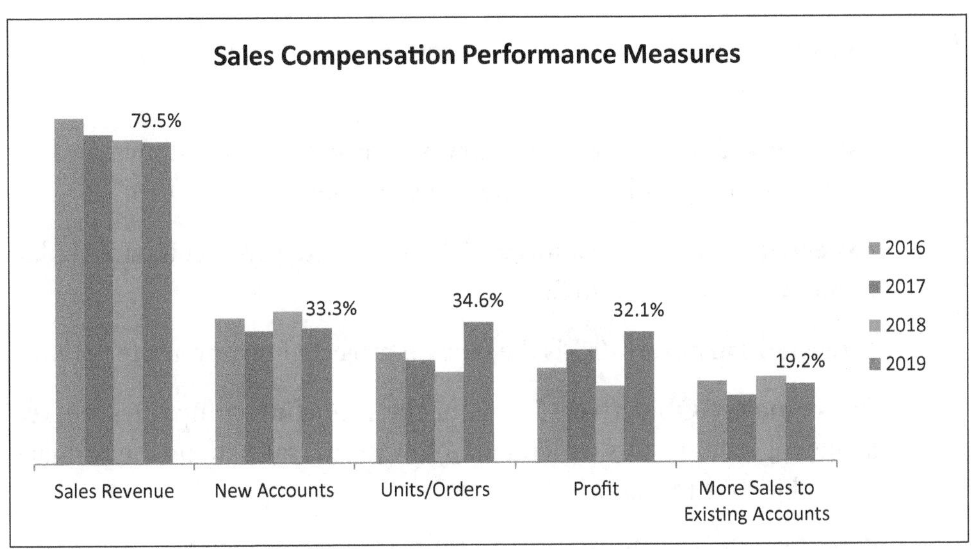

SALES DEPARTMENT TRENDS

Sales department practices vary by business conditions and market ambitions of each individual company. Gathering observations from many companies, however, can provide a summary overview of market movement, prevailing practices and general trends.

2018

- **Actual Percent Revenue Performance:** 6% was the *median* increase in revenue for 2018.
- **Sales Compared to Budget:** 100% was the *median* sales performance compared to sales budget in 2018.
- **Headcount Changes:** 66.3% of the surveyed companies increased headcount in 2018.
- **Open Positions:** 62% of the reporting companies had 1% to 5% open sales positions in 2018.
- **Turnover:** 10% was the *median* turnover rate in 2018. 46.1% had turnover of less than 9%.

2019

- **Revenue Expectations:** 6% is the expected *median* increase in revenue for 2019.
- **Sales Strategic Focus:** 28.8% cite grow existing business as the primary sales objective for 2019.
- **Sales Confidence:** 57% of the survey respondents have above-average confidence they will achieve their revenue objective for 2019.
- **Expected Headcount Changes:** 59% of the surveyed companies plan to increase headcount in 2019.
- **Projected Turnover:** 10% is the *median* projected turnover rate for 2019.
- **Performance Objectives:** 75.9% of the reporting companies ranked achieving sales results (revenue/bookings/unit sales) to be the primary sales objective for 2019.
- **Sales Effectiveness Initiatives:** 60.8% listed improving sales productivity as the primary sales effectiveness initiative for 2019.

Summary Observations

Revenue Performance. Revenue growth projections provide an indicator of the overall economic health of a company. Accurate estimates of revenue growth help ensure that sales management correctly resources sales programs and fairly assigns goals. Sales projections affect many sales management programs, including productivity improvement efforts such as staffing and training and reward programs such as sales compensation. Additionally, revenue projections will affect the size of assigned sales quotas, which, of course, affect incentive payouts.

55.9% of the reporting companies achieved between 95% and 104% of their sales budget for 2018. The 6% actual performance matches the expected growth number of 6%. A 6% median projected increase in revenue for 2019 matches 2018 performance. 57% of the survey respondents have above-average confidence they will achieve their revenue objective for 2019. The top three sales objectives for 2019 include achieving sales results (revenue/bookings/unit sales), ensuring account growth and managing profit/price/discounting.

Headcount Changes. Headcount changes are also another indicator of financial health. Comparisons to headcount changes, including growth and turnover rates, provide a reference for sales force planning. We consider staffing growth above 50% a positive economic indicator, and staffing growth below 50% a negative indicator.

2018 recorded a jump in staff sales expansion. While turnover remained consistent with previous years, companies adding head count increased from 47.1% in 2017 to 66.3% in 2018. For 2019, 59% of the companies plan to add staff, continuing the staff expansion trend. Turnover for 2018 was 10%, consistent with past years. Management expects this number to remain at 10% in 2019.

Performance Initiatives for 2019. These are the top three sales improvement objectives for 2019: improving sales productivity, improving sales process and increasing performance accountability.

2018 Actual Percent Revenue Performance: For your division sales unit, what percentage change in revenue performance occurred from 2017 to 2018?

10th Perc	25th Perc	50th Perc	75th Perc	90th Perc	Average
–1	2	6	11	24	12.3

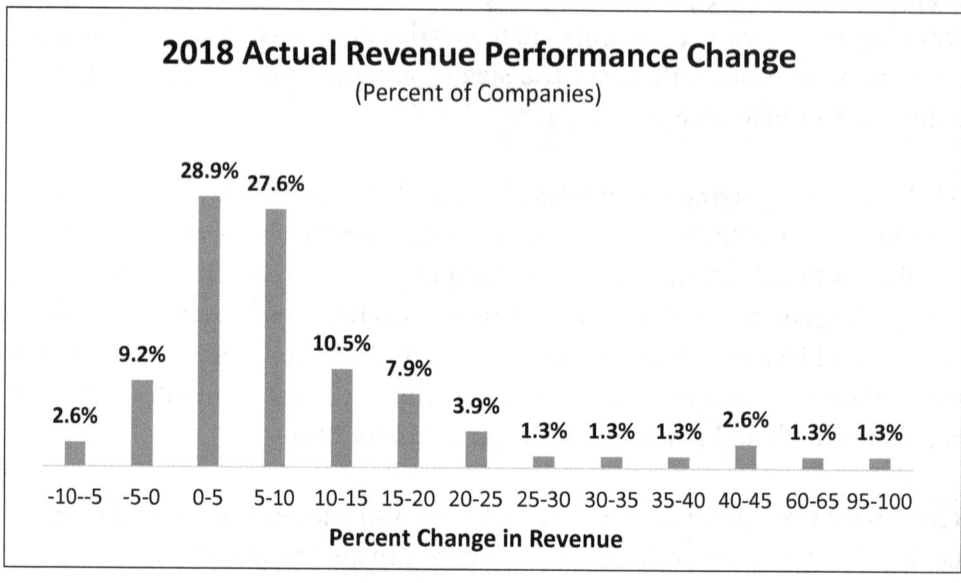

Survey Findings. 6% was the *median* increase in revenue for 2018. 56.5% of the reporting companies had revenue increases of 0 to 10% in 2018.

Observations. A 6% *median* increase in revenue for 2018 is a minor improvement from 5% for the previous year.

2018 Sales Compared to Budget: How did your actual sales performance compare to budget?

10th Perc	25th Perc	50th Perc	75th Perc	90th Perc	Average
90	95	100	103	112.4	100.8

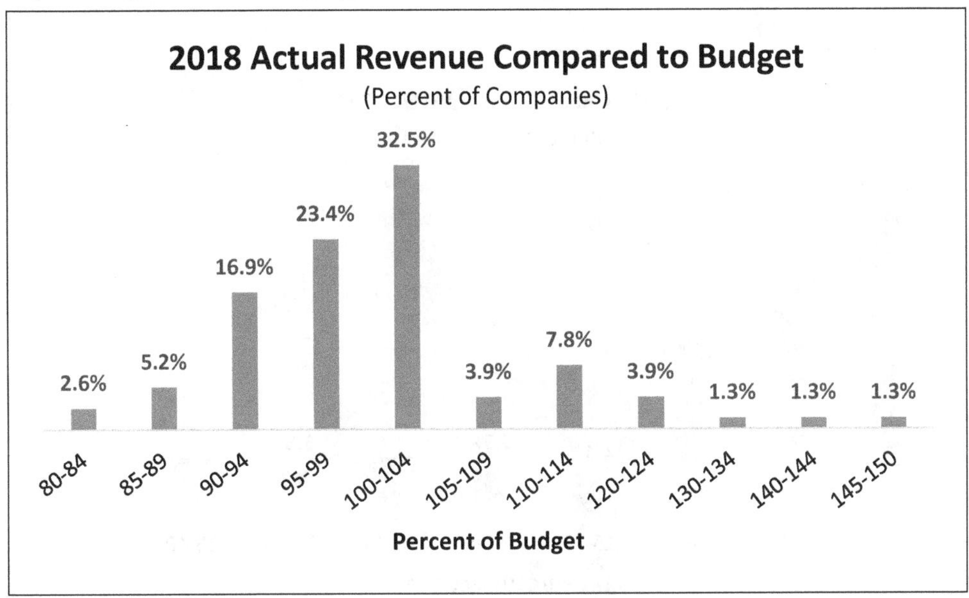

Survey Findings. 100% was the *median* sales performance compared to sales budget in 2018. 100.8% of budget was the *average* sales performance of the reporting companies in 2018. 32.5% of the companies were at 100% to 104% of their sales budgets for 2018.

Observations. 55.9% of the reporting companies were within 95% and 104% of the 2018 sales budget. 51.9% of the companies met or exceeded their sales goal budget.

2019 Revenue Expectations: For your division sales force, 2019 fiscal year revenue performance is forecasted to increase or decrease by what percent as compared to 2018?

10th Perc	25th Perc	50th Perc	75th Perc	90th Perc	Average
2	4	6	10	26.8	10.1

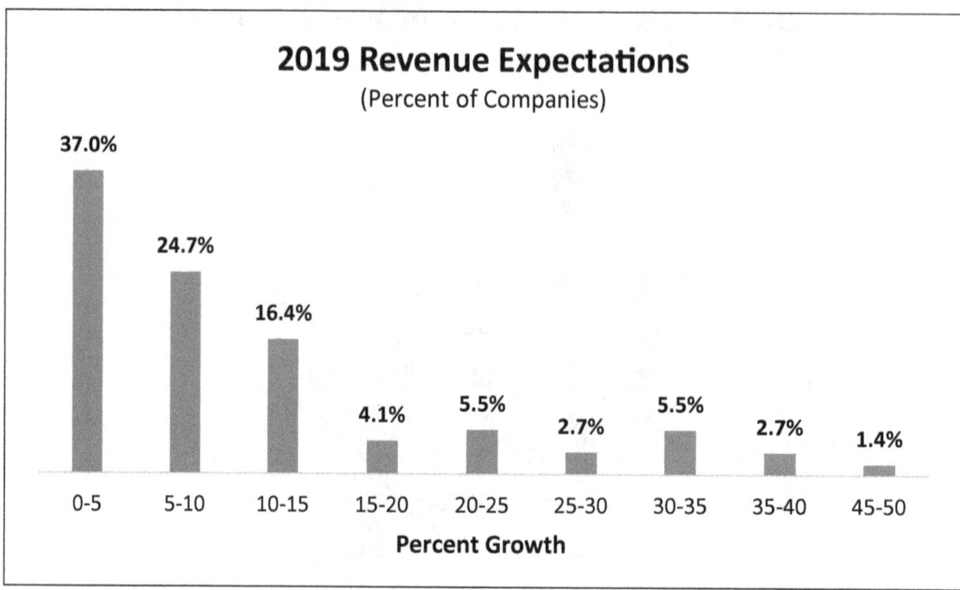

Survey Findings. 6% is the expected *median* increase in revenue for 2019. 10.1% is the *average* expected increase in revenue. 61.7% expect revenues to increase between 0 and 10% in 2019.

Observations. A 6% *median* projected increase in revenue for 2019 is a modest growth assumption. This year's sales growth projection matches last year's sales growth projection of 6%.

Sales Strategic Focus: In your opinion, what is the primary (top) strategic focus of senior management?

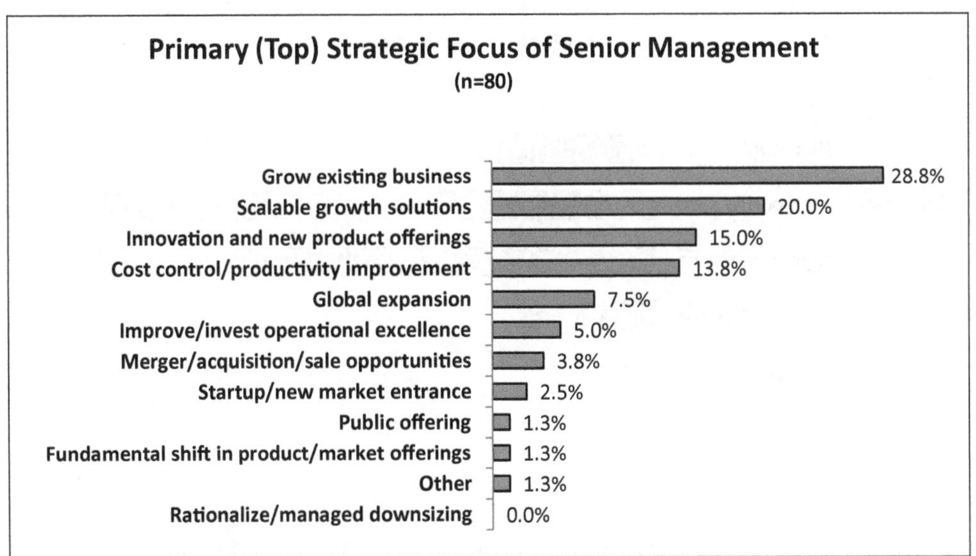

Survey Findings. 28.8% cite grow existing business as the primary sales objective for 2019. 20% indicate scalable growth solutions as the second most important objective. 15% list innovation and new product offerings as the third most important strategic objective.

Observations. Senior management wants the sales function to focus on revenue growth.

2019 Sales Confidence: How would you rate your company's sales confidence—the ability to meet and exceed goals for 2019?

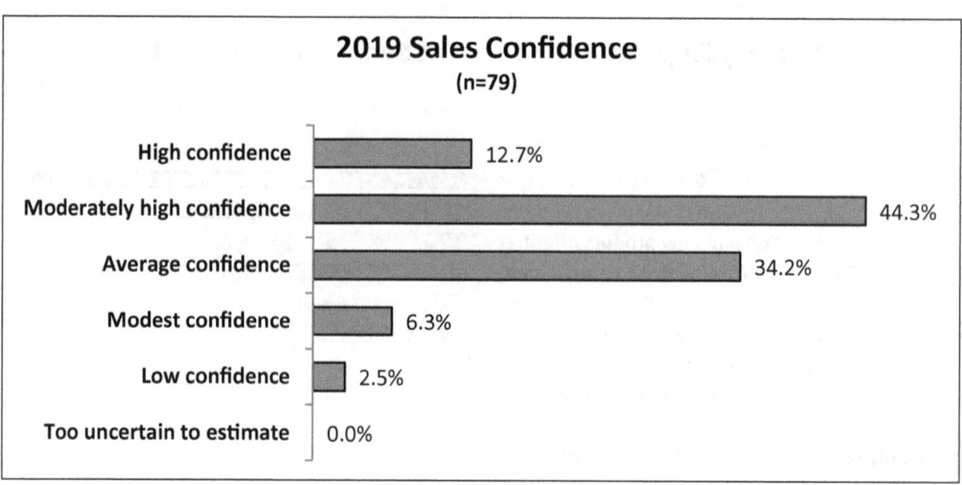

Survey Findings. 57% of the survey respondents have above-average confidence they will achieve their revenue objective for 2019. 34.2% have average confidence they will reach their 2019 sales revenue number.

Observations. Sales confidence continues to increase, improving from 42.3% last year to 57% this year for above-average expectations. As sales confidence increases, sales leaders are willing to make greater sales investments to improve sales outcomes, including revenue growth and sales for productivity.

2018 Headcount Changes: Did your sales force headcount change in 2018 for the division sales unit? (Exclude changes for supervisors and managers, but include all other customer contact jobs.)

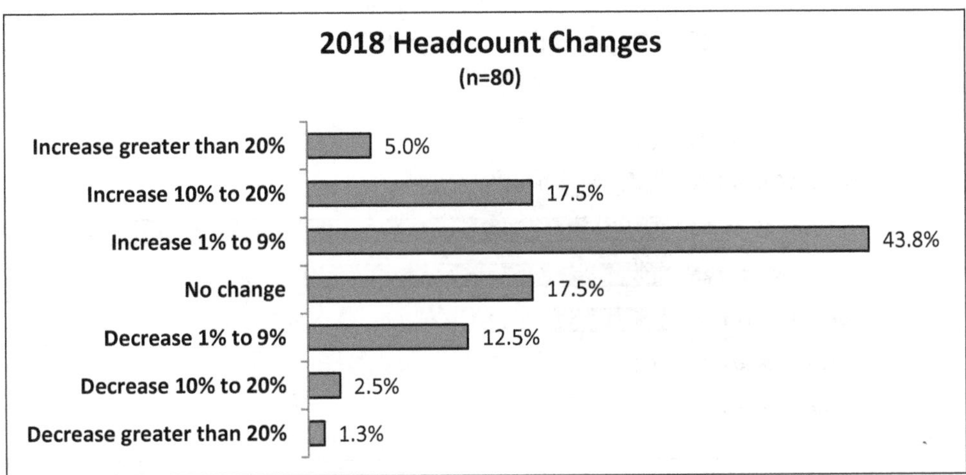

Survey Findings. 66.3% of the surveyed companies increased headcount in 2018. 17.5% made no change in headcount, and 16.3% decreased sales headcount in 2018.

Observations. Hiring increased in 2018 as compared to 2017. 2018 saw a 66.3% increase in headcount. 47.1% had an increase in headcount in 2017; whereas, 40.6% increased headcount in 2016. The hiring trend line is "up" over the last three years.

2019 Expected Headcount Changes: How do you expect 2019 sales force staffing levels to change as compared to 2018 for the division sales unit? (Exclude supervisors and managers, but include all other customer contact jobs.)

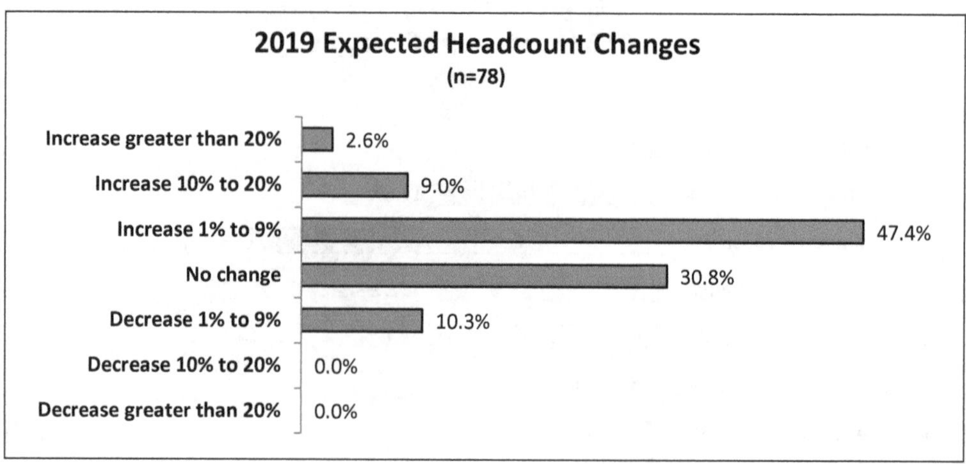

Survey Findings. 59% of the surveyed companies plan to increase headcount in 2019. 30.8% plan no change in headcount in 2019. 10.3% expect a reduction in headcount in 2019.

Observations. Almost 60% of the surveyed companies plan to increase headcount in 2019. This is a substantial increase from 49.6% in 2018.

2018 Open Positions: At any given time during 2018, what was the average percent of open sales positions compared to the total approved headcount?

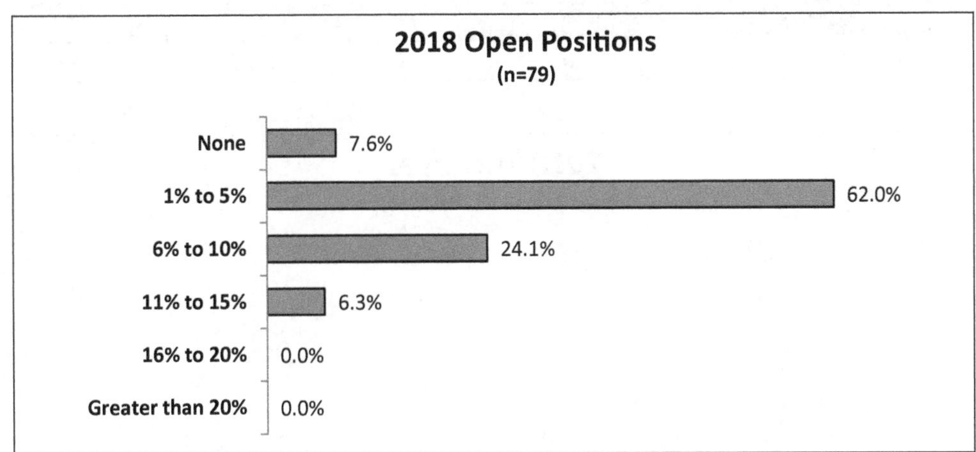

Survey Findings. 62% of the reporting companies had 1% to 5% open sales positions in 2018. 24.1% of the reporting companies had 6% to 10% open sales positions on average in 2018.

Observations. 86.1% of the reporting companies had 1% to 10% open positions of the approved headcount during 2018. This is an increase over 2017 when 79.1% of the reporting companies had 1% to 10% open sales positions.

2018 Turnover: What was your turnover percent rate (voluntary and involuntary) for sales personnel in 2018 for the division sales unit?

10th Perc	25th Perc	50th Perc	75th Perc	90th Perc	Average
3	5	10	15.2	22.5	11.4

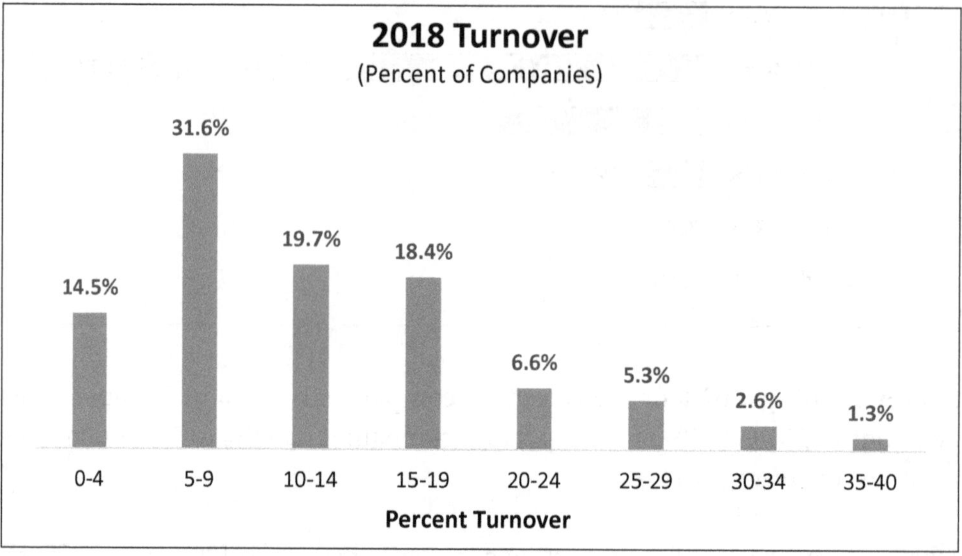

Survey Findings. 10% was the *median* turnover rate in 2018. 46.1% had turnover of less than 9%. 11.4% was the average turnover rate in 2018.

Observations. A 10% *median* turnover rate aligns with historical practices. While hiring is increasing, turnover remains constant.

2019 Projected Turnover: What is your anticipated/projected turnover percent rate (voluntary and involuntary) for sales personnel in the division sales unit?

10th Perc	25th Perc	50th Perc	75th Perc	90th Perc	Average
3	5	10	15	20	10

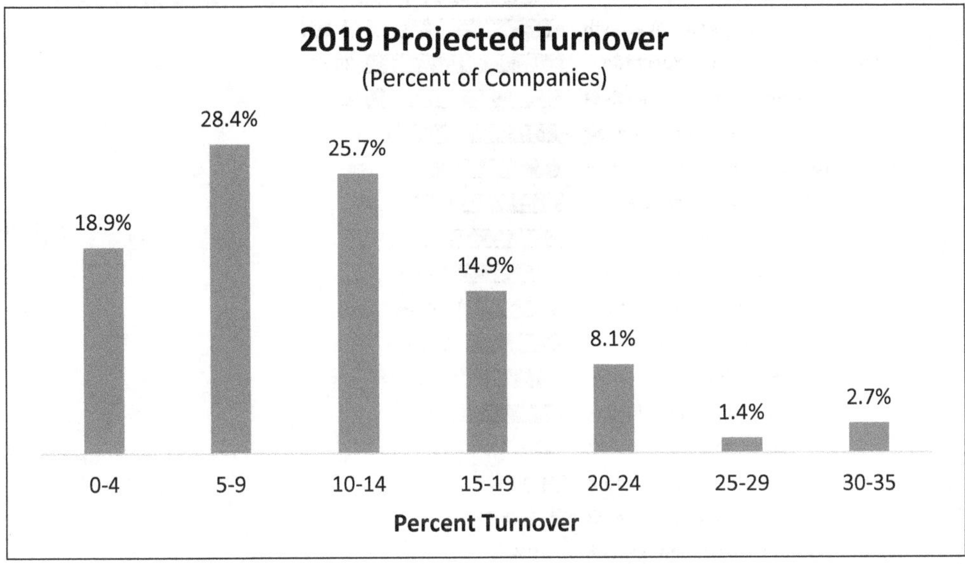

Survey Findings. 10% is the *median* projected turnover rate for 2019. 10% is the estimated *average* turnover rate for 2019. 47.3% of the reporting companies expect turnover to be less than 10%.

Observations. The reporting companies expect a 2% increase in turnover for 2019 as compared to the estimate for 2018.

2019 Performance Objectives: What are the top achieve and exceed sales performance objectives for 2019?

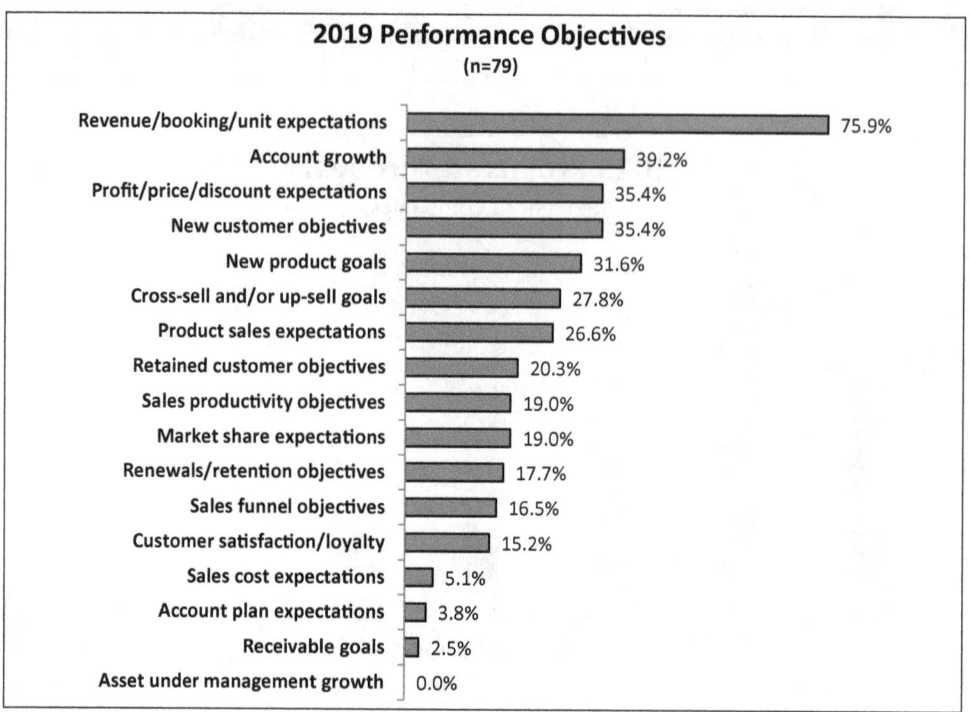

Other Performance Objectives

- Multiyear contracts
- Variable contribution margin
- MBOs
- Operational effectiveness metrics
- Corporate goals indirectly related to sales: online presence and client survey results
- Strategic products focus
- Top account growth
- Multi-product quotas
- Renewals/retention objectives
- CRM compliance targets
- Tonnage

Survey Findings. 75.9% of the reporting companies ranked achieving sales results (revenue/bookings/unit sales) to be the primary sales objective for 2019. 39.2% selected account growth. 35.4% selected profit/price/discounting as the primary sales objectives in 2019.

Observations. The top three sales objectives for 2019 include sales objectives, growth and profit measures.

2019 Sales Effectiveness Initiatives: What are the expected top three key sales effectiveness initiatives for the sales department in 2019?

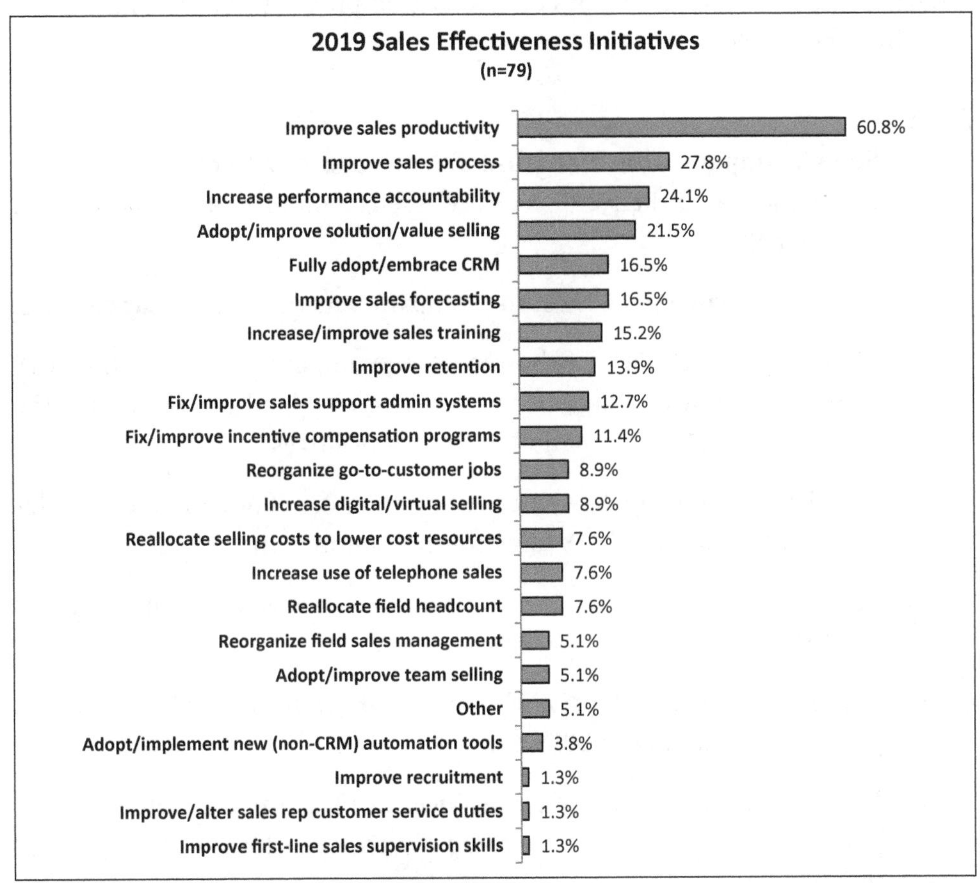

Other Sales Effectiveness Initiatives

- Improve team member capabilities
- Complaint resolution, price realization, customer loyalty
- Integrated quota management

Survey Findings. 60.8% listed improving sales productivity as the primary sales effectiveness initiative for 2019. 27.8% listed improving sales process and 24.1% selected increase performance accountability.

Observations. 2019 confirms improving sales productivity as a year-after-year enduring objective for the sales department. The top three objectives are to improve sales productivity, execute the sales process and hold sales personnel accountable for their results.

SALES COMPENSATION—WHAT HAPPENED IN 2018?

Sales compensation programs operate on an annual fiscal basis. Each year, we ask participants to rate their sales compensation programs on various factors including those below.

2018

- **Sales Compensation Program Effectiveness:** 91% of the reporting companies rated their 2018 sales compensation program as acceptable or better.
- **Mid-Year Changes:** 38.8% of the companies made no mid-year changes.
- **Plan Alignment:** 76% of the reporting companies assessed the 2018 sales compensation plans to be completely aligned or aligned for the most part with the company's business objectives.
- **Plan Understanding:** 87.4% reported that most, if not all, of their sales force understood the 2018 sales compensation plan.
- **Plan Rewards:** 87.4% of the surveyed companies noted that payouts mostly or fully aligned with seller results.
- **Incentive Payments Costs:** 3% was the *medi*an increase in incentive payments from 2017 to 2018.
- **Payout Estimate:** 100% of target incentive was the estimated *median* payout of the 2018 plan if the company achieved 100% of its sales goal in 2018.

Summary Observations

Sales Compensation Program Effectiveness Observations. 91% of companies assessed their 2018 sales compensation program to be acceptable or better. 42.5% made a few minor changes to the sales compensation plans mid-year. Most companies assessed their sales compensation plans to be aligned with company objectives and reported plan understanding among the sales personnel as high. Overall, the pay plans for 2018 receive good marks for ensuring that payouts matched seller sales results. Many of these numbers reflect improvement ratings when compared to 2017.

Incentive Payments Change Observations. The 3% growth in incentive payments was consistent with trends post-recession. Most companies noted the good health of the incentive plans by confirming the plans will pay 100% of target incentive for 100% performance. However, numerous outliers will require management attention in 2019. More accurate sales projections improve the ratings for the sales compensation plan.

2018 Sales Compensation Program Effectiveness: In 2018, how effective was the overall sales compensation program?

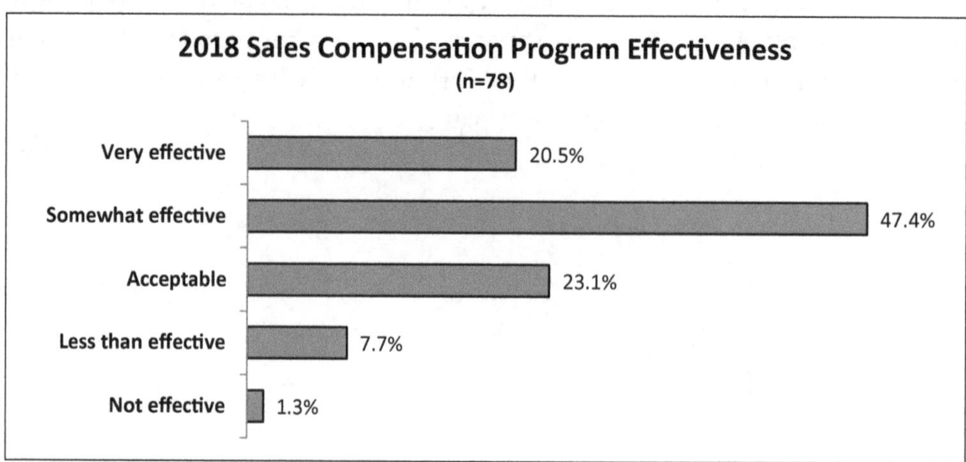

Survey Findings. 91% of the reporting companies rated their 2018 sales compensation program as acceptable or better. 9% of the reporting companies judged their incentive plans to be less than effective.

Observations. Most companies assessed their 2018 sales compensation program to be acceptable or better. These high ratings are consistent with the assessment of the 2017 program.

2018 Mid-Year Changes: During 2018, did you have to make any mid-year changes to the sales compensation program?

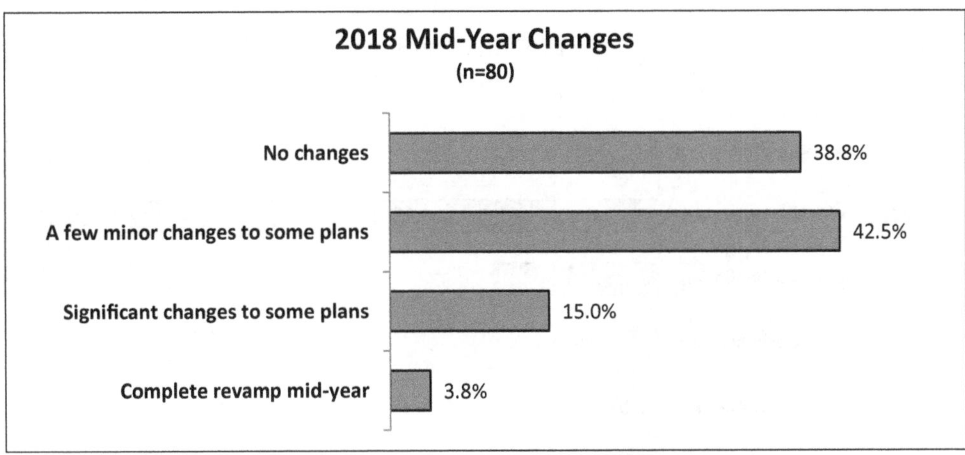

Survey Findings. 38.8% of the companies made no mid-year changes. 42.5% of the companies had a few minor changes to some of the plans. In addition, 15% had significant changes to some of the plans.

Observations. More than one-third of the companies did not change their sales compensation plans mid-year in 2018, reflecting market stability and the effectiveness of the 2018 plans. Very few companies (3.8%) had to make complete mid-year changes to their 2018 sales compensation program. Yet, 15% had to make significant changes to their sales compensation plans mid-year.

2018 Plan Alignment: How well did the 2018 sales compensation program align sales efforts with company business objectives?

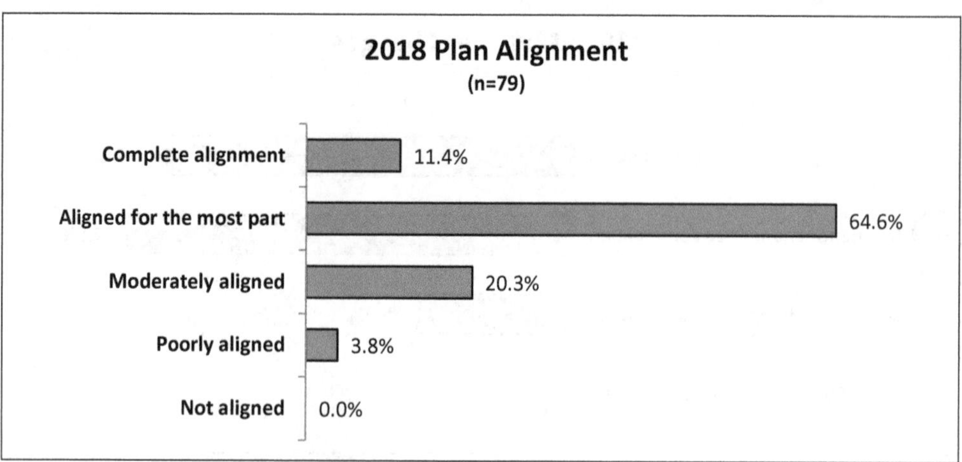

Survey Findings. 76% of the reporting companies assessed the 2018 sales compensation plans to be completely aligned or aligned for the most part with the company's business objectives. 20.3% assessed their 2018 sales compensation plans to be moderately aligned with the company's business objectives.

Observations. In more than 75% of the cases, sales management ensures sales compensation plan alignment with company objectives.

2018 Plan Understanding: How well did sales personnel understand their 2018 sales compensation plan?

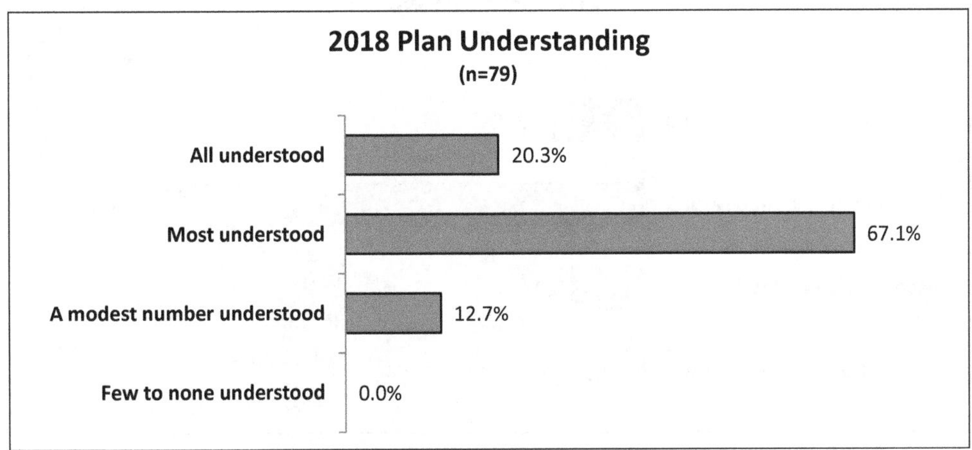

Survey Findings. 87.4% reported that most, if not all, of their sales force understood the 2018 sales compensation plan. 12.7% said only a modest number of sales personnel understood their plans.

Observations. Plan understanding among the reporting companies is high. This outcome reflects both good plan design and effective communication. These numbers are equal to, if not better than, the understanding assessment from the 2017 plan year.

2018 Plan Rewards: How well did payouts match performance?

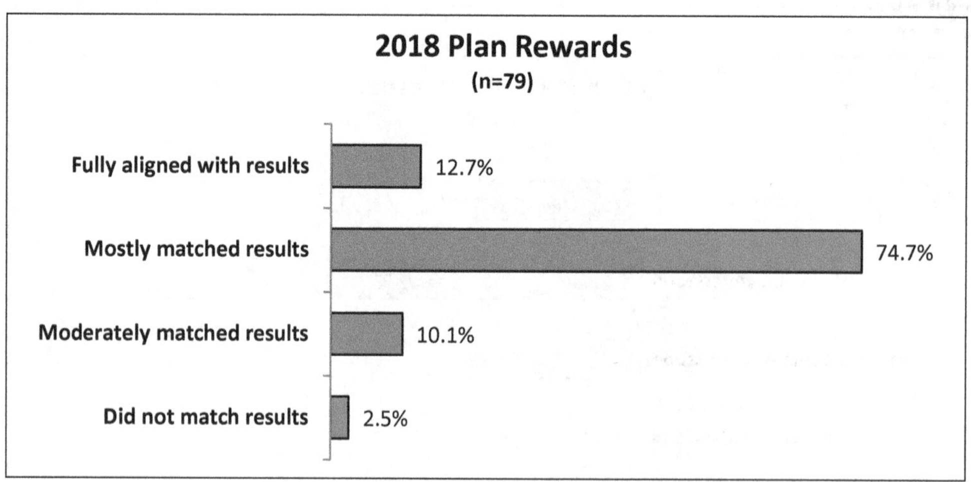

Survey Findings. 87.4% of the surveyed companies noted that payouts mostly or fully aligned with seller results. 10.1% of the companies selected "moderately matched results." 2.5% said the payouts did not match results.

Observations. Overall, the pay plans for 2018 receive good marks for ensuring that payouts matched seller sales results. These positive results are consistent with and improve upon the results for 2017.

2018 Incentive Payments Costs: By what percentage did actual incentive payouts for sales personnel change from 2017 to 2018?

10th Perc	25th Perc	50th Perc	75th Perc	90th Perc	Average
−5	0	3	9.5	17.6	4.7

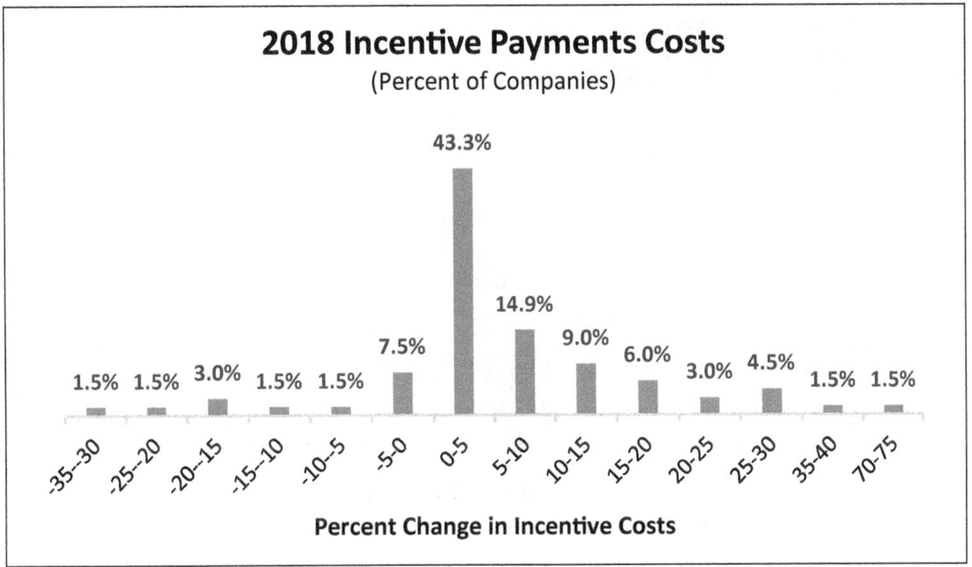

Survey Findings. 3% was the *median* increase in incentive payments from 2017 to 2018. 4.7% was the *average* increase in incentive payments from 2017 to 2018. 58.2% reported 0 to 10% changes in incentive payments from 2017 to 2018.

Observations. Growth in incentive payments modestly improved in 2018 by 1% (2% to 3%) when compared to 2017 payouts.

Payout Estimate: If your company achieved 100% of its sales objective, how much would the incentive plan pay compared to the incentive plan target budget?

10th Perc	25th Perc	50th Perc	75th Perc	90th Perc	Average
95.2	100	100	105.5	120	103.2

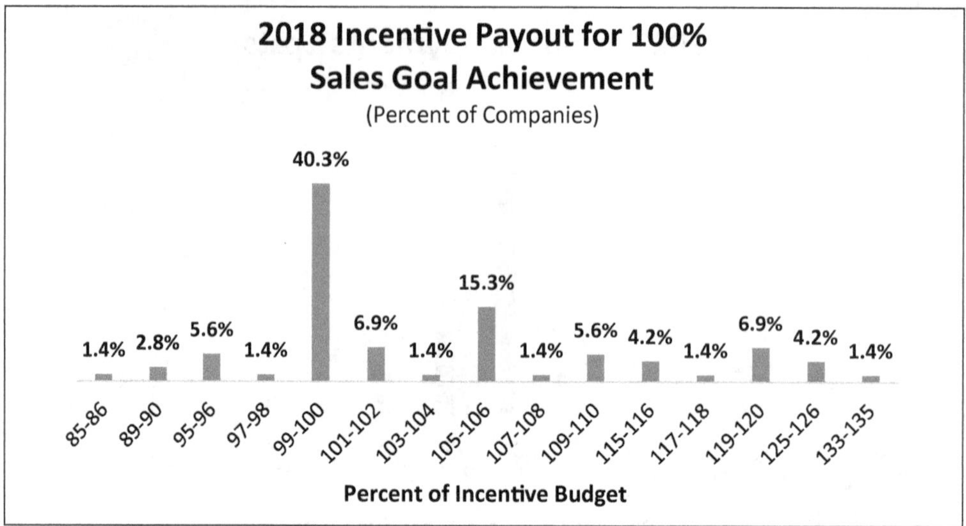

Survey Findings. 100% of target incentive was the estimated *median* payout of the 2018 plan if the company achieved 100% of its sales goal in 2018. 103.2% was the estimated *average* payout of the target incentive for the company reaching 100% of its goal in 2018.

Observations. For 2018, most companies planned to pay 100% of the target incentive for achieving 100% of the company goal. This is an appropriate design objective and consistent with the outcome in the previous 2017 plan year.

SALES COMPENSATION PROGRAM—WHAT WILL HAPPEN IN 2019?

Sales compensation planning for 2019 requires planning for base pay and incentive plan increases plus making changes to the plans to ensure alignment of sellers' objectives with company objectives.

2019

- **Base Pay Changes:** 71.3% of the reporting companies plan to give base pay increases in 2019, an increase from 67.4% in 2018.
- **Average Percent Change in Base Pay:** 3% is the *median* pay increase for companies planning base pay increases in 2019.
- **Sales Compensation Program Changes:** 96.2% of the reporting companies plan to make changes to the sales compensation program in 2019.
- **Sales Compensation Challenges:** 58.8% reported correct quota setting as the major challenge for the sales compensation program in 2019.
- **Plan Revision Reason:** 43.8% seek to improve sales objective alignment with business strategy as the primary change to the incentive plan for 2019.

Summary Observations

Sales Compensation Program Changes. The extent of plan changes to the 2019 sales compensation program is consistent with the extent of changes reported in previous surveys. To maintain alignment with company objectives, sales management normally updates the plans on an annual basis. 96.2% plan to change their incentive plans for 2019. The reasons companies plan to make changes in 2019 include the following: improve sales objective alignment with business strategy, improve sales productivity and better manage costs.

Base Pay Changes. 71.3% plan to increase base pay in 2019 providing a 3% *median* increase, the same target amount from last year.

Sales Compensation Challenges. Correct quota setting is the most challenging factor for the 2019 sales compensation plan, retaining its unbroken record as the No. 1 issue for sales compensation since the inception of this survey in 2003.

2019 Base Pay Changes: Will you make base pay changes for eligible employees in 2019?

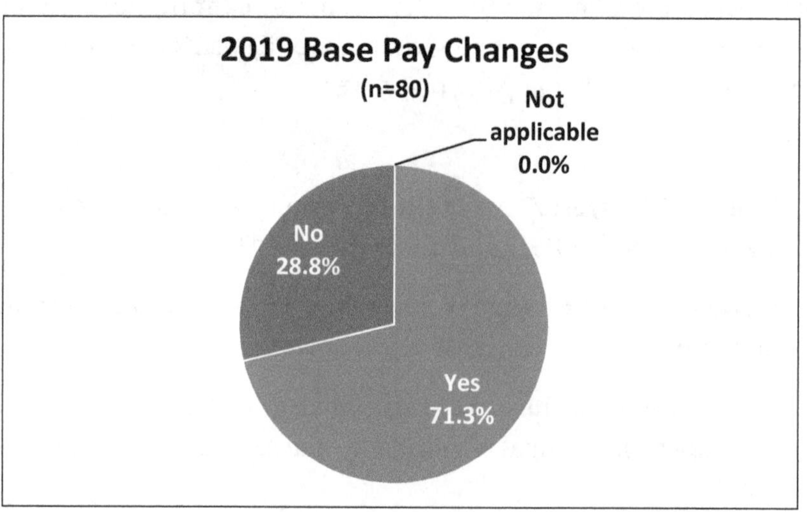

Survey Findings. 71.3% of the reporting companies plan to give base pay increases in 2019, an increase from 67.4% in 2018.

Observations. To maintain parity with the labor market, many companies are providing base pay increases. We would expect this number to continue to rise if wage inflation increases, or wage compression occurs. Wage compression occurs when new hires make more money than existing staff.

2019 Average Percent Change in Base Pay: If you answered yes to making a base pay change in 2019, what do you expect the average percent change in base pay to be for those receiving an increase?

10th Perc	25th Perc	50th Perc	75th Perc	90th Perc	Average
2	3	3	3	4	3.3

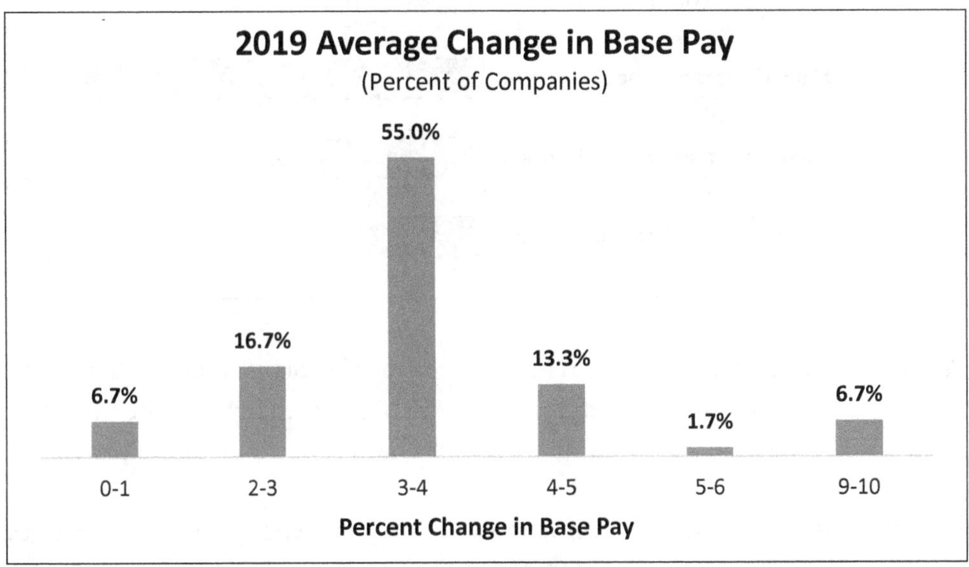

Survey Findings. 3% is the *median* pay increase for companies planning base pay increases in 2019. 3.3% is the *average* base pay increase for companies planning base pay increases for 2019. 55% of the reporting companies will be giving base pay increases between 3% and 4% in 2019.

Observations. Expected base pay increases will remain modest, consistent with low-labor market inflation. The increases in base pay for 2019 are similar to that of 2018.

2019 Sales Compensation Program Changes: For 2019, what are the extent of changes you plan to make to your sales compensation program?

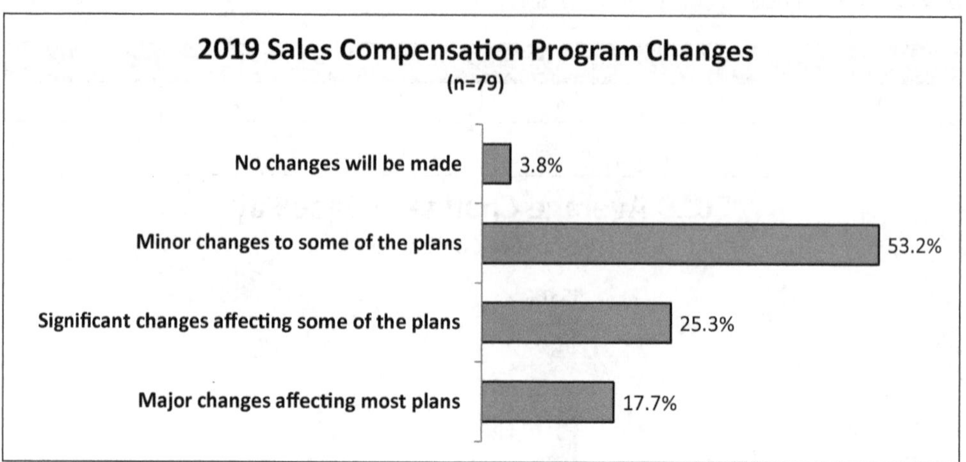

Survey Findings. 96.2% of the reporting companies plan to make changes to the sales compensation program in 2019. 3.8% plan no changes to the incentive plans for 2019. 53.2% expect to make minor changes to some of the plans.

Observations. The number of companies making plan changes to the 2019 sales compensation program is the highest rate in the 17-year history of this survey.

2019 Sales Compensation Challenges: What sales compensation challenges do you expect for 2019?

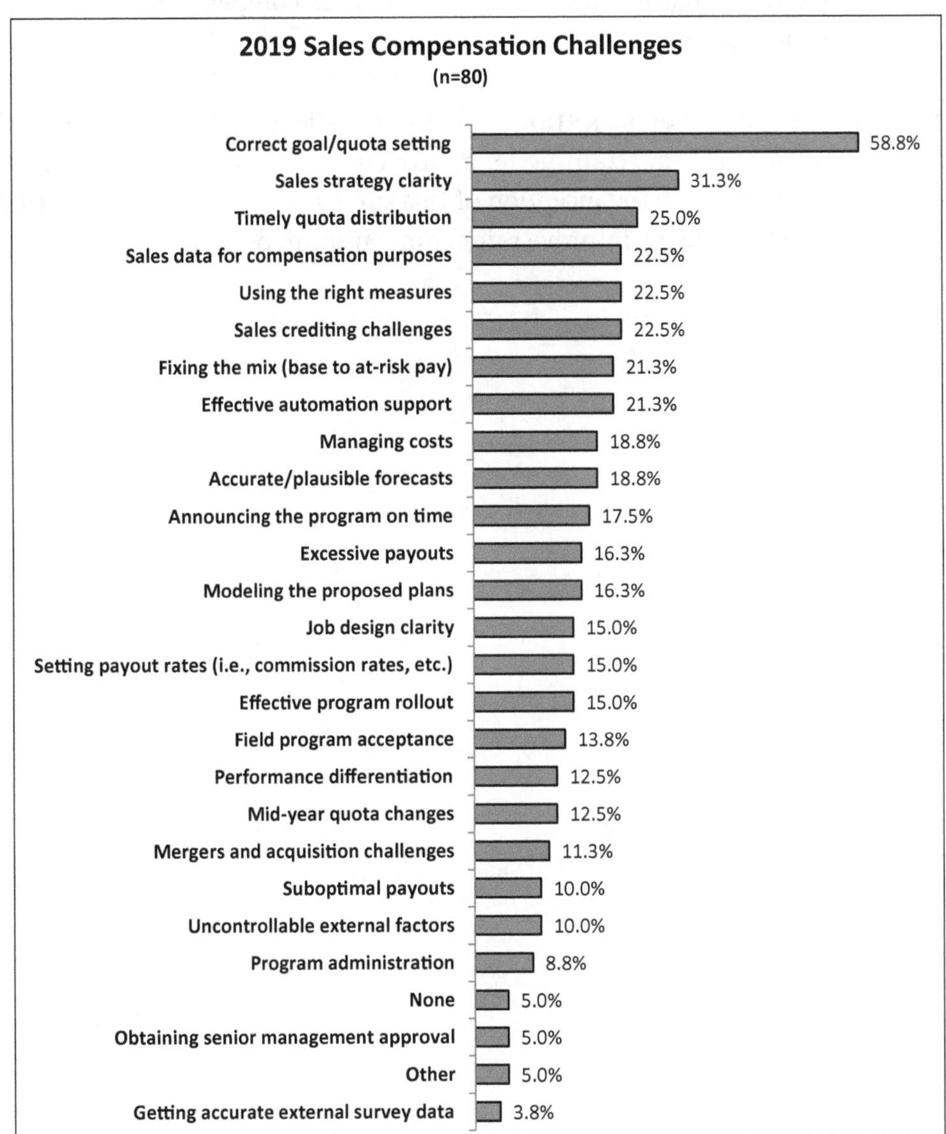

Other Sales Compensation Challenges

- High growth rate expectations
- Increase target payout by up to 25%
- Creating brand new plan for new role
- Aligning rep focus with business needs

Survey Findings. 58.8% reported correct quota setting as the major challenge for the sales compensation program in 2019. 31.3% noted sales strategy clarity as the second most significant challenge to the sales compensation plan. 25% said timely quota setting.

Observations. Correct quota setting is the most challenging factor for the 2019 sales compensation plan, retaining its unbroken record as the No. 1 issue for sales compensation since the inception of this survey in 2003. However, getting sales strategy clarity helps improve sales compensation design.

2019 Plan Revision Reason: Why will you change your sales compensation plan for next fiscal year?

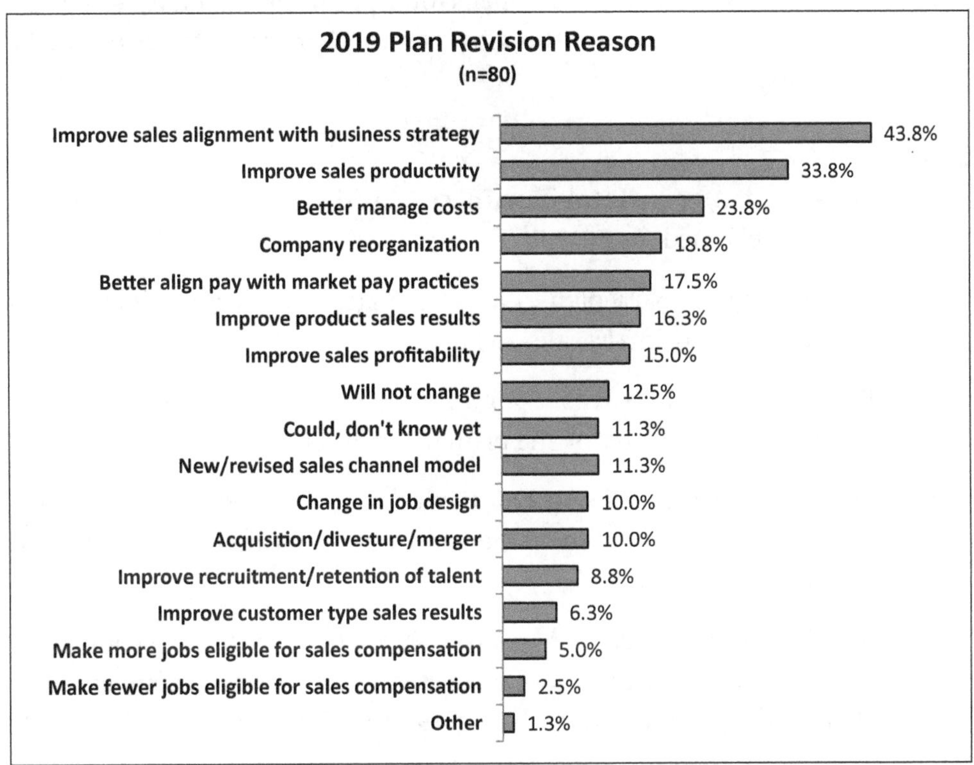

Survey Findings. 43.8% seek to improve sales objective alignment with business strategy as the primary change to the incentive plan for 2019. 33.8% cited improving sales productivity. 23.8% selected better manage costs as a reason to make changes to the 2019 sales compensation plan.

Observations. As the business strategy changes, so must the sales compensation plans to ensure alignment.

SALES COMPENSATION CHANGES PLANNED FOR THE PRIMARY SALES JOB IN 2019

Sales entities review their sales compensation programs annually to ensure program effectiveness. Here are the most common practices for 2019 for the primary sales job.

2019

- **Percent Change in Total Earnings:** 3% is the *median* increase in total earnings planned for 2019.
- **Plan Changes:** 43.6% plan to make changes to performance measures in 2019 for the primary sales job plan.
- **Performance Measures:** 79.5% reported sales revenue as the key performance measure for the primary sales job.
- **Measurement and Payment Period:** 34.6% reported their 2019 measurement and payment period to be an annual objective with monthly payments.
- **Number of Performance Measures:** 89.8% of the reporting companies will use three or fewer performance measures in the sales compensation plan for the primary sales job in 2019.
- **Individual Versus Team Performance:** 85.8% report individual performance as the largest accountability component in the 2019 plan.
- **MBO Component:** 87% of the reporting companies will not use a management by objectives (MBO) component in the 2019 sales compensation plan.
- **Calculation Method:** 38.4% of the reporting companies use a bonus formula paid against quota achievement as the calculation method for the key component in the sales compensation program for the primary sales job.
- **Pay Mix:** 26% of the reporting companies use a 50/50 (base/incentive) pay mix for the primary sales job.
- **Pay Caps:** 78.9% do not have an absolute cap on compensation earnings for the primary sales job.
- **Leverage/Upside:** 24.7% of the reporting companies provide 3x the target incentive for outstanding performance, the 90th percentile.

- **Threshold:** 55.8% have a threshold on the primary measure for the sales compensation plan for the primary sales job.
- **Clawbacks:** 58.4% use a clawback to recover monies already paid to sales personnel in the primary sales job.
- **New Hires:** 27.3% place new hires on a fixed guarantee.

Summary Observations

Budget. The sales compensation budget will increase 3% for 2019.

Plan Changes. 96.2% of the companies plan to make changes to the sales compensation plan in 2019. Changing performance measures is the modification done on an annual basis. Other changes include changing the formula rates and accelerators.

Performance Measures. Most companies have three or fewer performance measures for the incentive plan. Sales revenue, units/orders and new accounts are the primary drivers for the 2019 sales compensation plan. Top-line growth is a key focus in the incentive plan for the primary seller.

Individual Versus Team Performance. 85.5% use individual performance as the sole basis for incentive purposes.

MBO (Management by Objectives). An MBO incentive element is not a prevalent component for the primary sales job among the reporting companies.

2019 Calculation Method. 38.4% of the reporting companies use a bonus formula paid against quota achievement as the calculation method for the key component in the sales compensation program for the primary sales job.

Plan Features. 34.6% reported their 2019 measurement and payment period to be an annual objective with monthly payments. 50/50 is the most common pay mix for the primary sales job. The preferred approach is not to cap sales compensation earnings. Practices vary, but the two most common upside ratios are 2x and 3x the target incentive amount. About half use a threshold. A majority of survey participants have a clawback practice. Sales management places new hires on the incentive plan at time of employment.

Type of Sales Job: Select your primary sales job type used in this section.

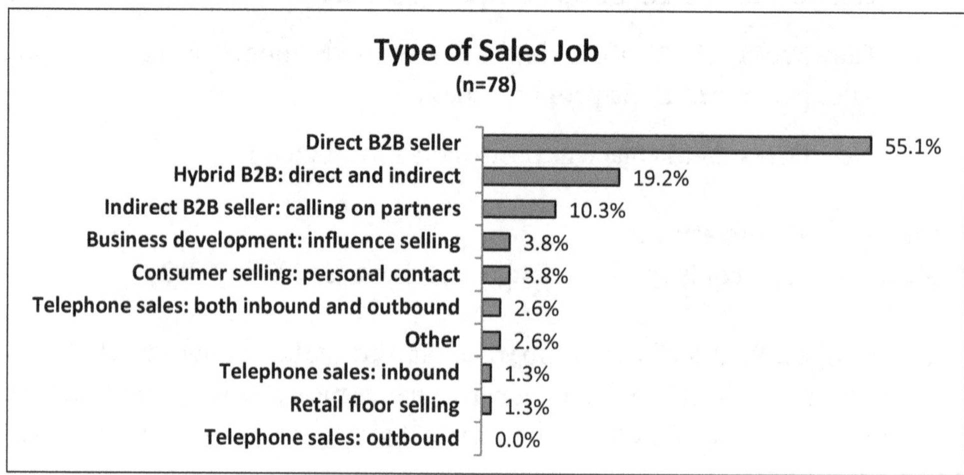

2019 Percent Change in Total Earnings: In 2019, what percent will the official (or unofficial) target earnings (base salary plus amount of incentive an average performer will earn) for the primary sales job change from 2018?

10th Perc	25th Perc	50th Perc	75th Perc	90th Perc	Average
0	0	3	4	9.1	2.8

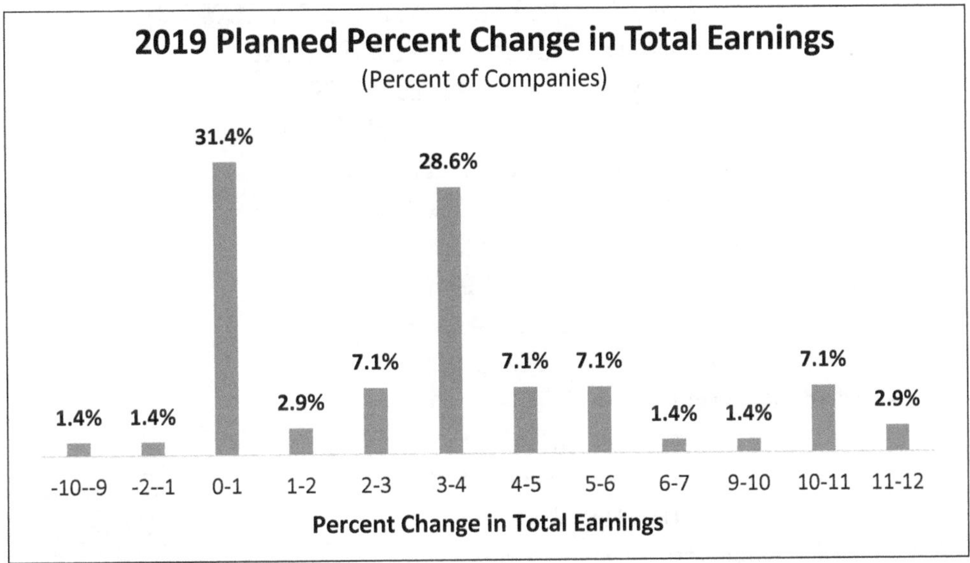

Survey Findings. 3% is the *median* increase in total earnings planned for 2019. 2.8% is the *average* increase in total earnings planned for 2019.

Observations. While pay cost increases remain modest, they are incrementally increasing at a positive rate.

2019 Plan Changes: For the primary sales job, the following elements of the incentive plan will be changed in 2019 (exclude quota changes):

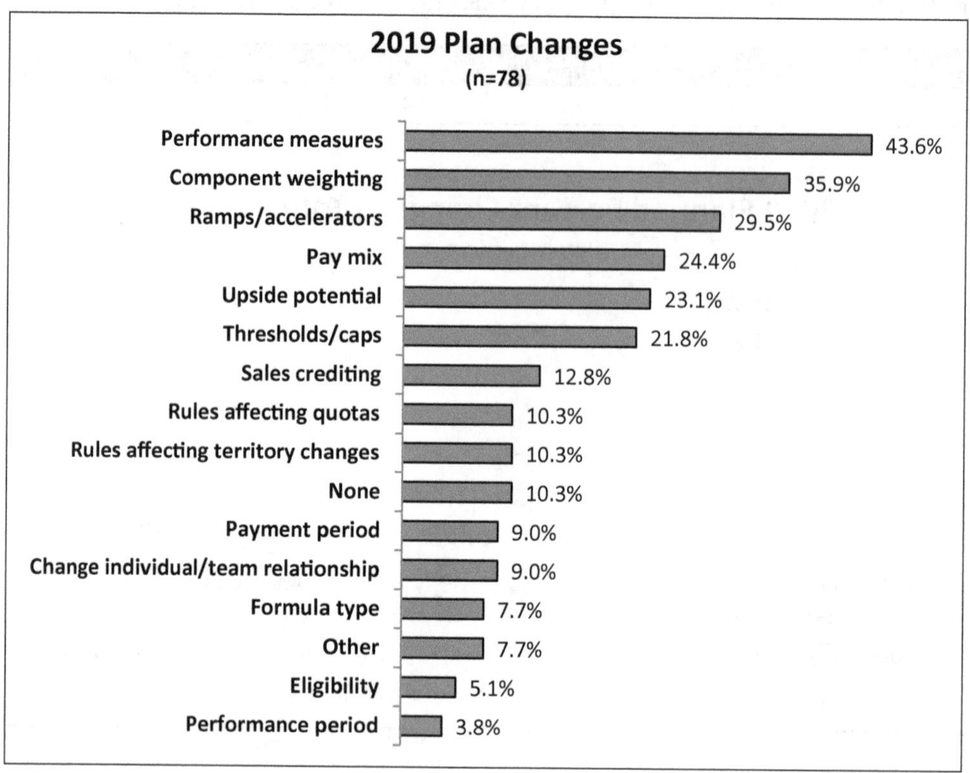

Other Plan Changes

- Additional incentive oppty for strategic initiatives
- Adding product spiffs
- Product modifiers
- Move from paying on MRR to ARR
- Adding new plans for new roles

Survey Findings. 43.6% plan to make changes to performance measures in 2019 for the primary sales job plan. 35.9% plan to change the component's weighting and 29.5% plan to change the incentive ramps and accelerators.

Observations. As noted elsewhere in this survey, more than 96% of the companies plan to make changes to the sales compensation plan in 2019. Changing performance measures, component weightings and ramps/accelerators are common modifications done on an annual basis.

2019 Performance Measures: In 2019, the sales compensation plan for the primary sales job will use which of the following distinct performance measures:

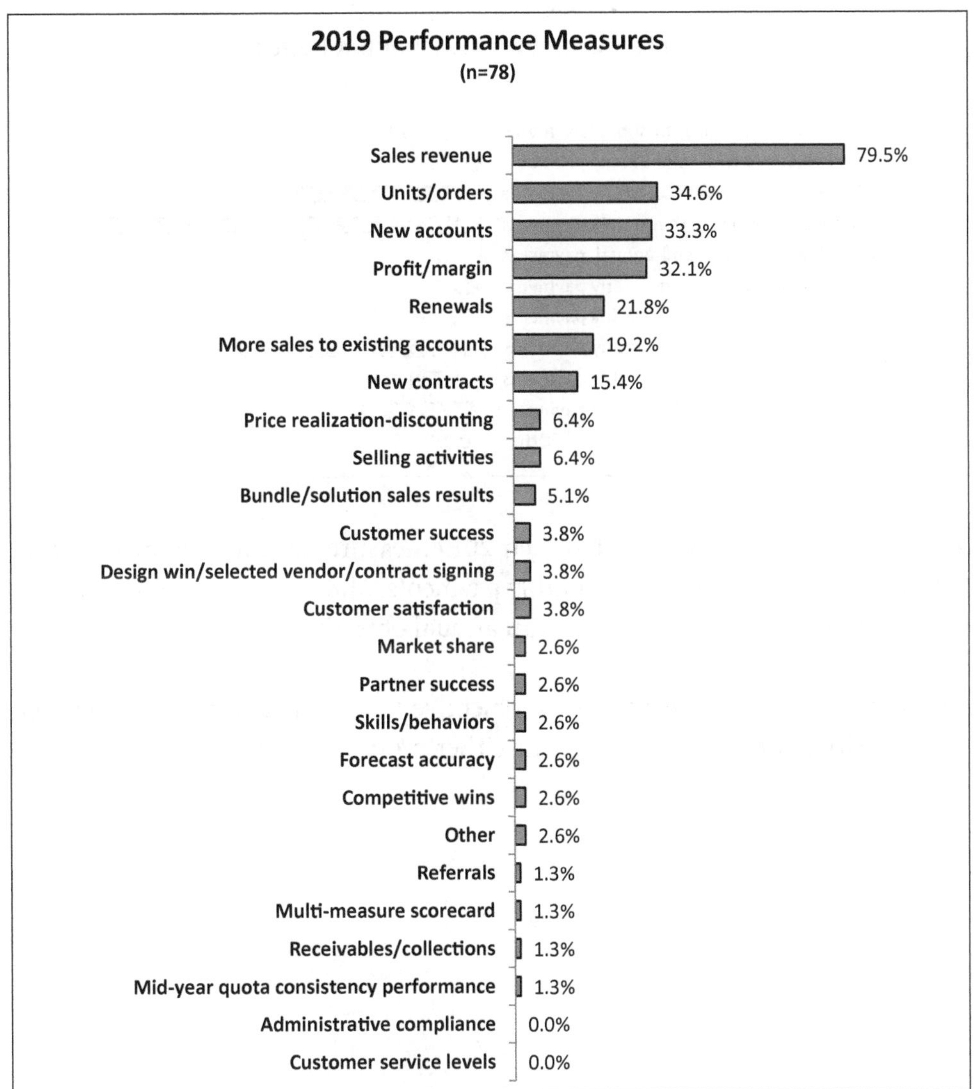

Survey Findings. 79.5% reported sales revenue as the key performance measure for the primary sales job. 34.6% selected units/orders as the next most important measure in 2019. In addition, 33.3% selected new accounts as the third most prevalent measure in the sales compensation plan.

Observations. Top-line growth is a key focus in the incentive plan for the primary seller. Revenue growth, units/orders and new accounts are the key drivers for the 2019 sales compensation plan for the primary sales job.

2019 Measurement and Payment Period: In 2019, the primary performance measure will be measured and paid primarily in the following fashion:

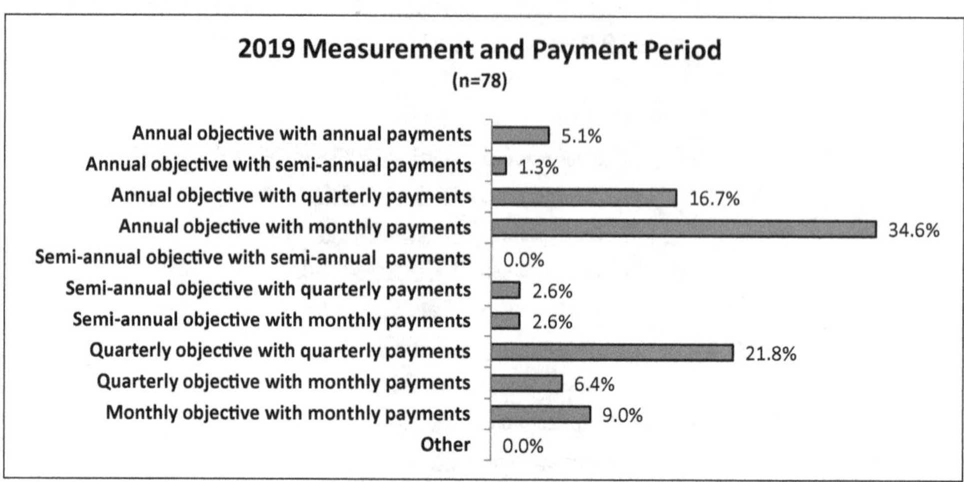

Survey Findings. 34.6% reported their 2019 measurement and payment period to be an annual objective with monthly payments. 21.8% use a quarterly objective with quarterly payments. 16.7% use an annual objective with quarterly payouts.

Observations. 57.7% use an annual objective for the incentive plan; however, the majority of annual payouts occur either monthly or quarterly.

2019 Number of Performance Measures: The incentive plan for the primary sales job has how many distinct performance measures?

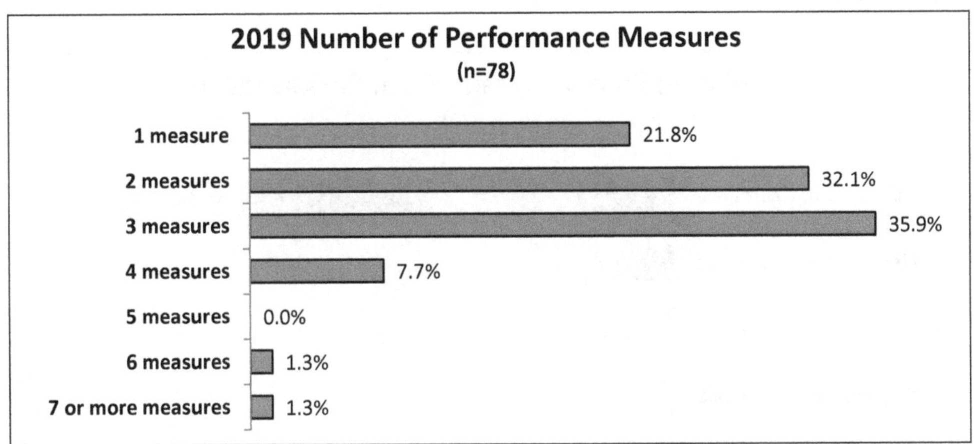

Survey Findings. 89.8% of the reporting companies will use three or fewer performance measures in the sales compensation plan for the primary sales job in 2019. 35.9% will use three measures. 32.1% will use two measures and 21.8% will use one measure in the incentive program for the primary sales job in 2019.

Observations. Sales compensation programs work best with three or fewer performance measures. Almost 90% of the reporting companies follow this practice.

2019 Individual Versus Team Performance: The individual versus team performance will be a mix of what percent? Enter the percentage; all five must sum to 100 percent.

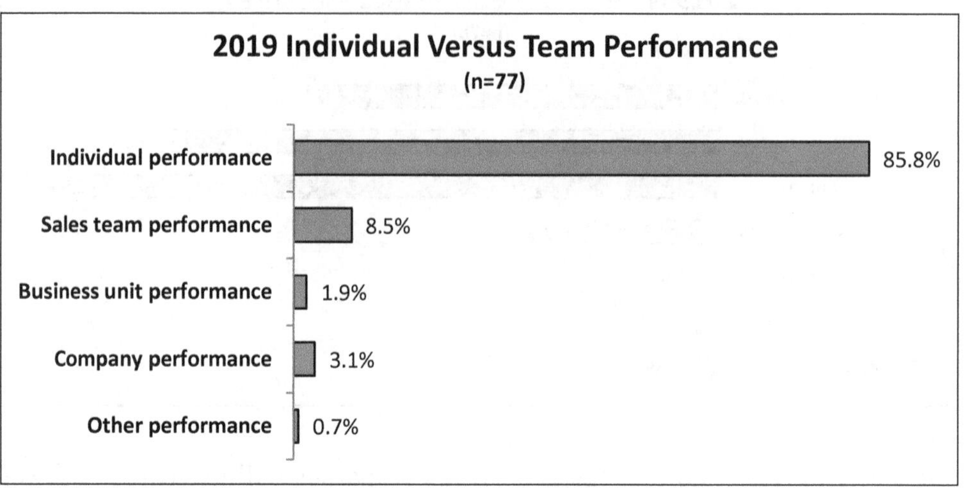

Survey Findings. 85.8% report individual performance as the largest accountability component in the 2019 plan. 8.5% represent sales team performance.

Observations. Sales compensation programs generally focus on individual performance; teaming is a minor factor.

2019 MBO Component: Does the incentive plan for the primary sales job have an MBO (management by objectives) component?

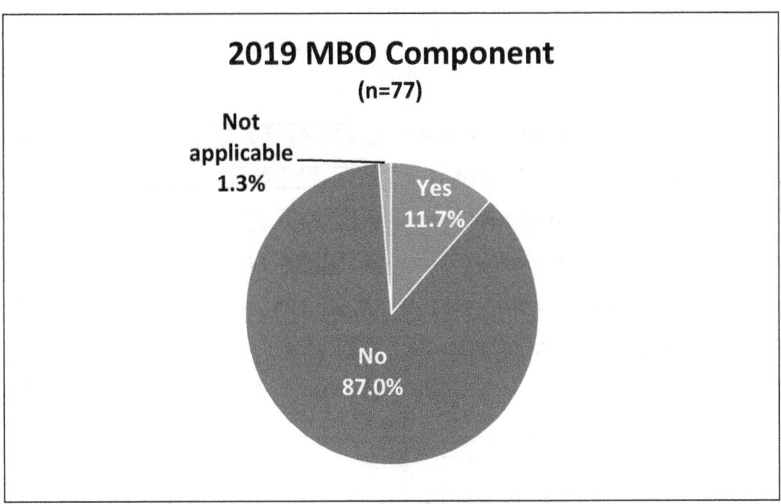

Survey Findings. 87% of the reporting companies will not use a management by objectives (MBO) component in the 2019 sales compensation plan. 11.7% of the reporting companies will use an MBO component.

Observations. An MBO or KSO (key sales objectives) incentive element is not a prevalent component for the primary sales job among the reporting companies.

2019 Calculation Method: What is the calculation method for the key performance measure of the primary sales job?

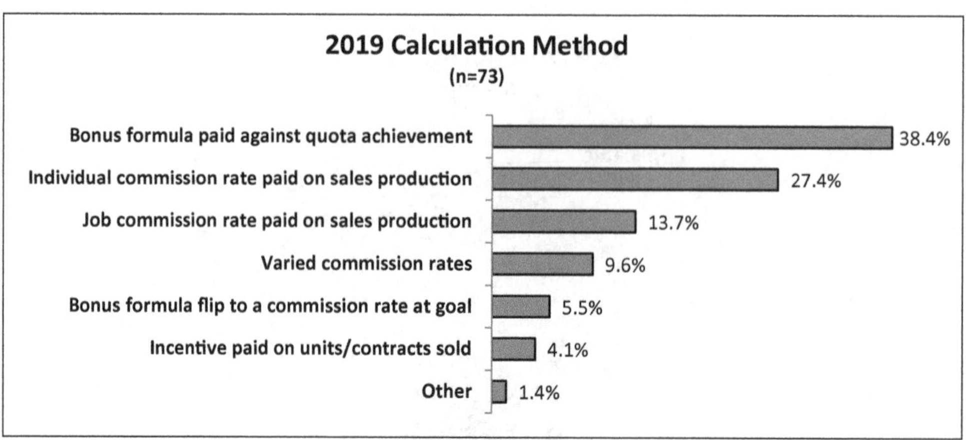

Survey Findings. 38.4% of the reporting companies use a bonus formula paid against quota achievement as the calculation method for the key component in the sales compensation program for the primary sales job. 27.4% of the reporting companies use an individual commission rate paid on sales production. In addition, 13.7% use a job commission rate paid on sales production as the calculation method.

Observations. The use of bonus formula paid against achievement to quota suggests that the territories are dissimilar in size; yet, sales management seeks to reward sales personnel alike for achieving 100% of sales goal although absolute sales goals differ by individual. This is the same rationale for individual commission rates, a common practice, too.

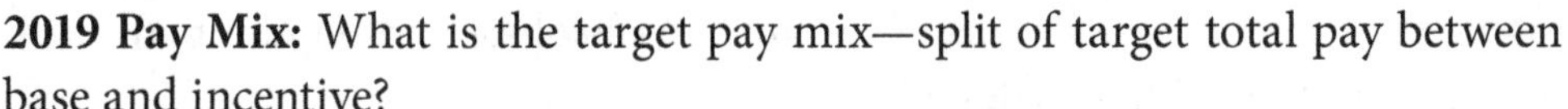

2019 Pay Mix: What is the target pay mix—split of target total pay between base and incentive?

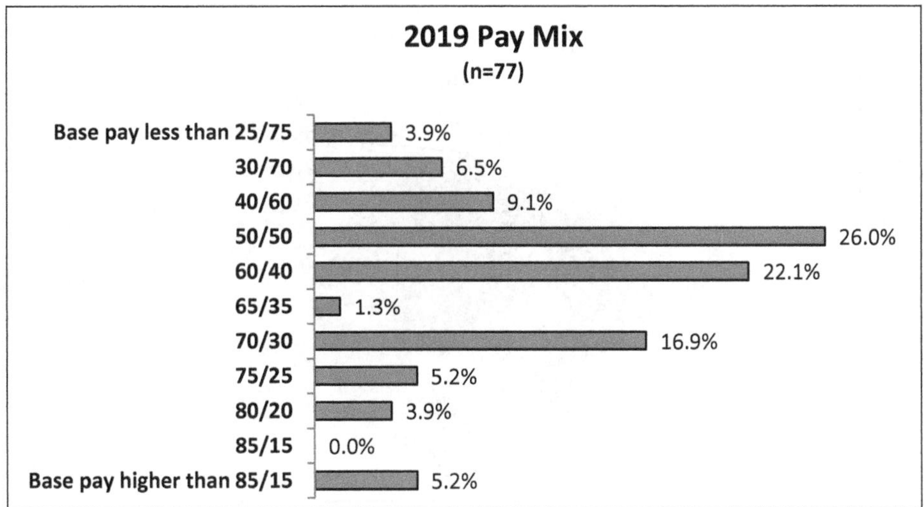

Survey Findings. 26% of the reporting companies use a 50/50 (base/incentive) pay mix for the primary sales job. 22.1% of the reporting companies use a 60/40 (base/incentive) pay mix for the primary sales job. 16.9% of the reporting companies use a 70/30 (base/incentive) pay mix for the primary sales job.

Observations. 50/50 is the most common pay mix for the primary sales job. A 60/40 pay mix is the second most popular pay mix. Combined, these two practices represent 48.1% of the reporting companies.

2019 Pay Caps: Does the pay plan have an absolute cap on compensation earnings for the primary sales job?

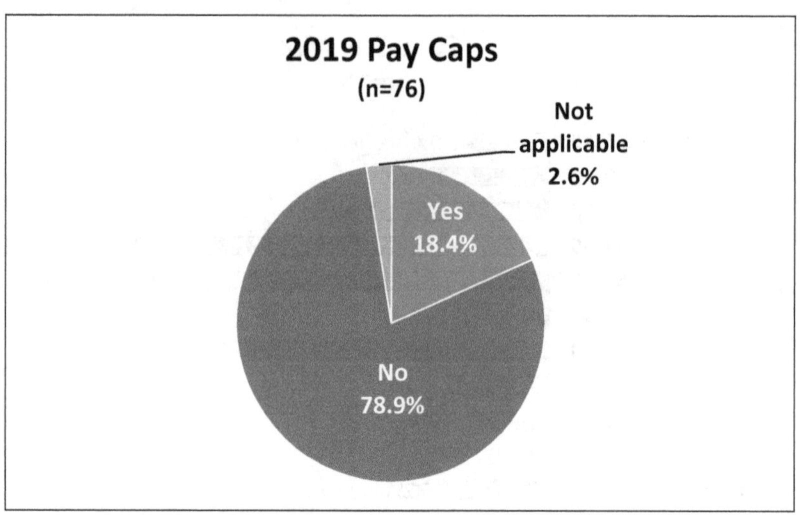

Survey Findings. 78.9% do not have an absolute cap on compensation earnings for the primary sales job. 18.4% do have an absolute cap on sales compensation earnings.

Observations. However, for some companies, the use of caps supports the company's pay philosophy. In other cases, it offsets the negative consequences of poor quota setting or the booking of unpredictable mega orders.

2019 Leverage/Upside: The best performers (~90th percentile of performance) in the primary sales job can earn how many total incentive dollars as a multiple of the at-risk target incentive dollars?

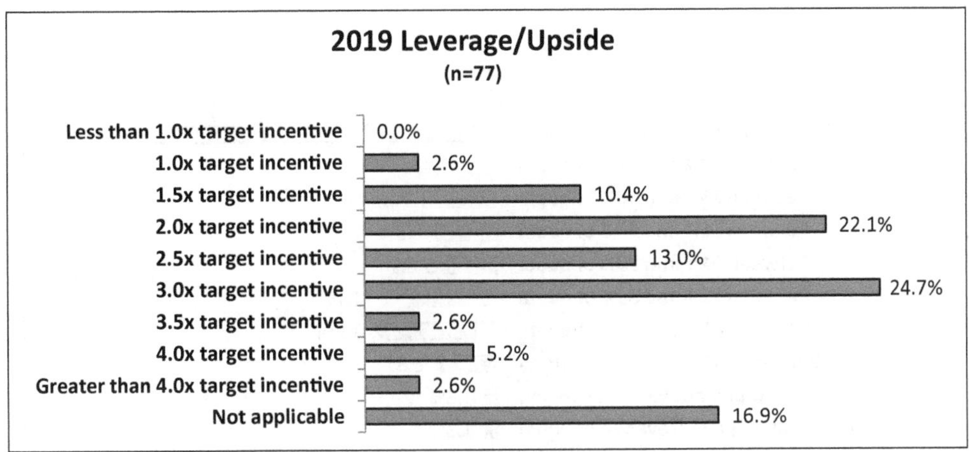

Survey Findings. 24.7% of the reporting companies provide 3x the target incentive for outstanding performance, the 90th percentile. 22.1% provide 2x the target incentive for outstanding performance.

Observations. Upside earnings provide the motivation to drive additional efforts. Practices vary, but the two most common upside ratios are 3x and 2x the target incentive amount. Confirm upside potential with market pay surveys.

2019 Threshold: Does the 2019 sales compensation plan for the primary sales job have a threshold—a minimum level of revenue performance before sellers earn incentive?

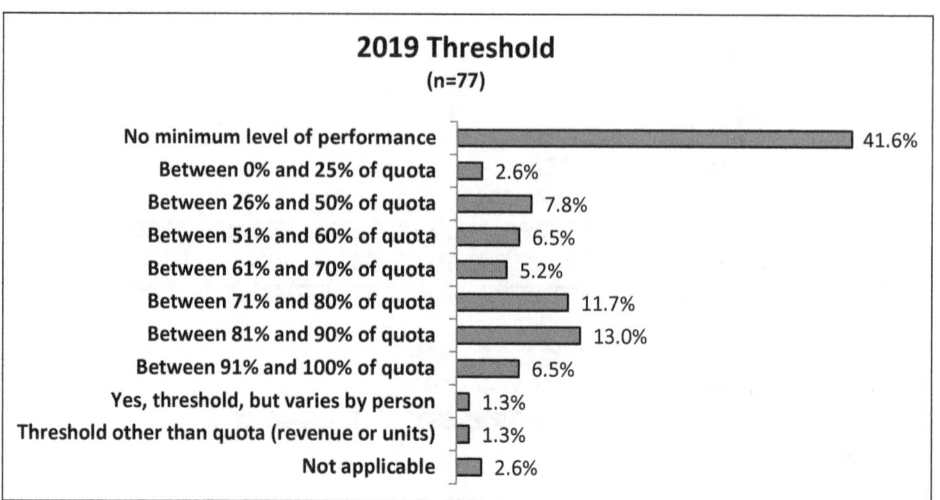

Survey Findings. 55.8% have a threshold on the primary measure for the sales compensation plan for the primary sales job. 41.6% do not have a threshold.

Observations. More than half of the respondents use a threshold. A simple rule to follow suggests that thresholds should sit at or above previously sold recurring/assured revenue.

2019 Clawbacks: Can all or any part of the incentive payment be clawed back (repaid to the company) for any reason?

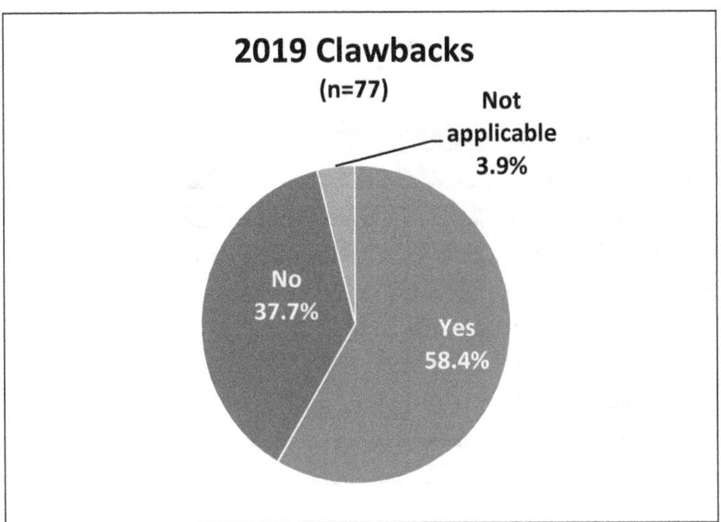

Survey Findings. 58.4% use a clawback to recover monies already paid to sales personnel in the primary sales job. 37.7% do not claw back paid monies.

Observations. A majority of survey participants have a clawback practice. A general rule is to claw back or recover paid monies in instances where the company is not paid for the order, regardless of the reason.

2019 New Hires: What is your incentive practice for new hires into the primary sales job?

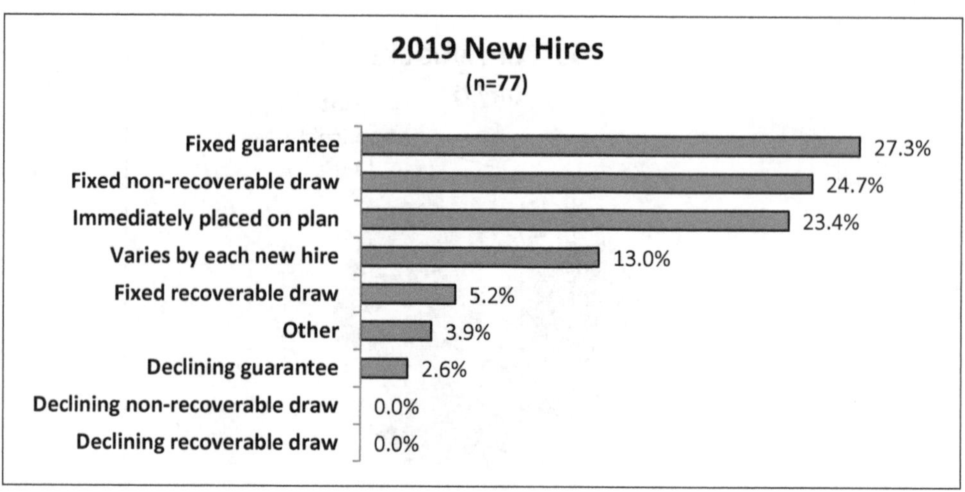

Other Practices for New Hires

- Put on plan after a 30-59-day grace period
- Immediately placed on plan with first two months of guarantee due to system reporting lags to pay

Survey Findings. 27.3% place a new hire on a fixed guarantee. Another 24.7% provide a fixed non-recoverable draw. 23.4% immediately place the new hire on the incentive plan.

Observations. 52% provide some "cushion" for new hires, either a guarantee or draw. Generally, the longer the ramp-up period, the more likely a company will provide some type of draw or guarantee until the seller is trained, acclimated and productive.

QUOTAS

Quotas are an integral part of most sales compensation plans. They provide management with the opportunity to calibrate and assign seller sales production. Unfortunately, there is no single approach, no proven method, which will assure 100% accurate quotas with 100% acceptance by the field organization. Most organizations make every effort to be fair and reasonable, while still being consistent with corporate sales expectations.

- **Quotas:** 50% was the *median* population of sales personnel reaching quota among the surveyed companies in 2018.
- **2018 Quotas Changes:** 38.5% of the companies did not have any mid-year quota changes for sales personnel in the primary sales job during 2018.
- **2018 Sales Crediting:** 100% is the *median* revenue performance for sales crediting purposes when compared to actual revenue.
- **2018 Quota Performance:** 95% was the *median* quota performance for sales personnel in 2018.
- **2019 Quotas Compared to Forecast:** 42.3% of the surveyed companies indicate sellers' goals exceed the sales department's objectives.
- **2019 Quota Allocation Method:** 30.4% use top-down allocation by field sales management

Summary Observations

Quotas. While companies often report they want 60% to 70% of their sales personnel to reach and exceed quota, the surveyed companies report approximately 50% of their sales personnel actually reached quota. A minimal to low level of mid-year quota changes reflects stable business conditions and a well-designed quota allocation method. 38.5% did not have any mid-year quota changes. The amount of double crediting appears minimal. In 2018, median quota performance was 95%. 42.3% over assign goals (sum of sellers' goals exceeds the sales department's sales objective). 30.4% use a top-down quota-setting method.

Quotas: What percent of sales personnel in the primary sales job met or exceeded quota in 2018?

10th Perc	25th Perc	50th Perc	75th Perc	90th Perc	Average
25	35	50	65	75	51.1

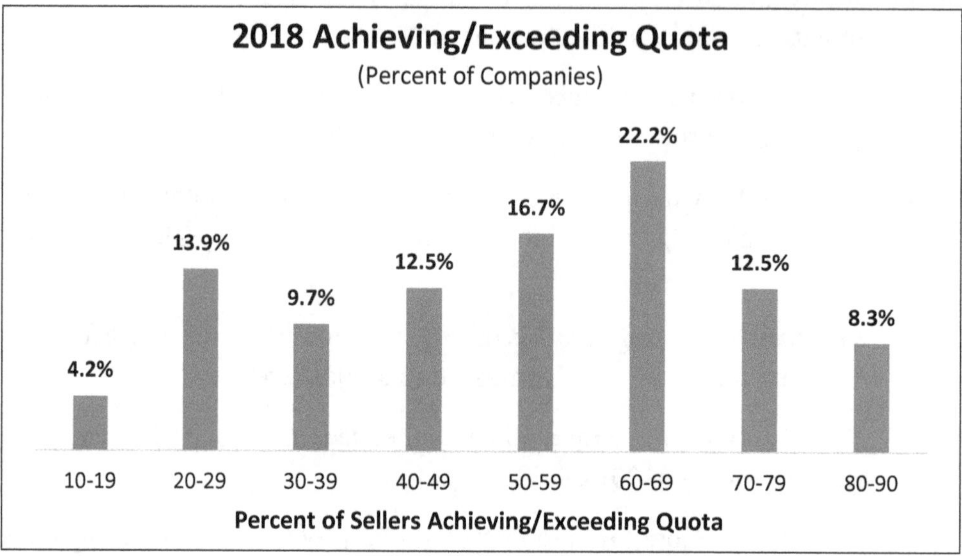

Survey Findings. 50% was the *median* population of sales personnel reaching quota among the surveyed companies in 2018. 51.1% was the *average* population of sales personnel reaching quota among the surveyed companies. 59.7% of the reporting companies had 50% or more of their sales personnel achieving quota.

Observations. When modeling plan costs, assumptions about quota performance should reflect the range of possible quota outcomes.

2018 Quotas Changes: In 2018, what percent of incumbents in the primary sales job had their quotas changed mid-performance period?

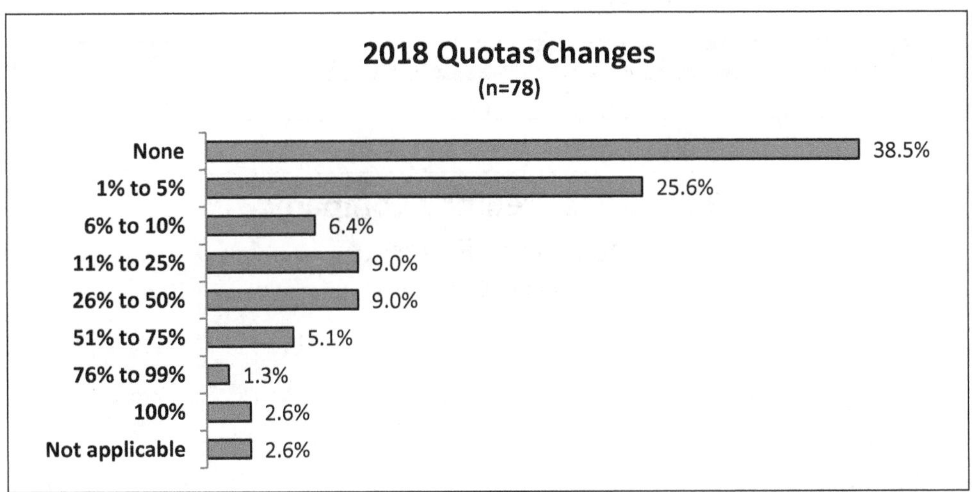

Survey Findings. 38.5% of the companies did not have any mid-year quota changes for sales personnel in the primary sales job during 2018. 25.6% reported that they made quota changes to 1% to 5% of sales personnel in the primary sales job.

Observations. A minimal to low level of quota changes reflects stable business conditions and a well-designed quota allocation and ongoing effective quota management process.

2018 Sales Crediting: Is your sales crediting for compensation purposes different than your actual revenue? In 2018, estimate the compensable revenue as a percent of actual revenue.

10th Perc	25th Perc	50th Perc	75th Perc	90th Perc	Average
86	95	100	100	104	95.1

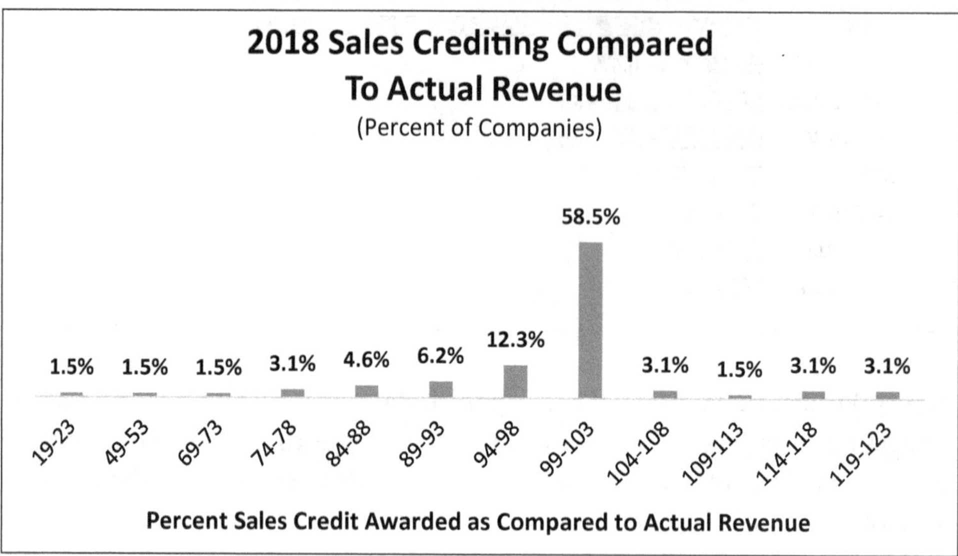

Survey Findings. 100% is the *median* revenue performance for sales crediting purposes when compared to actual revenue. 95.1% is the *average* revenue performance applied for sales crediting purposes when compared to actual revenue.

Observations. The amount of double crediting appears modest according to these results. Crediting above 100% is double crediting. Sales crediting below 100% of actual revenue often reflects sales credit caps or non-credited house accounts.

2018 Quota Performance: What was the average (not median) percent sales quota achievement in 2018 for incumbents in the primary sales job?

10th Perc	25th Perc	50th Perc	75th Perc	90th Perc	Average
55.5	86.2	95	100.8	104.9	89

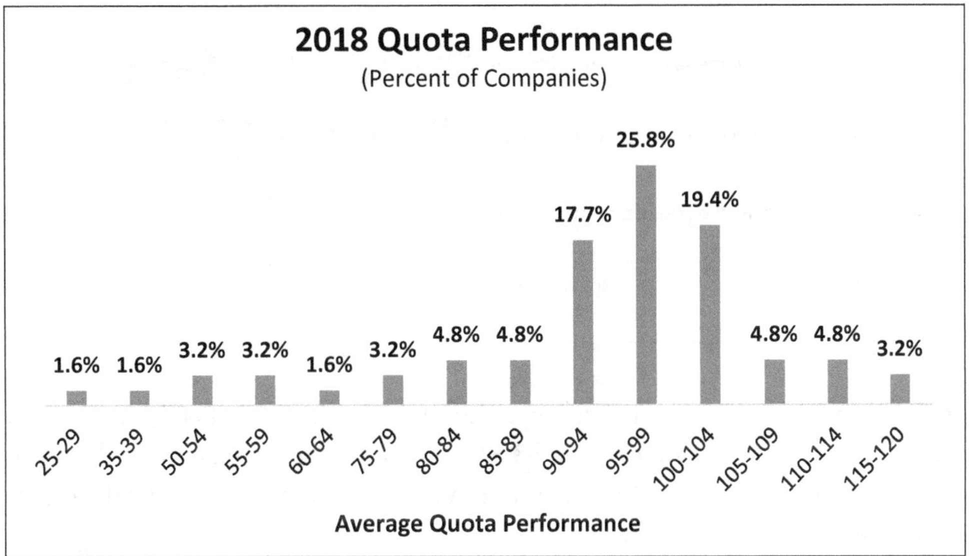

Survey Findings. 95% was the *median* quota performance for sales personnel in 2018. 89% was the *average* quota performance in 2018. 62.9% of the companies reported *average* performance between 90% and 104%.

Observations. 95% of target is the *median* average quota performance. Individual payouts will reflect this less than expected performance.

2019 Quotas Compared to Forecast: For 2019, how does the summation of assigned quotas to sales personnel compare to the sales department's objective (e.g., over assignment, match or under assignment)?

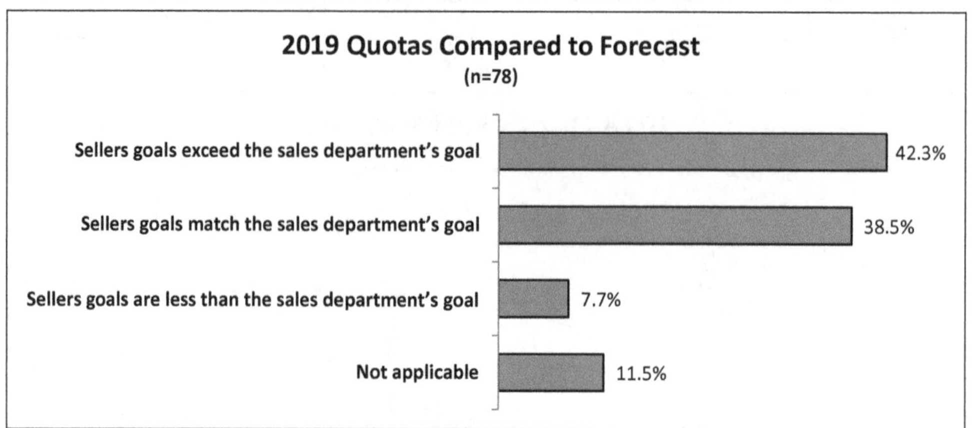

Survey Findings. 42.3% of the surveyed companies indicate sellers' goals exceed the sales department's objectives. 38.5% indicate sales management does not over-assign goals. And, 7.7% under assign the sales department's goal to sales personnel.

Observations. The most prevalent practice is to over-assign quotas as compared to the sales department's sales goal. However, only 42.3% of the reporting companies over-assign goals.

2019 Quota Allocation Method: Which of the following methods does the company use to allocate sales goals to sales personnel in the primary sales job?

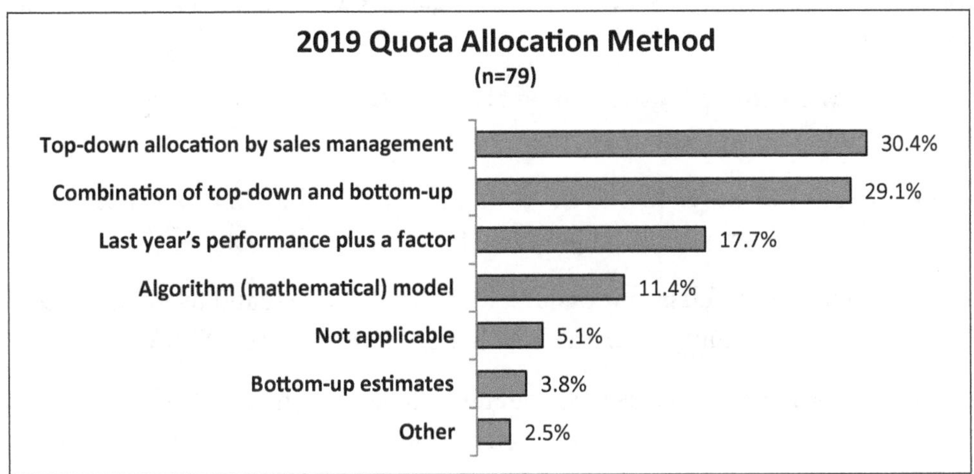

Survey Findings. 30.4% use top-down allocation by field sales management. 29.1% use a combination of top-down and bottom-up to assign sales quotas to sales personnel. 17.7% use last year's performance plus a factor to assign quotas to sales personnel.

Observations. Quota allocation is the process of assigning sales goals to sales personnel. Multiple quota allocation methods are available to sales management. We expect higher sales representative involvement in quota setting for territories with fewer accounts. Conversely, less sales representative participation occurs in the quota allocation process when sales personnel have a high number of indistinguishable accounts.

MOST ASKED QUESTIONS

We frequently get numerous questions about sales management and sales compensation practices. Curious too, we gathered responses on these often-asked questions.

- **New Product Launch Incentives:** 50.6% use a contest/spiff to help launch new product.
- **Profit Measure:** 62% of the companies do not have a profit measure in the sales compensation plan for the primary sales job.
- **Digital and Telephone Sellers:** 53.3% of the digital and telephone sellers are non-exempt under the Fair Labor Standards Act (FLSA).
- **FLSA Exemption Legal Challenge:** 95.6% have had no legal challenges to the exemption status of their inside telephone and digital sellers in the last five years.
- **Tariff/Trade Impact:** 86.5% of the companies have reported no impact on sales compensation due to tariff/trade global tensions and practices.
- **Sales Compensation Plan Eligibility:** 70% cite direct customer contact as the primary criteria for sales compensation eligibility.
- **Incenting New Versus Renewal Business:** 50% treat renewal business the same as new business for compensation purposes.
- **Formula Method:** 61.8% have made no changes to the formula method for their primary sales jobs in the last three years.
- **Duplicate Crediting:** 42.1% provide only the seller sales credit for a sale. 27.6% award sales credit to two sellers.
- **Sales Force Maturity:** 37.2% have seasoned, long-tenured sellers.
- **Young/Entry-Level Sellers:** 61% do not provide any special programs for young/entry-level sellers.
- **Millennial Values:** 75.3% say that "millennial values" have not affected sales management programs.
- **Millennial Values:** The majority of companies have not made any changes due to "millennial values." However, for those adopting new practices, the list varies: work from home, experience awards rather than cash, team-based selling, student loan repayment and more feedback, all offering interesting ideas for consideration.

- **Stock/Equity/Long-Term Incentive Eligibility:** 53.8% do not provide stock/equity/long-term incentives to sales personnel.
- **Long-Term Incentives—Frequency of Awards:** 57.5% who do provide stock, grant the long-term incentives annually, 30% provide at time of new hire.
- **All Sellers Program—Value of Long-Term Incentives:** $9,125 is the 50th percentile *median* value of the incentive awards if redeemed today.

Summary Observations

New Product Launch Incentives. 70.9% of the companies provide some type of "additional" incentive to reward new product results.

Profit Measure. 62% of the companies do not have a profit measure in the sales compensation plan for the primary sales job. However, sales management should use such a measure if the salesperson can materially affect profit outcomes.

Digital and Telephone Sellers. Only 53.3% of the digital and telephone sellers are non-exempt under the Fair Labor Standards Act (FLSA). Seek employment law legal assistance to correctly establish the exemption status of digital/telephone-based sellers. More than 4% of the reporting companies have had legal challenges to their exemption status.

Tariff/Trade Impact. 13.5% of the reporting companies have seen an impact on sales due to tariff/trade conflicts. Only 2.7% of the companies have changed quotas.

Sales Compensation Plan Eligibility. Companies use many factors to determine sales compensation eligibility. The most popular are: direct customer contact, sales quota responsibility and having an assigned sales territory.

Incenting New Versus Renewal Business. Half the companies treat new business the same as renewal business for sales compensation purposes. Only 23.7% reward more for new business versus renewal business.

Formula Method. 61.8% have made no changes to the formula method for their primary sales jobs in the last three years. After "other," the most prevalent change (7.9%) was to change a flat commission plan by adding payout ramps tied to quota performance.

Duplicate Crediting. Most companies limited the number of individuals getting sales credit for a single order. 42.1% provide sales credit only to the seller. 85.5% limit sales credit to three or fewer sellers.

Sales Force Maturity. Most reporting sales organizations have a mid-career or seasoned sales force. Generally, more experienced sellers are more productive. 61% do not provide any special programs for young/entry-level sellers.

Millennial Values. 75.3% say that "millennial values" have not affected sales management programs. While intentionally left undefined in the survey questionnaire, "millennial values" have had an impact on sales management programs for almost 25% of the reporting companies. Such changes include changes to work place policies and practices, increased use of teaming and collaboration and increased community volunteer events. Others include work from home, experience awards rather than cash, team-based selling, student loan repayment and more feedback.

Stock/Equity/Long-Term Incentive Eligibility. 53.8% do not provide stock/equity/long-term incentives to sales personnel. Only 17.9% provide awards to all sales personnel. 57.5% who do provide stock, grant the long-term incentives annually, 30% provide at time of new hire. Only half of the reporting companies provide any long-term incentives; of those, only half provide awards annually. The remaining companies identify other events such as promotions, significant sales events and achieving sales goals as triggers for long-term awards. The economic value of long-term incentives is relatively modest with 42.9% of the stock awards worth less than $5,099; the median is $9,125.

New Product Launch Incentives: What is the most common method to reward mid-year new product launches?

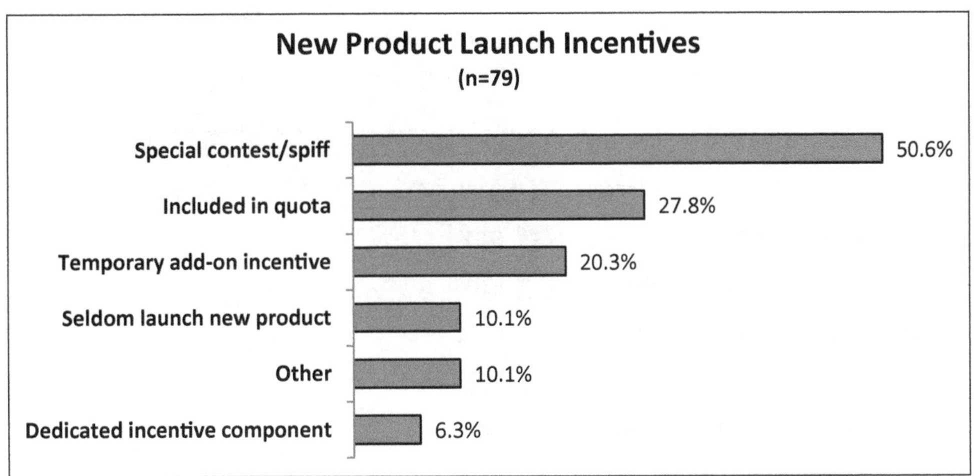

Other New Product Launch Incentives

- Have not addressed
- Provide quota credit uplift
- Pay commissions without changing quota
- Include sales in achievement, but not in quota
- Product launch billings are included in revenue
- Commission

Survey Findings. 50.6% use a contest/spiff to help launch new product. 27.8% include the new product in the sales compensation quota. 20.3% provide a temporary add-on incentive to support a new product launch.

Observations. When combined, special contest/spiff and temporary add-on incentive, 70.9% of the companies provide "additional" incentive to reward new product results.

Profit Measure: What profit measure do you use in the incentive program for the primary sales job?

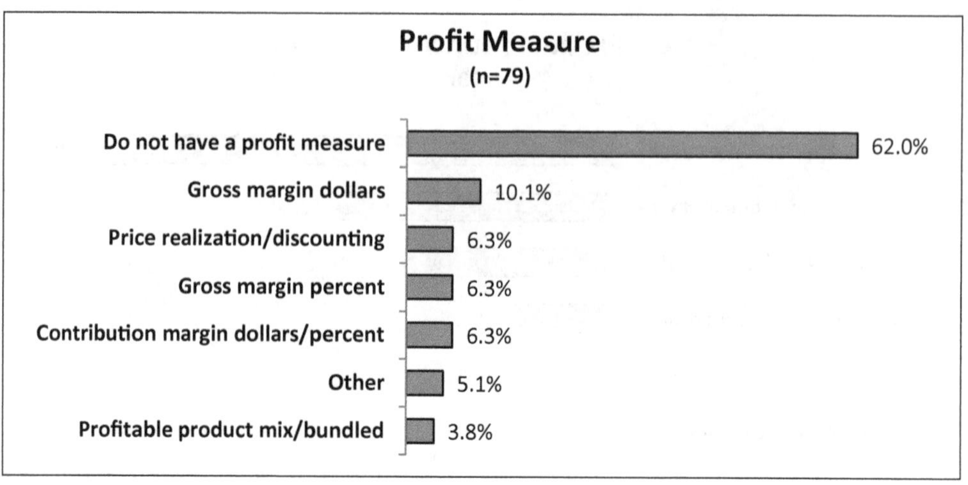

Other Profit Measures

- Operating profit
- Segment margin profit
- Profit index factor
- Standard margin

Survey Findings. 62% of the companies do not have a profit measure in the sales compensation plan for the primary sales job. 10.1% use a gross profit measure. 6.3% use a price realization/discounting measure.

Observations. More than 60% of the companies do not include a profit measure in the sales compensation plan. However, sales management should use such a measure if the salesperson can materially affect profit outcomes.

Digital and Telephone Sellers: What is the FLSA exemption status of the inside digital or telephone sales team? *FLSA: Fair Labor Standards Act

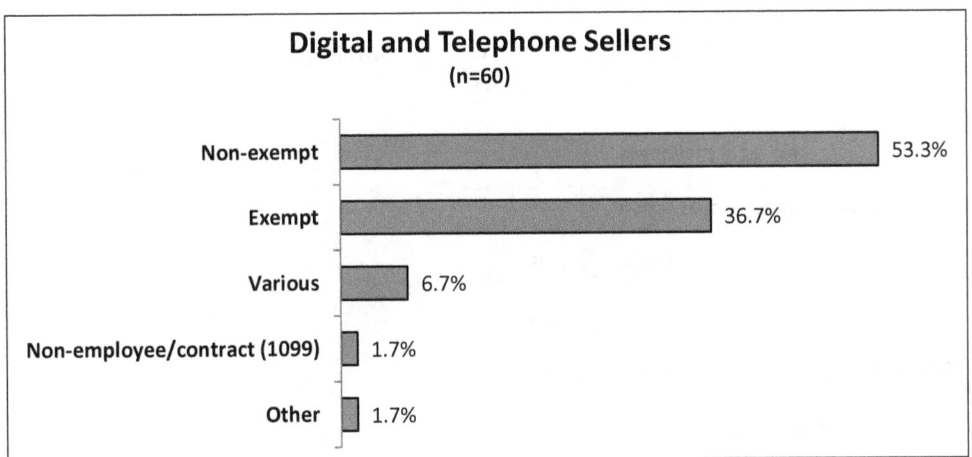

Survey Findings. 53.3% of the digital and telephone sellers are non-exempt under the Fair Labor Standards Act (FLSA). 36.7% are classified exempt and 6.7% have a variety of practices.

Observations. Most telephone-based sellers do not quality for exemption status; however, 36.7% of the companies have found a means to classify their telephone-based selling jobs as exempt.

FLSA Exemption Legal Challenge: Have you had any legal challenges to your exemption status for inside telephone and digital sellers in the last five years?

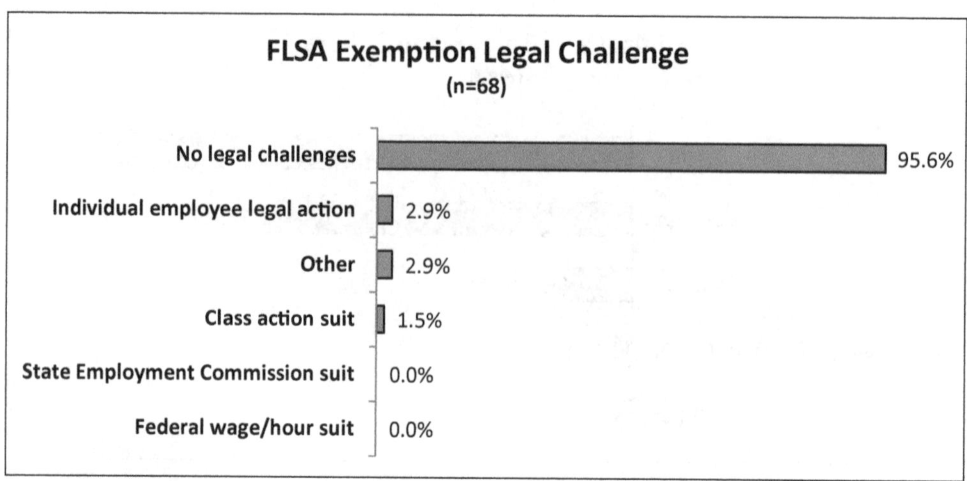

Survey Findings. 95.6% have had no legal challenges to the exemption status of their inside telephone and digital sellers in the last five years.

Observations. As reflected in the low incidence of legal challenges, management has successfully classified inside and digital sellers into the right Fair Labor Standards Act exemption status.

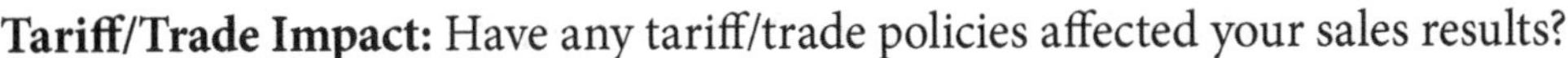

Tariff/Trade Impact: Have any tariff/trade policies affected your sales results?

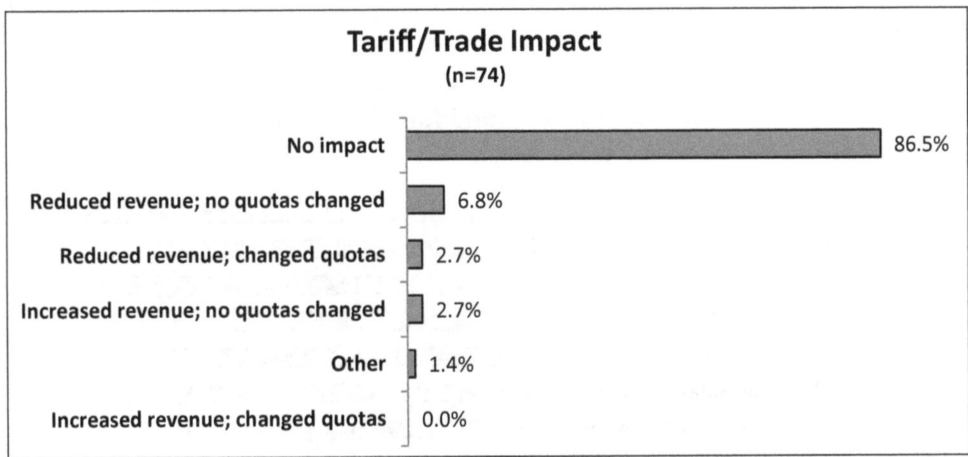

Survey Findings. 86.5% of the companies have reported no impact on sales compensation due to tariff/trade global tensions and practices.

Observations. Tariff and trade conflicts have impacted the revenues of 13.5% of the surveyed companies. If tariff and trade conflicts expand, we would expect to see adjustments to quotas, either up or down. To date, only 2.7% of the companies have changed quotas.

Sales Compensation Plan Eligibility: What criteria do you use to determine which jobs participate in the sales compensation plan (at-risk; with upside) eligibility?

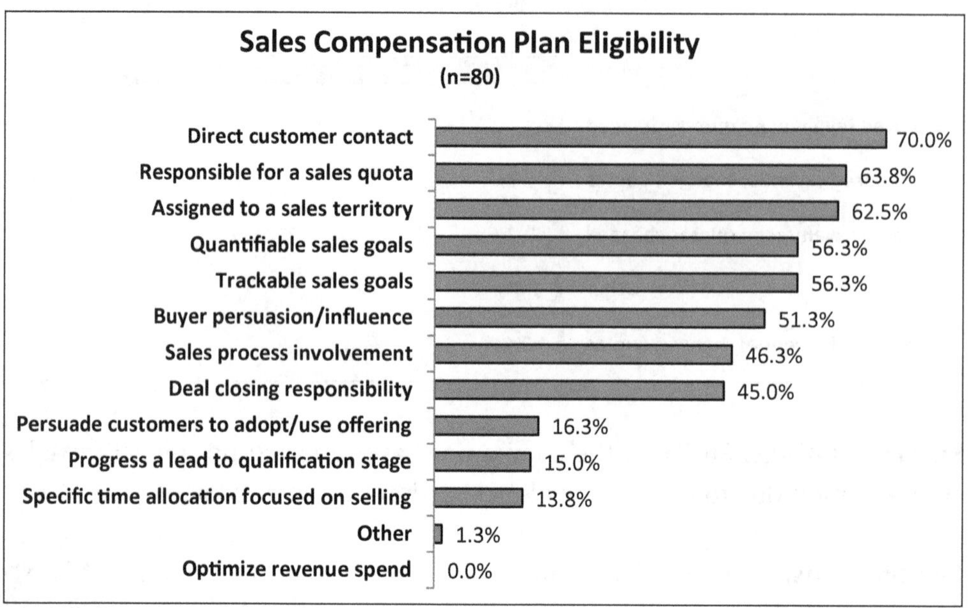

Survey Findings. 70% cite direct customer contact as the primary criteria for sales compensation eligibility. 63.8% list responsibility for a sales quota as the second criteria. 62.5% selected assigned a sales territory as the third most important criteria for determining sales compensation eligibility.

Observations. Sales compensation plan eligibility is driven by customer sales responsibility: contact, quota and territory assignment.

Incenting New Versus Renewal Business: For sales compensation purposes, do you treat new sales different from renewals?

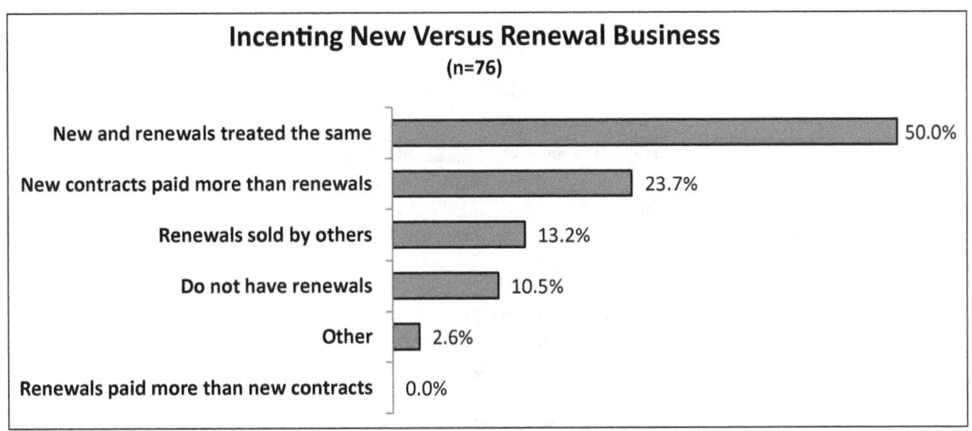

Other Methods for Incenting New Versus Renewal Business

- Managed by different teams
- Different roles have a different mix of new/renewals pay rates

Survey Findings. 50% treat renewal business the same as new business for compensation purposes. 23.7% pay new contracts more. 13.2% have renewals sold by others.

Observations. Generally, incentives reward more difficult selling. For 50% of the companies, sales management considers both new and renewals of equal value and difficulty. Only 23.7% reward more for new business versus renewal business.

Formula Method: For your primary sales job, have you changed the formula method within the last three years? *ICR: individual commission rate. What is the most recent change?

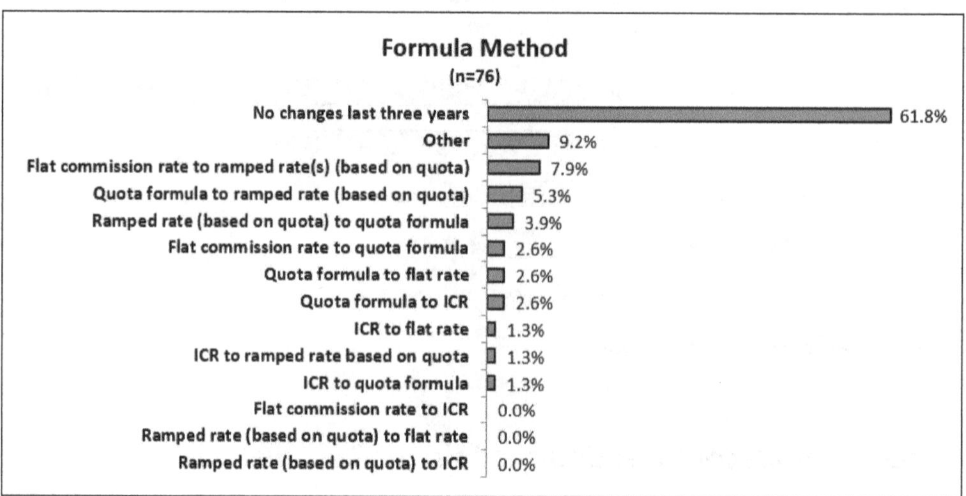

Other Formula Methods

- 2018 was the first year for the sales incentive plan
- Lowered the amount of commissions earned within the first 50% of quota
- Have mixed flat and ICR rates
- No commission
- Removed MBO
- Multiple changes
- Added MBO component of 10%
- Blended average attainment of quotas

Survey Findings. 61.8% have made no changes to the formula method for their primary sales jobs in the last three years. After "other," the most prevalent change (7.9%) was to change a flat commission plan by adding payout ramps tied to quota performance.

Observations. Companies keep their incentive formula for an extended period of time. The varied changes reflect either adopting a quota feature or discounting the use of a quota element.

Duplicate Crediting: For the typical sales deal, how many individuals (excluding managers) will get some form of sales credit?

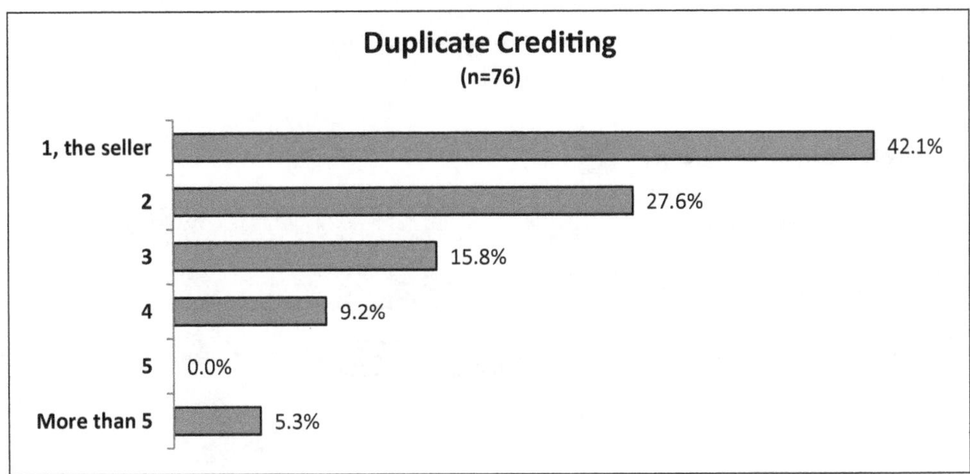

Survey Findings. 42.1% provide only the seller sales credit for a sale. 27.6% award sales credit to two sellers. 15.8% provide credit to three sellers.

Observations. Sharing sales credit should reward those who contribute to the sales outcome. Surprisingly, 5.3% of the companies report more than five people can earn sales credit on the same order.

Sales Force Maturity: How would you best describe your sales team's maturity for the primary sales job?

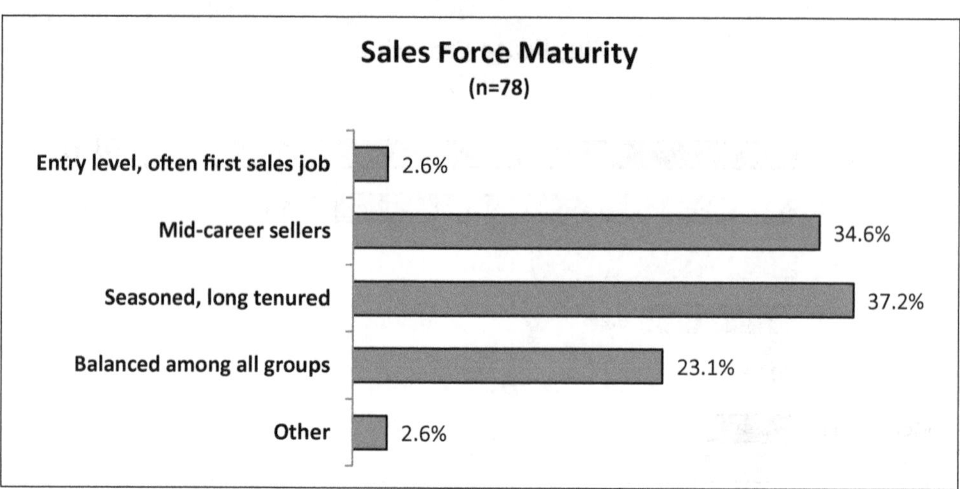

Survey Findings. 37.2% have seasoned, long-tenured sellers. 34.6% have mid-career sellers. 23.1% have a balanced maturity among entry-level, mid-career and seasoned, long-tenured sellers.

Observations. Most reporting sales organizations have a mid-career or seasoned sales force. Generally, more experienced sellers are more productive.

Young/Entry-Level Sellers: For any sales job, do you offer any special pay programs for your young/entry-level sellers?

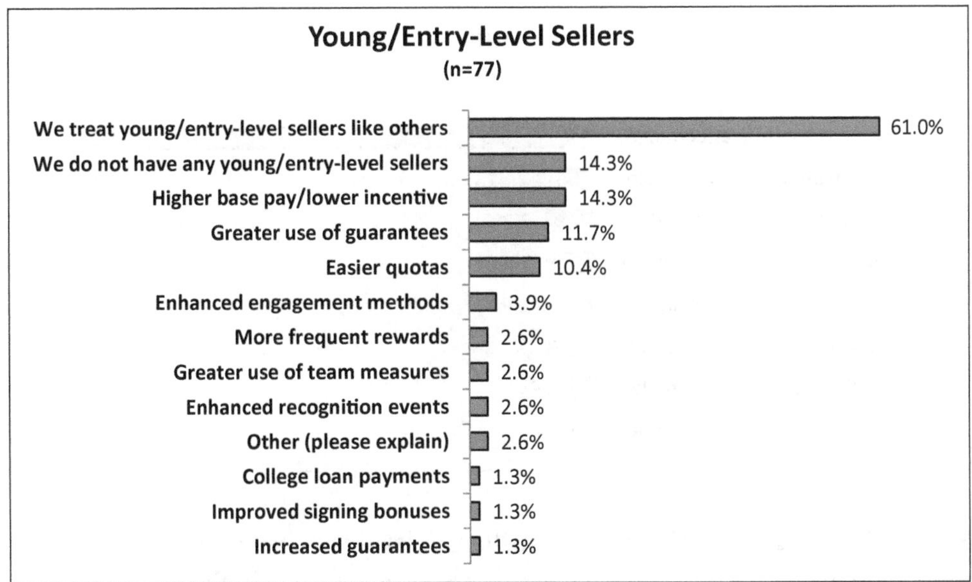

Survey Findings. 61% do not provide any special programs for young/entry-level sellers. 14.3% provide a less aggressive pay mix (higher base pay/lower incentive), and another 11.7% use guarantees to a greater extent.

Observations. While 61% do not provide any special sales compensation treatment for new hires, the rest of the companies use a variety of techniques to help onboard new sellers.

Millennial Values: Have millennial values affected any of the management programs for your sales team?

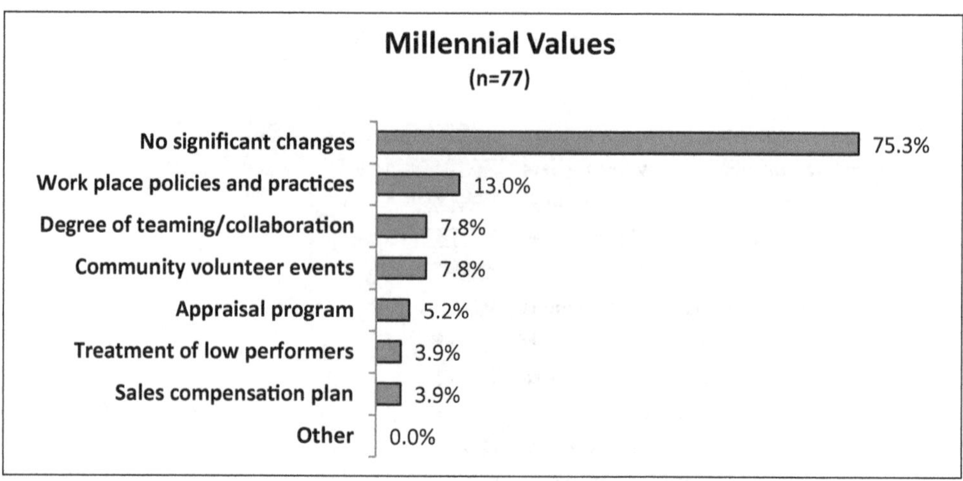

Survey Findings. 75.3% say that "millennial values" have not affected sales management programs. 13% have made changes to work place policies and practices. 7.8% have increased the use of teaming and collaboration. Another 7.8% have increased community volunteer events.

Observations. While intentionally left undefined in the survey questionnaire, "millennial values" have had an impact on sales management programs for almost 25% of the reporting companies.

Millennial Values: Describe the most significant change you have made based on millennial values.

- Work from home
- None at this time, but will need to in the near future as we attract more millennials
- More team-based selling
- Added student loan repayments
- More frequent information updates and feedback
- Accessible restrooms on each floor
- More hedonistic awards/ "experiences" versus cash
- Incentive contests
- Introduced more structure and processes to avoid miscommunication and improve individual accountability
- Flexible work hours
- Comp ratio, higher fixed

Survey Findings and Observations. The majority of companies have not made any changes due to "millennial values." However, for those adopting new practices, the list varies: work from home, experience awards rather than cash, team-based selling, student loan repayment and more feedback, all offering interesting ideas for consideration.

Stock/Equity/Long-Term Incentive Eligibility: Are sales personnel in the primary sales job eligible for long-term incentives (e.g., stock options, restricted stock, stock units)? Exclude stock savings and 401k plans.

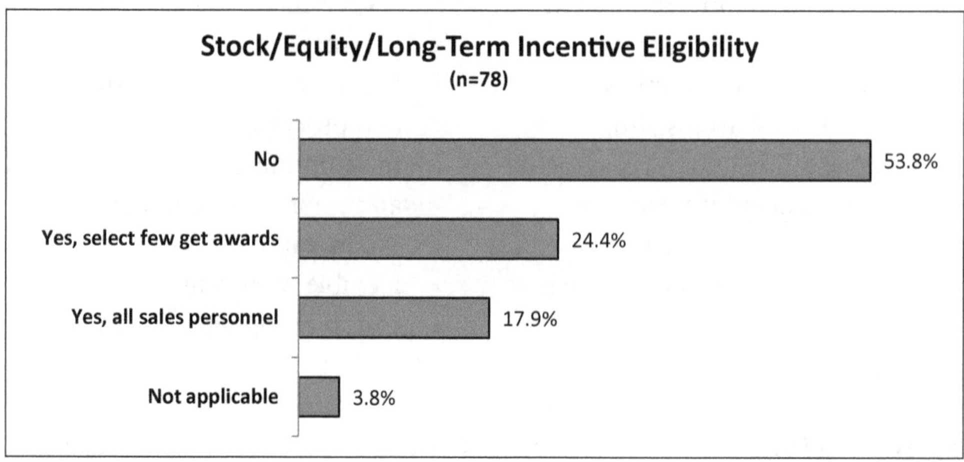

Survey Findings. 53.8% do not provide stock/equity/long-term incentives to sales personnel. 24.4% provide select awards. Only 17.9% provide awards to all sales personnel.

Observations. Only 17.9% of the reporting companies grant stock/equity/long-term incentives for sales personnel on an ongoing basis.

Long-Term Incentives—Frequency of Awards: If you provide long-term incentives to all sales personnel, how often do sellers get awards? If you do not provide long-term incentives to sales personnel, leave blank.

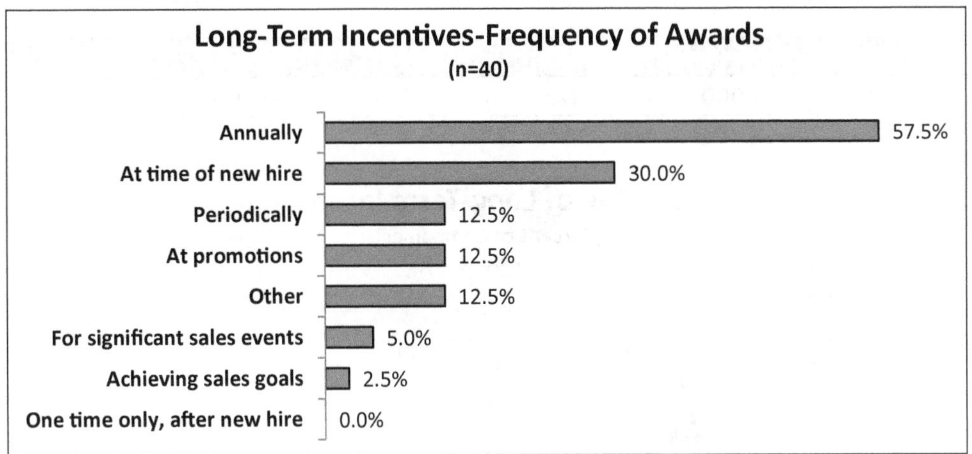

Other Long-Term Incentives—Frequency of Awards

- Retention awards for high potentials
- Only sales directors have LTI and it's awarded annually

Survey Findings. 57.5% who do provide stock, grant the long-term incentives annually. 30% provide at time of new hire.

Observations. Only half of the reporting companies provide any long-term incentives; of those, only half provide awards annually. The remaining companies identify other events such as promotions, significant sales events and achieving sales goals as triggers for long-term awards.

All Sellers Program—Value of Long-Term Incentives: If you provide long-term incentives to all sales personnel, what is the "average total cash value" in dollars per person for those incentives if redeemed today? Provide average estimate. If you do not provide long-term incentives to sales personnel, leave blank.

10th Perc	25th Perc	50th Perc	75th Perc	90th Perc	Average
650	2000	9125	12375	28500	12096.4

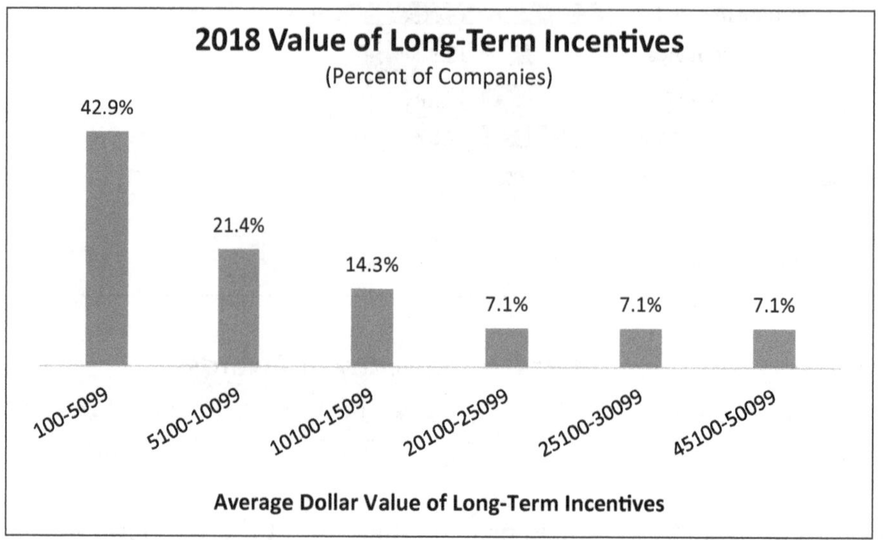

Survey Findings. $9,125 is the 50th percentile *median* value of the incentive awards if redeemed today. $12,096.40 is the *average* value.

Observations. The economic value of long-term incentives is relatively modest with 42.9% of the stock awards worth less than $5,099.

DEMOGRAPHICS

Fiscal Year: In what month does your fiscal 2019 year begin?

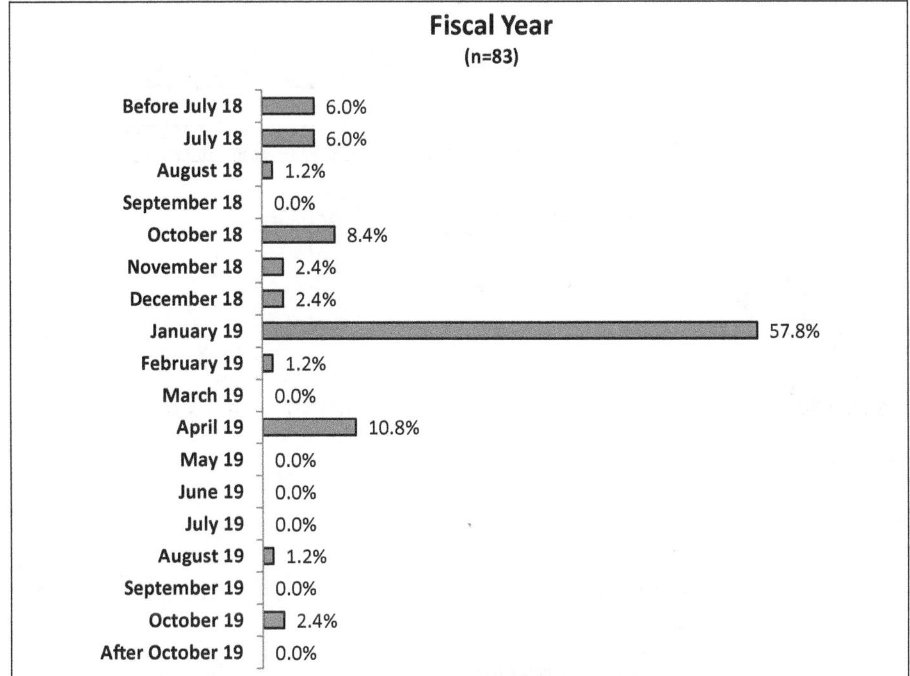

Number of Eligible Participants: For your division sales unit, how many employees are eligible to participate in the sales compensation program?

10th Perc	25th Perc	50th Perc	75th Perc	90th Perc	Average
33.6	100	214	675	1200	454.3

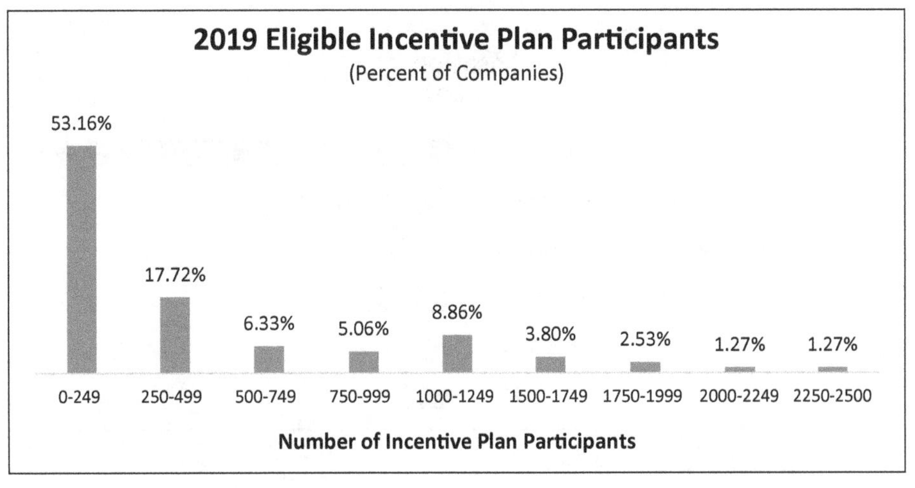

Type of Product/Service: Your division sales unit is primarily selling a:

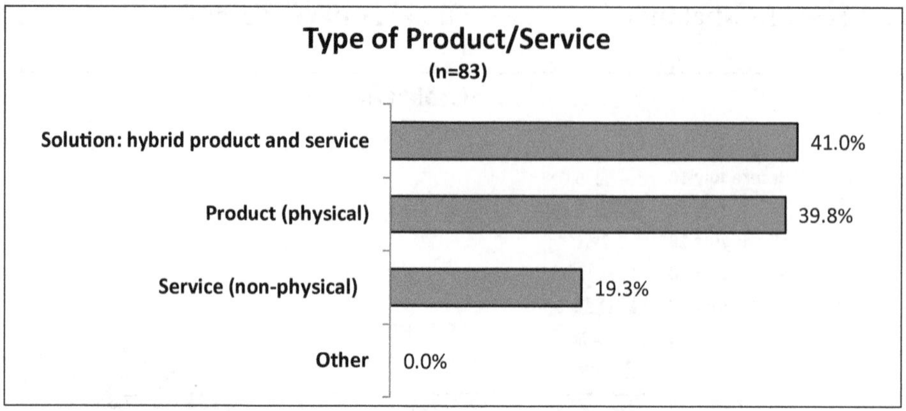

Sales Model: Your primary sales model for the division sales unit is:

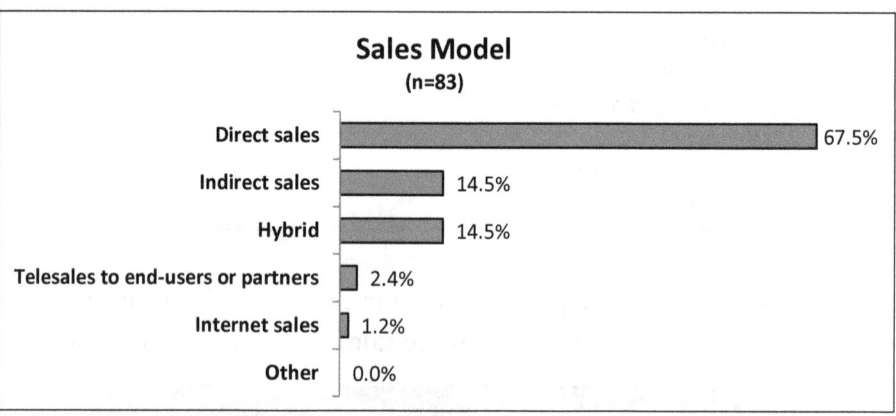

Location: Your sales division sales unit is located in:

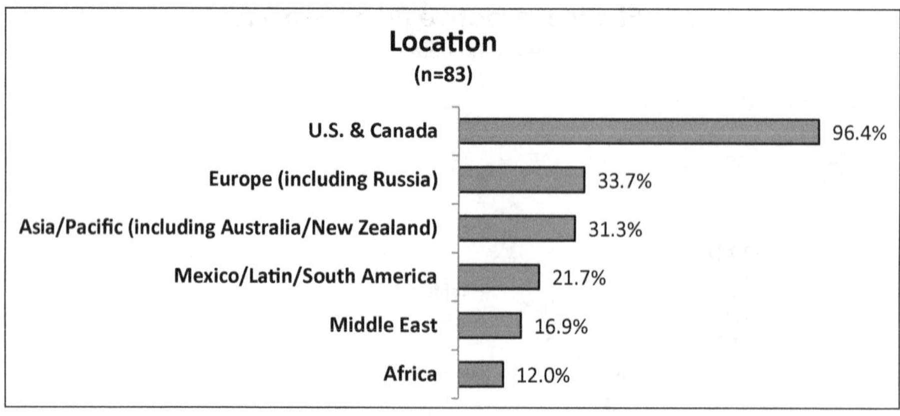

Industry Category: For the division sales unit, your industry is (if possible, avoid selecting "Other"):

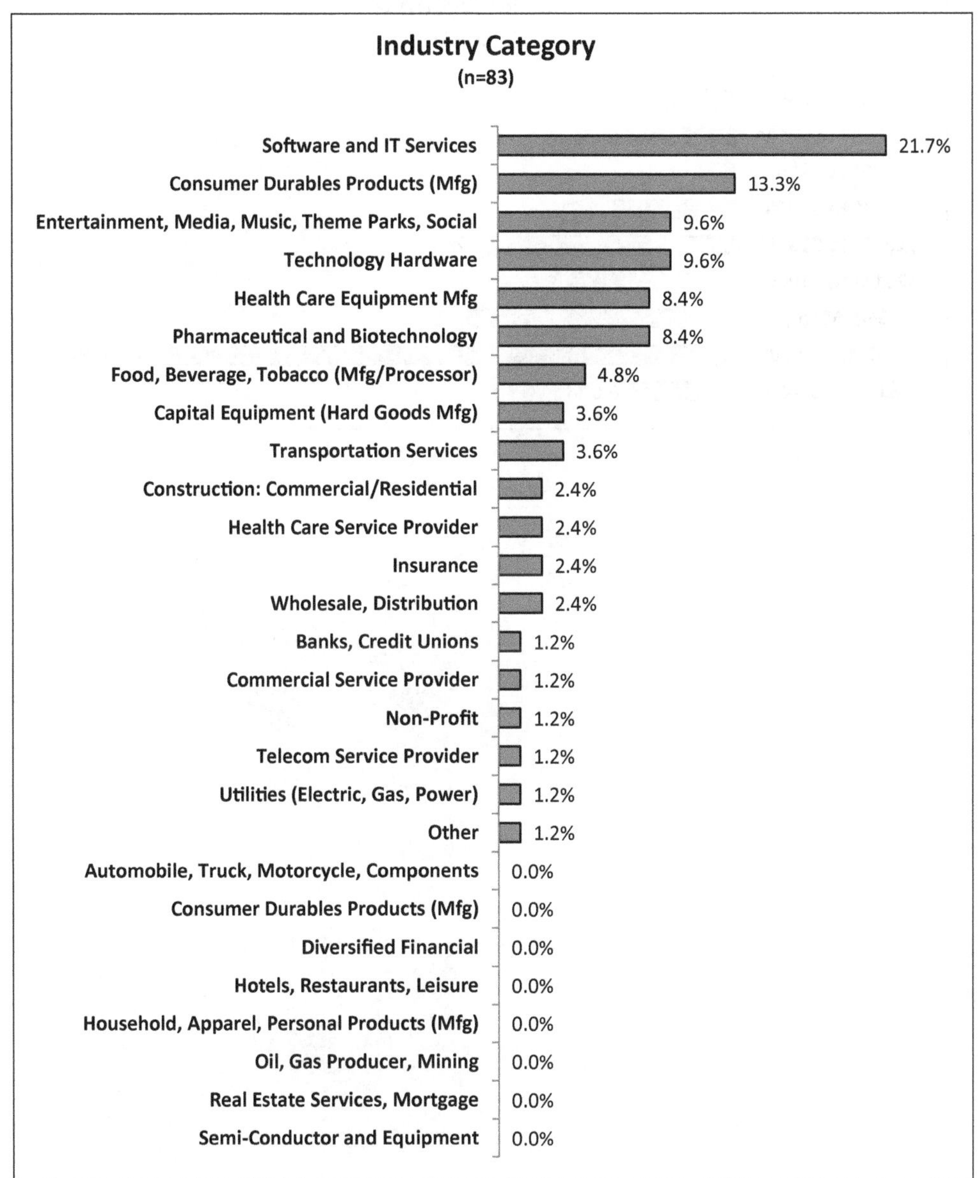

Other Industry Category

- Water Quality
- Health Care Insurance
- Med Device Capital & Consumable

Sales Volume: The division's sales for 2018 will be (approximately):

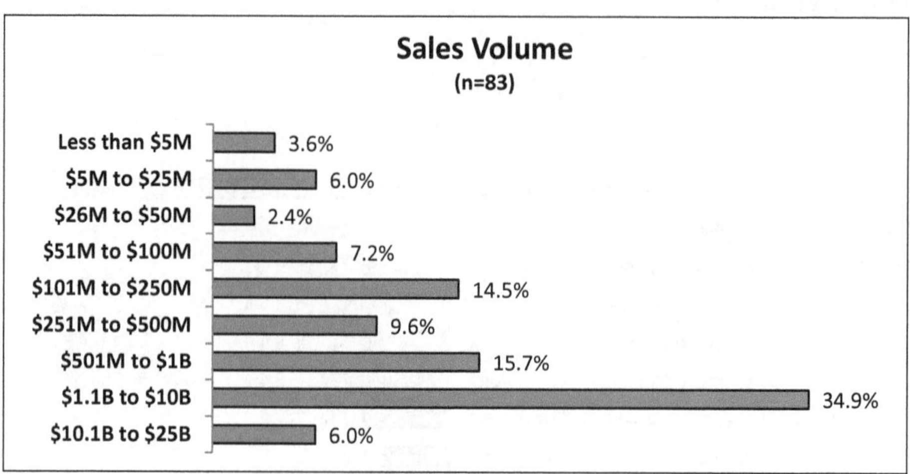

SALES COMPENSATION: MULTIYEAR TRENDS

SALES COMPENSATION ALMANAC • 2020

MULTIYEAR TRENDS DATA

Conducted each year since 2003, the *Sales Compensation Trends Survey* captures a moving history of sales compensation program trends. Economic cycles affect certain outcomes such as revenue, quota performance and pay increase amounts. The data and charts reveal the impact of these cycles. Other practices, such as annual revisions to the sales compensation program, remain relatively constant.

LISTING OF CHARTS

- Change in Annual Revenue—Projected Versus Actual
- Actual Headcount Changes
- Turnover Rate
- Sales Compensation Program Effectiveness
- Payouts and Performance
- Most Common Sales Compensation Challenges
- Extent of Program Changes
- Average Quota Achievement
- Percent Achieving Quota
- Projected Change in Total Earnings
- Actual Change in Incentive Payments

Change in Annual Revenue—Projected Versus Actual

Each year, the Alexander Group (AGI) asks survey participants two questions: How much do you expect revenue to grow next year? And, how much did revenue grow for the previous year? Revenue projections affect quota setting, which affects sales compensation plan payouts. The more accurate the revenue forecast (as compared to the actual), the more likely sales personnel will have stretch but achievable sales quotas. When the two numbers vary (either, the actual is above or below the projected revenue growth), variance in plan payouts will most likely occur. **Observations:** 2018 saw the projected and actual increase in revenue to be equal (6%). The two numbers were the same in 2017, too (5%). This outcome suggests that the quotas were realistic and sales personnel had a reasonable chance to reach and exceed goal. Overall, 2018 program effectiveness ratings are positive, most likely influenced in the alignment of projected and actual sales revenue outcome.

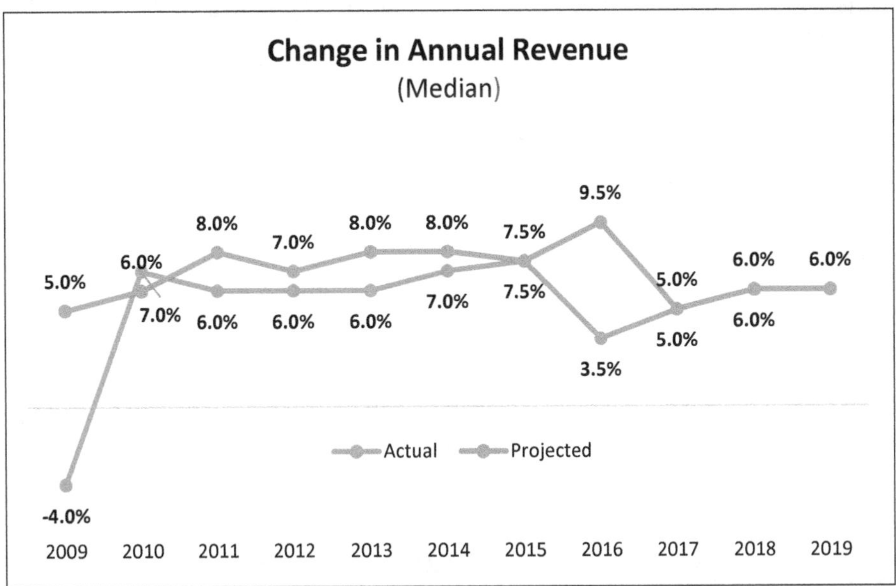

Actual Headcount Changes

Overall, sales entities continue to increase headcount. In 2018, 52.5% of the companies increased headcount. 21.8% decreased headcount. 26.1% had no change. Confidence in hiring is related to sales growth opportunity expectations. **Observations:** 2018 builds on the last four years of positive headcount growth.

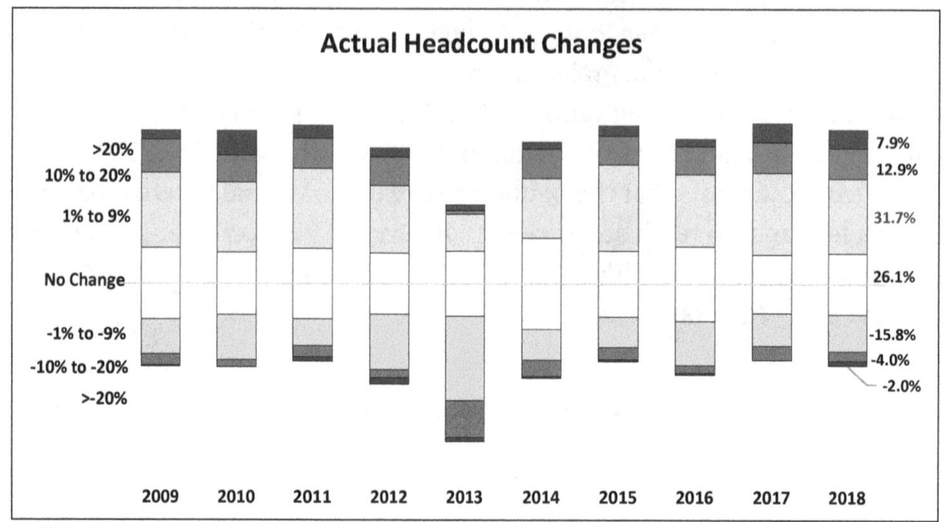

Turnover Rate

Many factors affect turnover rate and these vary by company. These turnover statistics represent both voluntary and involuntary turnover. **Observations:** A typical turnover rate for sales teams is close to 10 percent, with examples of higher and lower turnover rates in select years. 2018 saw a slight increase in turnover rates.

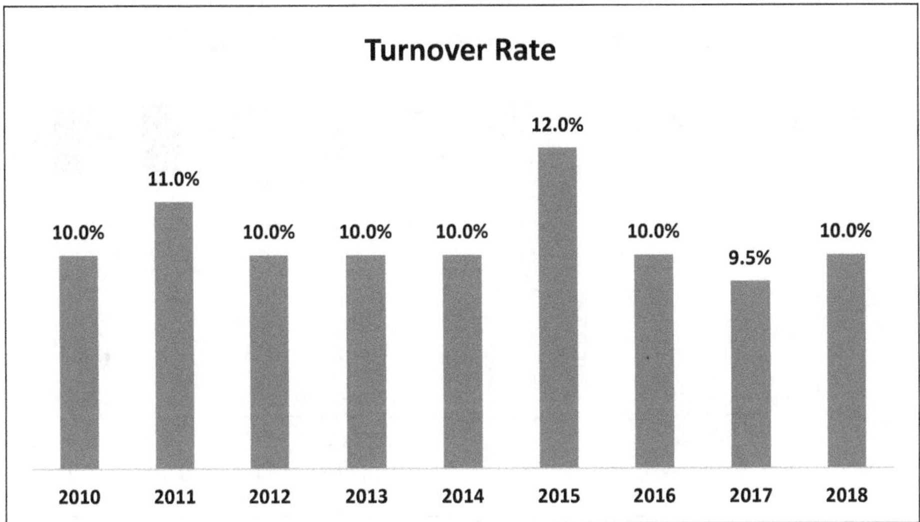

Sales Compensation Program Effectiveness

Most companies believe their sales compensation plans are acceptable and better. For 2018, the population of companies assessing their sales compensation programs as effective or better matched 2017. **Observations:** Companies normally make changes to their sales compensation plans on an annual basis. Generally, most companies find their sales compensation plans to be effective.

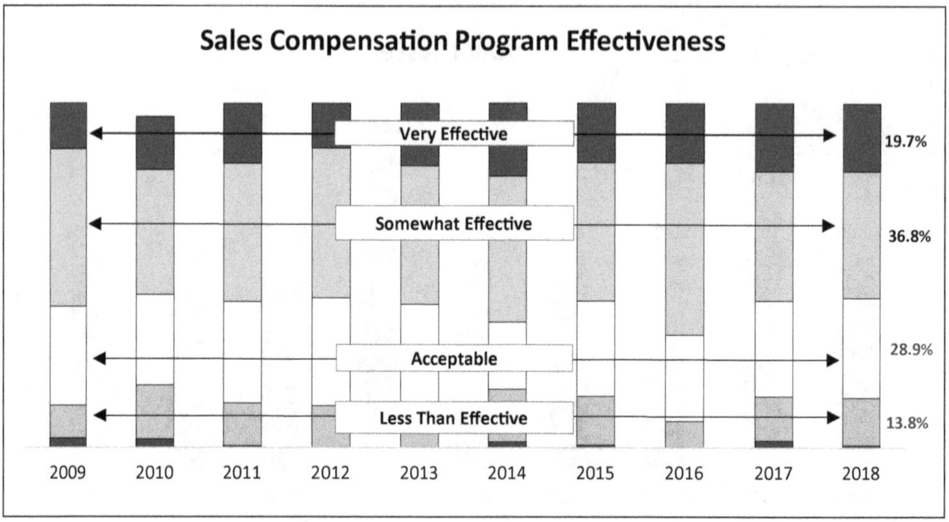

Payouts and Performance

Examining how well payouts matched performance helps assess program effectiveness. The closer payouts match performance, the more effective the program. **Observations:** Only a small percentage of companies found that the payouts did not match performance. In 2018, 12.7% of the companies observed that payouts fully aligned with performance down from 23.7% in 2017. However, payouts mostly matching results improved from 61.9% to 74.7%.

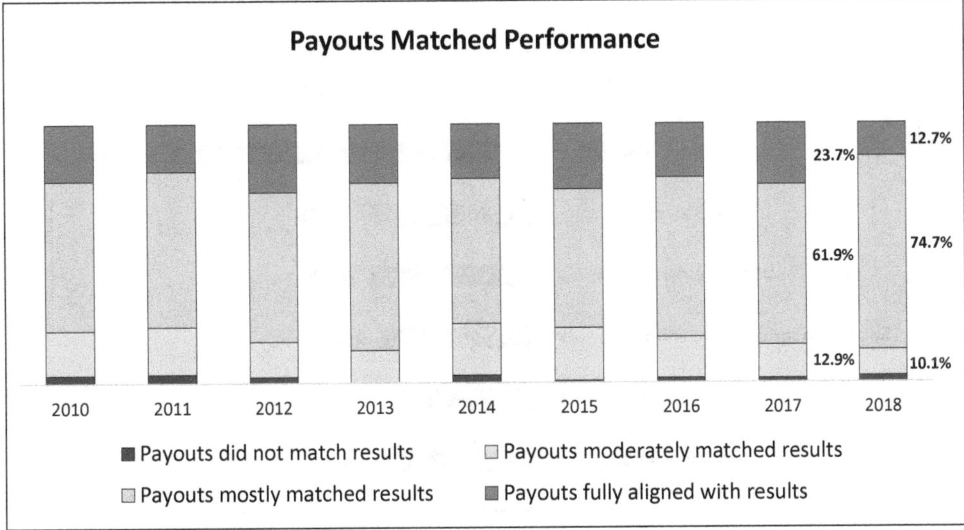

Most Common Sales Compensation Challenges

Each year, AGI asks participants to identify the most common challenges with their sales compensation plans. While there are slight variations of ratings from topic to topic each year, the cited factors in the chart are the top six issues since 2013. The chart provides an average response for the years 2013 through 2018. **Observation:** Correct goal setting remains the number one challenge affecting sales compensation plans.

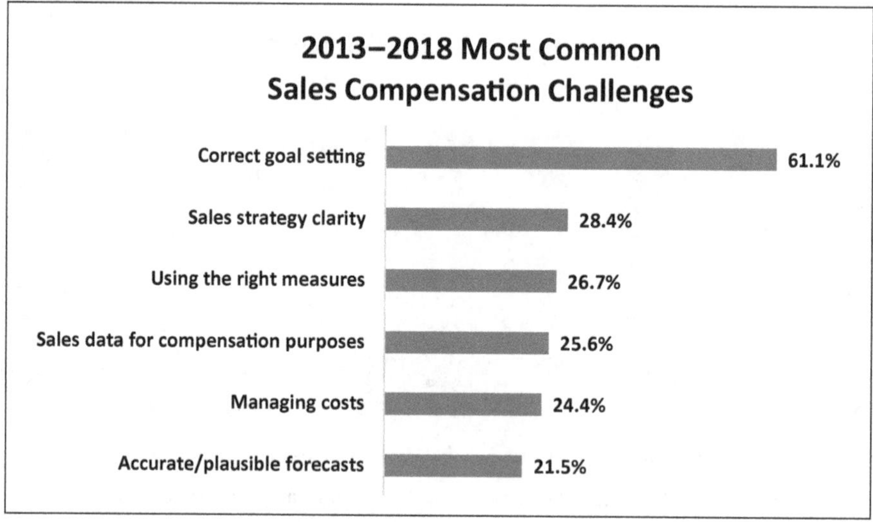

Extent of Program Changes

Sales management makes sales compensation program changes to keep the pay program aligned with sales objectives. Often, management makes changes to the performance measures to ensure strategic alignment. We support these efforts. **Observations:** More than 90 percent of the companies make changes to their sales compensation plans on an annual basis. About 13 percent make major changes to their pay programs each year.

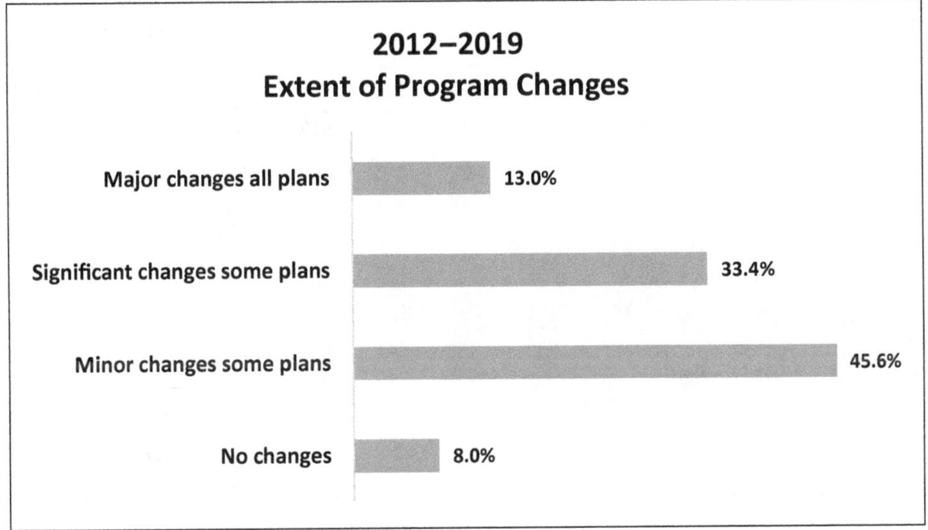

Average Quota Achievement

Average quota achievement gives an overall summary of the sales team's sales success. The average quota achievement includes all participants, both low performers and high performers. **Observation:** 2018 average quota achievement was 95%, the same as 2017.

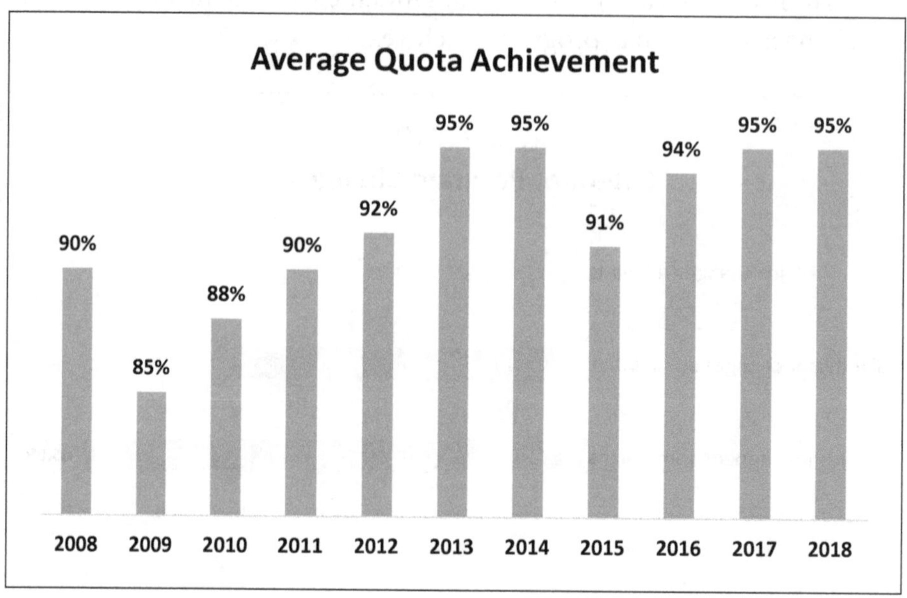

Percent Achieving Quota

Most companies target 60 percent to 70 percent of all sellers to achieve quota. **Observation:** The more typical outcome is for approximately 50 percent of all sellers to reach and exceed quota.

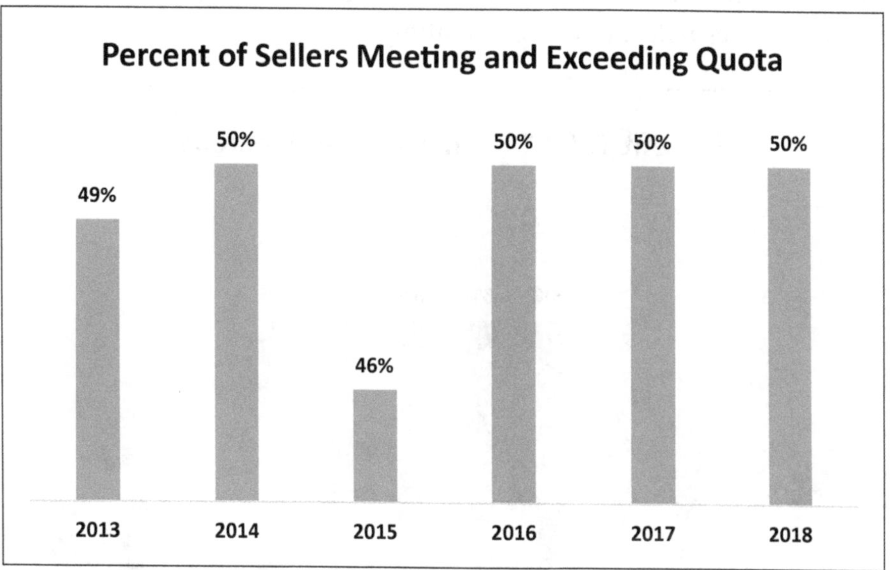

Projected Change in Total Earnings

Each year's wage inflation moves total earnings for all sellers. **Observations:** For the most part, estimated wage inflation (the increase in total earnings including base pay and incentive earnings) tracked at 3 percent since 2011 then declined to 2% starting in 2017 and 2018 and now is back at 3% for 2019. These modest planned increases reflect low wage inflation.

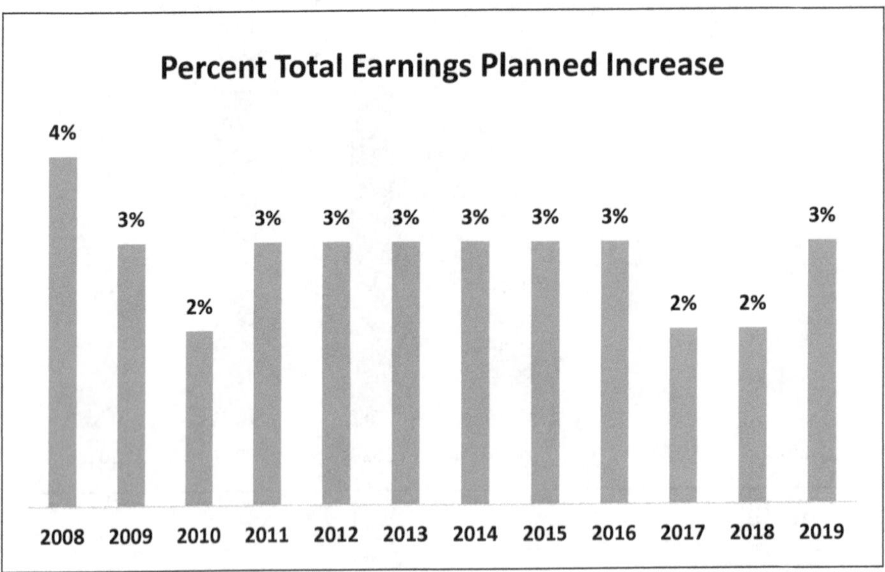

Actual Change in Incentive Payments

Year-to-year change in incentive payments (median) fluctuates. **Observations:** The change in actual incentive payments is an outcome of sales performance affected by market trends, competitor actions and quota difficulty. 2018 recorded a 3% increase in actual incentive payments.

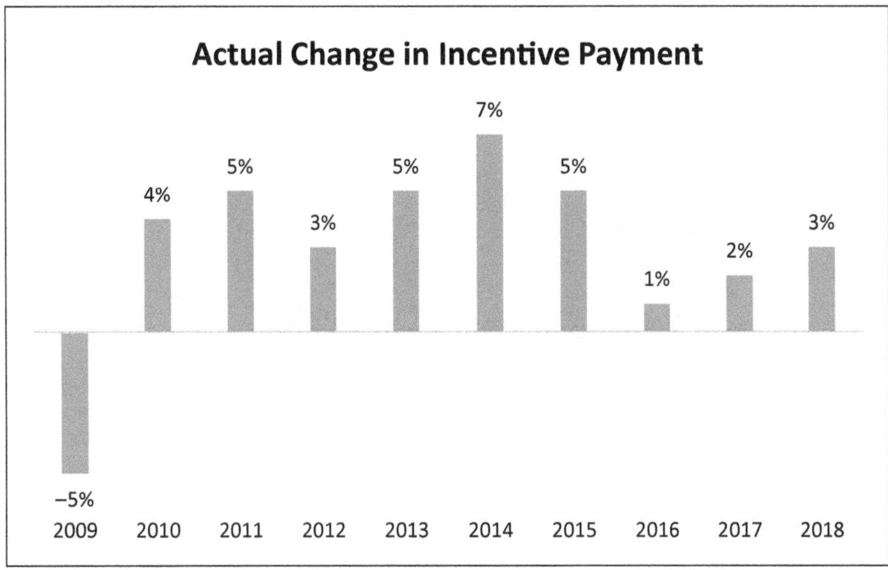

SALES COMPENSATION HOT TOPICS SURVEY

SALES COMPENSATION ALMANAC • 2020

2018 SALES COMPENSATION HOT TOPICS SURVEY

Each year, the sales compensation "hot topics" survey provides in-depth insight into select sales compensation practices. The *Sales Compensation Hot Topics Survey* examined recent and popular topics in sales compensation practices.

IN THIS SECTION

- Executive Summary
- Sales Personnel—New Hires
- Equity Incentives
- Specialty Customer Contact Jobs—Deployment and Pay Practices
- New FASB Regulations—Revenue Recognition: ASC 606
- Performance Measure Categories: Used in Primary Sales Job
- Sales Compensation Practices for the First-Line Sales Manager (FLSM)

EXECUTIVE SUMMARY

Each year, the Alexander Group conducts the *Sales Compensation Hot Topics Survey* to capture current trends, answer popular questions and examine topics of interest. We ask both our clients and our consultants to suggest topics for consideration. Thank you to the 107 participating companies that contributed their professional perspectives on the following topics: demand for new sellers, use of stock, pay practices of specialty customer contact jobs, ASC 606 and first-line sales manager pay programs.

We gathered data from July to August 2018 and published in September 2018. Participants receive a full copy of the survey results.

Noteworthy Highlights

- **Sales Personnel—New Hires:** With the improving economy, we asked participants if sales personnel labor shortages were emerging. At this time, the results suggest: "not yet."
- **Specialty Customer Contact Jobs—Pay Practices:** Jobs with more customer "influence/persuasion" are more likely to have more dollars of target compensation devoted to incentive compensation. Product and vertical sales specialist jobs have the highest portion of pay devoted to incentive among 14 sales affiliated jobs.
- **New FASB Regulations—Revenue Recognition: ASC 606:** While these new guidelines will affect accounting practices, they have yet to alter sales crediting practices for sales compensation purposes.
- **Performance Measure Categories: Used in Primary Sales Job:** Among seven performance categories (production, strategic, productivity, customer experience, activities, citizenship and compliance), production is the dominant performance criterion for sales compensation purposes.
- **Sales Compensation Practices for the First-Line Sales Manager:** For the most part, sales leadership aligns the incentive program of first-line sales managers (FLSMs) with the sellers they supervise.

SALES PERSONNEL—NEW HIRES

Summary: With the improving economy, we asked participants if sales personnel labor shortages were emerging. At this time, the results suggest: "not yet." Typical recruiting challenges remain constant. Open positions remain at historical levels. No significant investments in sales development programs have emerged. Signing bonuses remain muted. Most companies try to place new hires immediately on the incentive plan with a fully assigned quota. However, most provide some temporary guarantee to new hires—a traditional practice.

- **Finding Sales Personnel:** 40% indicate that finding new sales personnel continues with current, typical challenges. *Observations:* Regardless of the improving economy, only 24.8% say getting the right staff is becoming more challenging. Qualified candidates still seem available in the marketplace. We suspect those who reported "increasingly more difficult" need to recruit sellers with scarce availability such as those with relevant work experience, or, perhaps, specialized technical or engineering competencies.

- **Staffing Levels:** 33.3% have 3% to 5% of their sales positions open. *Observations:* Having 5% of the territories "open" and waiting for a salesperson is consistent with previous survey findings. These results indicate that the labor shortage pressures for sales personnel are not increasing substantially, yet. However, companies with sales openings greater than 5% of the work force should consider making investments to increase readily available sales personnel.

- **Sales Development Program:** 32.1% have a limited scope sales development program to train new sales personnel. *Observations:* Sales development programs train a cadre of available internal candidates waiting for management to assign them to an open territory. When labor shortages arise due to an expanding economy and shortage of workers, companies invest in such programs to quickly deploy replacements as turnover increases.

- **Signing Bonus:** 63.8% use a signing bonus in select cases when making an employment offer to a seller. *Observations:* 63.8% have the option to provide a signing bonus. This optional practice represents a moderate use of signing bonuses. Signing bonuses become more prevalent in tight labor markets. This does not seem to be the case for the reporting companies at this time.

- **Signing Bonus Amount:** 22% of the companies that provide signing bonuses provide between $5,001 and $10,000. *Observations:* Generally, the market for talent at this time does not require extravagant signing bonuses. Those that do provide signing bonuses to new sales personnel usually offer less than $15,000 with most bonuses between $5,001 and $10,000.
- **New Hires:** 24.5% of the companies immediately place the new sellers on the incentive program. *Observations:* Sales teams like to get new sales personnel onto the incentive program as quickly as possible. Companies provide a temporary cushion, such as a draw or guarantee, but the sentiment is to have new sellers fully participating in the incentive program as soon as possible.
- **New Hire—Amount of Draw or Guarantee:** 32.4% provide a 100% incentive pay guarantee for new sellers. *Observations:* A 100% guarantee is a generous pay package for new sales hires. 32.4% think it is a new hire onboarding necessity. For those who provide less than a 100% guarantee, the amounts vary substantially from company to company. Still, almost 25% provide no guarantee at all.
- **New Hire—Quota Treatment:** 33% of the respondents place new hires on full quotas when hired. *Observations:* The quota treatment is a function of whether a company provides a draw or a guarantee. Those without draws or guarantees are usually placed on full quota immediately. Absent a draw or a guarantee, management can provide a graduated ramp-up of the quota as reported by 17.9% of the companies.

Finding Sales Personnel: How difficult is it to find the right sales talent in the current labor market?

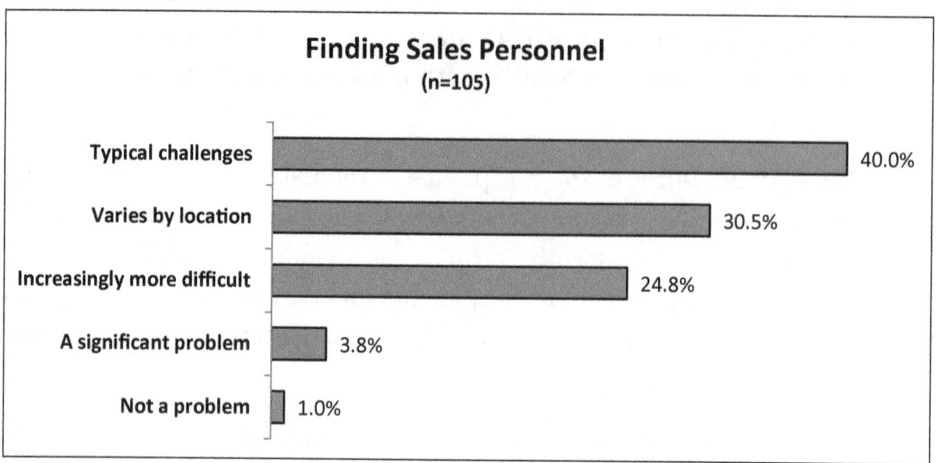

Survey Findings. 40% indicate that finding new sales personnel continues with current, typical challenges. 30.5% indicate staffing challenges vary by location. 24.8% find it increasingly more difficult to find the right talent.

Observations. Regardless of the improving economy, only 24.8% say getting the right staff is becoming more challenging. Qualified candidates still seem available in the marketplace. We suspect those who reported "increasingly more difficult" need to recruit sellers with scarce availability such as those with relevant work experience, or, perhaps, specialized technical or engineering competencies.

Staffing Levels: What percentage of your sales positions are now "open" waiting for an assigned incumbent?

10th Perc	25th Perc	50th Perc	75th Perc	90th Perc	Average
1	4	5	10	12	6.9

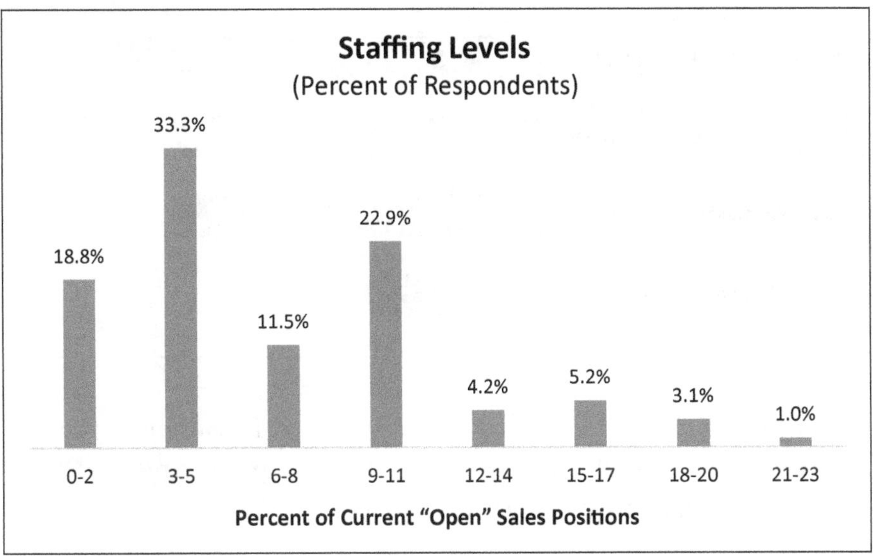

Survey Findings. 33.3% have 3% to 5% of their sales positions open. 22.9% have 9% to 11% of their sales positions open. And, 18.8% have 2% or less of their sales positions open.

Observations. Having 5% of the territories "open" and waiting for a salesperson is consistent with previous survey findings. These results indicate that the labor shortage pressures for sales personnel are not increasing substantially, yet. However, companies with sales openings greater than 5% of the work force should consider making investments to increase readily available sales personnel.

Sales Development Program: Do you have a sales training "bench" program for new sales personnel prior to assignment to open territories?

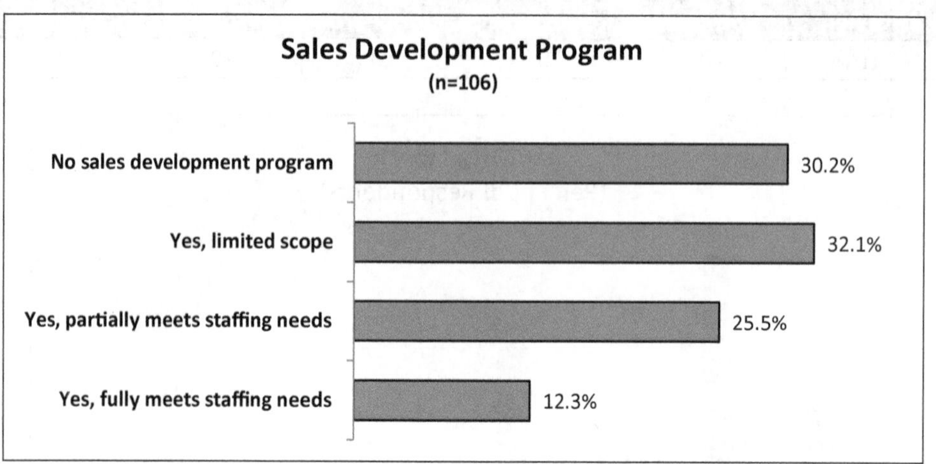

Survey Findings. 32.1% have a limited scope sales development program to train new sales personnel. 30.2% have no such program. And, 25.5% have a program that partially meets their staffing needs.

Observations. Sales development programs train a cadre of available internal candidates waiting for management to assign them to an open territory. When labor shortages arise due to an expanding economy and shortage of workers, companies invest in such programs to quickly deploy replacements as turnover increases.

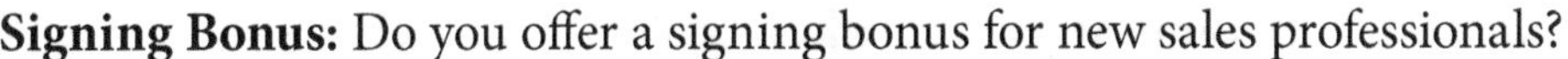

Signing Bonus: Do you offer a signing bonus for new sales professionals?

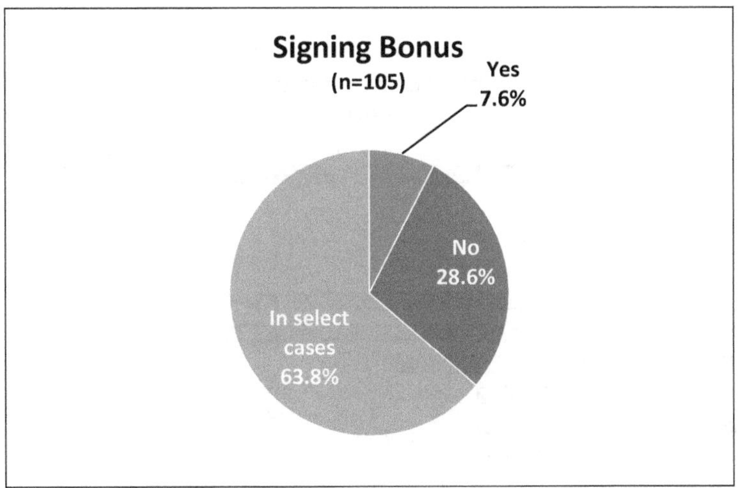

Survey Findings. 63.8% use a signing bonus in select cases when making an employment offer to a seller. 28.6% do not offer a signing bonus. Only 7.6% provide a signing bonus to all new sellers.

Observations. 63.8% have the option to provide a signing bonus. This optional practice represents a moderate use of signing bonuses. Signing bonuses become more prevalent in tight labor markets. This does not seem to be the case for the reporting companies at this time.

Signing Bonus Amount: If you provide a signing bonus, what is the average/ typical amount?

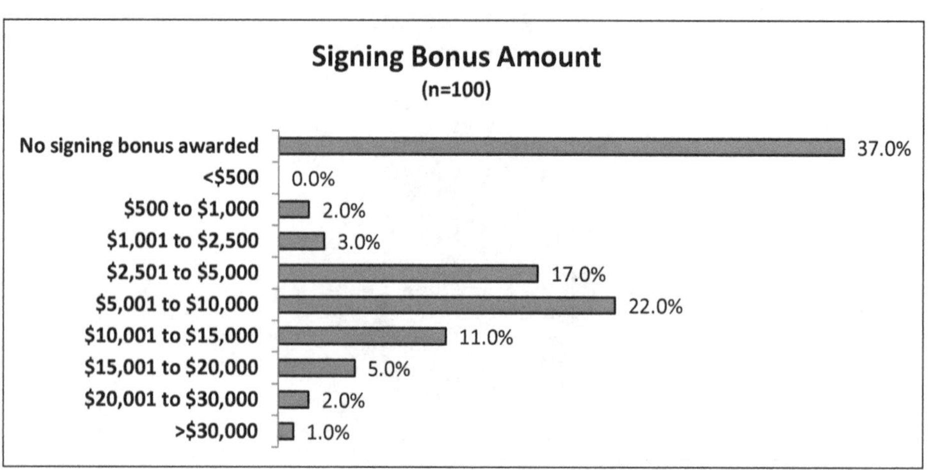

Survey Findings. 22% of the companies that provide signing bonuses provide between $5,001 and $10,000. 17% provide between $2,501 and $5,000. And, 11% provide between $10,001 and $15,000.

Observations. Generally, the market for talent at this time does not require extravagant signing bonuses. Those that do provide signing bonuses to new sales personnel usually offer less than $15,000 with most bonuses between $5,001 and $10,000.

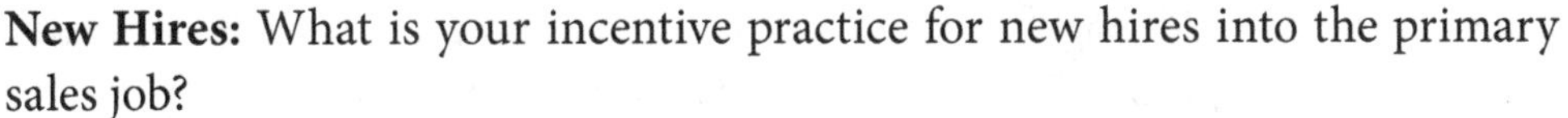

New Hires: What is your incentive practice for new hires into the primary sales job?

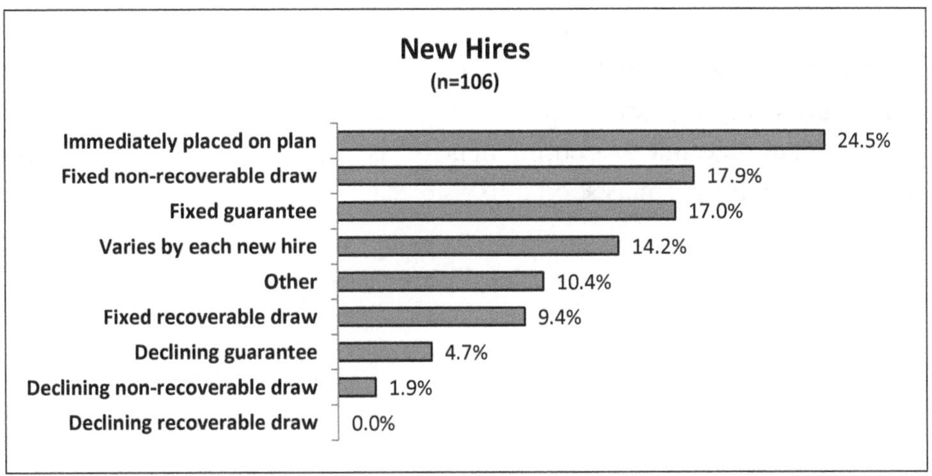

Other Incentive Practices for New Hires

- Ramped quota that progresses to full quota; increases base rate against variable in beginning
- Quarterly guarantee with sales plan paid if earned above guarantee
- Most go on plan immediately—in a few cases, we pay a fixed guarantee
- Base plus incentive
- Mostly on plan with recoverable draw, guarantee for up to 3 months as an exception
- Performance bonus: if they achieve their quarterly quota, achieve performance bonus (4 quarters)
- Generally—immediately placed on a plan (within 1 month of hire)—guarantee/draw varies by GEO
- Placed on plan after 30–60 days
- Greater of guarantee or actuals
- Immediately placed on plan with a guarantee for the first 2 months due to delay in financial reporting
- We normally plan on sales plan immediately, but provide 3 months of 100% non-recoverable draw
- Varies by location, rules on country level

Survey Findings. 24.5% of the companies immediately place the new sellers on the incentive program. 17.9% provide a fixed non-recoverable draw (payment in advance). And, 17% provide a fixed guarantee.

Observations. Sales teams like to get new sales personnel onto the incentive program as quickly as possible. Companies provide a temporary cushion, such as a draw or guarantee, but the sentiment is to have new sellers fully participating in the incentive program as soon as possible.

New Hire—Amount of Draw or Guarantee: If you provide a draw or guarantee for the primary sales job, what percent of the target incentive does the new hire receive as an initial draw or guarantee?

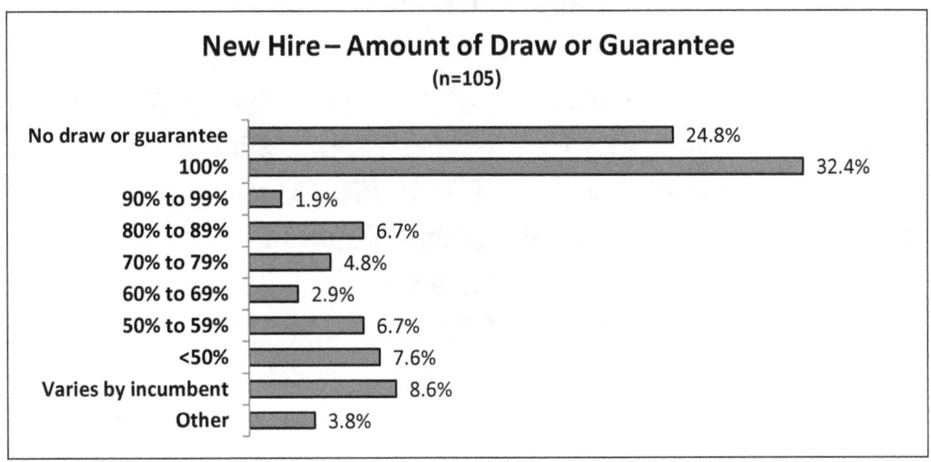

Other Draw or Guarantee Amounts

- $1,000 subsidy per period for a varying amount of pay periods
- $20k—$5k each quarter
- 30% or 20%/target for quarter is 100%
- <15%
- Varies by location, rules on country level

Survey Findings. 32.4% provide a 100% incentive pay guarantee for new sellers. The other guarantee amounts vary from 50% to 99% of target incentive.

Observations. A 100% guarantee is a generous pay package for new sales hires. 32.4% think it is a new hire onboarding necessity. For those who provide less than a 100% guarantee, the amounts vary substantially from company to company. Still, almost 25% provide no guarantee at all.

New Hire—Quota Treatment: If you provide a draw or guarantee for the primary sales job, do you assign a quota during that draw or guarantee period?

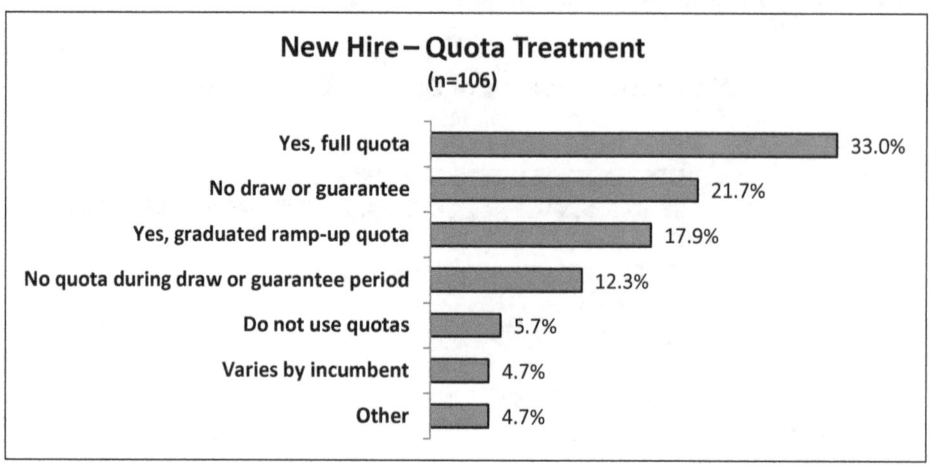

Other New Hire—Quota Treatments

- Issue prorated quota based on seasonality of business
- Full quota month Q1 to Q3, no quota in Q4
- Quota if on draw, no quota if on guarantee
- Varies by business unit
- No draw or guarantee, but ramp quota 5 months
- Draw is a minimum amount to be paid; quota provides upside during the transition period

Survey Findings. 33% of the respondents place new hires on full quotas when hired. 17.9% have a ramped-up quota.

Observations. The quota treatment is a function of whether a company provides a draw or a guarantee. Those without draws or guarantees are usually placed on full quota immediately. Absent a draw or a guarantee, management can provide a graduated ramp-up of the quota as reported by 17.9% of the companies.

EQUITY INCENTIVES

Summary: Almost two-thirds of the companies do not offer equity awards to sales personnel. Companies that do provide awards, only grant awards to a subset of sellers. The value of the awards, if redeemed today, averages about $25,000. Most of the respondents in the survey have modest growth rates, often a condition that precludes generous stock grants.

- **Equity Award Eligibility:** 60.7% of the reporting companies do not provide equity awards to sellers. *Observations:* Providing equity grants to sellers is a popular topic, yet almost two-thirds of the reporting companies do not grant such awards to sales personnel. Often young, fast-growing companies will grant restricted stock awards to employees. However, as growth slows, the use of generous stock grants declines to preclude diluting current shareholders' equity holdings.
- **Equity Award Participation:** 28.6% of the companies granting equity awards provide 91% to 100% of all sellers an award. *Observations:* Of the 30% that provide stock grants to sellers, less than 30% of those companies have a (near) universal stock grant program.
- **Equity Award Value:** 56.5% provide equity awards to sales personnel valued up to $25,000. *Observations:* Granting equity awards to sales personnel is not common. When stock awards are granted, the amounts seldom contribute substantially to incumbents' net worth.
- **2017 Company Revenue Growth Rate:** 53.8% of the reporting companies had sales growth last year of 1% to 9%. *Observations:* Growth rates affect many sales effectiveness programs. Most of the reporting companies in our survey had moderate growth rates. Moderate growth rates, for example, reduce the need for dramatic headcount expansion and supporting programs such as signing bonuses.

Equity Award Eligibility: Are sales personnel in the primary sales job eligible for equity awards (e.g., stock options, restricted stock or stock units)? Exclude stock savings and 401k plans.

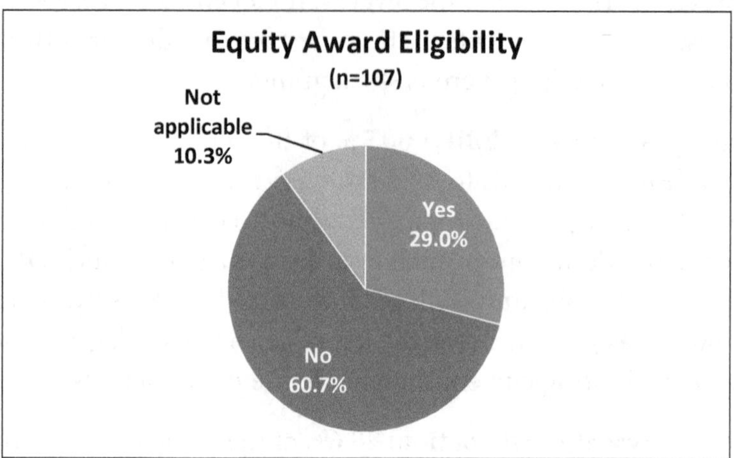

Survey Findings. 60.7% of the reporting companies do not provide equity awards to sellers. 29% do provide equity awards to sellers.

Observations. Providing equity grants to sellers is a popular topic, yet almost two-thirds of the reporting companies do not grant such awards to sales personnel. Often young, fast-growing companies will grant restricted stock awards to employees. However, as growth slows, the use of generous stock grants declines to preclude diluting current shareholders' equity holdings.

Equity Award Participation: If you provide equity awards to sales personnel, what percent of sales personnel have been granted awards? If you do not provide equity awards to sales personnel, leave blank.

10th Perc	25th Perc	50th Perc	75th Perc	90th Perc	Average
10	18.8	43	92.2	100	49.2

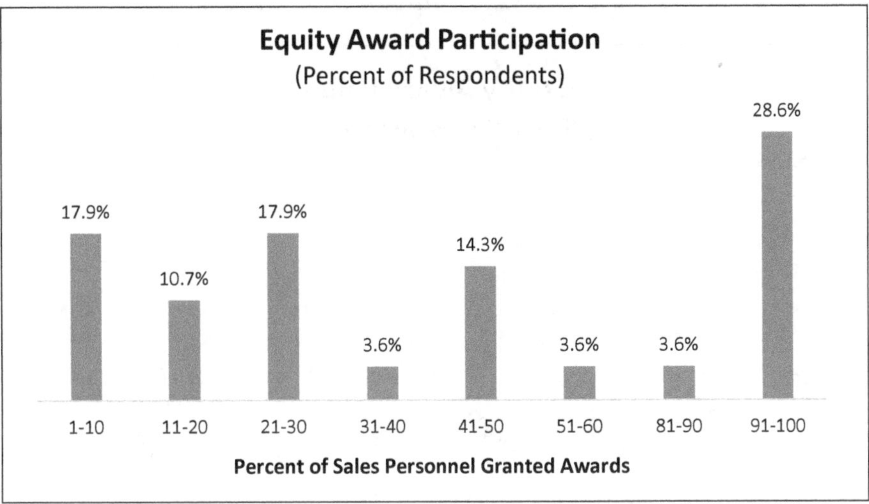

Survey Findings. 28.6% of the companies granting equity awards provide 91% to 100% of all sellers an award. The other 71.4% of the companies grant varied levels of equity awards.

Observations. Of the 29% that provide stock grants to sellers, less than 30% of those companies have a (near) universal stock grant program.

Equity Award Value: If you provide equity awards to sales personnel, the average total cash value among those holding equity awards would be worth how many dollars if redeemed today? Provide average estimate. If you do not provide equity awards to sales personnel, leave blank.

10th Perc	25th Perc	50th Perc	75th Perc	90th Perc	Average
10400	17000	20000	40000	88112	43223.5

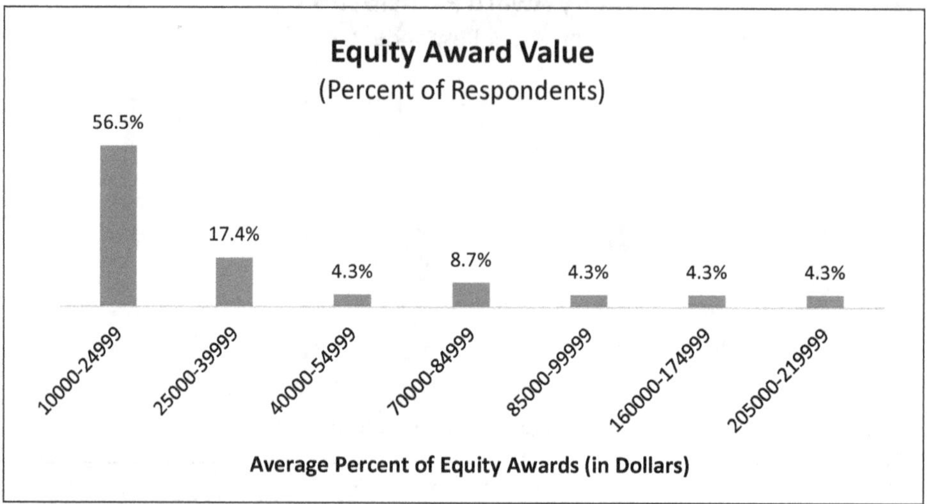

Survey Findings. 56.5% provide equity awards to sales personnel valued up to $25,000. The median is $20,000. There are a few companies with equity awards worth more than $200,000. Our conjecture: These rare, large amounts are for incumbents who will/did benefit from an IPO event, thus giving their stock awards substantial value.

Observations. Granting equity awards to sales personnel is not common. When stock awards are granted, the amounts seldom contribute substantially to incumbents' net worth.

2017 Company Revenue Growth Rate: What was the growth rate for your company in 2017?

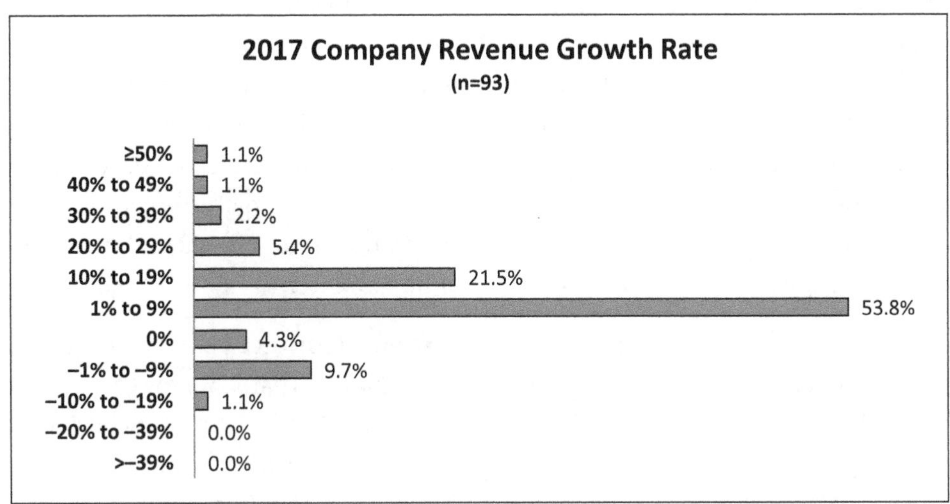

Survey Findings. 53.8% of the reporting companies had sales growth last year of 1% to 9%. 21.5% had growth of 10% to 19% in 2017. And, 9.7% had a sales decline of –1% to –9%.

Observations. Growth rates affect many sales effectiveness programs. Most of the reporting companies in our survey had moderate growth rates. Moderate growth rates, for example, reduce the need for dramatic headcount expansion and supporting programs such as signing bonuses.

SPECIALTY CUSTOMER CONTACT JOBS—DEPLOYMENT AND PAY PRACTICES

Summary: Beyond sales jobs, many other jobs have customer contact responsibilities. Some of these jobs have selling responsibilities, too. The participants reported their incentive compensation practices for 14 jobs. Jobs with more customer "influence/persuasion" are more likely to have more dollars of target compensation devoted to incentive compensation. Both product and vertical sales specialist jobs have the highest portion of target total pay devoted to incentive compensation. Customer support; non-sales efforts and post-sales technical support have the least amount of pay tied to incentive compensation.

- **Incentive Compensation for Customer Contact Jobs:** 58.1% of the companies provide a target incentive of greater than 25% for the Overlay Product Specialist. 56.7% provide the same level of target incentive for the Overlay Market/Vertical Specialist. *Observations:* Jobs with more "selling duties" have a higher target incentive than those with less selling, more service responsibilities. Practices vary from company to company.

Specialty Customer Contact Jobs—Deployment and Pay Practices: Does your company have any of these jobs? If yes, identify the approximate target incentive (percent of base pay) for each job.

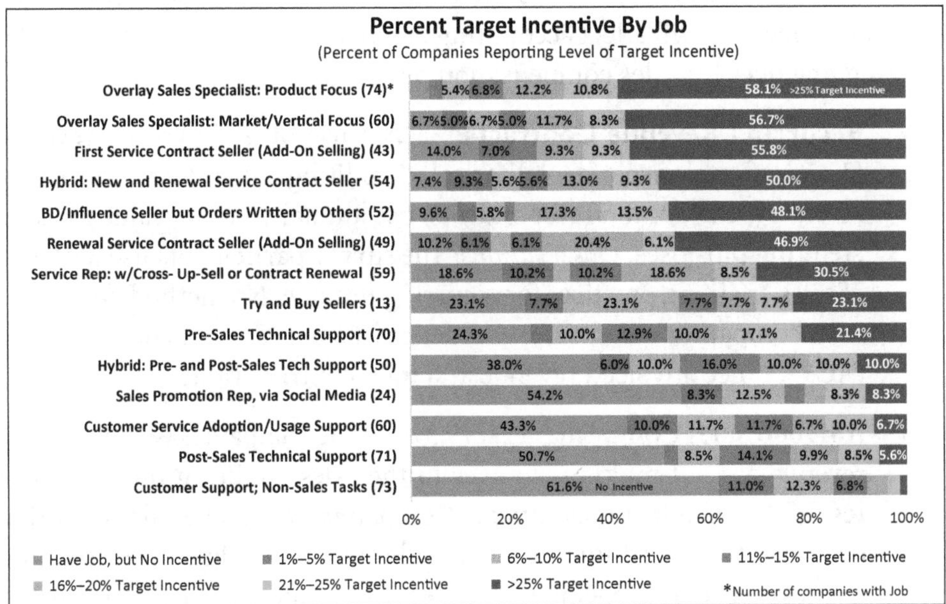

Survey Findings. 58.1% of the companies provide a target incentive of greater than 25% for the Overlay Product Specialist. 56.7% provide the same level of target incentive for the Overlay Market/Vertical Specialist. 61.6% provide no incentive for the Customer Support; Non-Sales Tasks Job. 50.7% provide no incentive for the Post-Sales Technical Support Job. (Blank band entries have less than 5% of the companies reporting.)

Observations. Jobs with more "selling duties" have a higher target incentive than those with less selling, more service responsibilities. Practices vary from company to company.

NEW FASB REGULATIONS—REVENUE RECOGNITION: ASC 606

Summary: Accounting Standards Codification (ASC) 606 specifies revenue and expense recognition for types of revenue and related selling expenses. While these new guidelines will affect accounting practices, they have yet to alter sales crediting practices for sales compensation purposes.

- **Recurring Revenue Contracts:** 22.2%* use billed/invoiced revenue (22.5% of total respondents) for sales crediting. 22.2%* with recurring revenue (22.5% of total respondents) use annual contract value for sales crediting purposes. *Observations:* The survey participants use a variety of sales crediting practices for recurring revenue. No method dominates with companies using diverse practices such as annual contract value (ACV), billed/invoiced revenue and total contract value (TCV).

- **ASC 606 Sales Comp Changes:** 79.3%* of the companies with recurring revenue are not making changes to the sales crediting practices as a result of ASC 606. *Observations:* Companies will make sales crediting decisions to reward for successful sales outcomes. For sales crediting purposes, sales management can select from different types of recurring revenue measures. ASC 606 specifies when finance recognizes revenue for recurring and other types of revenue. Sales compensation crediting practices do not have to follow accounting standards.

- **ASC 606 Behavior/Practice Changes:** 84%* of the companies *with* recurring revenue (74.5% of the total) have not made any sales practice changes as a result of ASC 606. *Observations:* While ASC 606 has affected financial reporting, it has not had a material impact on sales compensation practices.

*Calculated by removing those that do not have recurring revenue

Recurring Revenue Contracts: Do your sales personnel secure recurring revenue contracts with customers? If yes, what is the primary measure event you use for those recurring revenue contracts? Select all that apply.

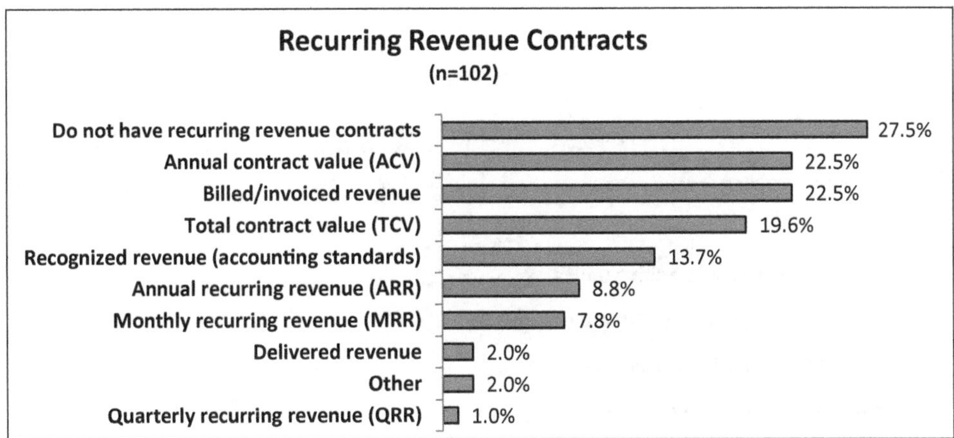

Survey Findings. 22.2%* use billed/invoiced revenue (22.5% of total respondents) for sales crediting. 22.2%* with recurring revenue (22.5% of total respondents) use annual contract value for sales crediting purposes. And, 19.4%* with recurring revenue (19.6% of total respondents) use total contract value for sales crediting.

Observations. The survey participants use a variety of sales crediting practices for recurring revenue. No method dominates with companies using diverse practices such as annual contract value (ACV), billed/invoiced revenue and total contract value (TCV).

*Calculated by removing those that do not have recurring revenue

ASC 606 Sales Comp Changes: Have you made or will you make any changes to the sales compensation plan for the primary sales job as a result of ASC 606? Select all that apply.

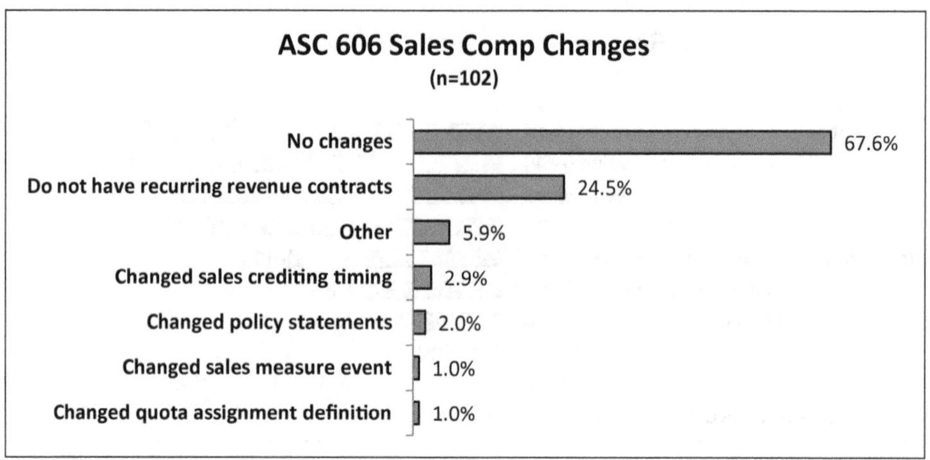

Other ASC 606 Sales Comp Changes

- Canada
- Does not apply in Canada
- Unsure at this time
- May change to ARR and add in multiyear payments. Quota will change if we go to ARR as well
- Changed from measuring on TCV to ACV/ARR, substitution clauses added
- Unaware of ASC 606 and the impact it will have on sales compensation
- Yes, but more of accounting treatment, which is held by corporate finance

Survey Findings. 79.3%* of the companies with recurring revenue are not making changes to the sales crediting practices as a result of ASC 606.

Observations. Companies will make sales crediting decisions to reward for successful sales outcomes. For sales crediting purposes, sales management can select from different types of recurring revenue measures. ASC 606 specifies when finance recognizes revenue for recurring and other types of revenue. Sales compensation crediting practices do not have to follow accounting standards.

*Calculated by removing those that do not have recurring revenue

ASC 606 Behavior/Practice Changes: Is your organization changing any of its sales practices or processes as a result of ASC 606?

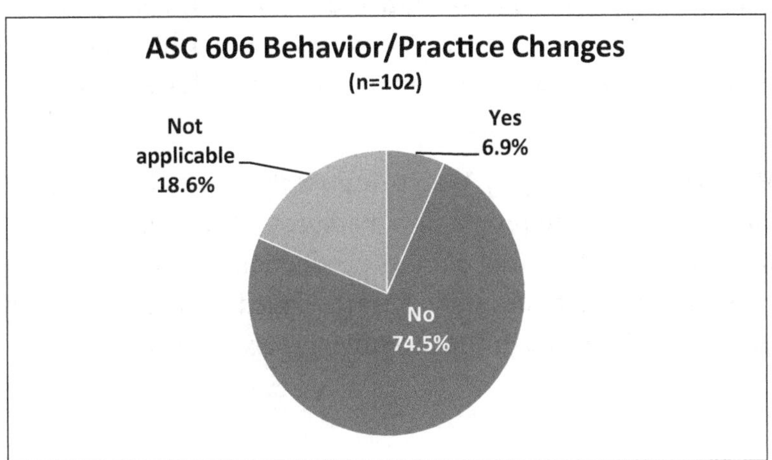

Other ASC 606 Behavior/Practice Changes

- Sales credit and financial recognition disconnect
- Simply adapting to the adjusted rev rec changes
- More emphasis on selling subscription, reduction in pull forwards
- We may—not sure just yet
- Support processes; no impact to salespeople
- Changed revenue recognition timing
- Financial reporting

Survey Findings. 84%* of the companies *with* recurring revenue (74.5% of the total) have not made any sales practice changes as a result of ASC 606.

Observations. While ASC 606 has affected financial reporting, it has not had a material impact on sales compensation practices.

*Calculated by removing those that do not have recurring revenue

PERFORMANCE MEASURE CATEGORIES: USED IN PRIMARY SALES JOB

Summary: Among seven performance categories (production, strategic, productivity, customer experience, activities, citizenship and compliance), production is the dominant performance criterion for sales compensation purposes.

- **Performance Category Weighting:** 81.8% of the target incentive dollars are allocated to production measures. *Observations:* Sales incentive plans are highly focused on sales production measures such as revenue, profit dollars, unit sales and contracts signed. Almost all other measures occupy a minor role in the incentive program for sellers.

Performance Category Weighting: What is the (approximate) weighting of performance measure categories for the primary sales job? Distribute 100% among the categories.

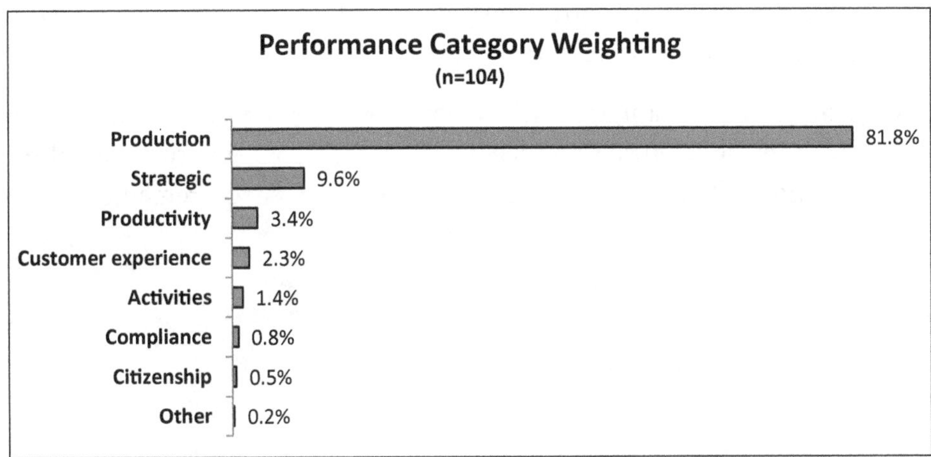

Survey Findings. 81.8% of the target incentive dollars are allocated to production measures. 9.6% of the incentive dollars are allocated to strategic measures. And, 3.4% of the incentive dollars are allocated to productivity measures.

Observations. Sales incentive plans are highly focused on sales production measures such as revenue, profit dollars, unit sales and contracts signed. Almost all other measures occupy a minor role in the incentive program for sellers.

Categories of performance measures:

- **Production.** Examples: sales revenue, profit dollars, unit sales, contracts signed
- **Strategic.** Examples: product mix, account performance, gross profit percent, discounting, price realization, cross-sell, contract length, receivables
- **Productivity.** Examples: close rate, balanced performance among accounts/partners, sales progression/pipeline performance, order linearity, quota accuracy, customer churn, customer/market share, scorecard
- **Customer Experience.** Examples: customer evaluation, customer success, net promoter score, social media scores, customer loyalty

- **Activities.** Examples: calls made, proposals written, business plan creation, buyer milestones, customer/market events
- **Citizenship.** Examples: team work, collaboration, personal/professional development, coaching/training, corporate values, ethics, social workplace awareness, professional conduct
- **Compliance.** Examples: CRM submissions, expense submissions—accuracy/timing, contract and legal compliance, ISO security regulations, training schedule, forecasting, other regulatory requirements

SALES COMPENSATION PRACTICES FOR THE FIRST-LINE SALES MANAGER (FLSM)

Summary: For the most part, sales leadership aligns the incentive program of first-line sales managers (FLSMs) with the sellers they supervise. The most common span of control is seven to eight direct reports. FLSMs are paid on the sales compensation plan. Sales revenue is the most common measure. Their payouts are tied to their team's performance and they are paid as frequently as their direct reports. Just like their direct reports, they have a similar pay mix, do not have caps and are paid at the same intervals using a bonus formula to reward quota performance. Almost all companies expect some sellers' annual earnings to exceed the target compensation of their supervisor: the first-line sales manager.

- **Span of Control:** 33.7% of the reporting companies indicate that the first-line sales manager has seven to eight direct reports. *Observations:* Seven to eight direct reports for first-line sales managers is a historical ratio. This span of control has remained unchanged for a long time. Of interest, new technologies and communication tools have not altered this traditional ratio.

- **FLSM Type of Incentive Plan:** 88.6% of the surveyed companies use a sales incentive plan to reward first-line sales managers. *Observations:* The overwhelming majority of the reporting companies have their first-line sales manager on a sales incentive plan, keeping them closely aligned with their subordinates.

- **FLSM Performance Measures:** 89.5% of the surveyed companies use sales revenue in the incentive plan for the first-line sales manager. *Observations:* Survey participants identified all the measures in the first-line sales manager incentive plan. The overwhelming preference in all incentive plans was sales revenue performance. Beyond sales revenue (89.5%) and profit (26.7%), companies use a limited number of other measures in the first-line sales manager incentive plan.

- **FLSM Measurement and Payment Period:** 32.4% of the companies pay sales managers monthly on performance against an annual objective. *Observations:* Among the surveyed companies, incentive plan pay frequency is split between monthly (43.2%) and quarterly (44.1%) payments.

- **FLSM Number of Performance Measures:** 36.6% report two measures in the first-line sales managers' incentive plan. *Observations:* Sales leadership instills high focus in the first-line sales managers' incentive plan by keeping the number of measures to three or fewer.
- **FLSM Average Target Payout:** 69.4% of the first-line sales managers are paid on their team's performance. *Observations:* The correct measure is to have the first-line sales manager paid on their team's performance. When a manager has his or her own accounts, they will carry an individual objective, too.
- **FLSM MBO Component:** 86% do not have an MBO component in the first-line sales managers' incentive plan. *Observations:* MBO (management by objectives) components are seldom used in the first-line sales managers' incentive plans.
- **FLSM MBO Weighting:** 20% is the median weighting for an MBO component, if employed in the first-line sales manager plan. *Observations:* Use of an MBO (management by objective) element is relatively rare (13%) and generally worth less than 25% of the incentive plan for 77% of the reporting companies using an MBO component.
- **FLSM Calculation Method:** 54.6% use a bonus formula paid against quota achievement to reward first-line sales managers. *Observations:* Sales leadership uses unique quotas or ICRs to manage target incentive for the first-line sales managers. The intent is to provide comparable earning opportunities for dissimilar sized goals driven by the varied composition of assigned sellers and their sales quotas.
- **FLSM Pay Mix:** 36% use a 60/40 (base/incentive) pay mix for their first-line sales managers. *Observations:* A 60/40 pay mix is a highly variable pay mix confirming management's belief that the first-line sales manager is a critical variable in seller success aligning rewards consistent with the team's performance.
- **Pay Mix Comparison to Direct Report:** 48% of the companies provide the same pay mix (base/target incentive) to first-line sales managers, as given to the sales personnel they supervise. *Observations:* Sales leadership aligns first-line sales managers' pay practices, such as pay mix, with the sellers they supervise.
- **FLSM Pay Caps:** 68% of the respondents do not cap first-line sales managers' incentive payouts. *Observations:* More than two-thirds of

the companies do not believe in capping incentive earnings for first-line sales managers.

- **FLSM Leverage/Upside:** 39.4% of the companies provide 2.0x target incentive to first-line sales managers for outstanding performance (best: 90th percentile). *Observations:* 2.0x target incentive for outstanding performance is the most common upside earning amount for first-line sales managers; however, practices vary.
- **Seller Payouts Compared to FLSM Target Total Pay:** 93.5% of the reporting companies confirm that sales personnel can earn more than the target total compensation of first-line sales managers. *Observations:* A reasonable policy provision would accommodate up to one-third of the sales personnel to reach and exceed the target total compensation of the first-line sales manager. Note: Most likely, in good years, the first-line sales managers' actual payments will exceed their own "target" compensation amount for the job.

Type of First-Line Sales Manager (FLSM): Supervises what types of sellers?

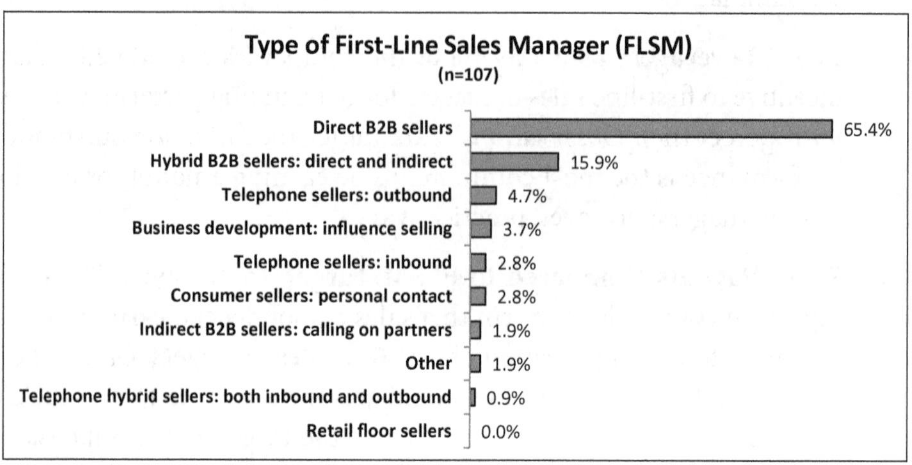

Span of Control: What is the average number of direct reports for the FLSM who supervises the primary sales job?

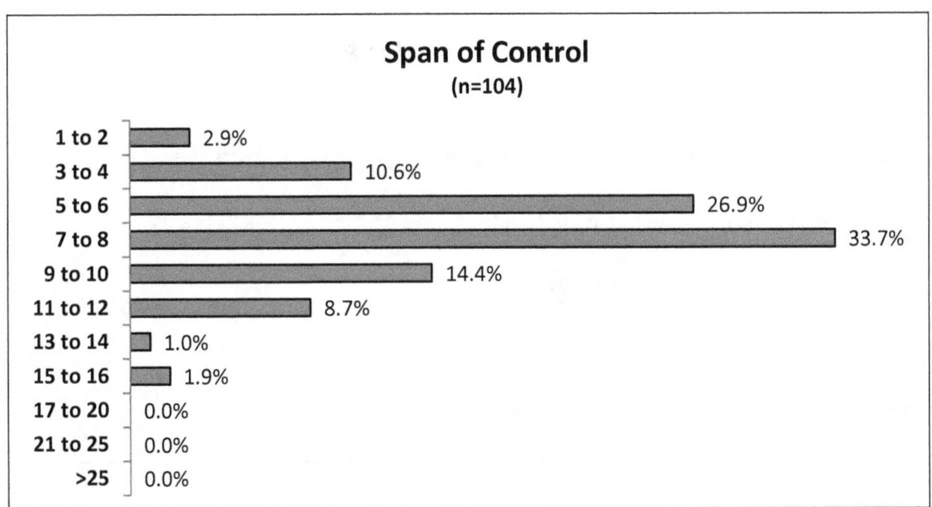

Survey Findings. 33.7% of the reporting companies indicate that the first-line sales manager has seven to eight direct reports. 26.9% of the first-line sales managers have five to six direct reports. 14.4% have nine to 10 direct reports.

Observations. Seven to eight direct reports for first-line sales managers is a historical ratio. This span of control has remained unchanged for a long time. Of interest, new technologies and communication tools have not altered this traditional ratio.

FLSM Type of Incentive Plan: The FLSM participates in what type of incentive plan?

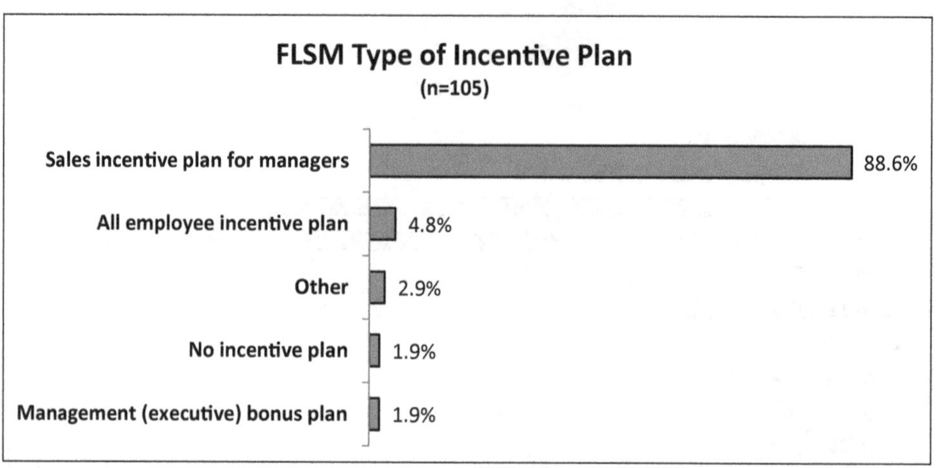

Other FLSM Incentive Plans

- Same incentive plan design as direct reports
- Sales incentive and management bonus plan
- 50% SIP & 50% mgmt. bonus plan

Survey Findings. 88.6% of the surveyed companies use a sales incentive plan to reward first-line sales managers.

Observations. The overwhelming majority of the reporting companies have their first-line sales manager on a sales incentive plan, keeping them closely aligned with their subordinates.

FLSM Performance Measures: The incentive plan for the FLSM uses which of the following distinct performance measures:

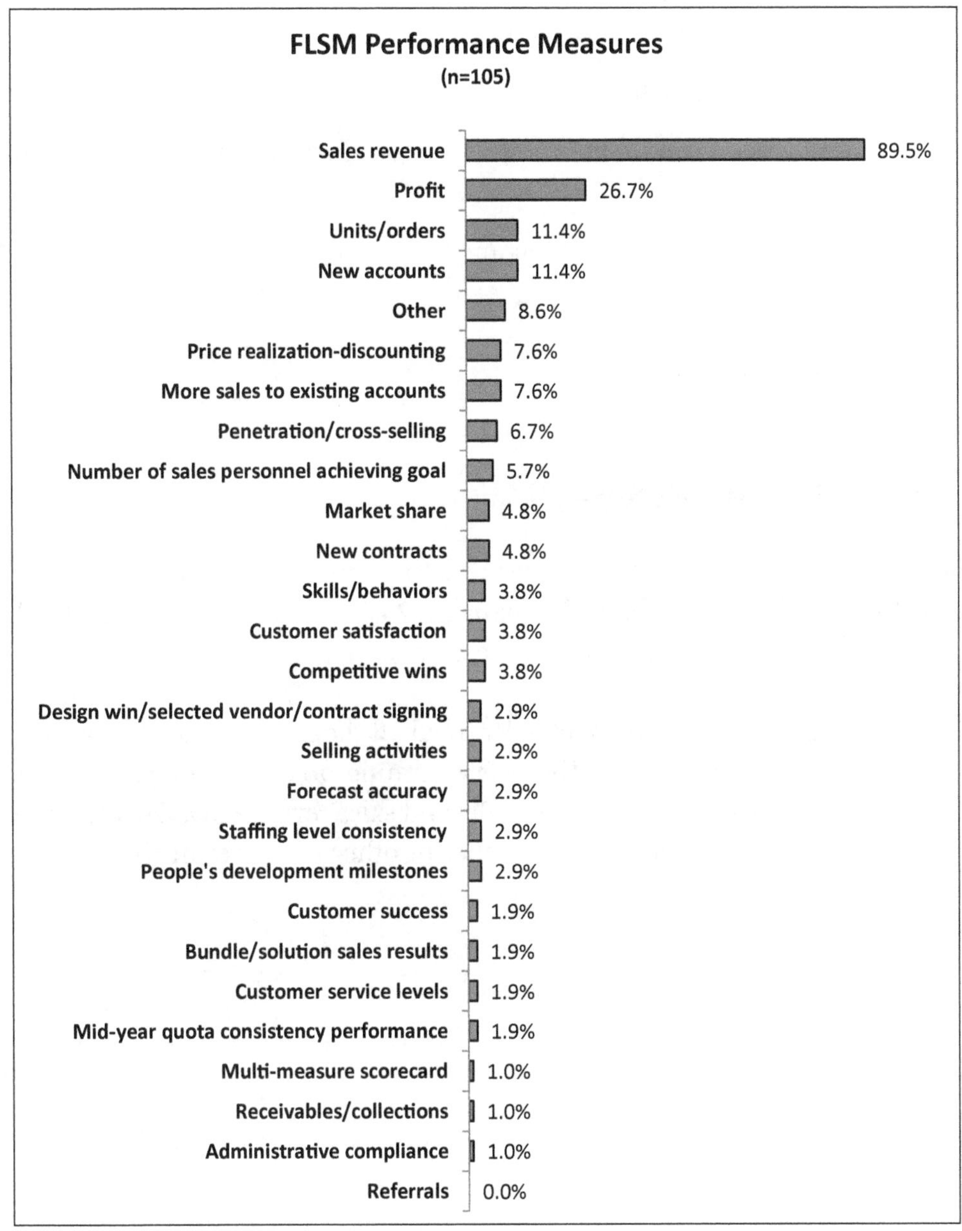

Other FLSM Performance Measures

- Connect yield rate (stack ranking)
- 50% IBO; 50% revenue performance to goal
- Gross margin, MBO
- Commission modifiers for strategic products and price realization/ discounting
- Product mix & operating income
- Revenue growth
- Net new bookings $
- Department and individual goals
- EBIT strategic objective

Survey Findings. 89.5% of the surveyed companies use sales revenue in the incentive plan for the first-line sales manager. 26.7% use a profit measure; 11.4% use units/orders; and another 11.4% use new accounts.

Observations. Survey participants identified all the measures in the first-line sales manager incentive plan. The overwhelming preference in all incentive plans was sales revenue performance. Beyond sales revenue (89.5%) and profit (26.7%), companies use a limited number of other measures in the first-line sales manager incentive plan.

FLSM Measurement and Payment Period: The primary performance measure is measured and paid primarily in the following fashion:

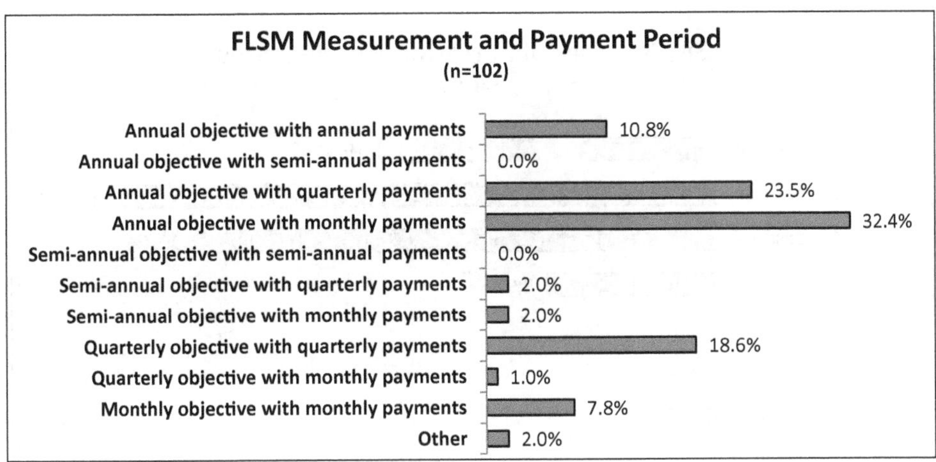

Other FLSM Measurement and Payment Period

- Annual metrics with quarterly advances
- Majority are on quarterly objective with quarterly payments, remainder are on semi-annual

Survey Findings. 32.4% of the companies pay sales managers monthly on performance against an annual objective. 23.5% pay quarterly on an annual objective. 18.6% pay quarterly for achievement of quarterly goals.

Observations. Among the surveyed companies, incentive plan pay frequency is split between monthly (43.2%) and quarterly (44.1%) payments.

FLSM Number of Performance Measures: The incentive plan for the FLSM has how many distinct performance measures?

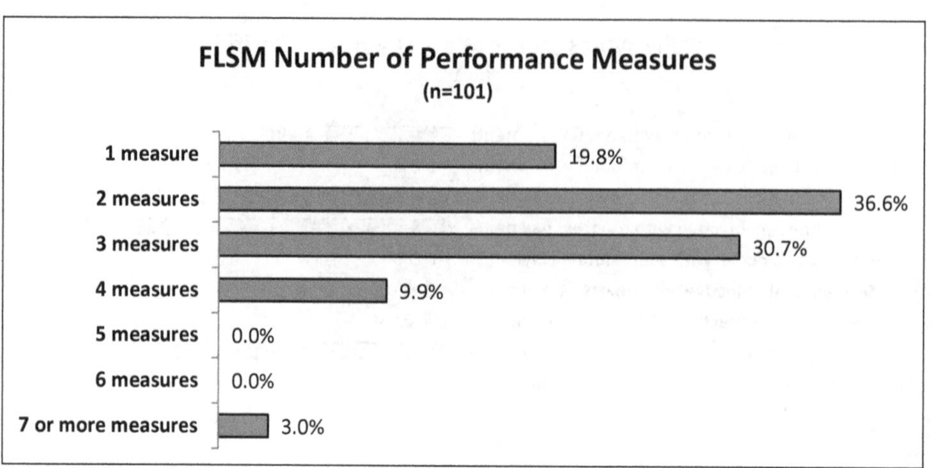

Survey Findings. 36.6% report two measures in the first-line sales managers' incentive plan. 30.7% have three measures. And, 19.8% have only one measure.

Observations. Sales leadership instills high focus in the first-line sales managers' incentive plan by keeping the number of measures to three or fewer.

FLSM Average Target Payout: The average target incentive payout will be a mix of what percent? Enter the percentage; all five must sum to 100 percent.

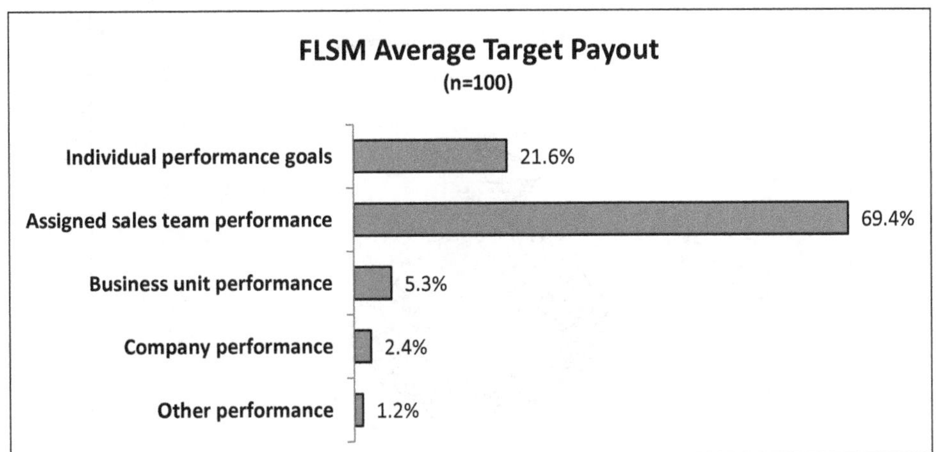

Survey Findings. 69.4% of the first-line sales managers are paid on their team's performance. 21.6% have individual performance goals. And, 5.3% have business unit performance as part of their incentive plan.

Observations. The correct measure is to have the first-line sales manager paid on their team's performance. When a manager has his or her own accounts, they will carry an individual objective, too.

FLSM MBO Component: Does the incentive plan for the FLSM have an MBO (management by objectives) component?

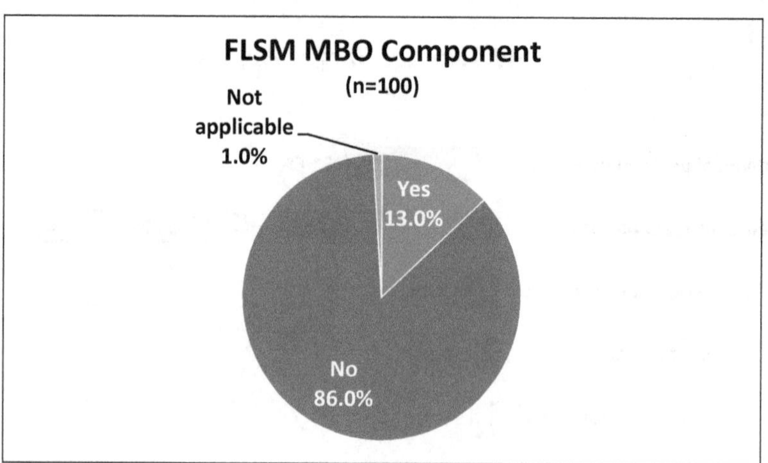

Survey Findings. 86% do not have an MBO component in the first-line sales managers' incentive plan. 13% have an MBO component.

Observations. MBO (management by objectives) components are seldom used in the first-line sales managers' incentive plans.

FLSM MBO Weighting: If the FLSM job has an MBO component, what percent of target incentive does it represent? (Leave blank if you do not have an MBO component; enter whole number percent.)

10th Perc	25th Perc	50th Perc	75th Perc	90th Perc	Average
6	10	20	25	46	23.8

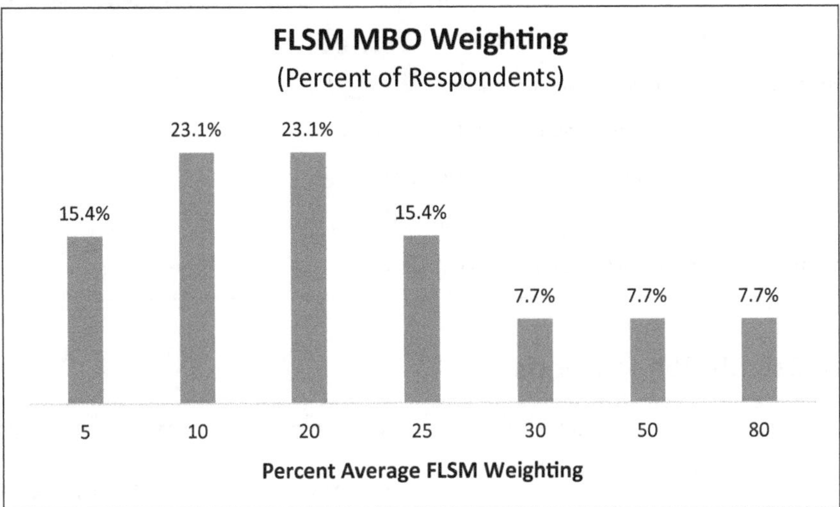

Survey Findings. 20% is the median weighting for an MBO component, if employed in the first-line sales manager plan.

Observations. Use of an MBO (management by objective) element is relatively rare (13%) and generally worth less than 25% of the incentive plan for 77% of the reporting companies using an MBO component.

FLSM Calculation Method: What is the calculation method for the key performance measure of the FLSM job?

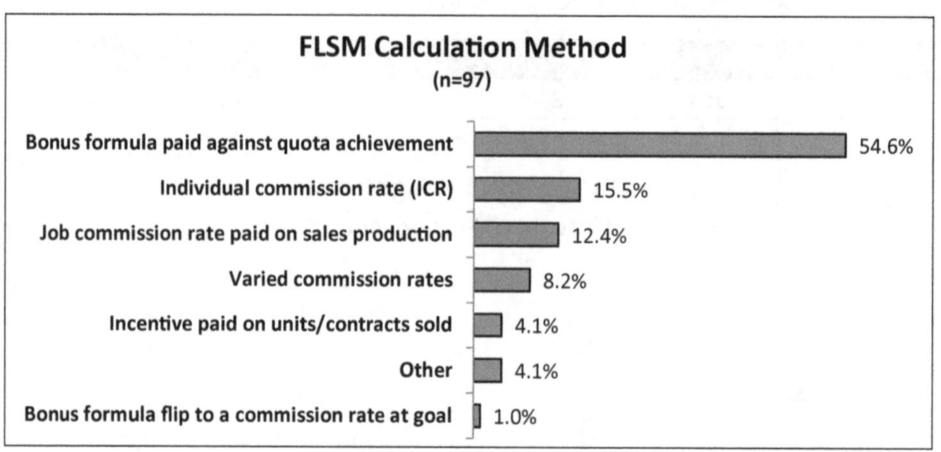

Other Calculation Methods

- Component weight based on target comp and stack ranking
- Target comp/ICR
- Achievement % on key sales objectives
- Commission on revenue growth
- Scorecard grade to bonus % of base salary

Survey Findings. 54.6% use a bonus formula paid against quota achievement to reward first-line sales managers. 15.5% use an individual commission rate (calculated by dividing the target incentive by the manager's quota). 12.4% have a uniform commission rate paid on sales production.

Observations. Sales leadership uses unique quotas or ICRs to manage target incentive for the first-line sales managers. The intent is to provide comparable earning opportunities for dissimilar sized goals driven by the varied composition of assigned sellers and their sales quotas.

FLSM Pay Mix: What is the target pay mix—the split of target total pay into base and target incentive (e.g., 60/40)?

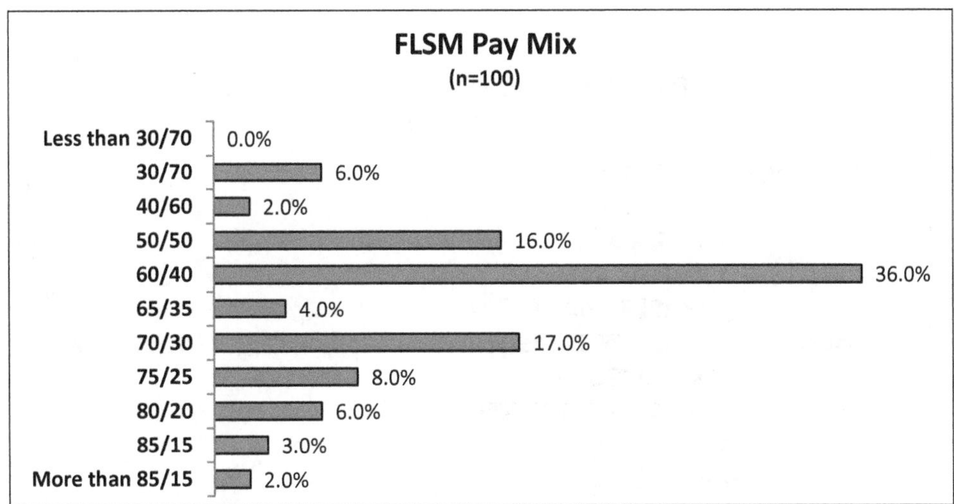

Survey Findings. 36% use a 60/40 (base/incentive) pay mix for their first-line sales managers. 17% use a 70/30 pay mix. And, 16% use a 50/50 pay mix.

Observations. A 60/40 pay mix is a highly variable pay mix confirming management's belief that the first-line sales manager is a critical variable in seller success aligning rewards consistent with the team's performance.

Pay Mix Comparison to Direct Report: For the FLSM who supervises the primary sales job, how does the target pay mix compare to the pay mix of the direct sellers (approximately)?

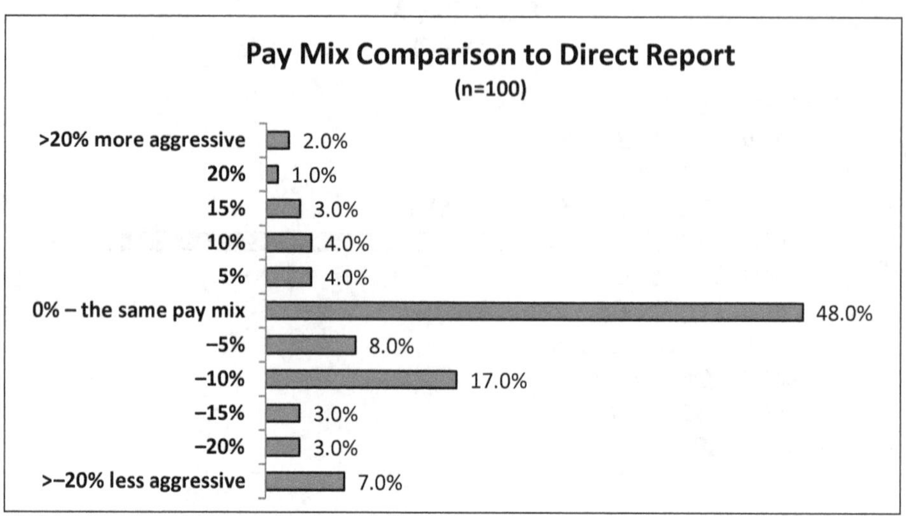

Survey Findings. 48% of the companies provide the same pay mix (base/target incentive) to first-line sales managers, as given to the sales personnel they supervise. 38% have a less aggressive pay mix, and a surprising 14% have a more aggressive pay mix for first-line sales managers as compared to their direct subordinates.

Observations. Sales leadership aligns first-line sales managers' pay practices, such as pay mix, with the sellers they supervise.

FLSM Pay Caps: Does the pay plan have an absolute cap on compensation earnings?

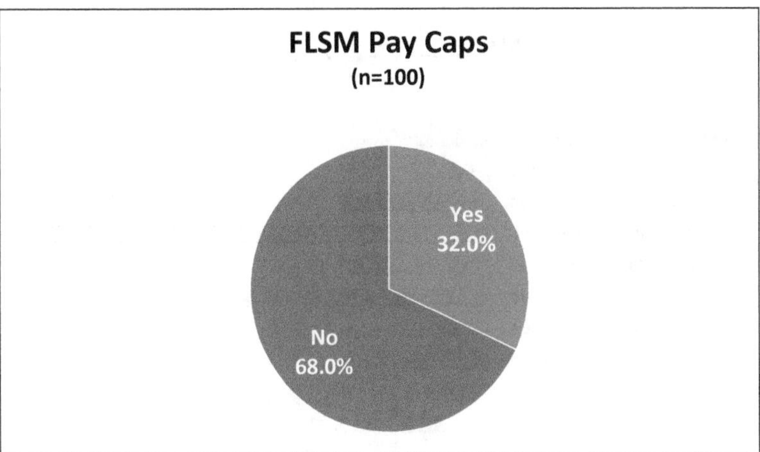

Survey Findings. 68% of the respondents do not cap first-line sales managers' incentive payouts. 32% cap payouts.

Observations. More than two-thirds of the companies do not believe in capping incentive earnings for first-line sales managers.

FLSM Leverage/Upside: The best performers (~90th percentile of performance) can earn how many times the at-risk target incentive?

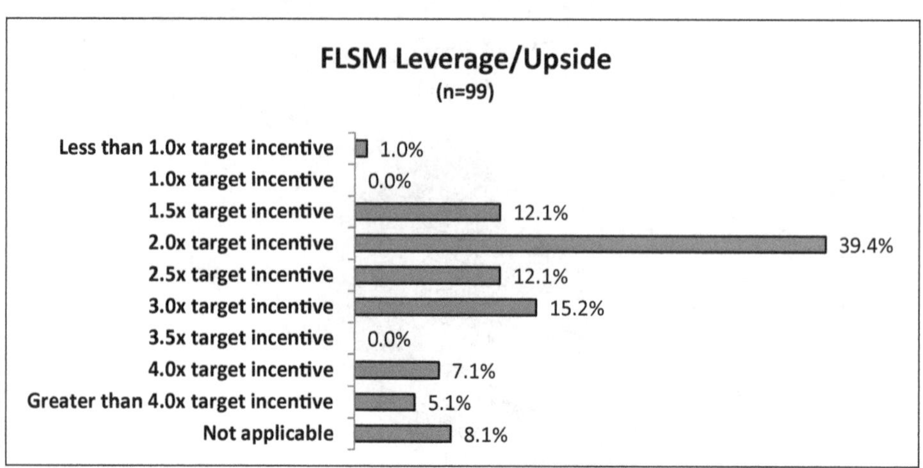

Survey Findings. 39.4% of the companies provide 2.0x target incentive to first-line sales managers for outstanding performance (best: 90th percentile). 15.2% provide 3.0x target incentive earnings for outstanding performance.

Observations. 2.0x target incentive for outstanding performance is the most common upside earning amount for first-line sales managers; however, practices vary.

Seller Payouts Compared to FLSM Target Total Pay: Approximately what percent of sales personnel earn greater than the FLSM's target total compensation amount?

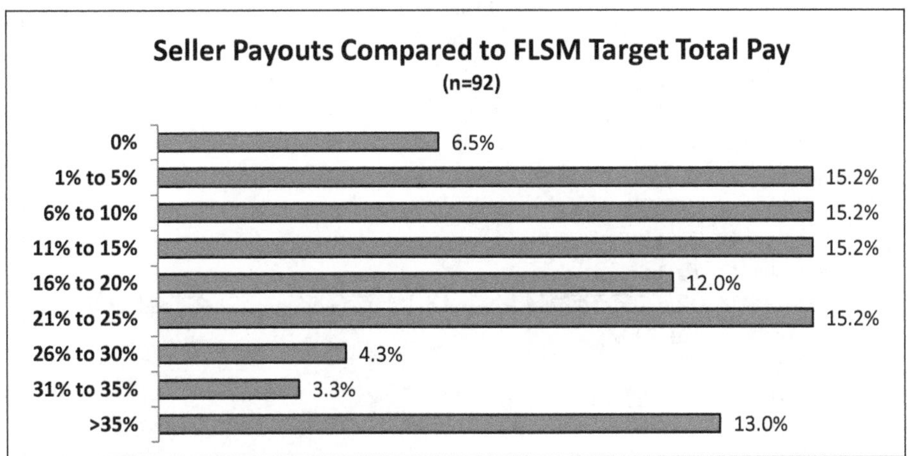

Survey Findings. 93.5% of the reporting companies confirm that sales personnel can earn more than the target total compensation of first-line sales managers.

Observations. A reasonable policy provision would accommodate up to one-third of the sales personnel to reach and exceed the target total compensation of the first-line sales manager. Note: Most likely, in good years, the first-line sales managers' actual payments will exceed their own "target" compensation amount for the job.

DEMOGRAPHICS

Fiscal Year: In what month does your fiscal 2018 year begin?

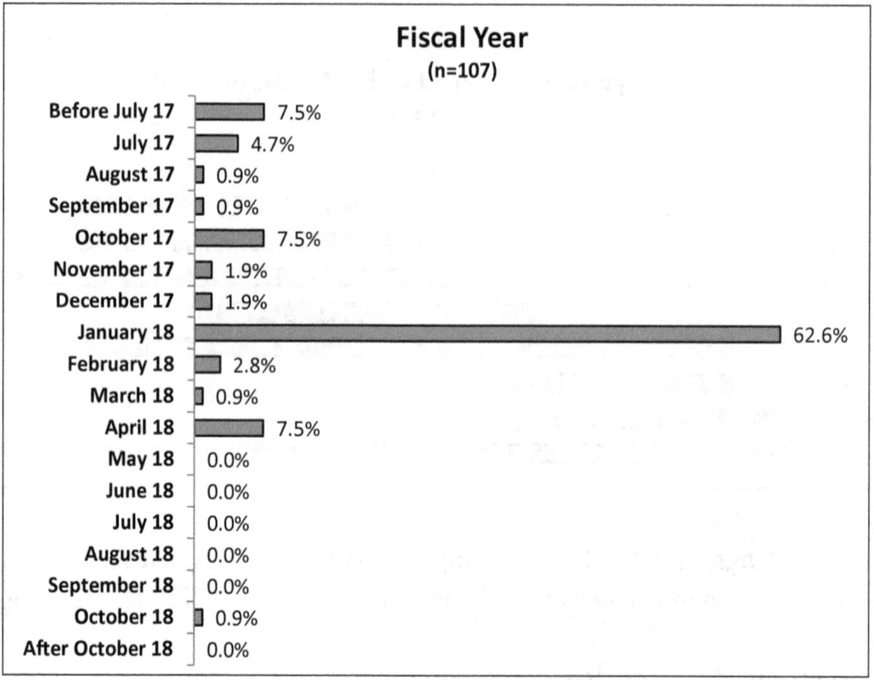

Number of Eligible Participants: For your division sales unit, how many employees are eligible to participate in the sales compensation program? (Enter a whole number, an estimate is acceptable.)

10th Perc	25th Perc	50th Perc	75th Perc	90th Perc	Average
61.2	115	268	775	2200	1489.6

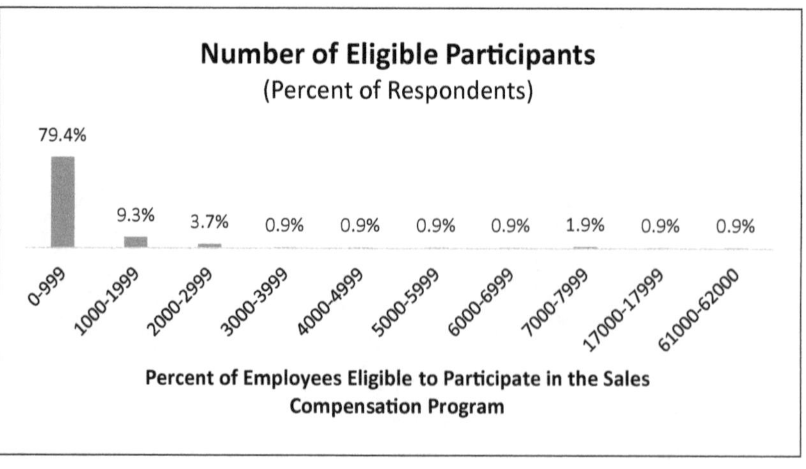

Type of Product/Service: Your division sales unit is primarily selling a:

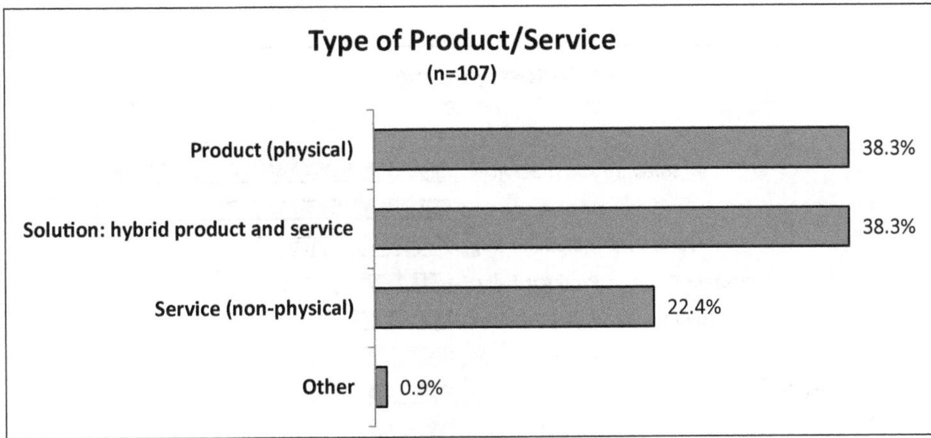

Sales Model: Your primary sales model for the division sales unit is:

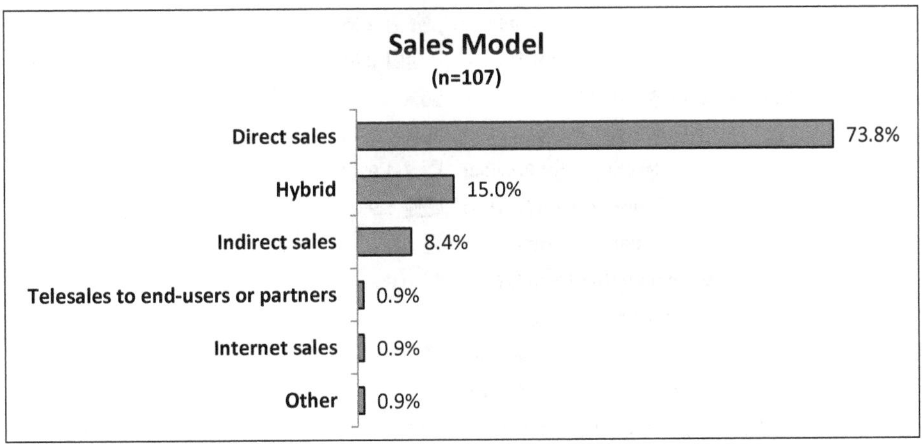

Industry Category: For the division sales unit, your industry is (if possible, avoid selecting "Other"):

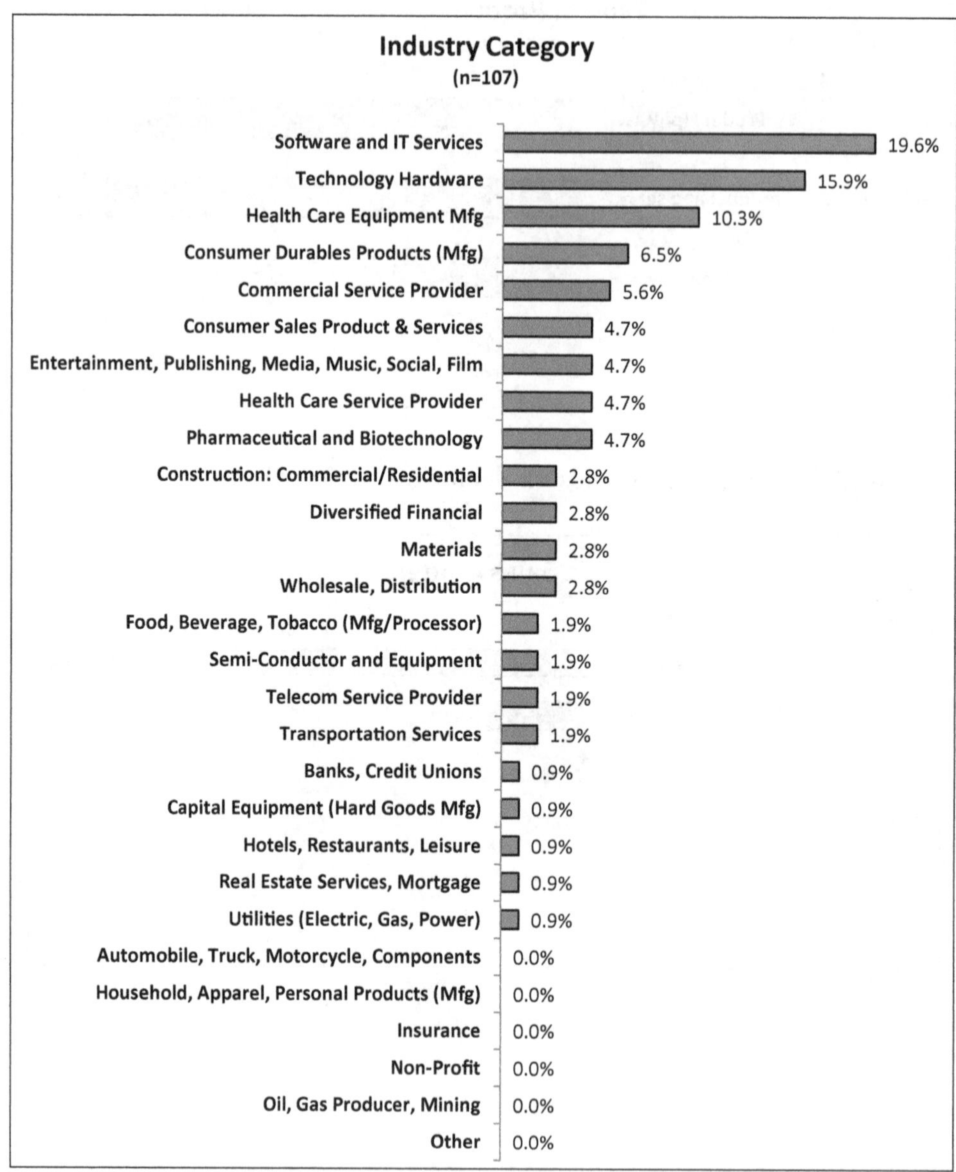

Country: Your division sales unit is located in:

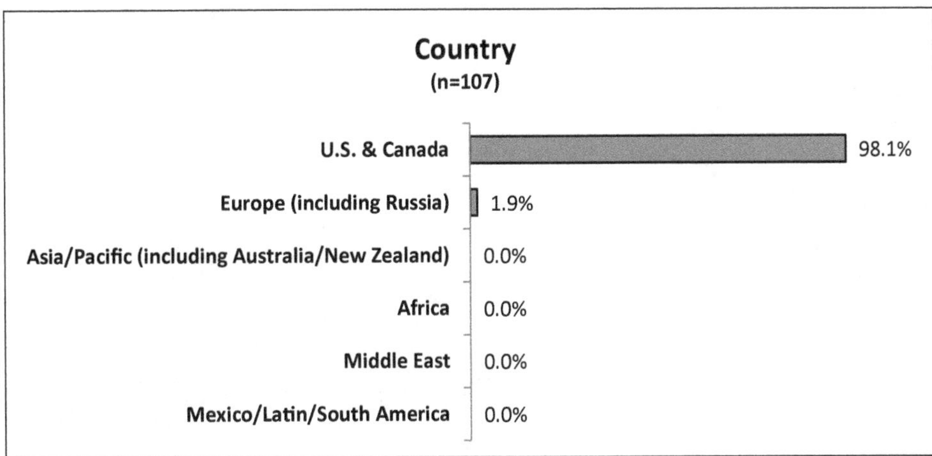

Sales Volume: The division's sales for 2018 will be (approximately):

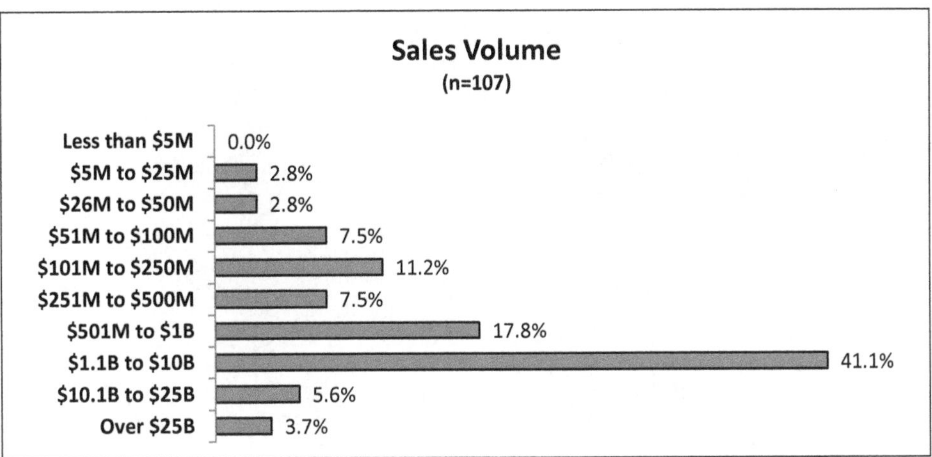

CAREERS IN SALES COMPENSATION SURVEY

2018 CAREERS IN SALES COMPENSATION SURVEY

The *Careers in Sales Compensation* Survey provides an in-depth profile of sales compensation professionals and advice for those interested in entering the field.

IN THIS SECTION

- Executive Summary
- Participant Profile
- Company Practices
- Advice for Sales Compensation Professionals

EXECUTIVE SUMMARY

Special thanks to all of the participants who contributed to this interesting study of sales compensation professionals. Sixty-two sales compensation practitioners provided personal background information, company practices and advice to those exploring a career in sales compensation. Also, we must thankfully acknowledge the informative and heart-felt comments provided to the questions that asked "what is good about working in sales compensation" and "what is not so good about such a job assignment." (These free-form comments appear at the end of the survey.)

The survey took place in September 2018 with participants receiving their full survey results in the same month.

Noteworthy Highlights

Here are some noteworthy highlights from the survey findings.

- **Senior management values sales compensation professionals.** Sales compensation is a specialized skill valued by management. Sales compensation design professionals often reside in the HR/compensation department. Sales compensation professionals may have other compensation program (non-sales) design and management duties. Some noted that the pay levels for sales compensation professionals are higher than similar-level jobs in HR. Most sales compensation professionals enjoy their work.
- **Finance/accounting experience and education provides a good foundation for sales compensation work.** Analytical skills, attention to detail and the ability to work with numerous stakeholders are key success factors.
- **Sales compensation functions have different owners.** Sales management and sales operations own the sales compensation program. Executive leadership often has final plan approval. HR/compensation helps with annual redesign efforts. Sales operations provides day-to-day management of the pay program. Most companies have limited headcount allocated to design and management of the sales compensation program. However, administration staff support often requires additional comparative headcount.

- **A sales compensation career offers interesting, challenging and rewarding work.** Sales compensation work plays a critical impact on company success. From executive engagement to successful program implementation, sales compensation offers numerous high visibility challenges and rewarding outcomes. However, during the annual redesign process, be prepared for hard work, long hours, deferred vacations and minimal appreciation. Overall, our survey participants report the rewards outweigh the shortcomings.

PARTICIPANT PROFILE

Summary. Most of the survey participants reside in the HR department. However, almost half of them have a finance/accounting employment background. Many have a finance/accounting education, some with an advanced graduate degree, often an MBA. Many of the respondents are individual contributors without supervisory duties. Most have sales compensation design responsibilities, but others have program management, administration and automation responsibilities. Few respondents have sales compensation as their sole responsibility; many have other compensation program duties, too. Scope of responsibilities includes either North American or global duties. Many of the respondents enjoy their sales compensation role. Less than 10 percent seek to leave their sales compensation role.

- **Your Department:** 59.7% reside in the human resources department. **Observations.** Most of the respondents reside in the HR department.
- **Employment Background:** 35.5% have a primary employment background in human resources prior to their sales compensation assignment. **Observations.** Surprisingly, while most of the respondents are located within the HR department, many have a finance/accounting background.
- **Academic Focus:** 33.9% have their highest degree focused on finance/accounting/marketing/logistics. **Observations.** Many of the professionals in sales compensation have either a finance/accounting/ marketing/logistics or general business/management academic training, confirming the need to understand and process "numbers."
- **Academic Degree:** 38.7% have a master of business administration degree. 32.3% have a bachelor of science degree. **Observations.** Degrees in master of business administration and bachelor of science account for 71% of the academic levels.
- **Your Job Level:** 42.6% of respondents indicate that their job level is manager/supervisor/leader. **Observations.** 81.9% of the survey respondents are either manager or director level professionals.
- **Supervision:** 43.5% have no design/management full-time equivalent professionals under their supervision. **Observations.** More than 40% of the respondents are individual contributors. Some noteworthy exceptions have more than five subordinates.

- **Current Duties:** 75.8% have design as their current sales compensation-related activity. **Observations.** Most respondents have a range of responsibilities spanning design, management, administration and automation.
- **Role Satisfaction:** 45.2% have a very high satisfaction with their sales compensation role. **Observations.** Sales compensation professionals like their work!
- **Career Ambitions:** 27.9% have career ambitions to remain in their current sales compensation role. **Observations.** Many respondents want to remain in sales compensation. Less than 10% said they wish to move out of sales compensation.
- **Compensation:** 17.7% have a current annual target total compensation of $200,000–$224,999; another 17.7% have $125,000–$149,999; and an additional 17.7% have $100,000–$124,999. **Observations.** Several respondents commented that they think sales compensation earns higher pay for similar job title levels within HR.
- **Region Scope:** 51.6% have their sales compensation responsibility in the U.S. and Canada. 50% have responsibilities globally. **Observations.** About half of the respondents stated North American sales compensation as their job focus. The other 50% had global sales compensation duties.
- **Other Duties:** 39.3% occupy more than 25% of their time on other compensation programs outside of sales compensation design/management. **Observations.** HR-based professionals often have other compensation program accountabilities. Sales strategy/sales operations have other sales performance program responsibilities. Only 21.3% had sales compensation design/management as their sole duty.

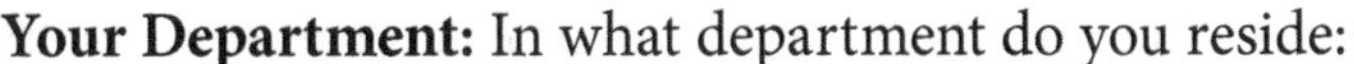

Your Department: In what department do you reside:

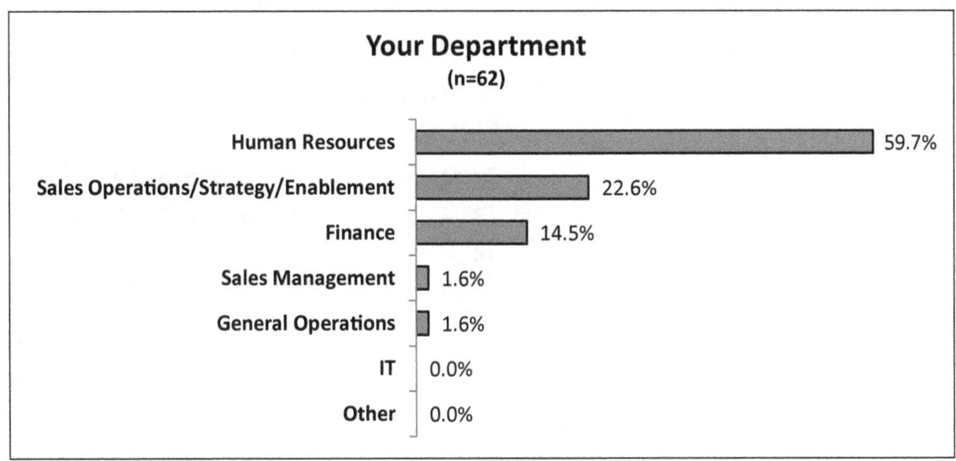

Survey Findings. 59.7% reside in the human resources department. 22.6% are located in the sales operations/strategy/enablement department. And, 14.5% are in the finance department.

Observations. Most of the respondents reside in the HR department.

Employment Background: Your primary employment background prior to your sales compensation assignment would be best described as:

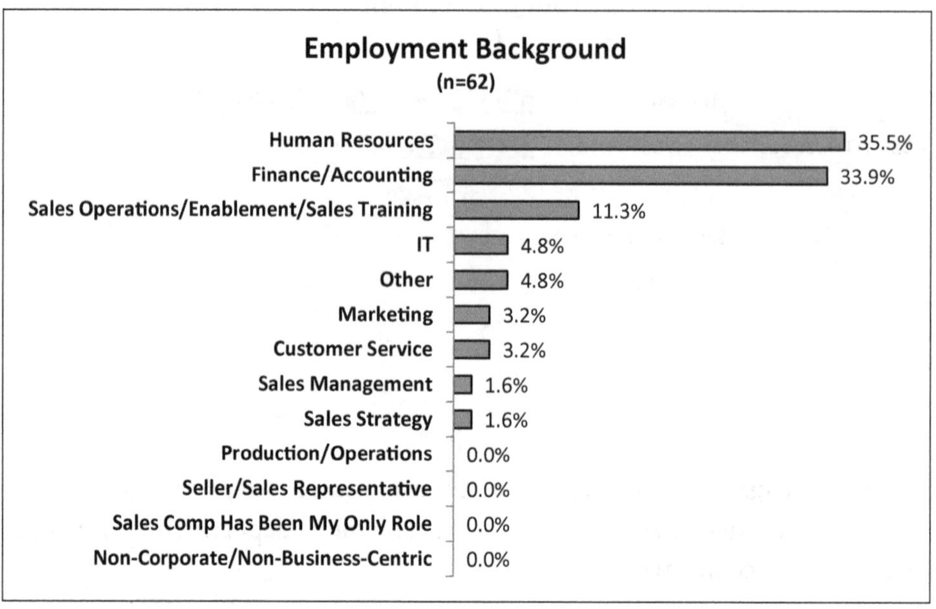

Other Employment Backgrounds

- Split between HR and sales operations
- Operations, compensation and sales
- Finance and HR

Survey Findings. 35.5% have a primary employment background in human resources prior to their sales compensation assignment. 33.9% have a finance/accounting background. And, 11.3% have experience in sales operations/enablement/sales training.

Observations. Surprisingly, while most of the respondents are located within the HR department, many have a finance/accounting background.

Academic Focus: What was/is your academic area of focus for your highest degree?

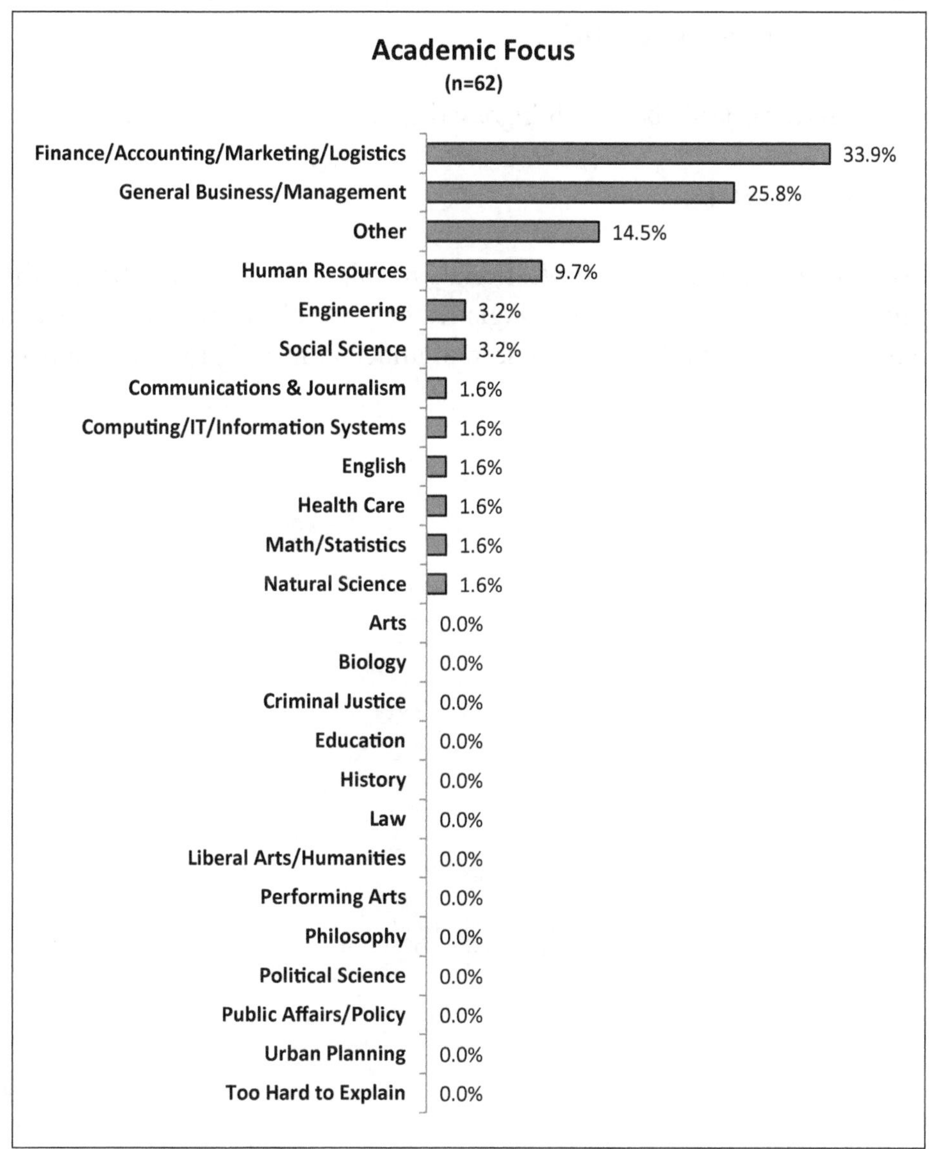

Other Academic Focuses

- Economics
- Industrial and org psychology/HR/business law
- I/O psychology
- Office management
- Psychology

- Economics
- BA Physics, BSEE, MBA
- Psychology
- Transportation/logistics

Survey Findings. 33.9% have their highest degree focused on finance/accounting/marketing/logistics. 25.8% in general business/management. And, 14.5% identify other academic areas.

Observations. Many of the professionals in sales compensation have either a finance/accounting/marketing/logistics or general business/management academic training, confirming the need to understand and process "numbers."

Academic Degree: Your highest Academic Degree earned is:

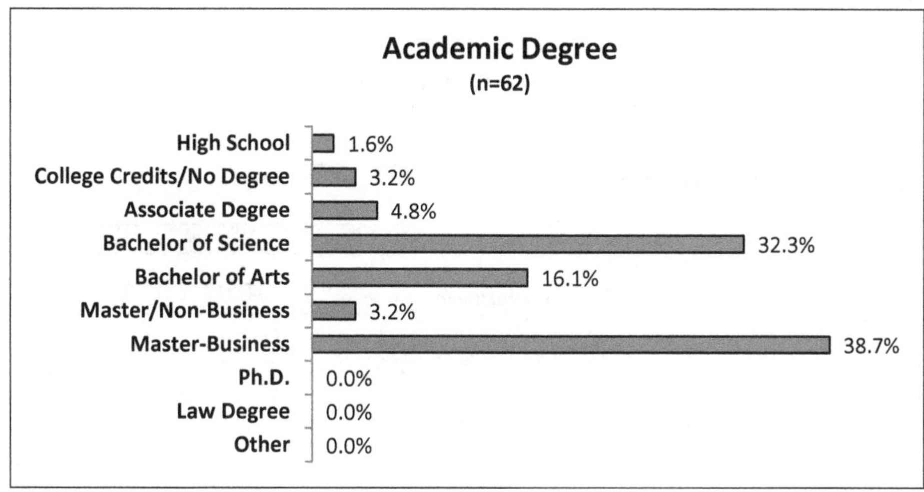

Survey Findings. 38.7% have a master of business administration degree. 32.3% have a bachelor of science degree. And, 16.1% have a bachelor of arts degree.

Observations. Degrees in master of business administration and bachelor of science account for 71% of the academic levels.

Your Job Level: Examples of additional designations include "senior," "executive" and others.

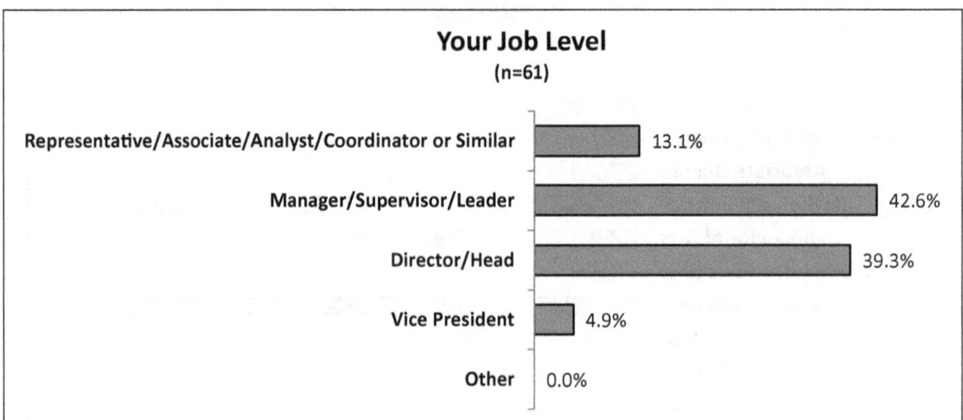

Survey Findings. 42.6% of respondents indicate that their job level is manager/supervisor/leader. 39.3% say they are a director/head. And, 13.1% chose representative/associate/analyst/coordinator or similar.

Observations. 81.9% of the survey respondents are either manager or director level professionals.

Supervision: How many design/management full-time equivalent professionals do you supervise?

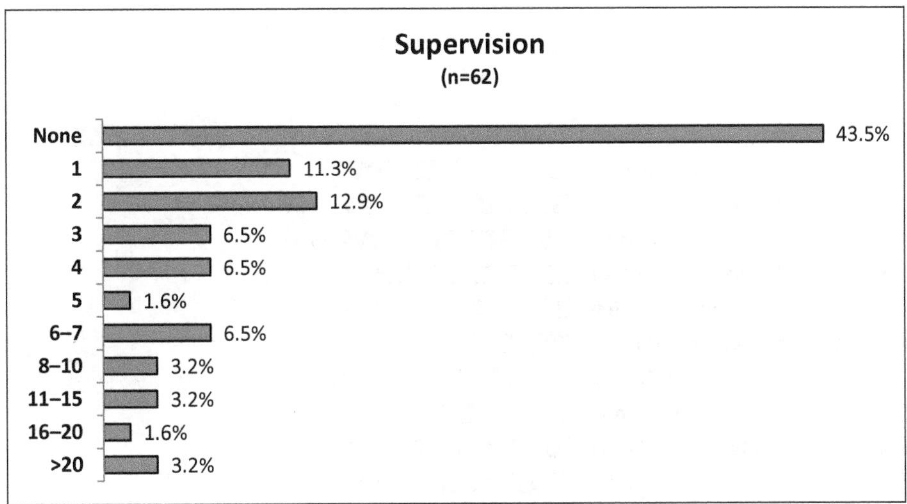

Survey Findings. 43.5% have no design/management full-time equivalent professionals under their supervision. 12.9% have two under their supervision. And, 11.3% have one.

Observations. More than 40% of the respondents are individual contributors. Some noteworthy exceptions have more than five subordinates.

Current Duties: Your current role includes the following sales compensation-related activities (select the best choice):

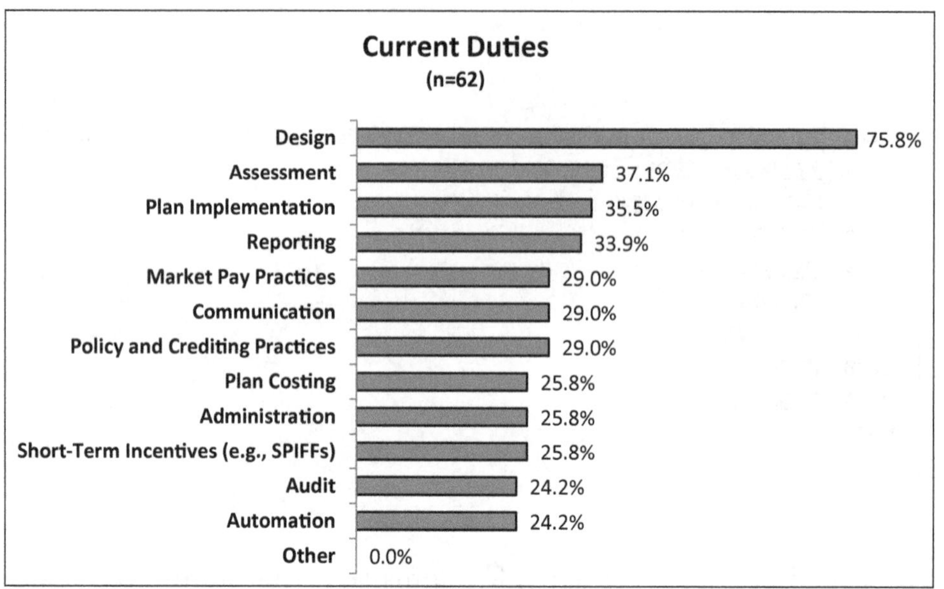

Survey Findings. 75.8% have design as their current sales compensation-related activity. 37.1% have assessment as their activity. And, 35.5% have plan implementation.

Observations. Most respondents have a range of responsibilities spanning design, management, administration and automation.

Role Satisfaction: Your satisfaction with your sales compensation role is:

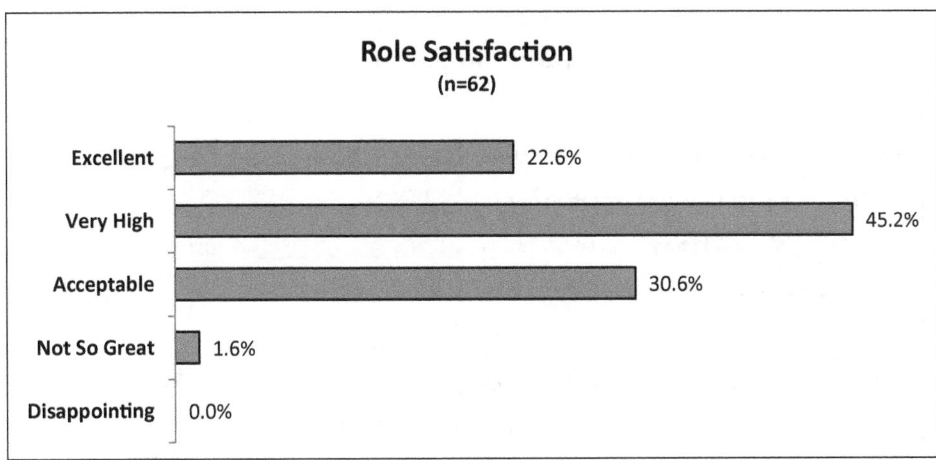

Survey Findings. 45.2% have a very high satisfaction with their sales compensation role. 30.6% find their role acceptable. And, 22.6% identify their satisfaction as excellent.

Observations. Sales compensation professionals like their work!

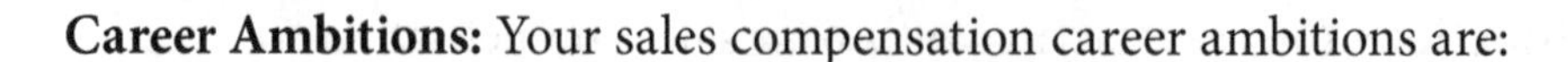

Career Ambitions: Your sales compensation career ambitions are:

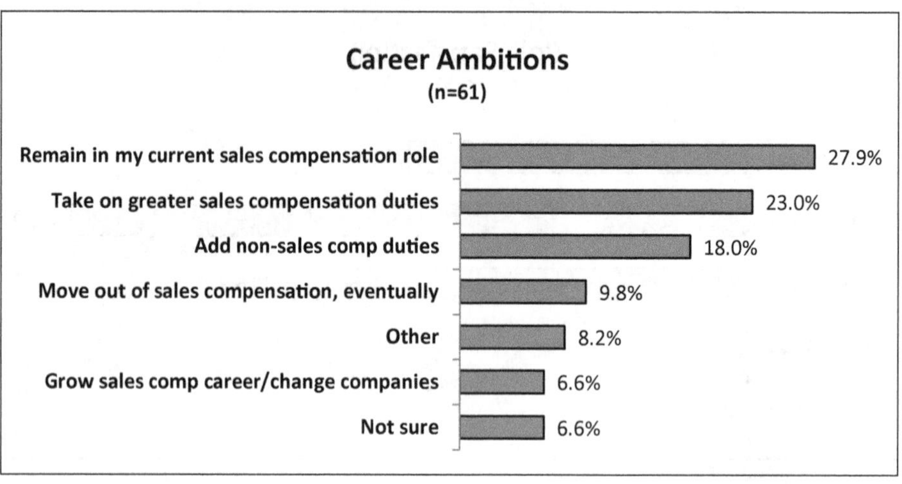

Other Career Ambitions

- Continue to lead while growing into VP role
- Look to move to an executive level role, either within or outside current organization
- More senior roles in total rewards, may or may not include sales comp
- Retiring in three months
- VP of compensation and benefits

Survey Findings. 27.9% have career ambitions to remain in their current sales compensation role. 23% want to take on greater sales compensation duties. And, 18% would like to add non-sales comp duties.

Observations. Many respondents want to remain in sales compensation. Less than 10% said they wish to move out of sales compensation.

Compensation: Your current annual target total compensation (base plus target incentive) is approximately:

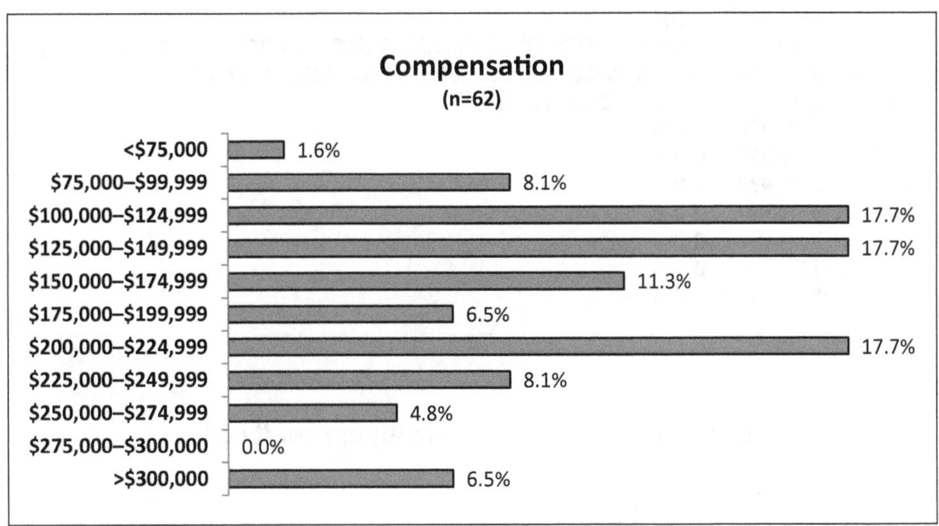

Survey Findings. 17.7% have a current annual target total compensation of $200,000–$224,999; another 17.7% have $125,000–$149,999; and an additional 17.7% have $100,000–$124,999. 11.3% have $150,000–$174,999. And, 8.1% have $75,000–$99,999, and another 8.1% have $225,000–$249,999 as their current annual target total compensation.

Observations. Several respondents commented that they think sales compensation earns higher pay for similar job title levels within HR.

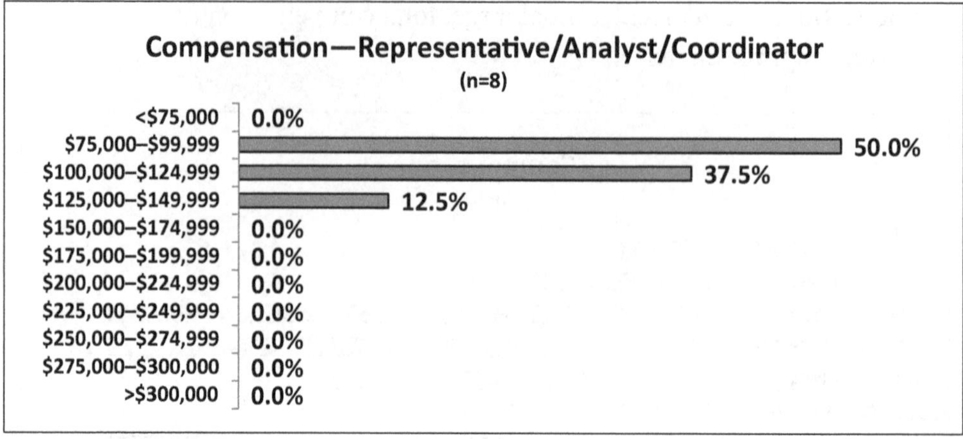
Compensation—Representative/Analyst/Coordinator
(n=8)
<$75,000 0.0%
$75,000–$99,999 50.0%
$100,000–$124,999 37.5%
$125,000–$149,999 12.5%
$150,000–$174,999 0.0%
$175,000–$199,999 0.0%
$200,000–$224,999 0.0%
$225,000–$249,999 0.0%
$250,000–$274,999 0.0%
$275,000–$300,000 0.0%
>$300,000 0.0%

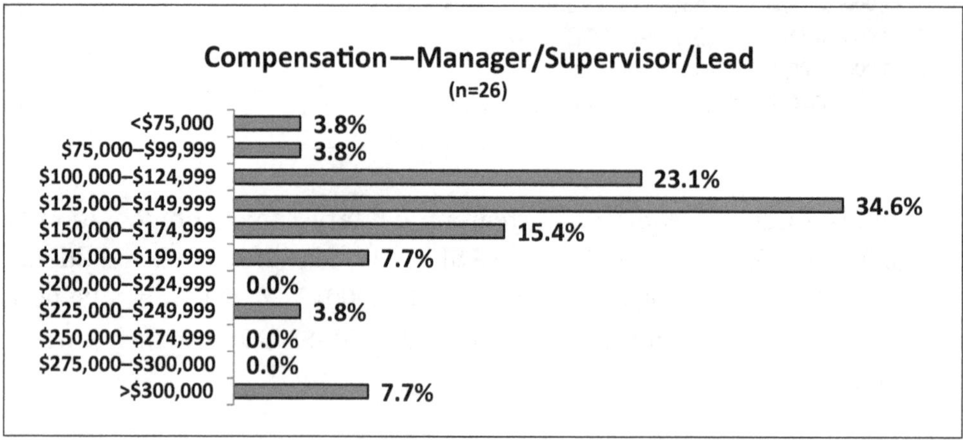
Compensation—Manager/Supervisor/Lead
(n=26)
<$75,000 3.8%
$75,000–$99,999 3.8%
$100,000–$124,999 23.1%
$125,000–$149,999 34.6%
$150,000–$174,999 15.4%
$175,000–$199,999 7.7%
$200,000–$224,999 0.0%
$225,000–$249,999 3.8%
$250,000–$274,999 0.0%
$275,000–$300,000 0.0%
>$300,000 7.7%

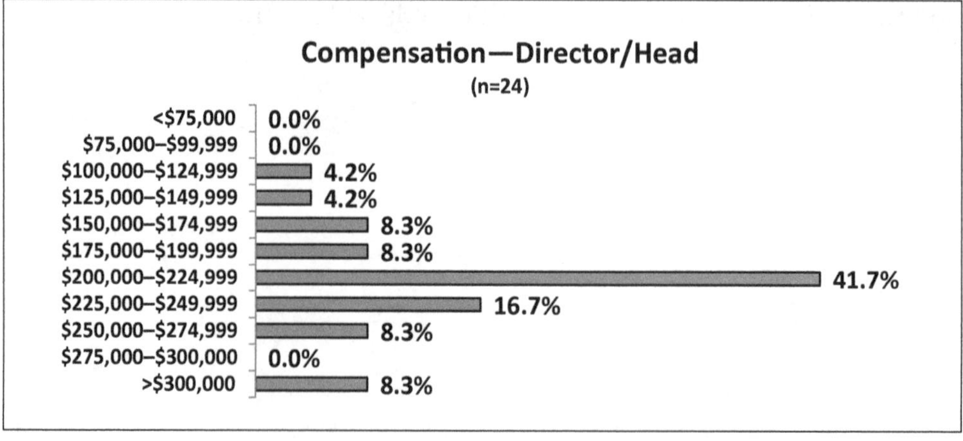
Compensation—Director/Head
(n=24)
<$75,000 0.0%
$75,000–$99,999 0.0%
$100,000–$124,999 4.2%
$125,000–$149,999 4.2%
$150,000–$174,999 8.3%
$175,000–$199,999 8.3%
$200,000–$224,999 41.7%
$225,000–$249,999 16.7%
$250,000–$274,999 8.3%
$275,000–$300,000 0.0%
>$300,000 8.3%

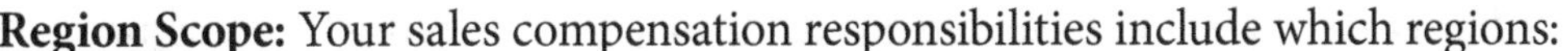

Region Scope: Your sales compensation responsibilities include which regions:

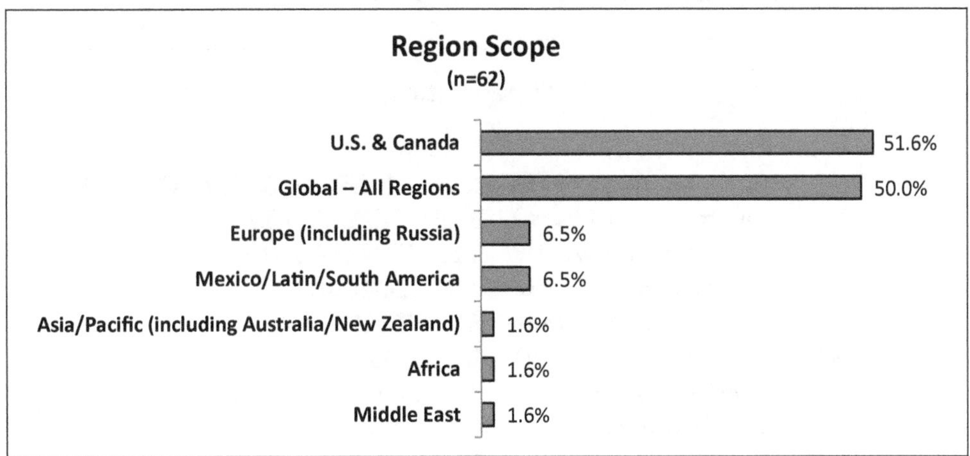

Survey Findings. 51.6% have their sales compensation responsibility in the U.S. and Canada. 50% have responsibilities globally. And, the regions of Europe and Mexico/Latin/South America are tied with 6.5%. (Multiple answers permitted.)

Observations. About half of the respondents stated North American sales compensation as their job focus. The other 50% had global sales compensation duties.

Other Duties: Do you have duties outside of sales compensation design/management occupying more than 25% of your time?

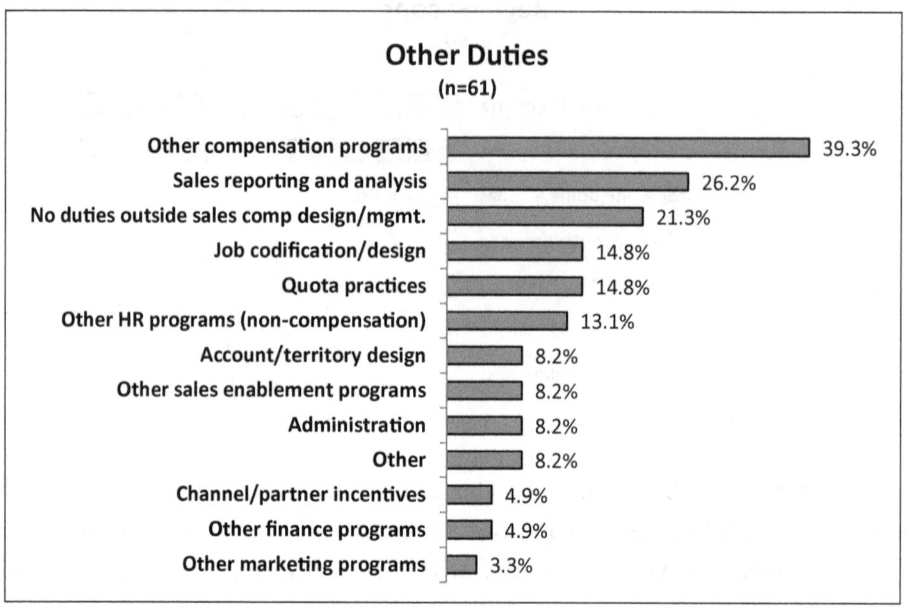

Other Duties

- Sales tools, sales strategy, sales process
- Variable pay program corporate governance
- Commission tool configuration
- Other HR/total rewards/compensation programs
- Deal review approval
- Manager of order management

Survey Findings. 39.3% occupy more than 25% of their time on other compensation programs outside of sales compensation design/management. 26.2% identify that sales reporting and analysis take more than 25% of their time. And, 21.3% have no duties outside sales comp design/management.

Observations. HR-based professionals often have other compensation program accountabilities. Sales strategy/sales operations have other sales performance program responsibilities. Only 21.3% had sales compensation design/management as their sole duty.

COMPANY PRACTICES

Summary. More than 50 percent of the companies report that sales compensation program ownership resides with sales management/sales operations or executive management. Companies will often use a redesign task force to make annual revisions. Executive management provides final program approval for plan changes. Sales operations provides the day-to-day management of the sales compensation program. Most companies have four or less professional FTEs supporting sales compensation design/management. For larger organizations, a high number of FTEs provide administration/automation support.

- **Sales Compensation Program Ownership:** 37.1% identify sales management/sales operations as the owner of the company's sales compensation program. **Observations.** Sales management/sales operations ranks at the top of the list for sales compensation program ownership as reported by 37.1% of the companies. Note the significant level of executive management ownership of the sales compensation program as found in 21% of the companies.

- **Sales Compensation Redesign Efforts:** 30.6% of the respondents use a sales compensation design task force as the responsible party for redesigning the sales compensation plan. **Observations.** We are encouraged to see that 30.6% use a design task force to revise the sales compensation plan. Another 30.6% of the companies rely on sales management/sales operations to shepherd the redesign effort.

- **Program Approval:** 48.4% identify CEO, COO, president or general manager as the ultimate/final approval authority for any program changes. **Observations.** For almost half of the companies, executive management rightfully wants to have final program approval, confirming the importance of the sales compensation program.

- **Program Management:** 40.3% say sales operations is responsible for day-to-day program management. **Observations.** In most cases, sales operations is responsible for day-to-day program management.

- **Highest Job Level:** 43.5% say that the highest job level with "sales compensation" in the title at their company is director/head. **Observations.** Many of the reporting companies (43.5%) have director level titles containing "sales compensation." These companies place a premium on an effective sales compensation program.

- **Design/Management Professional FTEs:** 32.8% have three to four full-time professionals working on sales compensation design/management at their company. **Observations.** Nearly 74% of the companies have four or fewer FTEs assigned to design/management of the sales compensation program.
- **Program Administration:** 32.8% indicate that finance is responsible for program administration. **Observations.** Finance and sales operations have the primary responsibility for program administration.
- **Administration/Automation Professional FTEs:** 22.6% have more than 20 full-time professionals working on sales compensation administration/automation. **Observations.** Administration of the sales compensation program requires numerous FTEs. In some cases, companies have a substantial headcount overseeing administration/automation with 22.6% of the reporting companies having more than 20 FTEs devoted to administration.

Sales Compensation Program Ownership: Who owns (final accountability) sales compensation at your company?

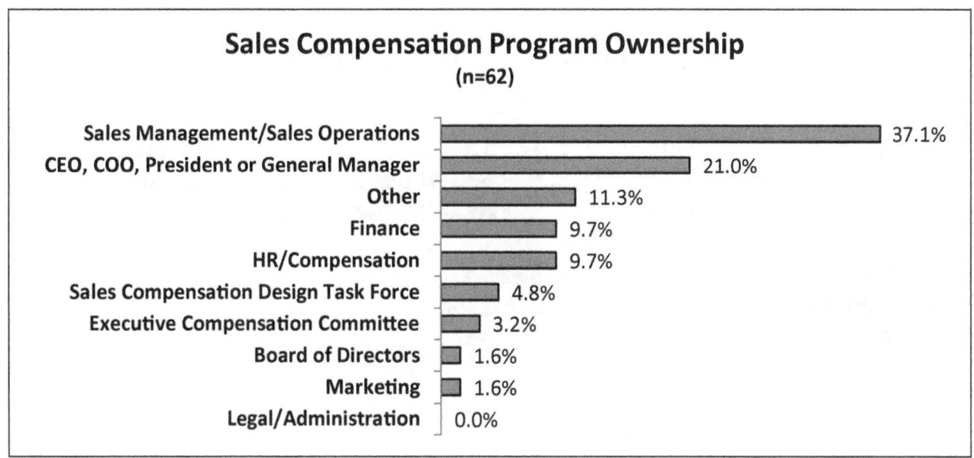

Other Owners of the Sales Compensation Program

- Vice chair of the business line
- CFO, top sales management and head of compensation
- CCO and CFO
- Payment is approved by finance and HR
- CSO, CMO
- CRO and CFO
- Sales compensation review board

Survey Findings. 37.1% identify sales management/sales operations as the owner of the company's sales compensation program. 21% said CEO, COO, president or general manager. And, 11.3% have an owner that was not listed.

Observations. Sales management/sales operations ranks at the top of the list for sales compensation program ownership as reported by 37.1% of the companies. Note the significant level of executive management ownership of the sales compensation program as found in 21% of the companies.

Sales Compensation Redesign Efforts: Who is responsible for the redesign of the sales compensation plan (leads process, suggests design upgrades)?

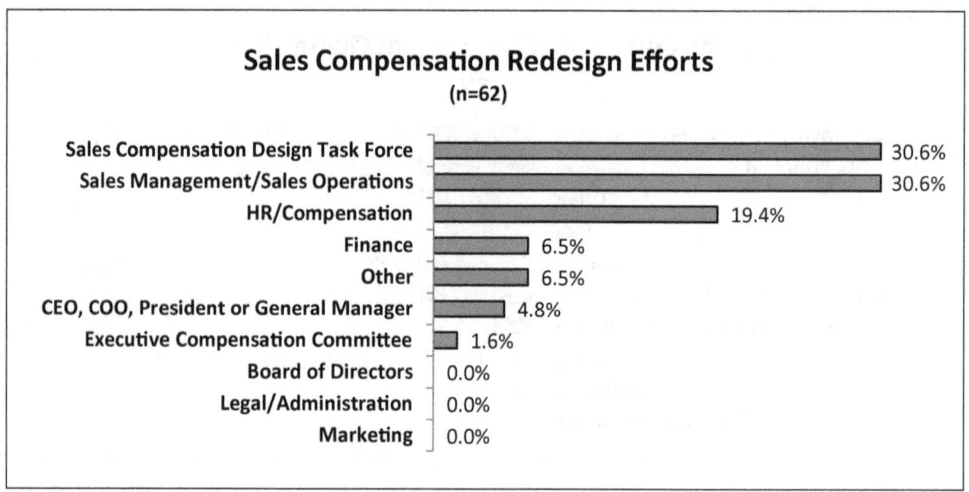

Other Sales Compensation Redesign Efforts

- Manager, sales compensation
- Sales compensation COE
- Currently sales management, moving to a model to include HR/sales comp
- SCRB

Survey Findings. 30.6% of the respondents use a sales compensation design task force as the responsible party for redesigning the sales compensation plan. Another 30.6% use sales management/sales operations. And, 19.4% identify HR/compensation as the party responsible. Finance and other tied with 6.5%.

Observations. We are encouraged to see that 30.6% use a design task force to revise the sales compensation plan. Another 30.6% of the companies rely on sales management/sales operations to shepherd the redesign effort.

Program Approval: Who has the ultimate/final approval authority for any program changes?

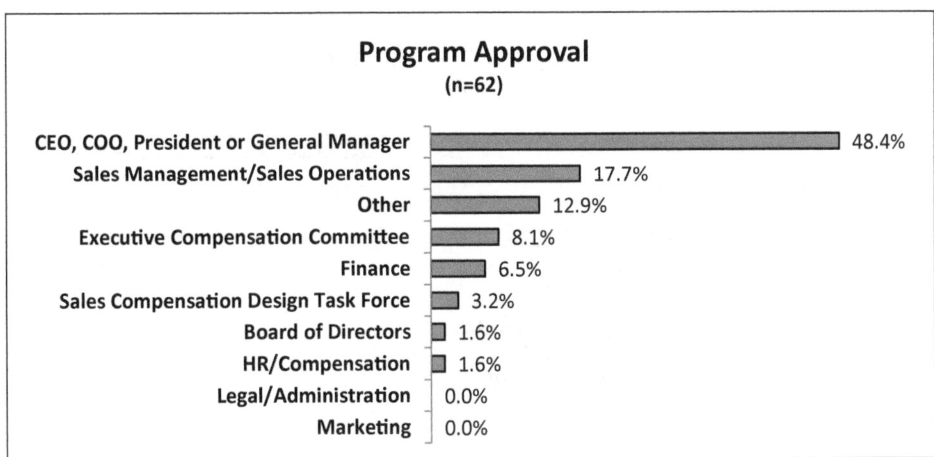

Other Program Approval Authorities

- Vice chair of the business line
- CFO, top sales management and head of compensation
- Total rewards committee
- CCO and CFO
- Committee made up of sales/marketing executives
- Regional SVPs
- CRO and CFO
- CEO & CFO

Survey Findings. 48.4% identify CEO, COO, president or general manager as the ultimate/final approval authority for any program changes. 17.7% say sales management/sales operations is the ultimate approval authority. And, 12.9% chose other.

Observations. For almost half of the companies, executive management rightfully wants to have final program approval, confirming the importance of the sales compensation program.

Program Management: Who is responsible for day-to-day program management, i.e., policy application, interpretation and field explanations/advice?

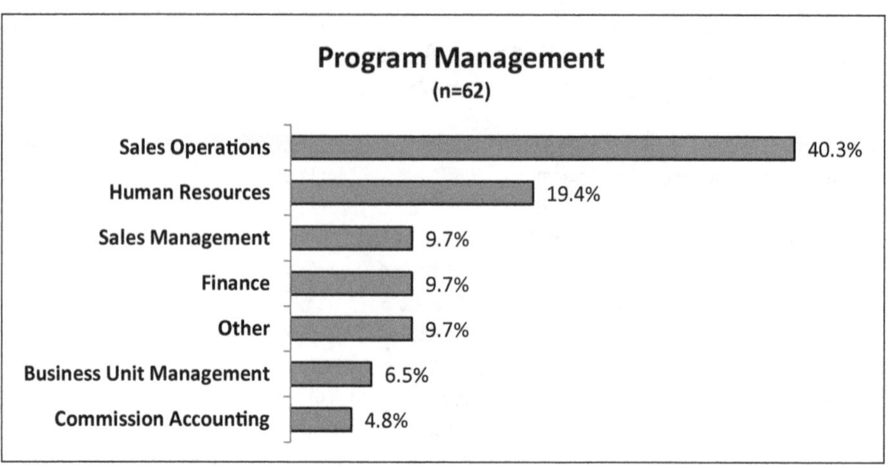

Other Day-to-Day Program Management

- Sales compensation team
- Incentive oversight committee: comprised of an incentive plan manager and various design team members
- Chief sales officer
- Sales compensation department
- Sales compensation
- My team

Survey Findings. 40.3% say sales operations is responsible for day-to-day program management. 19.4% say human resources. Sales management, finance and other tied with 9.7%.

Observations. In most cases, sales operations is responsible for day-to-day program management.

Highest Job Level: What is the highest job level with "sales compensation" in the title at your company? Examples of additional designations include "senior," "executive" and others:

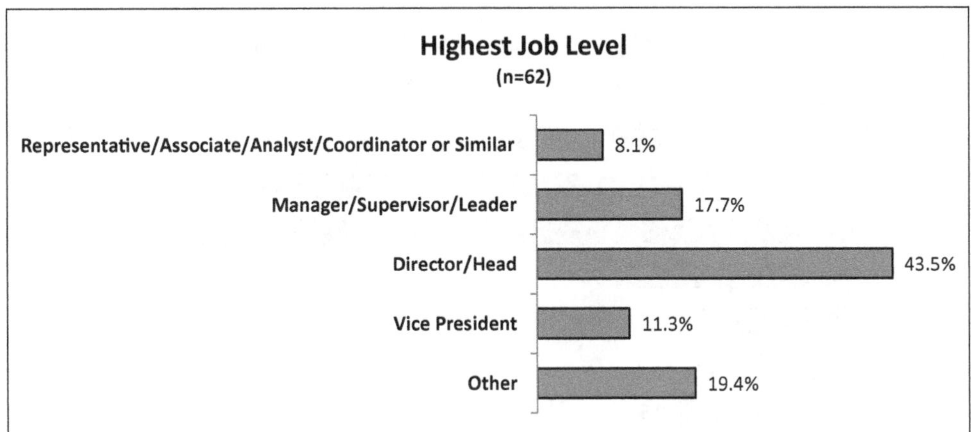

Other Highest Job Levels

- No one
- No positions focused solely on sales compensation
- NA
- None, embedded in responsibilities
- Senior director
- Falls under broad-based manager
- VP total rewards
- No one has the title sales compensation
- We use more generic titles, so none of our jobs has sales compensation in the title
- There are no titles with "sales" compensation in the title
- No one with that title
- None

Survey Findings. 43.5% say that the highest job level with "sales compensation" in the title at their company is director/head. 19.4% chose other. 17.7% have manager/supervisor/leader as their highest sales compensation job level.

Observations. Many of the reporting companies (43.5%) have director level titles containing "sales compensation." These companies place a premium on an effective sales compensation program.

Design/Management Professional FTEs: The number of full-time professionals (or equivalent) working on sales compensation design/management (not administration/automation) at your company is:

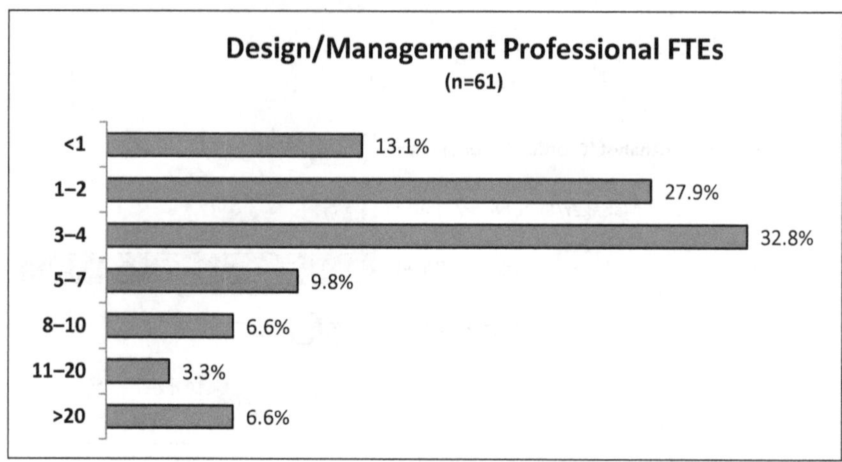

Survey Findings. 32.8% have three to four full-time professionals working on sales compensation design/management at their company. 27.9% have one to two. And, 13.1% have less than one.

Observations. Nearly 74% of the companies have four or fewer FTEs assigned to design/management of the sales compensation program.

Program Administration: Who is responsible for program administration, i.e., calculations, record keeping, reporting and payments?

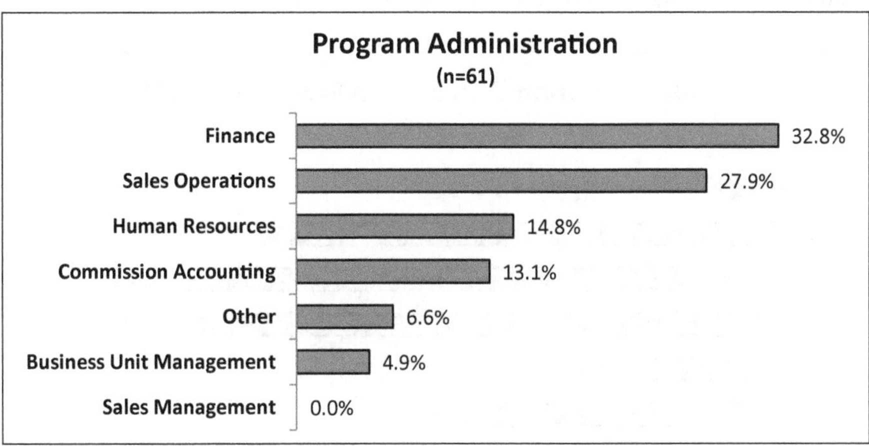

Other Program Administration

- Sales compensation team
- Incentive administration team
- Sales compensation department
- Sales compensation
- My global team

Survey Findings. 32.8% indicate that finance is responsible for program administration. 27.9% identify sales operations. And, 14.8% indicate human resources.

Observations. Finance and sales operations have the primary responsibility for program administration.

Administration/Automation Professional FTEs: The number of full-time professionals (or equivalent) working on sales compensation administration/automation (not design/management) at your company is:

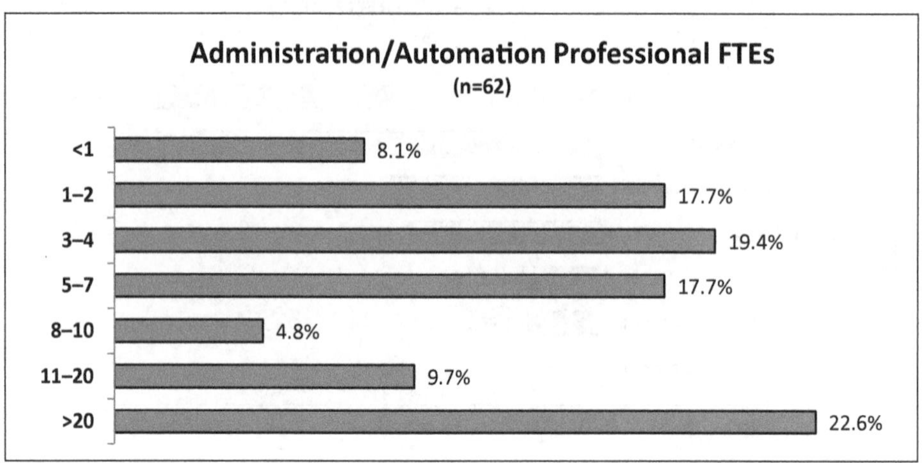

Survey Findings. 22.6% have more than 20 full-time professionals working on sales compensation administration/automation. 19.4% have three to four. One to two and five to seven each tied with 17.7%.

Observations. Administration of the sales compensation program requires numerous FTEs. In some cases, companies have a substantial headcount overseeing administration/automation with 22.6% of the reporting companies having more than 20 FTEs devoted to administration.

Industry Category: For the division sales unit, your industry is:

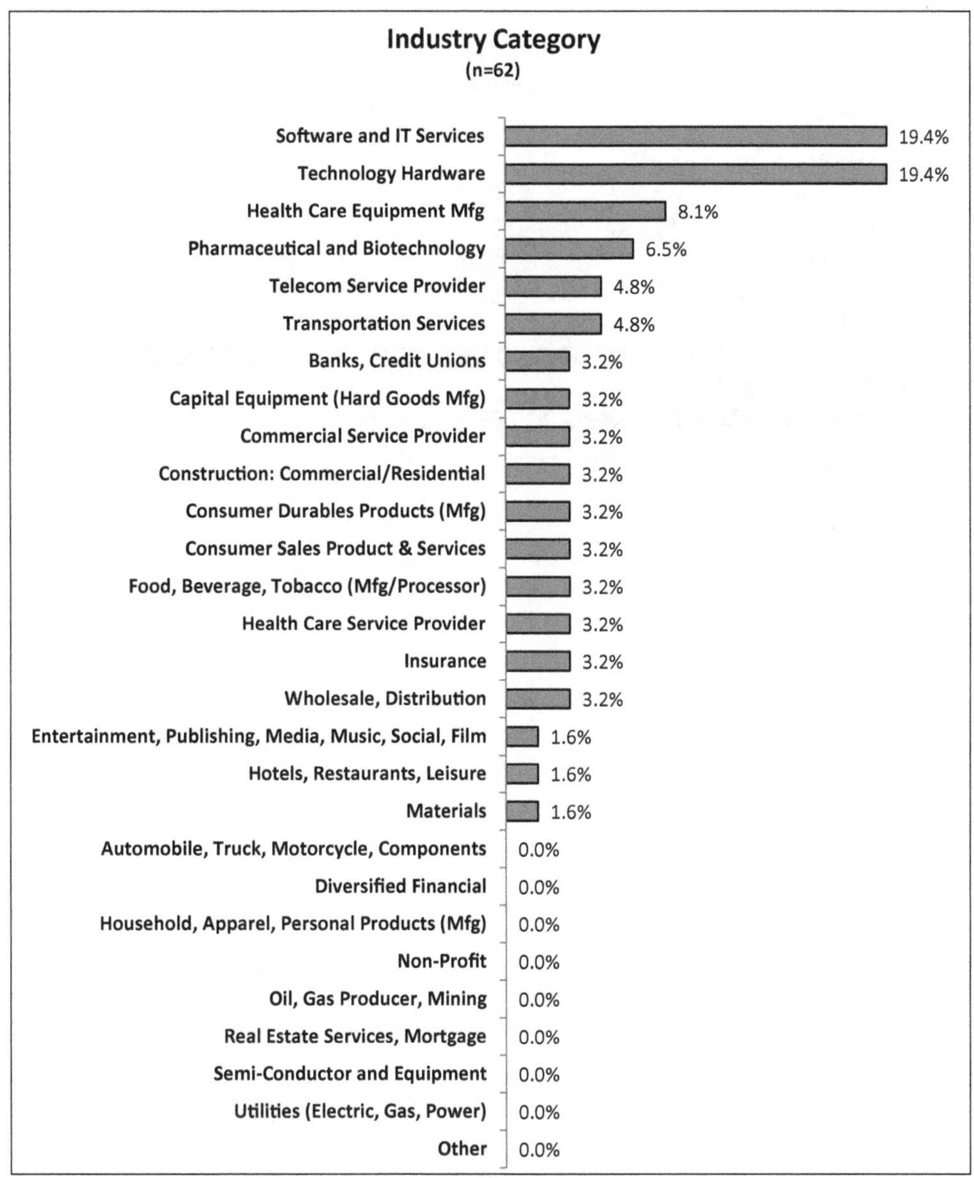

Sales Volume: The division's sales for 2018 will be (approximately):

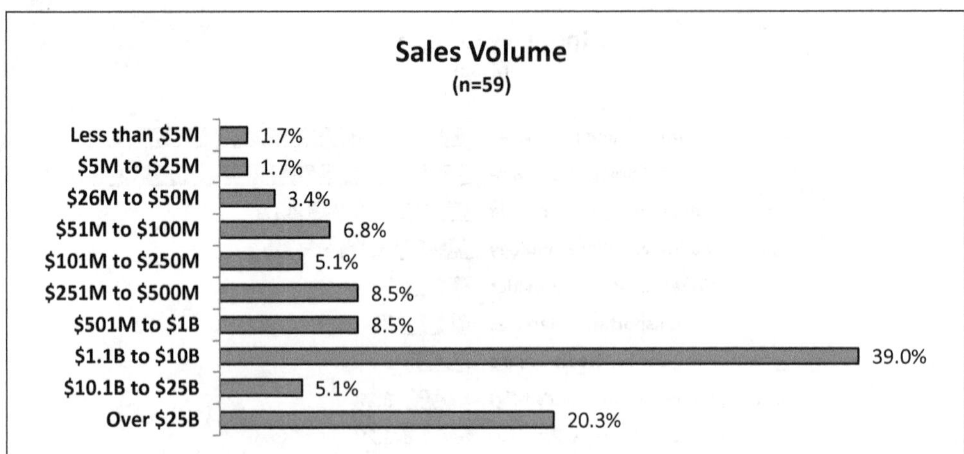

ADVICE FOR SALES COMPENSATION PROFESSIONALS

Summary. Preparing for a career in sales compensation includes developing the analytical skills to work with complex data, crediting and reporting systems. Study finance and accounting in school and gain work experience in sales operations and compensation. Read books, attend classes, connect with consultants and network with peers. It's a challenging, rewarding career, which pays well, but demands a lot.

- **Academic Advice:** 48.4% of the respondents suggest an academic career in finance/accounting/marketing/logistics for a sales compensation career. **Observations.** Most respondents encourage those seeking a career in sales compensation to be proficient with finance/accounting confirming that sales compensation work requires numeric competency.
- **Books to Read:** 75.9% chose *Compensating the Sales Force* by David Cichelli as the sales compensation book they would recommend. **Observations.** There are many great sales compensation books including Cichelli's *Compensating the Sales Force* and the annual *Sales Compensation Almanac.* DiMisa's book *Sales Compensation Made Simple* is a noteworthy sales compensation introductory text.
- **Classes:** 70.5% of the respondents suggest WorldatWork: Elements of Sales Compensation for learning about sales compensation. **Observations.** The two WorldatWork sales compensation classes were the only instruction-based programs cited by the participants. Many had attended these classes.
- **Sources:** 62.3% identify consulting firm(s) as the best source of information on sales compensation practices. 60.7% of the respondents say networking with peers. **Observations.** Consulting firms and networking with peers offers significant sales compensation content. Consulting firms offer vertical market conferences, research, benchmarks and applicable case studies. Peers can suggest timely observations and solutions.
- **What previous experience or activities can help someone be a successful sales compensation professional? Observations.** The survey participants suggest analytical training in finance, accounting or sales operations as a good technical foundation. Work experience with the sales team is a plus. Compensation training is helpful. Strong communications skills are important. The ability to ensure that the sales compensation plan serves the business objectives is most important.

- **Why should folks consider a career in sales compensation? Observations.** Sales compensation is a highly visible role working alongside senior management helping to solve strategic sales/business challenges. Requires engagement with diverse functional teams to solve pay alignment challenges. Offers interesting creative problem solving challenges that are always changing. Professionally rewarding to see positive business impact. Pays better than comparable level positions in HR/compensation.
- **What is a drawback to a career in sales compensation? Observations.** Drawbacks to a career in sales compensation include stressful work revising next year's plan requiring intense focus requiring long hours, often precluding year-end vacations. As a specialty skill, it is hard to enter; and difficult to leave. Outstanding efforts and results not fully appreciated. ***Participant Observation:*** *There are drawbacks and challenges in every role—nothing that cannot be overcome with a great attitude and willingness to learn, grow, teach and practice patience.*
- **Any additional comments? Observations.** Many professionals enjoy their sales compensation career.

Academic Advice: What academic career would you suggest for a sales compensation career?

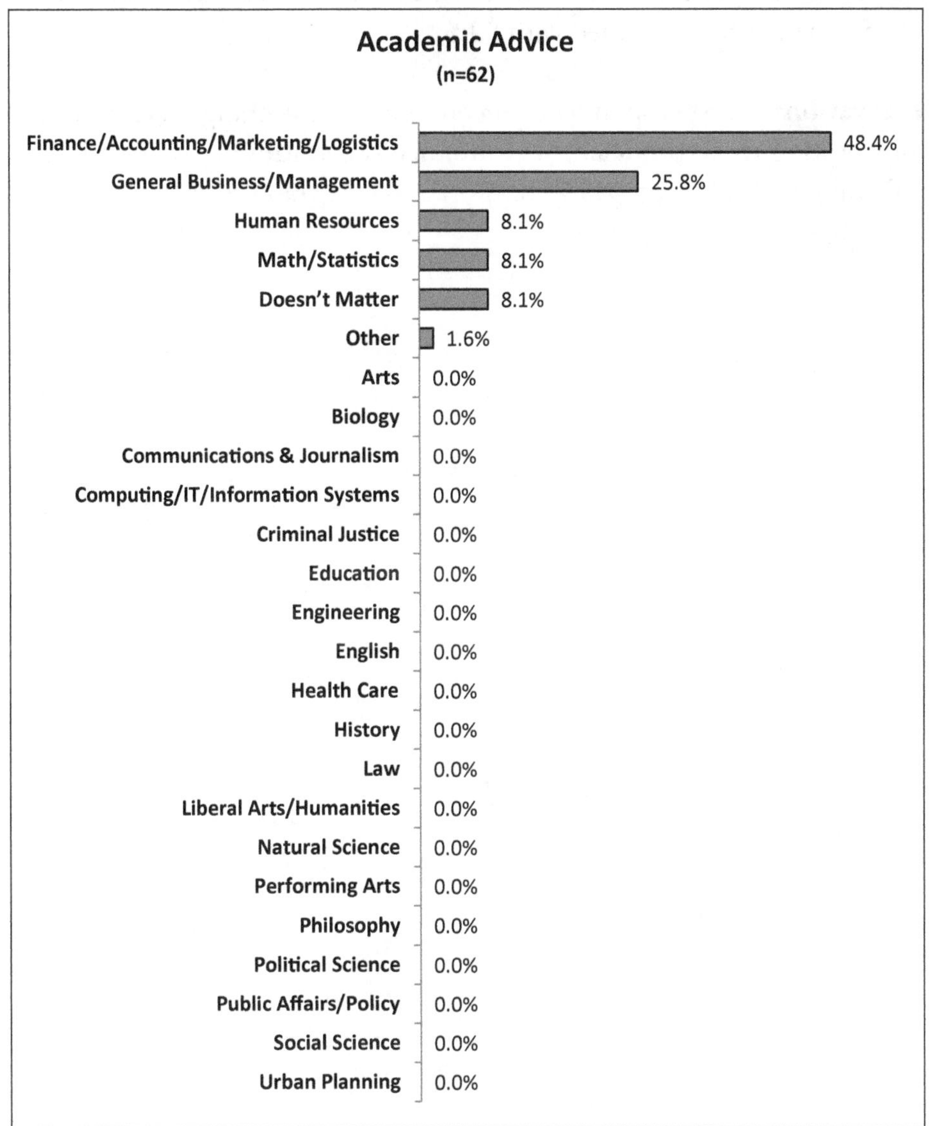

Other Academic Advice

- I know lots of people without "math-like" undergraduate degrees succeed in this field
- Economics

Survey Findings. 48.4% of the respondents suggest an academic career in finance/accounting/ marketing/logistics for a sales compensation career. 25.8% suggest general business/management. And, human resources, math/statistics and "doesn't matter" each tied with 8.1%.

Observations. Most respondents encourage those seeking a career in sales compensation to be proficient with finance/accounting/marketing/logistics confirming that sales compensation work requires numeric competency.

Books to Read: What sales compensation books would you recommend?

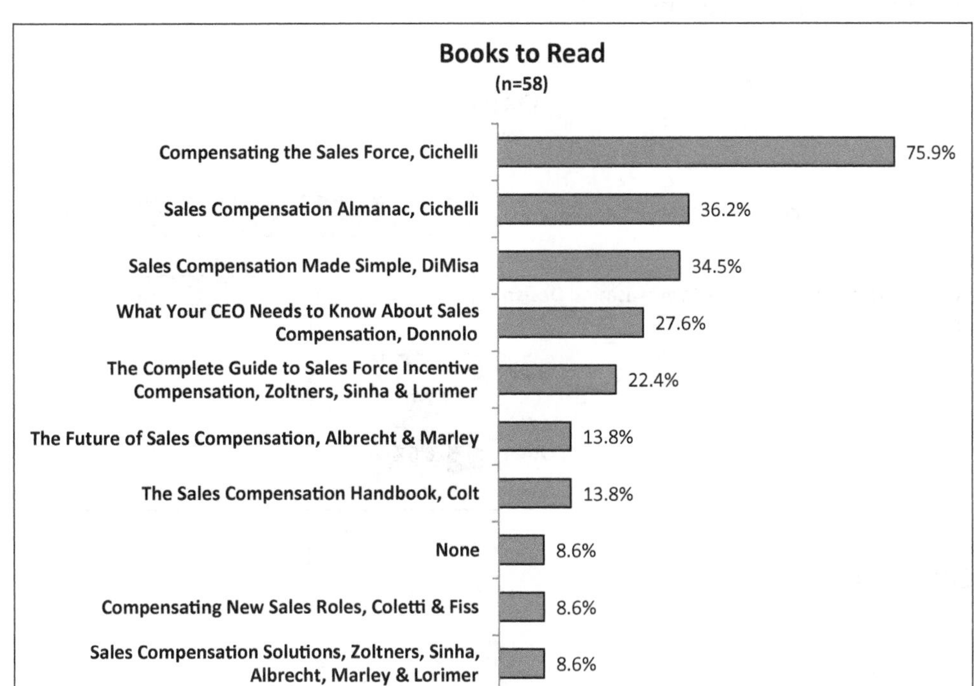

Other Books to Read

- If you want to be successful, you must constantly learn via books, seminars, whitepapers, mentors
- John Moynahan's book

Survey Findings. 75.9% chose *Compensating the Sales Force* by David Cichelli as the sales compensation book they would recommend. 36.2% chose *Sales Compensation Almanac* by David Cichelli. And, 34.5% chose *Sales Compensation Made Simple* by Joseph DiMisa.

Observations. There are many great sales compensation books, including Cichelli's *Compensating the Sales Force* and the annual *Sales Compensation Almanac*. DiMisa's book *Sales Compensation Made Simple* is a noteworthy sales compensation introductory text.

Classes: What classroom/e-courses, if any, would you recommend for learning about sales compensation?

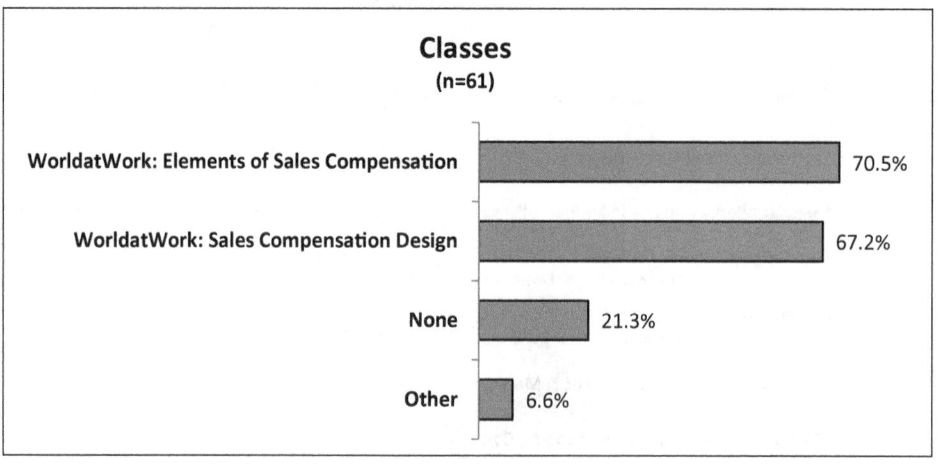

Other Classes

- Statistics, econometrics
- Anything you can find
- Korn Ferry, Pearl Meyer

Survey Findings. 70.5% of the respondents suggest WorldatWork: Elements of Sales Compensation for learning about sales compensation. 67.2% suggest WorldatWork: Sales Compensation Design. And, 21.3% selected none.

Observations. The two WorldatWork sales compensation classes were the only instruction-based programs cited by the participants. Many had attended these classes.

Sources: The best source(s) of information on sales compensation practices comes from:

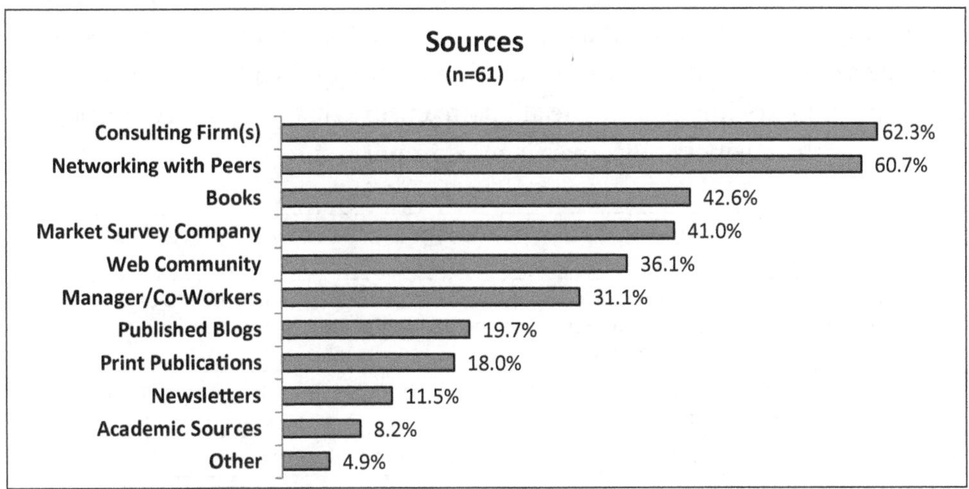

Other Sources

- I used the books I selected in the previous question and AGI as a primary consulting partner
- Books previously selected, Alexander Group for consulting, various blogs
- WorldatWork conferences
- Don't rely on one source
- Haven't found just one source. Have to pull from many
- AGI and Korn Ferry, Korn Ferry semi-annual gatherings
- WorldatWork; KFHG; Radford
- WorldatWork
- Trade shows

Survey Findings. 62.3% identify consulting firm(s) as the best source of information on sales compensation practices. 60.7% of the respondents say networking with peers. And, 42.6% identify books.

Observations. Consulting firms and networking with peers offers significant sales compensation content. Consulting firms offer vertical market conferences, research, benchmarks and applicable case studies. Peers can suggest timely observations and solutions.

What previous experience or activities can help someone be a successful sales compensation professional?

Observations: The survey participants suggest analytical training in finance, accounting or sales operations as a good technical foundation. Work experience with the sales team is a plus. Compensation training is helpful. Strong communications skills are important. The ability to ensure that the sales compensation plan serves the business objectives is most important.

Experience in sales, or in a role that supports and regularly interacts with sales. Strong analytical skills and math aptitude is a must
Understand the business. Volunteer to serve on cross-functional task forces to understand the role of sales in the company. Reach out to peers in the industry and network. Ask questions of your sales team and recruits
Any role that involves analysis; also in terms of the technology, a background in systems; experience with incentive pay
Financial analysis, broad-based compensation design/administration
For me, supporting the sales force in marketing created a firm foundation and understanding of the challenges of sales. Having an open and creative mind is important, as well
Consulting firms, networking with peers, courses
Broader compensation experience focused on maximizing connection of pay and performance have been helpful
Systems thinking, statistics, behavioral science and business analytics/visualization
Roles in sales operations
Prior work in finance or sales operations
Any analytical job, which requires good communication skills, and supports creativity, e.g., IT, operations, finance, logistics
Really, understand the business and how the business makes money. Understand motivation. The first is more finance; the second is psychology. Sometimes, the communication or involvement of the sales staff in design is more powerful than the computational design
Someone who likes to "fix" things—comp always has challenges
Consulting
Become a member of WorldatWork, be a sponge, read, get a mentor, and, if you're really serious, get your CSCP designation, having this will put you on the fast track for success
Good communication skills. It is not enough to simply calculate commissions correctly. To become a respected commissions' colleague, you need to be able to communicate the plan, as well as your calculations to salespeople, not other finance folks. So, learn how to communicate with salespeople, and they will become your allies not your enemies
Rotation in finance, accounting or sales operations. Listen in to sales "huddle" or any other meeting where sales/delivery talks about their business
Someone with prior sales or sales management experience with business acumen
Math/finance and advanced Excel/Access skills
Any job that teaches you to be creative within guidelines. To motivate and direct sales behavior towards meeting company objectives
Understanding the business strategy. Networking, analytics, communication and influence

Having worked in sales and been in sales comp; having worked in HR; having worked in finance
HR business partner/compensation/sales operations/sales rep/finance
Working in some facet of the sales organization is a critical underpinning for a successful role in sales compensation—especially for design and in a business-partnering role. This is important because it helps align incentives with the ability to understand go-to-market and strategy. This will differentiate someone in the eyes of the 'customer' rather than being seen as a calculation function
Experience in sales, finance or sales operations
Excel & PowerPoint, writing skills, financial modeling, critical thinking, project management skills, oral presentation skills
Sales operations role and understanding the limits of data
Take the perspective of the salesperson and try to take advantage of the system
Sales
Financial analysts, business analysts, data analysts, anyone with process experience and a good understanding of logic/math
Finance
Sales operations experience and analysis
Financial acumen; HR compensation; communication skills
Math skills, forecasting, psychology, consulting, WorldatWork classes
Finance background or sales
Sales or customer service experience. Wide range of HR activities
Strong Excel skills
Work is sales work in compensation
Must be very organized and detail oriented
Working in sales primarily, then get help from comp to understand that part
It may be easier to transition from the finance side, as someone who administers the plans, to the HR side, as someone who designs the plans, since sales compensation is unique
Stock market, anything that has to do with business operations
Math and finance, compensation classes, community college
Sales operations
Being a seller
It is helpful to understand the order management process and the systems used to process orders
Sales operations, order management, finance
Finance/accounting
Getting involved in the design process; networking with other comp professionals; interviewing individuals who are on a sales plan and understanding their job, how they are paid and what they do/don't understand about their compensation plan
Accounting/finance/economics, anything that forces one to have true attention to detail and the ability to analyze data to start with. Learning to manage and learning the ability to influence without authority. You have to be sure of what you are talking about and keeping up-to-date with industry trends and standards is helpful. You also have to be able to walk away, turn the other cheek, and not get upset if your ideas aren't listened to

Why should folks consider a career in sales compensation?

Observations: Sales compensation is a highly visible role working alongside senior management helping to solve strategic sales/business challenges. Requires engagement with diverse functional teams to solve pay alignment challenges. Offers interesting creative problem solving challenges that are always changing. Professionally rewarding to see positive business impact. Pays better than comparable level positions in HR/compensation.

Highly visible role in most companies with potential significant interaction with executives. Rewarding to be able to closely work with the sales organization and knowing your work directly impacts sales growth
If you like to think outside the box and apply different approaches to getting the best results, then sales comp may be the job for you
It's exciting and at the forefront of business. The skills you learn are applicable across many fields
Because it has a direct link to the success of the business, you are very visible, work directly with leaders in the organization and are involved in strategic discussions
For the right person, this job is very rewarding and challenging. Creating something from scratch that you then get to see in play and measure results is very rewarding
Close connection to business strategy, always changing
Great way to provide an expertise and to make an impact on business growth and rewards alignment to strategy
Interesting, challenging
It's rewarding to be informed about the sales strategy and be a part of the plan for how to achieve it
It is very broad...you have to know about the business, psychology of people, how to communicate, and it develops logic/analytical skills as well as gives chance to evolve (use creativity to automate, improve processes, drive sales behavior...)
It is an opportunity to partner with a team to drive topline performance and be recognized for outstanding work. Compensation for the role is generally high
Always things to fix—always a challenge
It's a highly visible, very important part of an organization; also very specialized, very few understand the mechanics and reasons why behind them
Your influence directly impacts (good or bad) a company's top line, and if done right positively impacts not only sales employees and their families but all employees
When you get it right, you feel like you are having an impact on the success of your company. That is a great feeling
I suppose it depends on the company and range of duties. I manage the compensation plan process from beginning to end and the rate of change is high. It's very interesting, challenging and rewarding work
Design can be very rewarding. Aligning business goals to sales force objectives. Modeling various outcomes. Ultimately, seeing the impact of your work

It's dynamic and fun!
It's a niche, close knit field and can be interesting
Because the industry is always changing, roles are always changing, and therefore how you pay those roles changes. Sales comp is never boring
The pay is good, and, if you want a challenge, working with salespeople will provide it
Tip of the spear converting business strategy to behaviors impacting the generation of results
You must stay actively involved, because it is an ever-changing environment, which provides the opportunity for challenging work and the ability to work with senior leadership
Sales compensation provides opportunity to engage in many aspects of an organization if all of the appropriate stakeholders are included, i.e., sales, operations, HR, finance, legal, even IT if a compensation platform is implemented. Also, it is a niche that many companies find difficult to fulfill so demand for truly qualified individuals is high. The compensation level can be significantly higher than other HR or sales operation roles
If you cannot sell, pay them!
Challenging, interesting, often the highest paying HR role at most companies, normally includes executive interaction, key function closely tied to company results
Unique expertise with exposure to the entire business and various leadership styles
Behaviors and the business are ever-changing
Critical role in sales
Lots of visibility to senior leadership; always changing
Challenging, creative, drive business results, provide competitive pay fairly
Opportunity to learn about the business end-to-end and have a meaningful impact in driving results and meeting the bottom line
There is more creativity involved in designing compensation plans than with standard accounting functions. Project management skills will be learned. There can be a lucrative career path within sales comp or moving to other parts of the organization
It's analytical yet psychological...therefore, there is a good balance of data and people
Creativity
Interesting
Offers the opportunity to develop creative solutions
It's interesting to see how changing a comp plan can drive behavior. It can also be very creative at times
Direct contribution to the business, understanding of not only the business but people and rewards levers
Getting sales compensation right is vital to the business. It is rewarding to design a plan and be able to assess the results at the end of the year. You also have the opportunity to collaborate across functions–sales, HR, marketing, legal, IT, etc.—and learn more about the business
It's always changing and evolving. A good sales comp analyst can have an impact beyond their title that would be difficult to achieve in other areas

What is a drawback to a career in sales compensation?

Observations: Drawbacks to a career in sales compensation include stressful work revising next year's plan requiring intense focus requiring long hours, often precluding year-end vacations. As a specialty skill, it is hard to enter and difficult to leave. Outstanding efforts and results are not fully appreciated. *Participant Observation: There are drawbacks and challenges in every role—nothing that cannot be overcome with a great attitude and willingness to learn, grow, teach and practice patience.*

Can be a thankless job. Who is ever happy with their commissions and bonuses? The ratio of complaints to compliments is about 99:1
Sales professionals can be difficult and challenging to work with at times
You get pigeonholed and the ability to leave your job can be more limited as there are less sales compensation specific roles available
The same reason why to consider it. Because of the importance of sales compensation and the visibility, the job can be very stressful
There are drawbacks and challenges in every role—nothing that cannot be overcome with a great attitude and willingness to learn, grow, teach and practice patience
Requires ability to work at high, strategic level as well as granular detailed level
Oversight
I can't think of any
It is a very expert job and once in it, very difficult to get out. If you do it well, you are seen as the expert and everyone depends on you, and wants to keep you there
If embedded in the sales organization, the role can be micromanaged and not fulfilling
Nobody is ever happy so the feedback scale is 0-negative
It's a thankless job; no one wants anything negative to happen; salespeople are relentless and think they are right about everything
Typically have three months of very stressful deadlines. If your company follows calendar year-end, then it's a bit stressful during holidays
When you get it wrong, the buck stops with you. So, take your time and get it right, each time. That can bring a lot of stress, but can also be very rewarding
There can be some seasonality to the work with a spike in Q4 and Q1. If that's when you like to vacation, that could be a downer
The admin side has its pitfalls—disputes, reporting issues, the cycle of calculations can become dull
The tendency to want to shoot from the hip rather than make decisions based on data. Also, dealing with individuals who believe everyone needs an incentive to do their job
Salespeople who complain
Everything schedules around pay dates. The associates must be paid, accurately and on time
Working with a sales team can get contentious. They like to "win" and you have to convince them that they can win with you

Everyone has an opinion and everyone is an expert; will never satisfy everyone
Sales compensation can be viewed as a hurdle where sometimes leaders will want to design their own plans because they know the roles best
Pressure and time are two aspects universal to sales compensation. Pressure because of the common myth that 'everything' can be fixed or managed through sales comp and balancing this knee jerk reaction to a sound sales compensation strategy. Time because of the nature of having to have plans designed, approved, implemented—it is an ongoing 'annual' cycle. Last point, sales compensation has a natural tension built into it requiring skills to build consensus and collaboration across all stakeholders while maintaining credibility with all groups
Depending on the role and company, it is an exhausting thankless job. Potentially tied to the financial calendars, which impacts holidays and vacations
Toughest and most difficult role in the HR family, executive presentation requirements can be difficult and time consuming, perfection is normally expected, the job often requires long hours and working weekends during design and plan implementation season
It's a niche and can be very subjective at times
Could turn to a liability in slow times
Support role
Process-oriented job meaning that there are times when vacation must be put on hold; expectation to adapt quickly to changes can be unrealistic; getting buy-in for investments into automated solutions for compensation is often difficult and the team is told to make do with spreadsheets for a temporary solution
Long hours
Requires senior level support and clear philosophy to be most successful
Can be a thankless job at times and many senior leaders don't really have an appreciation for the challenges or staffing needs
It does not necessarily help you get into "Sales." There can be a stigma about sales compensation where some see it as a dead-end job
Complainers

Any additional comments?

Observations: Many professionals enjoy their sales compensation career.

I've been managing sales incentive functions for almost 22 years, and I love the work. My background in sales and sales management has helped me to be successful in this field
It is not for the faint of heart!
Most people do not start out by dreaming of a career in sales compensation, but once they embark on one, they seldom leave it!
Being on a team of commission professionals at a large company is a good place to get started. You can learn the ropes and see if commissions is a good fit for you. Once you have some experience, look for a smaller company, where you can take on a bigger role. With luck, that company will grow, and you can grow a team there
I truly enjoy my job and would recommend a career in sales comp for accounting or finance folks who enjoy analysis and special projects more than journal entries and financial statements. That's how I got here
Balance being sensitive to the fact that you are dealing with people's pay with enforcing guidelines and deadlines. Must do well working within the gray areas of life
Great leaders respect and embrace sales compensation professionals for the role they play to helping achieve organizational success
My career path to sales compensation was not an intentional one, but it has provided me with excellent professional opportunities in the technology sector with the ability to work for some of the most dynamic companies in the world. Monetarily, this has been a career, which yielded high level of income based on some of the advice listed above, if you have the skill set and recognize the key of always learning, staying current, you can have a meaningful career
This survey is a great idea

REFERENCE GUIDE TO SALES COMPENSATION SURVEYS

SALES COMPENSATION MARKET PAY SURVEYS

Need to locate a sales compensation market pay survey? *The Reference Guide to Sales Compensation Surveys* catalogs many of the available surveys on sales compensation pay levels. Use these vendor products to price and manage your sales compensation costs.

IN THIS SECTION

- Compensation Surveys by Sector
- Survey Listings

Search of Surveys

Please let us know if you do not see your survey; or you use a survey not listed. We are interested in listing any survey that provides Compensation Data on sales jobs, U.S. and non-U.S. sources.

ABOUT THIS SURVEY REFERENCE GUIDE

Welcome to the *Reference Guide to Sales Compensation Surveys*©. This Guide is a resource for locating sales compensation surveys.

Published continually by the Alexander Group since 2000, the Guide profiles sales compensation surveys that provide benchmark pay data. The Guide also includes an index of compensation surveys by industry, allowing users to easily locate surveys that best meet their needs.

Inclusion—Survey Sources

Survey publishers provided the information in this Guide. In order to be included in the Guide, a survey must be administered by a third-party survey company, consulting firm or an association. The survey provider must publish the survey on a regular basis. Surveys must include pay information on customer contact jobs such as sales personnel, customer service, field technical support and related supervisory and management positions.

If you are aware of additional surveys that should be included in future editions, please contact me at david.cichelli@alexandergroup.com.

The Alexander Group would like to thank each individual at the survey organizations that contributed information to this Reference Guide.

Enjoy!
David Cichelli
Editor

TABLE OF CONTENTS

Compensation Surveys by Sector

Company Name/Survey Name	Media	IT/High-Tech	Manufacturing	General	Health Care/ Life Sciences/ Medical	Financial/ Insurance	Consumer/ Retail
American Society of Employers Office, Clerical and Technical Compensation Survey	✓		✓		✓	✓	✓
American Society of Employers Supervisory, Managerial and Professional Compensation Survey	✓		✓		✓	✓	✓
BDO USA, LLP BDO Annual Human Resource Outsourcing Compensation Survey				✓			
BDO USA, LLP BDO CRO Industry Global Compensation and Turnover Survey					✓		
BDO USA, LLP BDO Health Insurance Industry Sales Compensation Survey						✓	
Culpepper and Associates Culpepper Sales Compensation Survey	✓	✓		✓	✓		
DGL Consultants Annual Sales Compensation Survey & Analysis						✓	
DGL Consultants Defined Contribution (401k, 403b and 457 Plans) Retirement Plan Sales Compensation Survey: Large Plan Markets						✓	
DGL Consultants Defined Contribution (401k, 403b and 457 Plans) Retirement Plan Sales Compensation Survey: Small to Midsize Plan Markets						✓	
Economic Research Institute Sales and Marketing Salary Survey				✓			
Employer Associations of America National Sales Compensation Survey	✓		✓		✓	✓	✓
Fitzgerald's Compensation Consulting Services 2018 Agency/Brokerage Insurance Positions Survey						✓	
Fitzgerald's Compensation Consulting Services 2018 Call Center Insurance Positions Survey						✓	
Fitzgerald's Compensation Consulting Services 2018 Executive Insurance Positions Survey					✓	✓	
Fitzgerald's Compensation Consulting Services 2018 Health Insurance Positions Survey						✓	
MedReps.com 2018 Medical Sales Salary Report					✓		

Company Name/Survey Name	Media	IT/High-Tech	Manufacturing	General	Health Care/ Life Sciences/ Medical	Financial/ Insurance	Consumer/ Retail
Mercer Canadian Mercer Life Sciences Compensation Survey					✓		
Mercer US Mercer SIRS® Medical Device Sales Compensation Survey					✓		
Mercer | Comptryx Mercer | Comptryx		✓					
MRA—The Management Association Benchmark Compensation Survey	✓		✓		✓	✓	✓
Pearl Meyer CHiPS One World		✓	✓				
Pearl Meyer Forest Products Industry Compensation Survey			✓				
Pearl Meyer Global Engineering, Procurement & Construction Management Compensation Survey			✓				
Pearl Meyer HR Alliance Compensation Survey		✓					
Pearl Meyer National Engineering and Construction Salary Survey			✓				
Pearl Meyer The Executive Compensation and Benchmarking Survey				✓			
Radford Radford Global Sales Survey		✓		✓	✓		
Salary.com IPAS® Global Consumer Industry Survey							✓
Salary.com IPAS® Global High Technology Compensation Salary Survey		✓					
The Croner Company C2HR Cable and Satellite MSO Compensation Survey	✓						
The Croner Company C2HR Cable Programmers/Broadcast Networks Compensation Survey	✓						
The Croner Company Croner Digital Content and Technology Survey		✓					
The Croner Company Croner Entertainment Survey	✓						

Company Name/Survey Name	Media	IT/High-Tech	Manufacturing	General	Health Care/ Life Sciences/ Medical	Financial/ Insurance	Consumer/ Retail
The Croner Company Croner Local Media Survey	✓						
The Croner Company Croner Software Games Survey	✓						
Western Compensation & Benefits Consultants Marketing & Sales Compensation Survey			✓	✓	✓	✓	✓
Western Management Group Retail Sales Compensation Survey							✓
Western Management Group Sales and Service Compensation Survey	✓	✓					✓
Willis Towers Watson 2018 General Industry Sales, Marketing and Communications Compensation Survey Report—U.S.				✓	✓	✓	✓

American Society of Employers

Office, Clerical and Technical Compensation Survey
19575 Victor Parkway, Suite 100, Livonia, MI 48152
(248) 353-4500
www.aseonline.org

Survey Overview

The survey report is part of a three-volume set and is one of the most comprehensive compensation surveys in the state of Michigan. Covering data for over 100 positions across 17 job families, including Accounting/Financial, Administrative, Banking, Creative/Advertising, Design/Drafting, Engineering Support, Field Service/Sales, Human Resources, Information Systems, Legal, Medical, Quality Control/Assurance/Safety, Research/Scientific, Sales/Marketing, Scheduling, Supply Chain/Logistics and Technicians.

Survey Editor

Jason Rowe, jrowe@aseonline.org
(248) 223-8053

General Information

Industries Covered

Goods Producing, Non-Manufacturing (Natural Resources/Mining, Utilities, Construction), Non-Durable Goods Manufacturing, Durable Goods Manufacturing, Trade & Services (Retail Trade, Wholesale Trade, Transportation/Warehousing, Information (Communication/Broadcasting), Professional/Business Services, Leisure/Hospitality Services, Services not elsewhere classified), Government & Financial Services (Financial Activities & Public Administration), Educational & Health Services (Education Services, Health Services, Social Services)

Survey Specifications

Range of Revenue of Reporting Companies....... $0–$500M
Frequency of Survey Updates .... Annual/Specific Date
Annual Publication Date......................... Late May
First Year of Publication......................... 1952
Restrictions .... None
Data Delivery Methods .... Electronic/Soft Copy, Online
Non-Participant Report Available .... Yes
Custom Reporting............................... Online Access/User Defined
Data from World Regions .... North America
Number of Companies........................... 460

Number of Sales Jobs 9
Data Submitted . . . . Incumbent Level
Sales Volume by Job Title. . . . . No

Practices

Plan Performance Metrics. . . . . No
Formula Mechanics . . . . No
Benefits . . . . No
Allowances (e.g., Car, Mobile Devices, Internet) . . . No
Contests/Spiffs. . . . . No
Long-Term Incentives (e.g., Stock, RSU) . . . . No

Compensation Data

	Base Salary	Incentive Earnings	Total Compensation
Target	No	No	No
Actual	Yes	Yes	No

Major Sales/Customer Contact Job Families Featured in the Survey

Call Center Representative I, Call Center Representative II, Customer Service Representative I (Advanced), Customer Service Representative II (Experienced), Customer Service Representative III (Entry), Proposal Writer, Sales, Sales Order Clerk, Sales/Marketing Assistant, Social Media Coordinator

American Society of Employers

Supervisory, Managerial and Professional Compensation Survey

19575 Victor Parkway, Suite 100, Livonia, MI 48152
(248) 353-4500
www.aseonline.org

Survey Overview

This survey report is part of a three-volume set and is one of the most comprehensive compensation surveys in the state of Michigan. Covering data for over 290 positions across 22 job families, including Accounting/Financial, Administrative, Behavior Health, Construction Engineering Creative/Advertising, Design/Drafting, Engineering, Engineering Management, Engineering Program/Project Management, Engineering Support, Field Service/Sales, General Executive, Human Resources, Information Systems, Legal, Medical, Plant Management, Quality Control/Assurance/Safety, Research/Scientific, Sales/Marketing, Scheduling and Supply Chain/Logistics.

Survey Editor

Jason Rowe, jrowe@aseonline.org
(248) 223-8053

General Information

Industries Covered

Goods Producing, Non-Manufacturing (Natural Resources/Mining, Utilities, Construction), Non-Durable Goods Manufacturing, Durable Goods Manufacturing, Trade & Services (Retail Trade, Wholesale Trade, Transportation/Warehousing, Information (Communication/Broadcasting), Professional/Business Services, Leisure/ Hospitality Services, Services not elsewhere classified), Government & Financial Services (Financial Activities & Public Administration), Educational & Health Services (Education Services, Health Services, Social Services)

Survey Specifications

Range of Revenue of Reporting Companies....... $0–$500M
Frequency of Survey Updates .... Annual/Specific Date
Annual Publication Date....................... Late May
First Year of Publication....................... 1952
Restrictions .... None
Data Delivery Methods .... Electronic/Soft Copy, Online
Non-Participant Report Available .... Yes
Custom Reporting............................ Standard Report, Online Access/User Defined

Data from World Regions .... North America
Number of Companies......................... 490
Number of Sales Jobs 31
Data Submitted .... Incumbent Level
Sales Volume by Job Title....................... No

Practices

Plan Performance Metrics...................... No
Formula Mechanics .... No
Benefits .... No
Allowances (e.g., Car, Mobile Devices, Internet) . . . No
Contests/Spiffs................................ No
Long-Term Incentives (e.g., Stock, RSU) .... No

Compensation Data

	Base Salary	Incentive Earnings	Total Compensation
Target	No	No	No
Actual	Yes	Yes	No

Major Sales/Customer Contact Job Families Featured in the Survey

Advertising/Sales Promotions Manager, Business Development Manager, Call Center Manager, Customer Service Director, Customer Service Manager, Customer Service Supervisor, General Sales Manager (2nd Level of Management), Inside Sales Representative, International Sales Representative/Account Executive, Junior Outside Sales Representative, Marketing Director, Marketing Generalist I, Marketing Generalist II, Marketing Generalist III, Marketing Manager, Marketing Research Analyst I (Advanced), Marketing Research Analyst II (Experienced), Marketing Research Analyst III (Entry), Marketing Research Manager, National Accounts Manager, Order Processing Supervisor, Outside Sales Representative/Account Executive, Public Relations Manager, Public Relations Representative I, Public Relations Representative II, Sales Manager, Senior Inside Sales Representative, Senior Outside Sales Representative/Account Executive, Top International Sales Executive, Top Sales & Marketing Executive, Top Sales Executive

BDO USA, LLP

BDO Annual Human Resource Outsourcing Compensation Survey

1801 Market Street, Suite 1700, Philadelphia, PA 19103
(215) 636-5635
https://www.bdo.com/services/tax/global-employer-services/compensation-consulting

Survey Overview

Survey covers HR outsourcing positions.

Survey Editor

Judy Canavan, jcanavan@bdo.com
(215) 636-5635

General Information

Industries Covered

HR Outsourcing

Survey Specifications

Range of Revenue of Reporting Companies....... (Left Blank)
Frequency of Survey Updates .... Annual/Specific Date
Annual Publication Date...................... September
First Year of Publication...................... 2006
Restrictions .... Industry
Data Delivery Methods .... Electronic/Soft Copy
Non-Participant Report Available .... No
Custom Reporting............................ Standard Reporting
Data from World Regions .... North America
Number of Companies........................ 10–15
Number of Sales Jobs 5
Data Submitted .... Incumbent Level
Sales Volume by Job Title...................... No

Practices

Plan Performance Metrics . . . . No
Formula Mechanics . . . . No
Benefits . . . . No
Allowances (e.g., Car, Mobile Devices, Internet) . . . No
Contests/Spiffs . . . . (Left Blank)
Long-Term Incentives (e.g., Stock, RSU) . . . . No

Compensation Data

	Base Salary	Incentive Earnings	Total Compensation
Target	No	Yes	Yes
Actual	Yes	Yes	Yes

Major Sales/Customer Contact Job Families Featured in the Survey

Business Developers Top Job and Intermediate Level

BDO USA, LLP

BDO CRO Industry Global Compensation and Turnover Survey

BDO

1801 Market Street, Suite 1700, Philadelphia, PA 19103
(215) 636-5635
https://www.bdo.com/services/tax/global-employer-services/compensation-consulting

Survey Overview

Survey covers clinical research outsourcing companies.

Survey Editor

Judy Canavan, jcanavan@bdo.com
(215) 636-5635

General Information

Industries Covered

Clinical Research Outsourcing

Survey Specifications

Range of Revenue of Reporting Companies....... (Left Blank)
Frequency of Survey Updates .... Annual/Specific Date
Annual Publication Date...................... September
First Year of Publication...................... 1999
Restrictions .... Industry
Data Delivery Methods .... Electronic/Soft Copy
Non-Participant Report Available .... No
Custom Reporting............................ Standard Reporting
Data from World Regions .... North America, Europe, Asia, Middle East, Other Americas
Number of Companies......................... 20+
Number of Sales Jobs 30
Data Submitted .... Incumbent Level
Sales Volume by Job Title...................... No

Practices

Plan Performance Metrics...................... Yes
Formula Mechanics .... No
Benefits .... Yes
Allowances (e.g., Car, Mobile Devices, Internet) . . . Yes
Contests/Spiffs............................... (Left Blank)
Long-Term Incentives (e.g., Stock, RSU).......... Yes

Compensation Data

	Base Salary	Incentive Earnings	Total Compensation
Target	No	Yes	Yes
Actual	Yes	Yes	Yes

Major Sales/Customer Contact Job Families Featured in the Survey

Business Development: Contract Management, Project Budget Analysis, Proposal Writing, Sales, Strategic Account Management

BDO USA, LLP

BDO Health Insurance Industry Sales Compensation Survey
1801 Market Street, Suite 1700, Philadelphia, PA 19103
(215) 636-5635
https://www.bdo.com/services/tax/global-employer-services/compensation-consulting

Survey Overview

This is a Health Insurance Industry specific Sales Compensation Survey designed to assist companies by providing high-quality, industry-specific competitive sales compensation, pay levels and incentive plan design information. This survey covers multiple position levels within the sales job family.

Survey Editor

Judy Canavan, jcanavan@bdo.com
(215) 636-5635

General Information

Industries Covered

Health Insurance

Survey Specifications

Range of Revenue of Reporting Companies....... (Left Blank)
Frequency of Survey Updates .... Annual/Specific Date
Annual Publication Date........................ September
First Year of Publication........................ 2013
Restrictions .... Industry
Data Delivery Methods .... Electronic/Soft Copy
Non-Participant Report Available .... No
Custom Reporting............................ Standard Reporting
Data from World Regions .... (Left Blank)
Number of Companies......................... 25+
Number of Sales Jobs 45
Data Submitted .... Incumbent Level
Sales Volume by Job Title....................... Yes

Practices

Plan Performance Metrics . . . . Yes
Formula Mechanics . . . . Yes
Benefits . . . . No
Allowances (e.g., Car, Mobile Devices, Internet) . . . Yes
Contests/Spiffs . . . . Yes
Long-Term Incentives (e.g., Stock, RSU) . . . . Yes

Compensation Data

	Base Salary	Incentive Earnings	Total Compensation
Target	Yes	Yes	Yes
Actual	Yes	Yes	Yes

Major Sales/Customer Contact Job Families Featured in the Survey

New Sales Executives, Account Managers (renewals), Major/National/Large Group/ Small Group/Individual/FEP/Self Insured, Sales Management, Inside Sales, Sales Support

Culpepper and Associates, Inc.

Culpepper Sales Compensation Survey
3780 Mansell Road, Suite T-40, Alpharetta, GA 30022
(770) 641-5400
www.culpepper.com/SalesCompensation

Survey Overview

The *Culpepper Sales Compensation Survey* provides global market data to benchmark the compensation of your organization's sales talent. It includes 48 job families covering sales executives, sales management, sales representatives, sales engineering, and sales operations & administration.

Survey Editor

Leigh Culpepper, leigh@culpepper.com
(770) 641-5446

General Information

Industries Covered

Technology, IT, Digital Media/Advertising, Engineering, Life Sciences, Medical & Health Care and General Industry

Survey Specifications

Range of Revenue of Reporting Companies	$5M–$10B+
Frequency of Survey Updates	Evergreen
Annual Publication Date	Monthly updates with ability to view historical data by effective date
First Year of Publication	1981
Restrictions	None
Data Delivery Methods	Electronic/Soft Copy, Online
Non-Participant Report Available	No
Custom Reporting	Online Access/User Defined
Data from World Regions	North America, Europe, Asia, Middle East, Other Americas, Africa
Number of Companies	645+ Participating Companies
Number of Sales Jobs	48 Sales Job Families
Data Submitted	Incumbent Level
Sales Volume by Job Title	Yes

Practices

Plan Performance Metrics .... No
Formula Mechanics .... No
Benefits .... No
Allowances (e.g., Car, Mobile Devices, Internet) ... Yes
Contests/Spiffs .... No
Long-Term Incentives (e.g., Stock, RSU) .... Yes

Compensation Data

	Base Salary	Incentive Earnings	Total Compensation
Target	Yes	Yes	Yes
Actual	Yes	Yes	Yes

Major Sales/Customer Contact Job Families Featured in the Survey

Sales Executives: Top Sales Executive, Sales & Marketing Executive, Product Market/Segment/Channel Sales Executive, Sales Operations Executive, Sales Support Executive, Contracts Executive, Commercialization Executive, Product Management Executive

Sales Management: Sales & Professional Services Management, Inside & Outside Sales Management, Outside Sales Management, Inside Sales Management, Telesales Management, Renewal Sales Management, Strategic/Key Account Sales Management, Product Specialty Sales Management

Sales Representatives: Outside Sales Reps—New Business, Outside Sales Account Managers, Inside Sales Reps—New Business, Inside Sales Account Managers, Telesales Reps—Outbound, Telesales Reps—Inbound, Renewal Sales Reps, Strategic/Key Sales Account Managers, Product Sales Specialists

Sales Planning and Analysis: Sales Operations & Planning Management, Sales Commission Analysts, Sales Operations Analysts, Sales Force Effectiveness Analysts, Sales Planning Support Specialists

Sales Operations and Administration: Sales Administration Management, Sales Administrative Assistants, Order Processors

Contracts, Bids and Proposals: Contract Operations Management, Contract Specialists, Bid/Proposal Management, Bid/Proposal Specialists, Quote Coordinators

Sales Development: Sales Development Management, Sales Development Specialists, Telemarketing Representatives

Sales Engineering: Sales Engineering Management, Pre-Sales Engineering, Post-Sales Engineering, Pre- and Post-Sales Engineering, Sales Engineering Support Specialists

Sales Training: Sales Training Management, Sales Trainers

Related Jobs: Business Development and Marketing jobs are in the *Culpepper Operations Compensation Survey* and the *Culpepper Digital Marketing & Media Compensation Survey*

Post-Sales Client Engagement: Engagement jobs, including Client Relationship and Customer Success, are in the *Culpepper Operations Compensation Survey*

DGL Consultants, LLC

Annual Sales Compensation Survey & Analysis
3492 Hill Circle, Colorado Springs, CO 80904
(719) 634-7041
www.dglconsultants.com

DGL CONSULTANTS
compensation

Survey Overview

This survey provides relevant and comprehensive information supporting the marketing/sales strategies unique to: Annuity, ETF, Life Insurance, Managed Money, Mutual Fund and Pension/Retirement Services. The relationships among the various elements of the total pay program are examined position-specific to Product, Company Size, Distribution and Phase of Market Development including: Support, Field Sales and Staff Management Functions.

Survey Editor

Donald Lariviere, don@dglconsultants.com
(719) 634-7041

General Information

Industries Covered

Financial Services

Survey Specifications

Range of Revenue of Reporting Companies....... (Left Blank)
Frequency of Survey Updates .... Annual/Specific Date
Annual Publication Date........................ August
First Year of Publication........................ 1994
Restrictions .... Industry
Data Delivery Methods .... Electronic/Soft Copy, Online
Non-Participant Report Available .... Yes
Custom Reporting............................ Standard Reporting
Data from World Regions .... North America
Number of Companies......................... (Left Blank)
Number of Sales Jobs 10
Data Submitted .... Averages/Percentiles
Sales Volume by Job Title....................... Yes

Practices

Plan Performance Metrics . . . . (Left Blank)
Formula Mechanics . . . . (Left Blank)
Benefits . . . . Yes
Allowances (e.g., Car, Mobile Devices, Internet) . . . (Left Blank)
Contests/Spiffs . . . . (Left Blank)
Long-Term Incentives (e.g., Stock, RSU) . . . . Yes

Compensation Data

	Base Salary	Incentive Earnings	Total Compensation
Target	(Left Blank)	(Left Blank)	(Left Blank)
Actual	Yes	Yes	Yes

Major Sales/Customer Contact Job Families Featured in the Survey

Support Function: Internal Wholesaler, Sales Desk Manager, Compliance Officer, Operations Manager and Administrative

Field Sales Function: External Wholesaler

Staff Management Function: National Account/Channel Manager, Product Manager, Divisional Sales Manager and National Sales Manager

DGL Consultants, LLC

Defined Contribution (401k, 403b and 457 Plans) Retirement Plan Sales Compensation Survey: Large Plan Markets

DGL CONSULTANTS compensation

3492 Hill Circle, Colorado Springs, CO 80904
(719) 634-7041
www.dglconsultants.com

Survey Overview

This custom survey benchmarks the compensation levels for six key retirement plan sales and service roles. Distribution is primarily through plan sponsors, intermediaries and consultants in the large plan retirement markets.

Findings include:

- Drivers of Compensation
- Fixed and Variable Compensation
- Ranges and Dispersion of Compensation Paid
- Measure of Overall Productivity
- Cost of Sales in Basis Points
- Pay Progression Analysis
- Production Progression Analysis
- Tenure Distribution

Survey Editor

Donald Lariviere, don@dglconsultants.com
(719) 634-7041

General Information

Industries Covered

Financial Services

Survey Specifications

Range of Revenue of Reporting Companies....... (Left Blank)
Frequency of Survey Updates.................. (Left Blank)
Annual Publication Date...................... June, Biennial publication
First Year of Publication...................... 2016
Restrictions.................................. Industry
Data Delivery Methods........................ Electronic/Soft Copy
Non-Participant Report Available............... Yes
Custom Reporting............................ Standard Reporting
Data from World Regions..................... North America
Number of Companies........................ (Left Blank)

Number of Sales Jobs 6
Data Submitted .... Averages/Percentiles, Incumbent Level
Sales Volume by Job Title....................... Yes

Practices

Plan Performance Metrics....................... Yes
Formula Mechanics .... Yes
Benefits .... No
Allowances (e.g., Car, Mobile Devices, Internet) ... Yes
Contests/Spiffs .... Yes
Long-Term Incentives (e.g., Stock, RSU) .... Yes

Compensation Data

	Base Salary	Incentive Earnings	Total Compensation
Target	Yes	Yes	Yes
Actual	Yes	Yes	Yes

Major Sales/Customer Contact Job Families Featured in the Survey

Institutional Sales, Internal Sales Support, Relationship Manager/Client Service, Sales Desk Manager, Divisional Sales Manager, National Sales Manager

DGL Consultants, LLC

Defined Contribution (401k, 403b and 457 Plans) Retirement Plan Sales Compensation Survey: Small to Midsize Plan Markets

DGL CONSULTANTS compensation

3492 Hill Circle, Colorado Springs, CO 80904
(719) 634-7041
www.dglconsultants.com

Survey Overview

This custom survey benchmarks the compensation levels for six key retirement plan sales and service roles. Distribution is primarily through financial advisors (registered reps, RIA's, consultants, etc.) that sell retirement plans, investment only products and record-keeping services to small and mid-sized companies.

Findings include:

- Drivers of Compensation
- Fixed and Variable Compensation
- Ranges and Dispersion of Compensation Paid
- Measure of Overall Productivity
- Cost of Sales in Basis Points
- Pay Progression Analysis
- Production Progression Analysis
- Tenure Distribution

Survey Editor

Donald Lariviere, don@dglconsultants.com
(719) 634-7041

General Information

Industries Covered

Financial Services

Survey Specifications

Range of Revenue of Reporting Companies....... (Left Blank)
Frequency of Survey Updates.................. (Left Blank)
Annual Publication Date...................... June, Biennial publication
First Year of Publication..................... 2006
Restrictions................................ Industry
Data Delivery Methods........................ Electronic/Soft Copy
Non-Participant Report Available............... Yes
Custom Reporting............................ Standard Reporting
Data from World Regions...................... North America

Number of Companies........................ (Left Blank)
Number of Sales Jobs 6
Data Submitted .... Averages/Percentiles, Incumbent Level
Sales Volume by Job Title...................... Yes

Practices

Plan Performance Metrics...................... Yes
Formula Mechanics .... Yes
Benefits...................................... No
Allowances (e.g., Car, Mobile Devices, Internet) . . . Yes
Contests/Spiffs............................... Yes
Long-Term Incentives (e.g., Stock, RSU).......... Yes

Compensation Data

	Base Salary	Incentive Earnings	Total Compensation
Target	Yes	Yes	Yes
Actual	Yes	Yes	Yes

Major Sales/Customer Contact Job Families Featured in the Survey

External Wholesaler/Regional Pension Consultant, Internal Wholesaler/Inside Sales, Relationship Manager/Client Service/Enroller, National Accounts Manager/Channel Development & Implementation Manager, Regional Sales Manager, Divisional or National Sales Manager

Economic Research Institute (ERI)

Sales and Marketing Salary Survey
111 Academy Drive, Suite 270, Irvine, CA 92617
(800) 627-3697
www.erieri.com

Survey Overview

The *Sales and Marketing Salary Survey* documents market-based pay data for 183 benchmark jobs from up to three databases: digitized public sources, ERI Assessor Series data and direct participants. The following information is reported for each job title (salary data are shown in means, medians and percentile cuts): Annual Salary; Incentive/Variable Pay; Total Direct Annual Compensation; Job Description; and Selected Characteristics of the Occupation (SCO). Data collection begins October 1 and ends on March 31. Survey results are published annually in July, with an effective date of March 31 of the given survey year.

Survey Editor

Katherine Stewart, katherine.stewart@erieri.com
(800) 627-3697, ext. 300

General Information

Industries Covered

All Industries

Survey Specifications

Range of Revenue of Reporting Companies....... All Revenues
Frequency of Survey Updates .... Annual/Specific Date
Annual Publication Date........................ July 1
First Year of Publication........................ 2007
Restrictions .... None
Data Delivery Methods .... Online
Non-Participant Report Available .... Yes
Custom Reporting............................. No
Data from World Regions .... North America
Number of Companies......................... (Left Blank)
Number of Sales Jobs 183
Data Submitted .... Averages/Percentiles
Sales Volume by Job Title...................... No

Practices

Plan Performance Metrics...................... No
Formula Mechanics .... No
Benefits...................................... No
Allowances (e.g., Car, Mobile Devices, Internet)... No
Contests/Spiffs................................ No
Long-Term Incentives (e.g., Stock, RSU).......... (Left Blank)

Compensation Data

	Base Salary	Incentive Earnings	Total Compensation
Target	(Left Blank)	(Left Blank)	(Left Blank)
Actual	Yes	Yes	Yes

Major Sales/Customer Contact Job Families Featured in the Survey

Advertising, Marketing, Promotions, Public Relations and Sales Managers, Operations Specialties Managers, Other Sales and Related Workers, Retail Sales Workers, Sales Representative, Services Sales Representatives, Wholesale and Manufacturing Supervisors of Sales Workers

Employer Associations of America

National Sales Compensation Survey
N19 W24400 Riverwood Drive, Waukesha, WI 53188
(262) 696-3384
www.wagesalary.com

Survey Overview

This annual national survey reports on compensation throughout the U.S. covering 15 positions spanning a full (typical) sales force from executive to inside sales. This year's report contains 838 organizations representing 1,809 locations. Each job contains multiple compensation strategies (three types of strategies, plus combined compensation, which summarizes all three types).

Survey Editor

Cindy Mixon, cindy.mixon@mranet.org
(262) 696-3384

General Information

Industries Covered

Natural Resources/Mining, Utilities, Construction, Non-Durable Goods Manufacturing, Durable Goods Manufacturing, Retail Trade, Wholesale Trade, Transportation/Warehousing, Information (Communication and Broadcasting), Financial Activities, Professional/Business Services, Education Services, Health Services, Social Services, Leisure/Hospitality Services, Services not elsewhere classified

Survey Specifications

Range of Revenue of Reporting Companies....... $0–$250M+
Frequency of Survey Updates.................... Annual/Specific Date
Annual Publication Date........................ November
First Year of Publication...................... (Left Blank)
Restrictions................................... None
Data Delivery Methods.......................... Electronic/Soft Copy, Online
Non-Participant Report Available............... Yes
Custom Reporting............................... No
Data from World Regions........................ North America
Number of Companies............................ 840
Number of Sales Jobs........................... 15
Data Submitted................................. Incumbent Level
Sales Volume by Job Title...................... Yes

Practices

Plan Performance Metrics...................... No
Formula Mechanics .... No
Benefits...................................... No
Allowances (e.g., Car, Mobile Devices, Internet)... No
Contests/Spiffs............................... No
Long-Term Incentives (e.g., Stock, RSU).......... No

Compensation Data

	Base Salary	Incentive Earnings	Total Compensation
Target	No	No	No
Actual	Yes	Yes	Yes

Major Sales/Customer Contact Job Families Featured in the Survey

Top Sales & Marketing Executive, Top Sales Executive, Top International Sales Executive, General Sales Manager, Sales Manager, Sales Trainer, National Accounts Manager, International Sales Representative/Account Executive, Senior Outside Sales Representative/Account Executive, Outside Sales Representative/Account Executive, Junior Outside Sales Representative, Inside Sales Representative, Senior Inside Sales Representative, Order Processing Supervisor, Route Sales Representative

Additional Data on: Independent Sales Representatives

Fitzgerald's Compensation Consulting Services, Inc.

2018 Agency/Brokerage Insurance Positions Survey
714 Desert Willow Court Northwest, Concord, NC 28027
(704) 795-9800
www.ccs-consultants.com

Survey Overview

The purpose of this report is to provide insurance organizations with current benchmark position compensation levels for use by participating organizations in their program planning. The data contained in this report focuses on total direct compensation, including: Annual Base Salary, Annual Incentive Awards and expected value of recent long-term incentive grants or awards.

Survey Editor

Allan Fitzgerald, afitzgerald@ccs-consultants.com
(704) 795-9800

General Information

Industries Covered

Brokerage

Survey Specifications

Range of Revenue of Reporting Companies....... $25M–$6B
Frequency of Survey Updates .... Annual/Specific Date
Annual Publication Date...................... Early September
First Year of Publication..................... 2004
Restrictions .... None
Data Delivery Methods .... Paper, Electronic/Soft Copy, Online
Non-Participant Report Available .... Yes
Custom Reporting........................... Standard Reporting
Data from World Regions .... North America
Number of Companies........................ 10
Total Number of Survey Jobs 63
Number of Sales Jobs 11
Data Submitted .... Incumbent Level
Sales Volume by Job Title...................... No

Practices

Plan Performance Metrics . . . . No
Formula Mechanics . . . . No
Benefits . . . . No
Allowances (e.g., Car, Mobile Devices, Internet) . . . Yes
Contests/Spiffs . . . . No
Long-Term Incentives (e.g., Stock, RSU) . . . . Yes

Compensation Data

	Base Salary	Incentive Earnings	Total Compensation
Target	No	Yes	Yes
Actual	Yes	Yes	Yes

Major Sales/Customer Contact Job Families Featured in the Survey

Account Executive, Claims, Loss Control, Miscellaneous, Placement, Profit Center Management, Sales, Sales/Account Executive, Services, Technical Assistants, Top Insurance Management

Fitzgerald's Compensation Consulting Services, Inc.

2018 Call Center Insurance Positions Survey
714 Desert Willow Court Northwest, Concord, NC 28027
(704) 795-9800
www.ccs-consultants.com

Survey Overview

This statistical report presents the results from the 2018 Center Survey, which focuses on the pay elements of Total Cash Compensation (base salary, incentives and other cash compensation). Identifies and provides general information about the survey, survey participants, company characteristics, call center practices and geographic regions.

Survey Editor

Allan Fitzgerald, afitzgerald@ccs-consultants.com
(704) 795-9800

General Information

Industries Covered

Property Casualty Insurance Centers

Survey Specifications

Range of Revenue of Reporting Companies....... $700M–$14B
Frequency of Survey Updates .... Annual/Specific Date
Annual Publication Date........................ Mid-August
First Year of Publication........................ 2000
Restrictions .... None
Data Delivery Methods .... Paper, Electronic/Soft Copy, Online
Non-Participant Report Available .... Yes, and by Job
Custom Reporting............................. Standard Reporting
Data from World Regions .... North America
Number of Companies.......................... 27
Total Number of Survey Jobs 65
Number of Sales Jobs 16
Data Submitted .... Incumbent Level
Sales Volume by Job Title...................... No

Practices

Plan Performance Metrics .... No
Formula Mechanics .... No
Benefits .... No
Allowances (e.g., Car, Mobile Devices, Internet) ... Yes
Contests/Spiffs .... No
Long-Term Incentives (e.g., Stock, RSU) .... No

Compensation Data

	Base Salary	Incentive Earnings	Total Compensation
Target	No	Yes	No
Actual	Yes	Yes	Yes

Major Sales/Customer Contact Job Families Featured in the Survey

Claim Centers, Cross Centers Positions, Human Resource Service Centers, Insurance Telesales Centers, Processing Centers, Underwriting Centers

Fitzgerald's Compensation Consulting Services, Inc.

2018 Executive Insurance Positions
714 Desert Willow Court Northwest, Concord, NC 28027
(704) 795-9800
www.ccs-consultants.com

Survey Overview

Survey of executive roles in the insurance industry.

Survey Editor

Allan Fitzgerald, afitzgerald@ccs-consultants.com
(704) 795-9800

General Information

Industries Covered

P&C, Health and Specialty Lines Insurance

Survey Specifications

Range of Revenue of Reporting Companies....... $53M–$19.8B
Frequency of Survey Updates .... Annual/Specific Date
Annual Publication Date....................... Early August
First Year of Publication...................... 2012
Restrictions .... Industry
Data Delivery Methods .... Paper, Electronic/Soft Copy, Online
Non-Participant Report Available .... Yes
Custom Reporting.............................. Standard Reporting
Data from World Regions .... North America
Number of Companies Represented 17
Total Number of Jobs.......................... 178
Number of Sales Jobs 6
Data Submitted .... Incumbent Level
Sales Volume by Job Title....................... No

Practices

Plan Performance Metrics...................... No
Formula Mechanics .... No
Benefits...................................... No
Allowances (e.g., Car, Mobile Devices, Internet)... Yes
Contests/Spiffs................................ No
Long-Term Incentives (e.g., Stock, RSU).......... Yes

Compensation Data

	Base Salary	Incentive Earnings	Total Compensation
Target	(Left Blank)	Yes	Yes
Actual	Yes	Yes	Yes

Major Sales/Customer Contact Job Families Featured in the Survey

Top Sales & Marketing, Top Sales, Top Marketing, Top National Accounts, Top Field Sales, Regional Field Sales, Top Claims

Fitzgerald's Compensation Consulting Services, Inc.

2018 Health Insurance Positions Survey
714 Desert Willow Court Northwest, Concord, NC 28027
(704) 795-9800
www.ccs-consultants.com

Survey Overview

Fitzgerald's Compensation Consulting Services presents the results from the *2018 Health Insurance Positions Survey*, which focuses on cash compensation, pay practices and benefits. Competitive pay practices and information have been submitted from 27 health insurance companies participating in this year's survey.

Survey Editor

Allan Fitzgerald, afitzgerald@ccs-consultants.com
(704) 795-9800

General Information

Industries Covered

Accident, Claims, Dental, Disability, Health Care, Health Benefits, Health Care plus Life, Medical, Pharmaceutical, TPA, Vision

Survey Specifications

Range of Revenue of Reporting Companies....... $1.75M–$42B
Frequency of Survey Updates .... Annual/Specific Date
Annual Publication Date........................ Late June to Early July
First Year of Publication........................ 2006
Restrictions .... None
Data Delivery Methods .... Paper, Electronic/Soft Copy, Online
Non-Participant Report Available .... Yes, by Job Available
Custom Reporting............................. Standard & Custom Reporting
Data from World Regions .... North America
Number of Companies Represented 60
Total Number of Jobs.......................... 408
Number of Sales Jobs 40
Data Submitted .... Incumbent Level
Sales Volume by Job Title....................... No

Practices

Plan Performance Metrics...................... No
Formula Mechanics .... No
Benefits..................................... No
Allowances (e.g., Car, Mobile Devices, Internet)... Yes
Contests/Spiffs.............................. No
Long-Term Incentives (e.g., Stock, RSU).......... No

Compensation Data

	Base Salary	Incentive Earnings	Total Compensation
Target	No	Yes	No
Actual	Yes	Yes	Yes

Major Sales/Customer Contact Job Families Featured in the Survey

Accreditation, Actuarial, Appeals, Audit/Reimbursement, Behavioral Health, Business Change, Claims, Clinical Products & Programs, Community Health, Compliance, Congressional, Contracts, Credentialing, Customer Service, Dental/Vision, Direct Sales, Disease Management, EDI, Enrollment & Billing, Fraud Investigation, Media Communications, Medical Directors, Medical Policy, National Networks, Operations, Pharmacy, Provider Data, Provider Networks, Quality Initiatives, Recovery/Refunds, Review and Case Management, Sales & Sales Support, Underwriting

MedReps.com

2018 Medical Sales Salary Report
2655 Northwinds Pkwy, Alpharetta, GA 30009
(866) 619-1629
www.medreps.com/medical-sales-careers/medical-sales-salary-report/

Survey Overview

The *2018 8th Annual Medical Sales Salary Report* looks at the year-over-year income growth of medical sales professionals, and analyzes how income is affected by product sold, company size, age, experience, gender and other influential factors. Reports specific to each of the main product types—medical device, pharmaceutical, medical equipment and biopharma/biotech—are also available.

Survey Editor

Donald Richison, drichison@hcstaffingtech.com
(866) 619-1629

General Information

Industries Covered

(Left Blank)

Survey Specifications

Range of Revenue of Reporting Companies....... (Left Blank)
Frequency of Survey Updates .... Annual/Specific Date
Annual Publication Date........................ June
First Year of Publication........................ 2011
Restrictions .... Industry
Data Delivery Methods .... Electronic/Soft Copy
Non-Participant Report Available .... Yes
Custom Reporting............................. Standard Reporting
Data from World Regions .... North America
Number of Companies.......................... (Left Blank)
Number of Sales Jobs .... (Left Blank)
Data Submitted .... Average/Percentiles
Sales Volume by Job Title....................... No

Practices

Plan Performance Metrics...................... No
Formula Mechanics .... No

Benefits . . . . Yes
Allowances (e.g., Car, Mobile Devices, Internet) . . . Yes
Contests/Spiffs . . . . No
Long-Term Incentives (e.g., Stock, RSU) . . . . Yes

Compensation Data

	Base Salary	Incentive Earnings	Total Compensation
Target	No	No	No
Actual	Yes	Yes	Yes

Major Sales/Customer Contact Job Families Featured in the Survey

Medical Device Sales, Pharmaceutical Sales, Surgical Sales, Medical Equipment Sales, Biotech Sales

Mercer

Canadian Mercer Life Sciences Compensation Survey
400 West Market Street, Suite 700, Louisville, KY 40202
(800) 333-3070
www.imercer.com

Survey Overview

The *Canadian Mercer Life Sciences (MLS) Compensation Survey* is a valuable resource providing companies with need-to-know information about compensation practices in the life sciences industry to attract and retain top talent. The survey covers a broad selection of benchmark positions relevant to the industry ranging from pre-clinical and clinical research, medical affairs, sales, marketing, production and administration, as well as the full range of general infrastructure/support functions. Online and interactive report delivery through Mercer WIN® enables fully customized reporting with statistics and data elements according to your individual needs, including instant comparisons of your organization's data against the market.

Survey Editor

Christian Montemayor, christian.montemayor@mercer.com
(813) 207-6376

General Information

Industries Covered

Life Sciences

Survey Specifications

Range of Revenue of Reporting Companies	CAD$81M–CAD$530M (Interquartile Range)
Frequency of Survey Updates	Annual/Specific Date
Annual Publication Date	September
First Year of Publication	2011
Restrictions	Industry
Data Delivery Methods	Electronic/Soft Copy, Online
Non-Participant Report Available	No
Custom Reporting	Online Access/User Defined
Data from World Regions	North America, *Canada only*
Number of Companies	93
Number of Sales Jobs	33 jobs reportable (each job has multiple levels)/209 reportable jobs + level combinations
Data Submitted	Incumbent Level
Sales Volume by Job Title	No

Practices

Plan Performance Metrics.......................No
Formula Mechanics ....No
Benefits.......................................No
Allowances (e.g., Car, Mobile Devices, Internet)...Yes
Contests/Spiffs................................No
Long-Term Incentives (e.g., Stock, RSU)..........Yes

Compensation Data

	Base Salary	Incentive Earnings	Total Compensation
Target	No	Yes	Yes
Actual	Yes	Yes	Yes

Major Sales/Customer Contact Job Families Featured in the Survey

Sales Management, Sales Representatives, Technical Sales, Key Accounts, Sales Training, Sales Administration, Clinical Education, Customer Service

Mercer

US Mercer SIRS® Medical Device Sales Compensation Survey

400 West Market Street, Suite 700, Louisville, KY 40202
(800) 333-3070
www.imercer.com

Survey Overview

The *US Mercer SIRS® Medical Device Sales Compensation Survey* presents competitive compensation data for a select group of sales benchmark jobs in the medical device industry with the ability to analyze the data by primary product line, secondary product line, sales volume and sales quota. It focuses on compensation-related information and is delivered in both PDF and Excel format. This survey is very valuable for organizations that manage sales compensation by product line or would like to understand variation in compensation practices based on type or specialty of device being sold.

Primary product lines include Airway Management, Cardiac Rhythm Management & Valves, Clinical Chemistry & Diagnostic Products, Cosmetic Devices, Gastroenterology and Urology, General & Hospital Supplies, Ophthalmic Products, Orthopedic Products, Perfusion Systems/Cardiovascular Surgical Tools & Systems, Specialty Surgery and Vascular Devices. Secondary product lines include Capital Equipment, Consumables/Disposables, Durable Goods and Implantable Devices.

Survey Editor

Matthew Kreger, matthew.kreger@mercer.com
(212) 345-7720

General Information

Industries Covered

Life Sciences—Medical Devices

Survey Specifications

Range of Revenue of Reporting Companies	$214M–$2,583M (Interquartile Range)
Frequency of Survey Updates	Annual/Specific Date
Annual Publication Date	August
First Year of Publication	2000
Restrictions	Industry, Must Participate in *SIRS® Benchmark Survey*
Data Delivery Methods	Electronic/Soft Copy
Non-Participant Report Available	No

Custom Reporting. . . . . Online Access/User Defined—For an additional fee
Data from World Regions . . . . North America
Number of Companies. 112
Number of Sales Jobs 53
Data Submitted . . . . Incumbent Level
Sales Volume by Job Title. . . . . Yes

Practices

Plan Performance Metrics. . . . . No
Formula Mechanics . . . . No
Benefits . . . . No
Allowances (e.g., Car, Mobile Devices, Internet) . . . No
Contests/Spiffs. . . . . No
Long-Term Incentives (e.g., Stock, RSU) . . . . Yes

Compensation Data

	Base Salary	Incentive Earnings	Total Compensation
Target	No	Yes	Yes
Actual	Yes	Yes	Yes

Major Sales/Customer Contact Job Families Featured in the Survey

Sales – Medical Devices, Sales – National Accounts, Inside Sales, Training – Sales, Clinical Education, Engineering – Field, Technician – Field

Mercer | Comptryx

Mercer | Comptryx
17 Main Street, Hopkinton, MA 01748
(508) 435-3999
www.comptryx.com

Survey Overview

Mercer | Comptryx is a dynamic Global Salary Survey for the technology industry that uniquely reports both pay and on-demand workforce analytics market data. The survey covers virtually all jobs, all levels, all functions (including sales) and all standard compensation elements (base, allowances, STI, LTI, benefit fringe rates). Our state-of-the-art-reporting system provides in-depth workforce analysis using a menu of organizational metrics. Unlike simple salary surveys, which only let you price jobs, *Mercer | Comptryx* also helps you find the optimal size, shape, mix and cost for your company or sales organization.

Survey Editor

Roger Sturtevant, roger.sturtevant@mercer.com
(508) 435-3999, ext. 50

General Information

Industries Covered

Tech Sector, Aerospace and Defense, and Life Sciences

Survey Specifications

Range of Revenue of Reporting Companies....... $100M–$125B
Frequency of Survey Updates .... Evergreen
Annual Publication Date....................... (Left Blank)
First Year of Publication..................... 2011
Restrictions .... Industry
Data Delivery Methods .... Electronic/Soft Copy
Non-Participant Report Available .... No
Custom Reporting.............................. Online Access/User Defined
Data from World Regions .... North America, Europe, Asia, Middle East, Other Americas, Africa
Number of Companies........................... 300+
Number of Sales Jobs 1,600
Data Submitted .... Incumbent Level
Sales Volume by Job Title..................... No

Practices

Plan Performance Metrics .... No
Formula Mechanics .... No
Benefits .... Yes
Allowances (e.g., Car, Mobile Devices, Internet) ... Yes
Contests/Spiffs .... (Left Blank)
Long-Term Incentives (e.g., Stock, RSU) .... Yes

Compensation Data

	Base Salary	Incentive Earnings	Total Compensation
Target	Yes	Yes	Yes
Actual	Yes	Yes	Yes

Major Sales/Customer Contact Job Families Featured in the Survey

Service Contract, Distributor, Retail, Government, Territory, Key Account, Internet, Professional Services, Contract Renewal, OEM/VAR, Inside/Telesales

MRA—The Management Association

Benchmark Compensation Survey
N19 W24400 Riverwood Drive, Waukesha, WI 53188
(262) 696-3508
www.mranet.org

Survey Overview

This annual survey reports on compensation for employees in Illinois, Iowa, Minnesota, North Dakota, South Dakota and Wisconsin covering 445 core jobs in key business areas from staff level through leadership across 19 job families. This year's report contains 1,083 organizations reporting on over 60,000 employees.

Survey Editor

Kelly Greinke, kelly.greinke@mranet.org
(262) 696-3448

General Information

Industries Covered

Manufacturing—Union, Manufacturing—Non-Union, Services (Includes Retail Trade, Wholesale Trade, Transportation/Warehousing, Information/Communication/Broadcasting, Professional/Business Services, Education Services, Social Services, Leisure/Hospitality Services, Public Administration, and Services not elsewhere classified), Financial Activities, Health Care/Health Services, Goods Producing, Non-Manufacturing (Includes Natural Resources/Mining, Utilities and Construction)

Survey Specifications

Range of Revenue of Reporting Companies....... $0–$250M+
Frequency of Survey Updates .... Annual/Specific Date
Annual Publication Date........................ July
First Year of Publication........................ 1901
Restrictions .... None
Data Delivery Methods .... Electronic/Soft Copy, Online
Non-Participant Report Available .... Yes
Custom Reporting............................. Online Access/User Defined
Data from World Regions .... North America
Number of Companies.......................... 1,083
Number of Sales Jobs 32
Data Submitted .... Incumbent Level
Sales Volume by Job Title....................... Yes

Practices

Plan Performance Metrics . . . . No
Formula Mechanics . . . . No
Benefits . . . . No
Allowances (e.g., Car, Mobile Devices, Internet) . . . No
Contests/Spiffs . . . . No
Long-Term Incentives (e.g., Stock, RSU) . . . . No

Compensation Data

	Base Salary	Incentive Earnings	Total Compensation
Target	No	Yes	No
Actual	Yes	Yes	Yes

Major Sales/Customer Contact Job Families Featured in the Survey

Marketing Director, Marketing and Sales Senior Manager, Assistant Sales Manager, Sales Manager (Regional Administration), Sales Manager (Export), Government Accounts Manager, Marketing Manager, Marketing Generalist III (Advanced), Marketing Generalist II (Experienced), Marketing Generalist I (Entry), Public Relations Manager, Public Relations Representative II, Market Research Manager, Market Research Analyst III (Advanced), Market Research Analyst II (Experienced), Market Research Analyst I (Entry), Telemarketing Supervisor, Customer Service Director, Customer Service Manager, Customer Service Supervisor, Customer Service Representative I (Entry), Customer Service Representative II (Experienced), Customer Service Representative III (Advanced), Sales/Marketing Assistant, Order Processing Supervisor, Order Clerk, Sales Correspondent Senior, Sales Correspondent, Sales Representative – Telemarketing, Telemarketing Supervisor, Telephone Order Processing Representative, and Sales Representative – Inside Sales

Pearl Meyer

CHiPS One World
93 Worcester Street, Wellesley, MA 02481
(508) 460-9600
www.pearlmeyer.com

Pearl Meyer

Survey Overview

A comprehensive, global, total compensation survey focusing on technology firms and other firms with large technology populations.

Survey Editor

Rebecca Toman, rebecca.toman@pearlmeyer.com
(508) 630-1475

General Information

Industries Covered

A broad range of jobs from engineering to administrative functions to sales

Survey Specifications

Range of Revenue of Reporting Companies....... Small to Really Big
Frequency of Survey Updates .... Annual/Specific Date
Annual Publication Date........................ First Week of July
First Year of Publication........................ 1989
Restrictions .... Industry
Data Delivery Methods .... Electronic/Soft Copy, Online
Non-Participant Report Available .... No
Custom Reporting............................ Standard Reporting
Data from World Regions .... North America, Europe, Asia, Middle East, Other Americas, Africa
Number of Companies......................... 100+
Number of Sales Jobs .... 100+
Data Submitted .... Averages/Percentiles
Sales Volume by Job Title....................... (Left Blank)

Practices

Plan Performance Metrics...................... (Left Blank)
Formula Mechanics .... (Left Blank)
Benefits...................................... (Left Blank)
Allowances (e.g., Car, Mobile Devices, Internet) ... (Left Blank)
Contests/Spiffs............................... (Left Blank)
Long-Term Incentives (e.g., Stock, RSU).......... (Left Blank)

Compensation Data

	Base Salary	Incentive Earnings	Total Compensation
Target	(Left Blank)	Yes	Yes
Actual	Yes	Yes	Yes

Major Sales/Customer Contact Job Families Featured in the Survey

Field Sales – Direct – Commercial, Field Sales – Direct – Government, Field Sales – Direct – Combination, Field Sales – Direct Roll-Up, Field Sales – Indirect OEM, Field Sales – Indirect VAR, Field Sales – Indirect Distributor, Field Sales – Indirect Retail, Field Sales – Indirect Multiple Channels, Field Sales – Indirect Roll-Up, Field Sales – Direct and Indirect Combination, Field Sales – Direct and Indirect Roll-Up, Product/Service Sales Specialist (Overlay), Strategic Client Management, Global Account Management, National (Domestic) Account Management, Maintenance Contract Sales, Retail – Sales (Store), Inside Sales Representative – Consumer, Inside Sales Representative – B2B Supplies, Consumables, Packaged Offerings, Inside Sales Representative – B2B Product/Service/Solutions, Inside Sales Roll-Up

Pearl Meyer

Forest Products Industry Compensation Survey
93 Worcester Street, Wellesley, MA 02481
(508) 460-9600
www.pearlmeyer.com

Pearl Meyer

Survey Overview

The Forest Products Industry Compensation Association (FPICA) is comprised of approximately 40 forest products companies doing business in the United States. The FPICA members participate in a survey with respect to compensation matters. The survey is for the sole and exclusive use of participating members. An administrative consultant coordinates the administration of the survey and is the contact person for the survey provider with respect to matters relating to the conduct of the survey.

Survey Editor

Andrew Guigno, andrew.guigno@pearlmeyer.com
(508) 630-1508

General Information

Industries Covered

Forest Products Industry

Survey Specifications

Range of Revenue of Reporting Companies....... Small to Really Big
Frequency of Survey Updates .... Annual/Specific Date
Annual Publication Date...................... August 1
First Year of Publication...................... 11 Years Ago
Restrictions .... Industry
Data Delivery Methods .... Electronic/Soft Copy, Online
Non-Participant Report Available .... No
Custom Reporting............................ Standard Reporting
Data from World Regions .... (Left Blank)
Number of Companies......................... 40+
Number of Sales Jobs 18
Data Submitted .... Averages/Percentiles
Sales Volume by Job Title...................... (Left Blank)

Practices

Plan Performance Metrics....................... (Left Blank)
Formula Mechanics .... (Left Blank)
Benefits.................................... (Left Blank)
Allowances (e.g., Car, Mobile Devices, Internet)... (Left Blank)
Contests/Spiffs............................... (Left Blank)
Long-Term Incentives (e.g., Stock, RSU).......... (Left Blank)

Compensation Data

	Base Salary	Incentive Earnings	Total Compensation
Target	(Left Blank)	Yes	Yes
Actual	Yes	Yes	Yes

Major Sales/Customer Contact Job Families Featured in the Survey

Division Sales and Marketing Manager, Level II Sales Representative, Level III Sales Representative, Level IV National Account Executive, Regional Sales Manager, Inside Sales Representative I, Inside Sales Representative II, Inside Sales Representative III, Sales Manager, Sales Service Manager, Customer/Sales Service Representative, National/Divisional Sales Manager, Sales Supervisor/Manager, Customer Sales Service Manager, Customer/Sales Service Representative, Inside Sales/Customer Service Representative

Pearl Meyer

Global Engineering, Procurement & Construction Management Compensation Survey
93 Worcester Street, Wellesley, MA 02481
(508) 460-9600
www.pearlmeyer.com

Pearl Meyer

Survey Overview

The *Global Engineering, Procurement and Construction Management Compensation Survey (EPCM)* is a global compensation information source specifically focused on engineering and construction/construction management companies.

Survey Editor

Rebecca Toman, rebecca.toman@pearlmeyer.com
(508) 630-1475

General Information

Industries Covered

Engineering and Construction

Survey Specifications

Range of Revenue of Reporting Companies....... Large to Very Large
Frequency of Survey Updates .... Annual/Specific Date
Annual Publication Date....................... September 15
First Year of Publication..................... 5 Years Ago
Restrictions .... Industry
Data Delivery Methods .... Electronic/Soft Copy, Online
Non-Participant Report Available .... No
Custom Reporting.............................. Standard Reporting
Data from World Regions .... North America, Europe, Asia, Middle East, Other Americas
Number of Companies........................... 12+
Number of Sales Jobs 5
Data Submitted .... Averages/Percentiles
Sales Volume by Job Title..................... (Left Blank)

Practices

Plan Performance Metrics...................... (Left Blank)
Formula Mechanics .... (Left Blank)
Benefits.................................... (Left Blank)
Allowances (e.g., Car, Mobile Devices, Internet)... (Left Blank)
Contests/Spiffs.............................. (Left Blank)
Long-Term Incentives (e.g., Stock, RSU).......... (Left Blank)

Compensation Data

	Base Salary	Incentive Earnings	Total Compensation
Target	(Left Blank)	Yes	Yes
Actual	Yes	Yes	Yes

Major Sales/Customer Contact Job Families Featured in the Survey

Business Development – 5 Levels

Pearl Meyer

HR Alliance Compensation Survey
93 Worcester Street, Wellesley, MA 02481
(508) 460-9600
www.pearlmeyer.com

Pearl Meyer

Survey Overview

HR Alliance's (formerly WTPF) Compensation Survey is the most stable and reliable source of competitive regional pay information for human resources professionals supporting the government contracting, technology and professional services communities in the Washington, D.C., area. The survey has been conducted each year since 1989. In 2010, WTPF joined forces with the SAIC Security Cleared Federal Contracting Personnel Survey and now also gathers information on security clearances—at both the incumbent and policy level.

Survey Editor

Rebecca Toman, rebecca.toman@pearlmeyer.com
(508) 630-1475

General Information

Industries Covered

Geographic: Washington, D.C., only with a high proportion of government contracting organizations

Survey Specifications

Range of Revenue of Reporting Companies....... Small to Very Large
Frequency of Survey Updates .... Annual/Specific Date
Annual Publication Date........................ Late August
First Year of Publication........................ 10+ Years Ago
Restrictions .... Geography
Data Delivery Methods .... Electronic/Soft Copy, Online
Non-Participant Report Available .... No
Custom Reporting............................. Standard Reporting
Data from World Regions .... (Left Blank)
Number of Companies......................... 50+
Number of Sales Jobs .... 20+
Data Submitted .... Averages/Percentiles
Sales Volume by Job Title...................... (Left Blank)

Practices

Plan Performance Metrics . . . . (Left Blank)
Formula Mechanics . . . . (Left Blank)
Benefits . . . . (Left Blank)
Allowances (e.g., Car, Mobile Devices, Internet) . . . (Left Blank)
Contests/Spiffs . . . . (Left Blank)
Long-Term Incentives (e.g., Stock, RSU) . . . . (Left Blank)

Compensation Data

	Base Salary	Incentive Earnings	Total Compensation
Target	(Left Blank)	Yes	Yes
Actual	Yes	Yes	Yes

Major Sales/Customer Contact Job Families Featured in the Survey

Account Management, Business Development, Sales Engineering, Marketing, Marketing Communications, Customer Relationship Management, Customer Relationship Delivery Management, Delivery Management, Sales Management

Pearl Meyer

National Engineering and Construction Salary Survey

Pearl Meyer

93 Worcester Street, Wellesley, MA 02481
(508) 460-9600
www.pearlmeyer.com

Survey Overview

The *National Engineering and Construction Salary Survey (NECSS)* is a compensation information source specifically focused on engineering and construction/construction management companies with significant operations in both areas, primarily in the power, petrochemical, civil, environmental, transportation and/or mining and metals industries. The survey covers approximately 18 job families (109 jobs) and provides policy and practice information in areas of salary administration, turnover, overtime, college recruiting and hiring rates, as well as variable pay plans.

Survey Editor

Rebecca Toman, rebecca.toman@pearlmeyer.com
(508) 630-1475

General Information

Industries Covered

Engineering and Construction

Survey Specifications

Range of Revenue of Reporting Companies....... Large to Very Large
Frequency of Survey Updates.................... Annual/Specific Date
Annual Publication Date........................ August 15
First Year of Publication........................ 25+ Years Ago
Restrictions.................................. Industry
Data Delivery Methods......................... Electronic/Soft Copy, Online
Non-Participant Report Available............... No
Custom Reporting.............................. Standard Reporting
Data from World Regions...................... (Left Blank)
Number of Companies.......................... 30+
Number of Sales Jobs.......................... 5
Data Submitted............................... Averages/Percentiles
Sales Volume by Job Title...................... (Left Blank)

Practices

Plan Performance Metrics....................... (Left Blank)
Formula Mechanics .... (Left Blank)
Benefits....................................... (Left Blank)
Allowances (e.g., Car, Mobile Devices, Internet)... (Left Blank)
Contests/Spiffs................................ (Left Blank)
Long-Term Incentives (e.g., Stock, RSU).......... (Left Blank)

Compensation Data

	Base Salary	Incentive Earnings	Total Compensation
Target	(Left Blank)	Yes	Yes
Actual	Yes	Yes	Yes

Major Sales/Customer Contact Job Families Featured in the Survey

Business Development Job Family – 5 levels – Variable Compensation Reported

Pearl Meyer

The Executive Compensation and Benchmarking Survey

Pearl Meyer

93 Worcester Street, Wellesley, MA 02481
(508) 460-9600
www.pearlmeyer.com

Survey Overview

The report covers the complete top two layers of a firm's management team including over 70 executive positions. In addition to a traditional competitive pay summary by benchmark position, the report also gives data for non-benchmark positions (e.g., direct report to CEO, not matched elsewhere) allowing you to determine an appropriate survey match for each one of your top executives, even those with a unique range of responsibilities.

Survey Editor

Rebecca Toman, rebecca.toman@pearlmeyer.com
(508) 630-1475

General Information

Industries Covered

Broad Range

Survey Specifications

Range of Revenue of Reporting Companies....... Medium to Very Large
Frequency of Survey Updates .... Annual/Specific Date
Annual Publication Date........................ Early July
First Year of Publication........................ 20+ Years Ago
Restrictions .... Industry
Data Delivery Methods .... Electronic/Soft Copy, Online
Non-Participant Report Available .... No
Custom Reporting............................. Standard Reporting
Data from World Regions .... (Left Blank)
Number of Companies.......................... 300+
Number of Sales Jobs .... (Left Blank)
Data Submitted .... Averages/Percentiles
Sales Volume by Job Title....................... (Left Blank)

Practices

Plan Performance Metrics . . . . (Left Blank)
Formula Mechanics . . . . (Left Blank)
Benefits . . . . (Left Blank)
Allowances (e.g., Car, Mobile Devices, Internet) . . . (Left Blank)
Contests/Spiffs . . . . (Left Blank)
Long-Term Incentives (e.g., Stock, RSU) . . . . (Left Blank)

Compensation Data

	Base Salary	Incentive Earnings	Total Compensation
Target	(Left Blank)	Yes	Yes
Actual	Yes	Yes	Yes

Major Sales/Customer Contact Job Families Featured in the Survey

Top Sales, Top Marketing and Sales, Direct Report to Top Sales, Direct Report to Top Marketing and Sales.

Radford

An Aon Hewitt Company

Radford Global Sales Survey
2570 North First Street, Suite 500, San Jose, CA 95131
(408) 321-2500
https://radford.aon.com

Survey Overview

Sales professionals in the technology and life sciences sectors share a unique challenge: selling innovation. Meeting this mandate requires top talent, flexible incentives and intelligent sales targets. Our survey platform is designed to address these issues across multiple sales channels and industries. The *Radford Global Sales Survey* provides human resources and compensation professionals with access to rewards insights covering more technology and life sciences companies, incumbents and countries on a single survey platform than any other data provider.

Survey Editor

Julie Mills, jmills@radford.com
(408) 321-2540

General Information

Industries Covered

Technology, Life Sciences, Medical Devices, General Industry

Survey Specifications

Range of Revenue of Reporting Companies....... Less than $10M–$5B+
Frequency of Survey Updates .... Evergreen
Annual Publication Date....................... Monthly
First Year of Publication...................... 1986
Restrictions .... Industry
Data Delivery Methods .... Online
Non-Participant Report Available .... No
Custom Reporting............................ Standard Reporting, Online Access/User Defined
Data from World Regions .... North America, Europe, Asia, Middle East, Other Americas, Africa
Number of Companies......................... More than 1,650
Number of Sales Jobs .... 400+
Data Submitted .... Averages/Percentiles, Incumbent Level
Sales Volume by Job Title...................... Yes

Practices

Plan Performance Metrics....................... Yes
Formula Mechanics .... Yes
Benefits...................................... Yes
Allowances (e.g., Car, Mobile Devices, Internet)... Yes
Contests/Spiffs................................ Yes
Long-Term Incentives (e.g., Stock, RSU).......... Yes

Compensation Data

	Base Salary	Incentive Earnings	Total Compensation
Target	Yes	Yes	Yes
Actual	Yes	Yes	Yes

Major Sales/Customer Contact Job Families Featured in the Survey

Alliances & Partnerships, Contract Management & Renewal, Consulting Services, Customer Success, Field Sales (Direct, Retail, OEM/VAR, Multi-Channel), Global & Regional Sales Leadership, Global & Country Strategic Account Management, Inside Sales, Internet Ad Sales, Leasing & Finance Sales, Maintenance/Services, Managed Care, Medical Device Sales (Implantable, Non-Implantable), Pharmaceutical Sales (Hospital Pharma, Specialty/Non-Specialty Pharma, Oncology), Life Sciences Sales (Diagnostics, Animal Health, Life Sciences Products/Services), Relationship Management, Sales Administration & Support, Sales Engineering (Pre- & Post-Sale), Sales Executives, Sales Operations (Deal Desk, Commissions Analyst, Operations Analyst, Order Process Management), Sales Training, Sales Force Effectiveness/Sales Enablement, Telemarketing/Lead Development

Salary.com

IPAS® Global Consumer Industry Survey
610 Lincoln Street North Building, Suite 200,
Waltham, MA 02451
(781) 989-9488
www.salary.com

Survey Overview

Since 1996, we have offered several U.S. surveys, which opened the door to the world of pay and benefits in the consumer industry. In 2012, we combined three of our consumer surveys (Apparel & Footwear, Specialty Retail and Luxury Goods) into one comprehensive, global product. The *IPAS® Global Consumer Industry Survey* creates a single, comprehensive source of reliable market intelligence. In 2012, the survey expanded from U.S. only to Global and we are currently reporting jobs in 14 countries.

Survey Editor

Tricia Mulkeen, tricia.mulkeen@salary.com

General Information

Industries Covered

Apparel, Footwear, Luxury Goods, Consumer Goods

Survey Specifications

Range of Revenue of Reporting Companies	$150M–$10B (typical range)
Frequency of Survey Updates	Annual/Specific Date
Annual Publication Date	September
First Year of Publication	1996
Restrictions	Industry
Data Delivery Methods	Online
Non-Participant Report Available	Yes (For one-time only purchase/must participate next year)
Custom Reporting	Standard Reporting, Online Access/User Defined
Data from World Regions	North America, Europe, Asia (Mainly USA, recently expanded to global, 14 countries available in 2017 for certain jobs only)
Number of Companies	39 companies in 2018 (85 unique/premier brands)

Number of Sales Jobs .... 8 sales functions covered (wholesale) plus retail/store sales associate
Data Submitted .... Incumbent Level
Sales Volume by Job Title....................... No

Practices

Plan Performance Metrics....................... No (For retail positions only)
Formula Mechanics .... No
Benefits .... No
Allowances (e.g., Car, Mobile Devices, Internet) ... No
Contests/Spiffs................................. No
Long-Term Incentives (e.g., Stock, RSU).......... Yes (Eligibility and general information only, actual LTI values not collected)

Compensation Data

	Base Salary	Incentive Earnings	Total Compensation
Target	No	Yes	Yes
Actual	Yes	Yes	Yes

Major Sales/Customer Contact Job Families Featured in the Survey

Sales (Corporate/Wholesale): Dealer/Customer Relations, Key Account Sales, Sample Management, Sales & Marketing, Sales Planning/Analysis, Sales Support, Field Sales, Inside Sales Store Sales Associate and Lead Store Sales Associate

Store Management: Department Managers, Assistant Store Managers, Associate Store Managers, Store Managers

Salary.com

IPAS® Global High Technology Compensation Salary Survey
610 Lincoln Street North Building, Suite 200,
Waltham, MA 02451
(781) 989-9488
www.salary.com

Survey Overview

IPAS® is a unique single source of global market data focusing on the high technology industry. It allows participants to price jobs around the world and compare jobs in various countries using the same methodology, participants, currency and system.

Global compensation data is collected from the most prestigious firms in the industry and validated by a team of experts, so participants can be certain that they have the highest quality information available to build their compensation programs around the world.

Input requirements are kept minimal by focusing on key data elements and results are delivered via our web tool, easily accessible any time. Data is collected throughout the year based upon participants' focal review effective dates. Survey results are updated quarterly.

Survey Editor

Tricia Mulkeen, tricia.mulkeen@salary.com

General Information

Industries Covered

High-technology (computer systems/peripherals, software, electronics, semiconductors, tele-communications, networking, web/internet, professional services/consulting). Expanding to other industries

Survey Specifications

Range of Revenue of Reporting Companies	<$50M–>$10B
Frequency of Survey Updates	Evergreen
Annual Publication Date	Survey results updated quarterly
First Year of Publication	1998
Restrictions	Industry
Data Delivery Methods	Online
Non-Participant Report Available	No
Custom Reporting	Standard Reporting, Online Access/User Defined
Data from World Regions	North America, Europe, Asia, Middle East, Other Americas, Africa

Number of Companies........................ 350 companies in 2018
Number of Sales Jobs .... 383 Sales Job Function/Job Level Combinations
Data Submitted .... Incumbent Level
Sales Volume by Job Title...................... No

Practices

Plan Performance Metrics...................... No
Formula Mechanics .... No
Benefits.................................... No
Allowances (e.g., Car, Mobile Devices, Internet)... Yes
Contests/Spiffs.............................. No
Long-Term Incentives (e.g., Stock, RSU).......... Yes*

* *Long-Term Incentive* eligibility reported in standard survey results.

Compensation Data

	Base Salary	Incentive Earnings	Total Compensation
Target	No	Yes	Yes
Actual	Yes	Yes	Yes

Major Sales/Customer Contact Job Families Featured in the Survey

Sales: Advertising Sales, Federal Government Sales, Field Account/Territory Sales Management, Channel Sales (Distributor/Retail), Sales & Marketing, Product Leasing Sales, Key/Major Account Management, Contract Renewal Sales, OEM/VAR Sales, Professional Services/Outsourcing Sales, Partner Sales, Client Relationship Management, Services/Support Sales, Outbound Telesales

Sales Operations: Engagement/Bid Proposal, CRM Administration, Ad Campaign Support, Systems Engineering, Sales Forecasting & Analysis, Sales Operations, Inbound Telesales, Sales Order Administration/Processing, Sales Program Management, Sales Training, Telemarketing, Sales Support

Technical Support/Customer Service: Customer/Product Support, Technical Support Engineering, Field Customer Engineering, Customer/Technical Service Support Management, Call Center Scheduling, Program Management, Customer Support/Call Center Quality, Product Repair, Account Support Management, Customer Service (General)

Job Levels Reported (if applicable and/or when sufficient data):
8 Management Levels–Supervisor to Executive
8 Professional Levels–Entry to Fellow
5 Support Levels–Entry to Expert

The Croner Company

C2HR Cable and Satellite MSO Compensation Survey
1028 Sir Francis Drake Boulevard, Kentfield, CA 94904
(415) 485-5530
www.croner.biz

Survey Overview

The *C2HR Cable and Satellite MSO Compensation Survey* is a highly industry specific survey. Conducted annually to provide multiple systems operators (MSOs) with up-to-date, market competitive compensation data.

The participants in the MSO Survey include the large MSOs, as well as smaller, regional companies and satellite operators, telecommunications companies and home security companies.

Survey Editor

Hali Croner, (415) 485-5530

General Information

Industries Covered

Cable TV and Satellite Multiple System Operators

Survey Specifications

Range of Revenue of Reporting Companies....... (Left Blank)
Frequency of Survey Updates .... Annual/Specific Date
Annual Publication Date....................... September
First Year of Publication...................... 2001
Restrictions .... Industry
Data Delivery Methods .... Electronic/Soft Copy, Online
Non-Participant Report Available .... Yes
Custom Reporting............................. Standard Reporting, Online Access/User Defined
Data from World Regions .... North America
Number of Companies......................... 11
Number of Sales Jobs 64
Data Submitted .... Averages/Percentiles
Sales Volume by Job Title...................... Yes

Practices

Plan Performance Metrics .... Yes
Formula Mechanics .... Yes
Benefits .... No
Allowances (e.g., Car, Mobile Devices, Internet) ... No
Contests/Spiffs .... (Left Blank)
Long-Term Incentives (e.g., Stock, RSU) .... Yes

Compensation Data

	Base Salary	Incentive Earnings	Total Compensation
Target	Yes	Yes	Yes
Actual	Yes	Yes	Yes

Major Sales/Customer Contact Job Families Featured in the Survey

Carrier Sales, Channel Sales Management, Commercial Inside Sales, Commercial Sales Account Management, Commercial Sales Engineering, Commercial Sales Management, Direct Sales Management, Embedded Retail Sales, Home Security Sales, Inbound Sales, MDU Sales Account Management, Market Development/Access Management, National Enterprise Commercial Sales, Major Account/Enterprise Commercial Sales, Small-to-Medium Business Commercial Sales, Outbound Sales, Retail Sales, Regional Retail Sales, Sales Operations, Store Retail Sales

The Croner Company

C2HR Cable Programmers/Broadcast Networks Compensation Survey

1028 Sir Francis Drake Boulevard, Kentfield, CA 94904
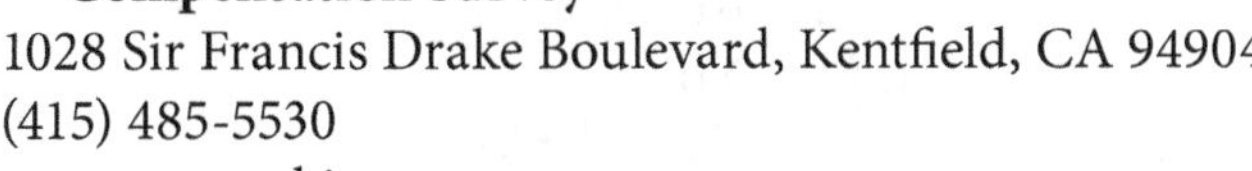
(415) 485-5530
www.croner.biz

Survey Overview

The *C2HR Cable Programmers/Broadcast Networks Compensation Survey* is a participant-only compensation survey conducted annually to provide cable programmers, broadcast networks, digital and other media companies with up-to-date, market competitive compensation data.

Participant companies include all five national broadcast networks and all of the leading cable programmers, as well as companies that create content for internet channels.

Survey Editor

Hali Croner, (415) 485-5530

General Information

Industries Covered

Broadcast Networks, Cable Programming

Survey Specifications

Range of Revenue of Reporting Companies	(Left Blank)
Frequency of Survey Updates	Annual/Specific Date
Annual Publication Date	September
First Year of Publication	2001
Restrictions	None
Data Delivery Methods	Electronic/Soft Copy, Online
Non-Participant Report Available	Yes
Custom Reporting	Standard Reporting, Online Access/User Defined
Data from World Regions	North America
Number of Companies	47
Number of Sales Jobs	55
Data Submitted	Averages/Percentiles
Sales Volume by Job Title	Yes

Practices

Plan Performance Metrics . . . . Yes
Formula Mechanics . . . . Yes
Benefits . . . . No
Allowances (e.g., Car, Mobile Devices, Internet) . . . No
Contests/Spiffs . . . . (Left Blank)
Long-Term Incentives (e.g., Stock, RSU) . . . . Yes

Compensation Data

	Base Salary	Incentive Earnings	Total Compensation
Target	Yes	Yes	Yes
Actual	Yes	Yes	Yes

Major Sales/Customer Contact Job Families Featured in the Survey

Advertisement Inventory, Advertisement Traffic, Advertising Sales, Advertising Sales Analysis, Advertising Sales Planning, Affiliate Marketing, Affiliate Sales, Integrated Sales and Marketing, Sales Operations

The Croner Company

Croner Digital Content and Technology Survey
1028 Sir Francis Drake Boulevard, Kentfield, CA 94904
(415) 485-5530
www.croner.biz

Survey Overview

The *Croner Digital Content and Technology Survey* is conducted annually to provide up-to-date market compensation data to companies conducting a material part of their business via internet platforms. The report is designed specifically for companies that develop and publish frequently updated internet content and/or provide consumers and businesses with internet transactions and services.

Participant companies in the *Croner Digital Content and Technology Survey* span multiple industry segments including digital advertising services, e-commerce retail, e-commerce transactions, media and entertainment, online/mobile gaming, publishing, search/social networks, web publishing and business products/services. Positions reported in the survey are specific to digital organizations or to digital units within a larger organization.

Survey Editor

Hali Croner, (415) 485-5530

General Information

Industries Covered

All Companies with Internet/Mobile Presence

Survey Specifications

Range of Revenue of Reporting Companies	(Left Blank)
Frequency of Survey Updates	Annual/Specific Date
Annual Publication Date	August
First Year of Publication	1996
Restrictions	None
Data Delivery Methods	Electronic/Soft Copy, Online
Non-Participant Report Available	Yes
Custom Reporting	Standard Reporting, Online Access/User Defined
Data from World Regions	North America, United Kingdom, China, France, Germany and Spain

Number of Companies........................ 135
Number of Sales Jobs 91
Data Submitted .... Averages/Percentiles
Sales Volume by Job Title...................... Yes

Practices

Plan Performance Metrics...................... Yes
Formula Mechanics .... Yes
Benefits...................................... No
Allowances (e.g., Car, Mobile Devices, Internet) . . . No
Contests/Spiffs............................... (Left Blank)
Long-Term Incentives (e.g., Stock, RSU).......... Yes

Compensation Data

	Base Salary	Incentive Earnings	Total Compensation
Target	Yes	Yes	Yes
Actual	Yes	Yes	Yes

Major Sales/Customer Contact Job Families Featured in the Survey

Advertising Traffic, Advertising Operations, Advertising Solutions, Digital Product Sales, Field Advertising Sales, Inside Advertising Sales, Local Advertising Sales, Offers Sales, Programmatic Sales, Sales Account Services, Sales Analytics, Sales Marketing, Sales Operations, Sales Strategy and Planning, Sales Training, Yield Analytics

The Croner Company

Croner Entertainment Survey
1028 Sir Francis Drake Boulevard, Kentfield, CA 94904
(415) 485-5530
www.croner.biz

Survey Overview

The *Croner Entertainment Survey* is an industry-specific survey conducted annually to serve as a comprehensive compensation resource for benchmark positions in the film, television, music and digital entertainment industries. It includes positions at all organizational levels, from executive to hourly, across a broad range of job families.

Survey Editor

Hali Croner, (415) 485-5530

General Information

Industries Covered

Theatrical, Television and Music Production/Post-Production, Distribution & Sales

Survey Specifications

Range of Revenue of Reporting Companies....... (Left Blank)
Frequency of Survey Updates .... Annual/Specific Date
Annual Publication Date...................... November
First Year of Publication...................... 2013
Restrictions .... Industry
Data Delivery Methods .... Electronic/Soft Copy, Online
Non-Participant Report Available .... Yes
Custom Reporting........................... Standard Reporting, Online Access/User Defined
Data from World Regions .... North America
Number of Companies........................ 37
Number of Sales Jobs 38
Data Submitted .... Averages/Percentiles
Sales Volume by Job Title...................... Yes

Practices

Plan Performance Metrics...................... No
Formula Mechanics .... No
Benefits.................................... No
Allowances (e.g., Car, Mobile Devices, Internet) ... Yes
Contests/Spiffs.............................. (Left Blank)
Long-Term Incentives (e.g., Stock, RSU).......... Yes

Compensation Data

	Base Salary	Incentive Earnings	Total Compensation
Target	Yes	Yes	Yes
Actual	Yes	Yes	Yes

Major Sales/Customer Contact Job Families Featured in the Survey

Distribution Sales

The Croner Company

Croner Local Media Survey
1028 Sir Francis Drake Boulevard, Kentfield, CA 94904
(415) 485-5530
www.croner.biz

Survey Overview

The *Croner Local Media Survey* is an industry-specific survey conducted annually to provide local advertising sales compensation, advertising sales plan design features and compensation for local television and radio station programming and operations across multiple industries, including cable, television, radio and digital media.

Survey Editor

Hali Croner, (415) 485-5530

General Information

Industries Covered

Cable, Television, Radio and Digital (Online and Mobile Media)

Survey Specifications

Range of Revenue of Reporting Companies....... (Left Blank)
Frequency of Survey Updates .... Annual/Specific Date
Annual Publication Date...................... September
First Year of Publication...................... 2010
Restrictions .... Industry
Data Delivery Methods .... Electronic/Soft Copy
Non-Participant Report Available .... Yes
Custom Reporting............................ Standard Reporting
Data from World Regions .... North America
Number of Companies........................ 14
Number of Sales Jobs 15
Data Submitted .... Averages/Percentiles
Sales Volume by Job Title..................... Yes

Practices

Plan Performance Metrics..................... Yes
Formula Mechanics .... Yes
Benefits.................................... No
Allowances (e.g., Car, Mobile Devices, Internet) . . . No
Contests/Spiffs.............................. (Left Blank)
Long-Term Incentives (e.g., Stock, RSU).......... Yes

Compensation Data

	Base Salary	Incentive Earnings	Total Compensation
Target	Yes	No	Yes
Actual	Yes	No	Yes

Major Sales/Customer Contact Job Families Featured in the Survey

Sales Management Structure A, Sales Management Structure B, Sales Individual Contributors, Sales Support, Traffic

The Croner Company

Croner Software Games Survey
1028 Sir Francis Drake Boulevard, Kentfield, CA 94904
(415) 485-5530
www.croner.biz

Survey Overview

The *Croner Software Games Survey* is the benchmark survey of the entertainment software industry. This leading-edge report provides compensation data for jobs in all gaming platform types, including mobile, social, console, PC, handheld, MMO and casino games. The survey has provided market data about positions in companies that publish and/or develop software for entertainment and education in the U.S. and Canada since 1990, its scope and content evolving each year casino gaming industry.

The North America Survey reports data and policies and practices such as bonus plans and selected benefits for companies and includes positions and cuts specific to mobile and social gaming. The International Supplement reports data for selected positions in the U.K and Europe.

Survey Editor

Hali Croner, (415) 485-5530

General Information

Industries Covered

Software Games: Including Entertainment, Educational and Casino

Survey Specifications

Range of Revenue of Reporting Companies	(Left Blank)
Frequency of Survey Updates	Annual/Specific Date
Annual Publication Date	December
First Year of Publication	1990
Restrictions	Industry
Data Delivery Methods	Electronic/Soft Copy, Online
Non-Participant Report Available	Yes
Custom Reporting	Standard Reporting, Online Access/User Defined
Data from World Regions	North America, United Kingdom
Number of Companies	52
Number of Sales Jobs	22
Data Submitted	Averages/Percentiles
Sales Volume by Job Title	Yes

Practices

Plan Performance Metrics....................... Yes
Formula Mechanics .... Yes
Benefits...................................... Yes
Allowances (e.g., Car, Mobile Devices, Internet)... Yes
Contests/Spiffs................................ (Left Blank)
Long-Term Incentives (e.g., Stock, RSU).......... Yes

Compensation Data

	Base Salary	Incentive Earnings	Total Compensation
Target	Yes	Yes	Yes
Actual	Yes	Yes	Yes

Major Sales/Customer Contact Job Families Featured in the Survey

Field Sales, In Game Advertising Sales, Sales Administration, Sales Analysis, Sales Management

Western Compensation & Benefits Consultants

Marketing & Sales Compensation Survey
595 Howe Street, Suite 502
Vancouver, BC, V6C 2T5 Canada
(604) 683-9155
www.wcbc.ca

Survey Overview

WCBC's *Marketing & Sales Compensation Survey*, conducted annually, provides salary and incentive data for over 80 positions. The survey covers a broad range of Canadian organizations in all sectors of the economy.

Survey Editor

Linda Reid, linda_reid@wcbc.ca
(604) 683-9155

General Information

Industries Covered

Professional, Scientific & Technical Services, Retail Trade, Educational Services, Health Care & Social Assistance, Associations & Regulatory Bodies, Finance & Insurance, Agriculture, Forestry, Fishing & Hunting, Mining, Quarrying and Oil & Gas Extraction, Manufacturing, Transportation & Warehousing, Arts, Entertainment, Recreation, Tourism, Hospitality, Wholesale Trade, Other

Survey Specifications

Range of Revenue of Reporting Companies....... $50M–>$100M
Frequency of Survey Updates .... Annual/Specific Date
Annual Publication Date....................... Published in September, data effective July 1
First Year of Publication...................... 1985
Restrictions .... None
Data Delivery Methods .... Paper, Electronic/Soft Copy, Online
Non-Participant Report Available .... Yes
Custom Reporting.............................. Online Access/User Defined
Data from World Regions .... North America
Number of Companies........................... 150+
Number of Sales Jobs .... 80+
Data Submitted .... Incumbent Level
Sales Volume by Job Title...................... No

Practices

Plan Performance Metrics .... No
Formula Mechanics .... No
Benefits .... No
Allowances (e.g., Car, Mobile Devices, Internet) ... No
Contests/Spiffs .... No
Long-Term Incentives (e.g., Stock, RSU) .... No

Compensation Data

	Base Salary	Incentive Earnings	Total Compensation
Target	No	No	No
Actual	Yes	Yes	Yes

Major Sales/Customer Contact Job Families Featured in the Survey

General Operations, Marketing/Media, Sales/Merchandising/Advertising, Art/Design/Media, Communications/Events/Community Relations, Customer Services/Technical Service/Call Centre, Retail, Member Relations/Fundraising, Business Development

Western Management Group

Retail Sales Compensation Survey
237 West Main Street, Los Gatos, CA 95030
(408) 399-4900
www.wmgnet.com

Survey Overview

This survey includes multiple levels for jobs in the Retail industry, and additional positions specific to the restaurant and grocery sectors. For each job, we collect Base Salary, Sales Incentives, Non-Sales Incentives and Targeted Incentive Compensation. Store type/channel, product category and geographic breakouts available.

Survey Editor

DeLynn Gentile, delynn@wmgnet.com
(408) 399-4900, ext. 227

General Information

Industries Covered

Retail Sales

Survey Specifications

Range of Revenue of Reporting Companies....... $25M–$150B
Frequency of Survey Updates.................. Annual/Specific Date
Annual Publication Date...................... July
First Year of Publication..................... 2004
Restrictions................................ None
Data Delivery Methods........................ Paper, Electronic/Soft Copy, Online
Non-Participant Report Available............... No
Custom Reporting............................ Standard Reporting, Online Access/User Defined
Data from World Regions...................... North America, Europe
Number of Companies......................... 156
Number of Sales Jobs......................... 315
Data Submitted.............................. Incumbent Level
Sales Volume by Job Title...................... No

Practices

Plan Performance Metrics...................... No
Formula Mechanics .... Yes
Benefits...................................... Yes
Allowances (e.g., Car, Mobile Devices, Internet)... Yes
Contests/Spiffs............................... Yes
Long-Term Incentives (e.g., Stock, RSU).......... Yes

Compensation Data

	Base Salary	Incentive Earnings	Total Compensation
Target	Yes	Yes	Yes
Actual	Yes	Yes	Yes

Major Sales/Customer Contact Job Families Featured in the Survey

Store and Sales Management, Visual Merchandising/Presentation, Merchandising Processing, Warehousing/Distribution/Transportation, Inventory/Logistics/Planning, Purchasing, Customer Service, Market/Advertising/Promotion, Indirect/Online/Internet Sales, Finance/Risk Management, Loss Prevention/Security, Human Resources, Facilities Support and Real Estate, Administration-Store Level, Franchise Sales/Operations, IT Systems, Store Operations/Communications, Executive/Senior Management, Pharmacy, Photography, Beauty/Fragrance, Optical, Grocery and Restaurant

Western Management Group

Sales and Service Compensation Survey
237 West Main Street, Los Gatos, CA 95030
(408) 399-4900
www.wmgnet.com

Survey Overview

The survey collects data for key Sales and Service positions in the Consumer Products, High-Technology Commercial and Media industries. Jobs include sales forces directly to end-users or retailers, business-to-business or indirectly through channels. Media industry and sales support jobs for companies that sell as space have been added to the survey. Data collected includes Total Cash Compensation in the form of Actual earned and Targeted Base Pay, Sales Incentives and Non-Sales Variable Pay for the previous and current sales plan. Industry product and revenue level breakouts are available.

Survey Editors

Toni McGrath, toni@wmgnet.com
(408) 399-4900, ext. 229

General Information

Industries Covered

Consumer Products, High-Technology, Commercial and Media Industries

Survey Specifications

Range of Revenue of Reporting Companies....... $33M–$163B
Frequency of Survey Updates .... Annual/Specific Date
Annual Publication Date .... July
First Year of Publication........................ 1985
Restrictions .... None
Data Delivery Methods .... Paper, Electronic/Soft Copy, Online
Non-Participant Report Available .... (Left Blank)
Custom Reporting............................. Standard Reporting, Online Access/User Defined
Data from World Regions .... North America
Number of Companies.......................... 150
Number of Sales Jobs 120
Data Submitted .... Incumbent Level
Sales Volume by Job Title....................... No

Practices

Plan Performance Metrics. . . . . No
Formula Mechanics . . . . Yes
Benefits . . . . Yes
Allowances (e.g., Car, Mobile Devices, Internet) . . . Yes
Contests/Spiffs . . . . Yes
Long-Term Incentives (e.g., Stock, RSU) . . . . Yes

Compensation Data

	Base Salary	Incentive Earnings	Total Compensation
Target	Yes	Yes	Yes
Actual	Yes	Yes	Yes

Major Sales/Customer Contact Job Families Featured in the Survey

General Sales, Product Specialty Sales, Retail Account Management, Government Sales, Business Development, Inside Sales, Media Sales, Sales Administration, Sales Automation, Sales Forecasting, Remote Support, Field Service, Education and Systems Engineering

Willis Towers Watson

2018 General Industry Sales, Marketing and Communications Compensation Survey Report—U.S.

WillisTowersWatson

44 South Broadway, 13th Floor,
White Plains, New York 10601
(800) 645-5771
www.wtwdataservices.com

Survey Overview

With the latest data offered by the *General Industry Sales, Marketing and Communications Compensation Survey Report*, you can ensure that your organization's compensation plan encourages your sales, marketing and communications teams to perform at optimum levels.

This survey report is a subset of the General Industry Middle Management, Professional and Support Compensation Survey Report—U.S. covering all your nonexecutive sales, marketing and communication jobs.

The 2018 survey report includes: compensation data reported by 890 organizations on more than 253,000 incumbents across all industries as well as straightforward leveling methodology for matching incumbents, covering sales jobs at all levels and industries.

New in 2019, the *Sales Compensation and Design Survey Report—U.S.* will focus exclusively on jobs directly involved in the sales function. Contact us for more information.

Survey Contact

Client Care, wtwusdata@willistowerswatson.com
(800) 645-5771

General Information

Industries Covered

Banking and Finance, Durable Goods, Health Care, Nondurable Goods, Retail, Services, Utilities and Energy

Survey Specifications

Range of Revenue of Reporting Companies....... $20M–$70B
Frequency of Survey Updates .... Annual/Specific Date
Annual Publication Date........................ September
First Year of Publication........................ Over 10 Years
Restrictions .... None
Data Delivery Methods .... Online

Non-Participant Report Available . . . . Yes
Custom Reporting. . . . . Standard Reporting
Data from World Regions . . . . North America
Number of Companies. 890
Number of Sales Jobs . . . . Nearly 100 Function/Level combinations and 29 Disciplines
Data Submitted . . . . Incumbent Level
Sales Volume by Job Title. . . . . No

Practices

Plan Performance Metrics. . . . . No
Formula Mechanics . . . . No
Benefits . . . . No
Allowances (e.g., Car, Mobile Devices, Internet) . . . No
Contests/Spiffs . . . . No
Long-Term Incentives (e.g., Stock, RSU) . . . . No

Compensation Data

	Base Salary	Incentive Earnings	Total Compensation
Target	No	Yes	Yes
Actual	Yes	Yes	Yes

Major Sales/Customer Contact Job Families Featured in the Survey

Account/Relationship Management, Bid Management, Client Service Delivery Management, Channel Sales, Direct Sales, Government Sales, Large Deal Acquisition Sales, New Account Acquisition Sales, Remote Sales, Sales Support and Administration, Technical Sales Support

SALES COMPENSATION AUTOMATION SOLUTIONS VENDOR GUIDE

Reprinted with permission from OpenSymmetry
www.opensymmetry.com

SALES COMPENSATION ADMINISTRATION VENDORS

Sales compensation administration software and service providers use powerful administration tools to track, report and model sales compensation transactions. Use this list of vendors to locate and assess the right administration software to help manage your pay program.

IN THIS SECTION

- Overview
- Vendors Listing

Acknolwedgment

This listing is updated each year by OpenSymmetry, which graciously allows us to reprint its vendor listing in this section.

OVERVIEW

The Sales Performance Management (SPM) market continues to grow. According to Gartner Research's 2019 Magic Quadrant for Sales Performance Management (SPM), the $950 million SPM software market continues yearly growth of 13% and is expected to reach $1.4 billion by 2022. SPM is a critical component of a sales organization's core enablement solutions because it provides the link between business strategy and selling behavior. The footprint of SPM is broadening from just compensating sales representatives to driving a more holistic approach. This includes sales talent acquisition through talent development, support for sales process, incentive design and administration, and the management of territories and quotas all in one solution. These integrated applications help enterprises improve the organization, direction and motivation of sales teams in order to achieve sustained improvements in growth and profitability.

With dozens of SPM solutions in the market, selecting the right solution or combination of solutions can be a complex and time-consuming task. The SPM Vendor Guide has been prepared by OpenSymmetry to introduce the leading suppliers of SPM systems and solutions.

As you read this guide, OpenSymmetry has four recommendations:

- Have a clear vision of the future state you desire to achieve. SPM technology is the enabler, but the design, process and approach need to be aligned.
- Automate incentive design in a way that will drive and reward the right behaviors from your sales team and modeled expected outcomes.
- Establish a realistic business case. It's not uncommon for organizations to have a robust platform that is much bigger than what is needed to achieve desired results.
- Have a rigorous selection process. This is a multiyear investment, requiring the right planning upfront.

The SPM software vendors included in this review were selected based on their customer base, corporate recognition and contribution to the field of SPM. Each has significant qualities within their services or software that should be reviewed when assessing the purchase of a solution.

Inclusion of vendors in this guide does not constitute endorsement or recommendation of any listed vendors. OpenSymmetry has not evaluated, prequalified or certified these vendors.

About OpenSymmetry

OpenSymmetry provides end-to-end sales performance management consulting services, from strategy work and data services to implementation and post-implementation services. With over 2 million payees enabled by OS solutions, OpenSymmetry is committed to creating the best possible user experience for sales technology solutions and enabling clients to become sustainable in terms of sales performance management, whether through operational self-sufficiency or through OS-managed systems.

Since 2004, OpenSymmetry has completed over 1,500 successful SPM projects for more than 500 clients ranging from SMBs to enterprise-level companies across four continents. Headquartered in Austin, Texas, OpenSymmetry has been recognized by Inc. as one of the 50 Best Workplaces in 2016 and 2017, and the Inc. 5000 Fastest Growing Private Companies in the U.S. for seven years in a row.

Disclosure Note: OpenSymmetry is an integration partner with the following software companies:

Anaplan	IBM	Oracle	SAP	Xactly

Anaplan

Date Founded: 2006	**Location:** San Francisco	**Phone:** (415) 742-8199
Employees: 1,300+	**Revenue:** $240M+	**Web:** anaplan.com

Anaplan (NYSE: PLAN) is pioneering the category of Connected Planning. Large and fast-growing global enterprises use the Anaplan solution to connect people, data and plans across the business, enabling real-time planning and decision-making in rapidly changing business environments. Anaplan was recognized by Gartner as a Leader in the 2019 Magic Quadrant for Sales Performance Management report for the third consecutive year.

Anaplan for Sales delivers a dynamic sales performance management (SPM) and sales effectiveness solution that empowers sales leaders to innovate the ways they sell. By connecting the entire sales strategy on a single platform, Anaplan gives sales leaders the power to anticipate market changes and act accordingly, while keeping sales objectives aligned to company goals. Leaders and executives can plan, predict and model the performance of the entire sales organization and improve alignment across teams of any size. Anaplan customers increase the value of their existing CRM systems by motivating the right sales behaviors, modeling future performance and optimizing sales activities across the enterprise. By coordinating these go-to-market processes on a single platform, Anaplan confers a unique competitive advantage that helps companies increase revenue, drive growth and confidently arm their sales teams, all while easily connecting with other enterprise systems.

Average # of Payees	Undisclosed
Primary Markets	Telecommunications, retail, pharmaceuticals, technology, CPG, manufacturing, insurance, oil and gas, financial services, life sciences
Delivery Model	SaaS
Total # of Participants	Undisclosed
Client Base	1000+
Managed Services	Yes
Training	Online classes/certification
Support	Live chat, email and phone
Pricing Model	Subscription-based, license per user
Technology	Patented HyperBlock architecture combines the best of relational, in-memory columnar, and cell-driven data models to deliver a powerful calculation engine in the cloud. The Anaplan platform integrates with enterprise systems including Salesforce, Informatica, MuleSoft, Dell Boomi, SnapLogic, Tableau and DocuSign

Sample Customers	DocuSign, HPE, Intel, Intuitive Surgical, Lexmark, McAfee, Motorola, Red Hat, Rogers Communications, Tableau, Telus, Tyco, VMware
Additional Offerings	Finance: strategic planning; budgeting and forecasting; operational planning; financial consolidation and corporate reporting. Supply chain: product portfolio management; demand planning; supply planning; sales and operations planning; strategic policy management.

IBM (IBM SPM/ICM)

Date Founded: 1911	**Location:** Armonk, NY	**Phone:** (914) 499-1900
Employees: 351,656	**Revenue:** $79.59B (2018)	**Web:** ibm.biz/ibm_spm

IBM Sales Performance Management (SPM) continues to be positioned in the Leaders quadrant of the Gartner 2019 Magic Quadrant for Sales Performance Management. The solution is comprised with capabilities to help organizations improve sales performance and operations with better incentive compensation plan management and smarter sales territories and quota administration. Organizations gain faster insights with data discover and advanced analytics capabilities through IBM Watson (i.e., Artificial Intelligence (AI), Machine Learning (ML) and Natural Language Processing (NLP)).

IBM Sales Performance Management (SPM)—including incentive compensation management (ICM), and territory and quota management can be deployed as a SaaS or on-premise offering. Combined with IBM Planning Analytics functionality, organizations have a comprehensive solution for sales planning, sales management and sales analytics. ICMobile enables access to sales metrics and reports, on any mobile device, at any time.

IBM Incentive Compensation Management (ICM) is a highly scalable solution that enables companies to automate the process of calculating, reporting & analyzing variable-based pay. IBM ICM provides tools and information for sales reps—ensuring accuracy and efficiency. Managers and administrators can take control of their operations, eliminate surprises and make better strategic choices for their variable incentive programs.

IBM Incentive Compensation Management has proven capabilities for handling very large transaction volumes and compensation complexity. In 2018, the user interface (UI) was updated for both the administer and end-users and now offers premium performance options for large and complex model calculation that requires speed and flexibility. Product development includes a client-driven roadmap that is facilitated through IBM Design Thinking workshops—giving customers a voice to help shape the solution to include capabilities that are most important to them. This is a unique strategy that gives customers an interactive opportunity to work with and directly affect the future functionality of the product.

Average # of Payees	100 to 5,000+; largest customer has over 30,000 payees
Primary Markets	Banking, insurance, telecom, life sciences, retail, industrial and others
Delivery Model	SaaS or on premise, enterprise or mid-market

Total # of Participants	N/A
Client Base	N/A
Managed Services	Yes
Training	Online certification/classes, On-site training offerings
Support	Online and phone, worldwide
Pricing Model	For cloud: subscription pricing based on payees. For on premise: perpetual license fee based on payees, plus annual maintenance fee. For both: implementation fee based on statement of work
Technology	Uses Microsoft SQL database, C# and Java, Spark
Sample Customers	Facebook, T-Mobile, Sprint, Capital One, EarthLink, Getty Images, PayPal, Kohl's, Samsung, Elavon
Additional Offerings	IBM Watson (i.e., artificial intelligence (AI), machine learning (ML) and natural language processing (NLP), IBM Planning Analytics (for planning, scenario modeling & forecasting)

Iconixx

Date Founded: 2010	**Location:** Austin, TX	**Phone:** (877) 426-6499
Employees: 100+	**Revenue:** $10M+	**Web:** iconixx.com

Iconixx offers an enterprise-class sales performance management solution enabling organizations to align their corporate strategy and planning with sales execution. Our highly configurable and scalable, cloud-based solution allows for improved operational efficiencies delivering commission payout accuracy with multiple currencies, plan modeling and optimization, quota and territory management, dependable forecasting, advanced analytics and regulatory compliance. Organizations are able to budget and plan more efficiently, increase sales productivity, improve overall profitability by automating, analyzing and optimizing commission and incentive processes with Iconixx.

Iconixx Sales™: A sales performance management (SPM) solution that makes it simple to design, configure and manage complex sales compensation plans. Iconixx Sales delivers value with: a native workflow engine, native territory management, pre-configured business rules and formulas library, configurable role-based dashboards, self-service analytical capabilities, compliance through a complete audit trail, accrual and forecasts of total incentive compensation expenses based upon historical trends with seasonality factors, and analysis of plan effectiveness with "what-if" modeling and payout forecasting.

The Iconixx ICM system can process the data set below in under one hour using a standard cloud production environment with no pre-processing, added costs or additional hardware for acceleration:

- 100,000 payees
- 20 million transactions
- 20 separate compensation plans
- 5 hierarchy levels of roll-up crediting
- 3 components per compensation plan
- 1 hour of less computation time
- 0 pre-processing, additional costs, extra hardware, errors or gimmicks

Iconixx Incentive™: An incentive compensation management (ICM) tool that easily manages complex quarterly and annual bonus programs, discretionary awards, MBOs and other variable incentive plans for the entire organization.

Iconixx Merit™: A solution to easily design, create and manage complex merit increase processes requiring workflow driven approvals and budget management.

Average # of Payees	100 to 100,000+
Primary Markets	Insurance, telecommunications, retail, technology, financial services, manufacturing, mortgage, life sciences, health care, communications, software
Delivery Model	SaaS
Total # of Participants	100,000+
Managed Services	Yes (internal team and partners)
Training	Classroom, virtual and on-site training for an Iconixx Compensation Administrator Certification
Support	Phone
Pricing Model	Subscription model (SaaS)
Technology	Cloud technology accessible through standard web browser
Sample Customers	Scholastic, Randstad, CBS, Datacolor, Raymond James, Phonak, Instrument Management Services, DISA Global, HUB International, Thule, WOW, Equipment Depot, First Bank, Bioventus
Additional Offerings	Business outsourcing services, technical support solutions, full business process outsourcing, expert services

Optymyze

Date Founded: 2013	Location: Global with resources in the North America, EMEA and APAC	Phone: (484) 490-9090 (USA)
Employees: 320+	Revenue: $70+ million	Web: optymyze.com

Optymyze transforms sales operations into a strategic competitive advantage–from improving individual business processes to building Centers of Excellence for sales operations management. Optymyze enables sales improvements with a set of integrated, no-code, highly scalable cloud platforms that help sales organizations easily and quickly adapt to change—including platforms for sales performance management (including sales compensation, quotas, territories and objectives), sales data management (including data repository and ETL management), application development (including enterprise planning, and reporting and analytics). With enabling cloud platforms and hundreds of experts in sales operations and business process management, Optymyze has built a solid track record of client success by enabling customers to:

- Deliver Rapid Impact
    - Optymyze eliminates risks and accelerates time to value by including best-in-class apps, setup services, operational support and cloud services in one annual subscription fee
- Adapt to Change
    - Through ongoing engagement, Optymyze provides strategic vision, helps companies continuously prioritize needs and enables them to rapidly adapt to change
- Expand as You Need
    - Optymyze goes beyond sales compensation and sales performance management to improve all aspects of sales operations

Optymyze was again named a leader in the Gartner 2019 Magic Quadrant for Sales Performance Management and achieved the highest score of all the vendors in each of the four Sales Performance Management (SPM) Use Cases in the Gartner 2019 Critical Capabilities for Sales Performance Management report. In addition, Optymyze received perfect 5.0 scores for Data Transformation (ETL) and Audit processes and is referenced as the vendor providing the "best customer experience."

Although its roots are in SPM, Optymyze has created a new market for sales operations management, rooted in our no-code data and end-user app development platforms—all part of one fully integrated solution. Companies looking for an SPM solution are often shopping for the wrong thing and missing out on the opportunity to make a bigger impact on their sales force productivity and sales effectiveness.

Average # of Payees	200 to over 100,000+
Primary Markets	Largest clients are in insurance, financial services, life sciences, banking, telecom, technology, manufacturing, distribution and retail; however, Optymyze serves all industries
Delivery Model	Cloud application deployments utilize AWS, with the associated global elasticity and scalability for both in-memory and batch processing
Pricing Model	Annual subscription fee includes setup services, operational support and cloud services
Technology	Browser-based, enterprise-scale cloud applications for managing sales operations. Platform as a service for building mobile apps for iOS and Android. Data repository integrates with Oracle, SAP, Salesforce, MS Dynamics and other ERP, CRM, HR, accounting, marketing, legacy systems and third-party data providers such as NIPR and IMS
Sample Customers	GE, McKesson, J&J, Office Depot, Alcon, Charter Communications, Zurich, Thomson Reuters, Charles Schwab, Cigna, Estee Lauder, PepsiCo, Sunovion, Sasktel, Desjardins (Canada), Maxis (Malaysia), and Telenet (Belgium)
Additional Offerings	In addition to core SPM solutions, Optymyze goes beyond sales performance management to improving any aspect of sales operations through its no-code data management and application development platforms.

Oracle

Date Founded: 1977	**Location:** Redwood Shores, CA	**Phone:** (800) 633-0738
Employees: 138,000+	**Revenue:** $37.728B (2017)	**Web:** oracle.com

Oracle Corporation provides a range of tools for managing business data, supporting business operations and facilitating collaboration and application development.

Oracle Sales Performance Management (SPM), which includes robust incentive compensation capabilities, is a component of the Oracle Engagement Cloud service and provides an integrated suite of rich sales planning tools allowing sales executives, managers and operations staff to collaborate and quickly deploy effective sales, territory and quota plans. Additionally, Oracle Sales Planning for Engagement Cloud is available for customers that wish to tap into advanced planning capabilities that draw from historical financial actuals and use powerful planning methodologies to quickly and easily create plans based on even the most complex statistical projections, complex formulas and custom metrics. By aligning the company's business and sales strategy, Oracle SPM provides the means to motivate the sales organization to achieve their sales objectives. Oracle SPM streamlines the rollout of new plan initiatives ranging from simple to complex, provides productivity tools to reduce administrative costs, generates intelligence-based plans, and presents relevant business insights to drive sales performance.

Oracle SPM, including incentive compensation, enables organizations to define measurable business objectives (MBO's) and model their compensation plans that align with their business strategy and sales performance goals. Organizations can leverage the solution to motivate their own sales force, service teams, third-party representatives, customers/suppliers, resellers, partners or any other compensated party using various monetary and non-monetary rewards such as commission, bonus, SPIFs, prizes, leaderboards and more. Ensuring that sales reps are consistently and constantly informed, each sales rep has access to interactive sales performance reports with real-time information on their performance to quota, earnings to target incentive and objective achievements. Sales reps are presented their potential commission and attainment on each opportunity, ensuring they are working those opportunities that are aligned most closely with Sales Strategy. Sales Performance data is also available in real-time on the go by accessing the Mobile Commissions application on their mobile devices.

Oracle Sales Performance Management is available with multiple editions of Oracle Engagement Cloud, and is fully integrated with other Oracle CRM/ERP/HCM applications and other third-party systems. Oracle Sales Planning Cloud is available as a separate, advanced solution, which is designed to work seamlessly with Oracle Engagement Cloud and Oracle EPM Cloud.

Average # of Payees	1,000 to 100,000+
Primary Markets	High-tech/manufacturing, retail, financial services, telecommunications, automotive, health care/pharma sales and more
Delivery Model	SaaS
Total # of Participants	N/A
Client Base	N/A
Managed Services	Yes
Training	Online classes/on-site classes/certification
Support	Online and phone
Pricing Model	Per user per month
Technology	Oracle DB, OBIEE, Oracle Engagement Cloud, Oracle EPM Cloud, Oracle HCM Cloud
Sample Customers	Motorola, Avaya, Emirates NBD, General Electric, Mazda Motors, Australia Finance Group, Priceline, Symantec
Additional Offerings	Oracle offers hundreds of applications, ranging from its well-known database, to its suite of cloud application services, platform as a service and infrastructure as a service.

SAP

Date Founded: 1972	**Location:** Global	**Phone:** (866) 812-5244
Employees: 96,000+	**Revenue:** $29.1B	**Web:** SAP.com

SAP is the market leader in enterprise application software, helping companies of all sizes and in all industries run at their best: 77% of the world's transaction revenue touches an SAP system. Our machine learning, Internet of Things (IoT) and advanced analytics technologies help turn customers' businesses into intelligent enterprises. Our end-to-end suite of applications and services enables our customers to operate profitably, adapt continuously and make a difference.

SAP Commissions (formerly CallidusCloud) delivers an end-to-end Sales Performance Management solution and has been recognized as a leader in the Gartner Magic Quadrant for Sales Performance Management for six consecutive years.

Average # of Payees	Not disclosed
Primary Markets	Financial services, high-tech, insurance, manufacturing, life sciences, telecommunications and more
Delivery Model	SaaS
Total # of Participants	Not disclosed
Client Base	Not disclosed
Managed Services	Yes
Training	E-learning, virtual instructor-led, on-site are available with classes and certifications
Support	Chat, phone, IM and email, to a designated technical support engineer
Pricing Model	Per payee per month
Technology	SAP Commissions runs on an SAP HANA Database Server with an Apache Tomcat application server. SAP Commissions, intelligent add-on extends core compensation functionality with territory and quota management and uses proprietary technology for embedded analytics and artificial intelligence. SAP Commissions integrates with SAP applications and all major 3rd party CRM, ERP and HR systems like Salesforce.com, Oracle/NetSuite, Microsoft, and Workday
Sample Customers	Verizon, EMC, ADT, Aetna, AXA, DirecTV, JPMorgan Chase, Lenovo, MetroPCS
Additional Offerings	SAP Sales Cloud provides a full suite of sales capabilities including CRM, Retail Execution, Pipeline Management, Configure Price Quote, Contract Lifecycle Management, Sales Enablement, Litmos Sales Training, Intelligent Sales Forecasting, Producer Lifecycle Management, Revenue Recognition, Subscription Billing, Entitlement Management, Data Mediation, Coaching and more.

Xactly

Date Founded: 2005	**Location:** San Jose, CA	**Phone:** (866) 469-2285
Employees: >600	**Revenue:** Privately Held, not reported	**Web:** xactlycorp.com

Xactly unleashes the human potential of sales teams by dramatically improving their sales planning, territory optimization and incentive compensation processes. With its distinct cloud applications suite and unique empirical sales performance data set collected over 14 years, Xactly increases sales productivity and revenue growth. The value of our interconnected suite is captured in the user's ability to Plan, Execute and Optimize their sales performance management operations:

PLAN: Empowering companies with a data-driven approach ensuring optimally staffed sales organizations, equally distributed quotas, balanced territories and benchmarked comp plans to drive 15% increase in revenues, 20% improvement in productivity and 10% greater quota attainment

- Xactly Sales Planning—Eliminate guesswork from resource planning to hit sales targets and drive top-line growth using analytics and artificial intelligence (AI).
- Xactly Advanced Quota Planning—complex quota planning solution supporting account-based and decentralized quota planning to create fair and equitable quotas for the enterprise.
- Xactly AlignStar—territory design and planning software to visualize, analyze and optimize sales territories
- Xactly Benchmarking—Empower sales leaders to proactively monitor incentive compensation programs. Compare performance in teams both company and industry wide. Ensure incentive programs retain top performers, align sales behavior and reduce undesired rep attrition.

EXECUTE: Driving desired sales behaviors through tailor made incentives and compensation plans. Automating crediting and commission calculations driving error-free commission payouts, increase forecast accuracy to 99.6% and lowering error disputes to less than 0.5%. Seamlessly integrate and comply commission expense accounting with latest ASC 606/IFRS 15 revenue standards

- Xactly Incent, Xactly Express & Xactly SimplyComp—Drive sales behaviors with error-free incentive compensation, increase operational efficiencies and improve productivity with on-demand commissions visibility.

- Xactly Commission Expense Accounting—Manage your commission accounting process and ensure compliance under the new ASC 606 (IFRS 15) revenue recognition standard.
- Xactly Objectives—Drive performance and revenue by aligning employee behaviors with company goals through employee performance management software to assign and track MBO plans.

OPTIMIZE: Optimizing sales performance with near real-time data insights and leveraging true AI/ML to predict sales rep attrition to proactively retain top performing reps. Improving sales ramp and productivity to increase win rates by 15%.

- Xactly Insights—The Sales Performance Management (SPM) industry's first-ever AI platform to provide the latest incentive compensation insights based on real pay and performance data to ensure competitive pay, effective plans and strategically aligned sales teams.
- Xactly Connect—Automate and streamline the critical flow of data across your entire sales performance management (SPM) suite with an open, standards-based data integration platform.

Average # of Payees	Varies by product, ranging from 10 to 10s of thousands of payees
Primary Markets	Manufacturing, retail, wholesale, business services, financial services, technology
Delivery Model	100% SaaS
Total # of Participants	Over 1,600 customers
Managed Services	Yes, through partners
Training	Online, at Xactly, or on-site classes
Support	Online, phone, specialist
Pricing Model	Per payee per month
Technology	True multi-tenant SaaS
Sample Customers	Salesforce, Viega, Workday, Cox Automotive, Hyatt, National Instruments, OpenText, Wood Maxkenzie, ServiceMax, SThree, Insperity, Docusign, Carestream, Cascade Orthopedic Supply
Additional Offerings	Xactly offers incentive compensation through Xactly Incent™, Xactly Express™ and Xactly SimpleComp™. The complete suite includes Xactly Sales Planning, Xactly Advanced Quota Planning, Xactly Alignstar, Xactly Benchmarking, Xactly Insights, Xactly Commission Expense Accounting, Xactly Objectives, and Xactly Connect.

Acquisitions

Xactly made two acquisitions in 2018. The first was Obero, a fast-growing sales performance management (SPM) company based in Canada. Obero has developed a number of key solutions, including rich sales planning and ASC 606/ IFRS 15 capabilities that are now part of Xactly. The second was OpsPanda, which delivers an AI-based sales resource and capacity planning solution. With these two acquisitions, Xactly now delivers a continuous and end-to-end, data-driven sales planning solution within our market-leading sales performance management (SPM) portfolio.

SALES COMPENSATION EDUCATION RESOURCES

EDUCATIONAL RESOURCES

Sales compensation is a constantly evolving topic. Use these resources to help learn and expand your knowledge about sales compensation concepts and principles.

IN THIS SECTION

- Courses
- Webinars
- Books

WORLDATWORK COURSES

Creating Sales Compensation Principles—A Stakeholder's Guide *Four-Hour Two-Day Seminar*

Elements of Sales Compensation *Two-Day Seminar*

Sales Compensation 101: Understanding Sales Compensation Essentials *Two-Day Seminar*

Sales Compensation Design—Developing Incentive Plans That Work *One-Day Seminar*

WORLDATWORK WEBINARS

Achieving World-Class Sales Compensation Design: How to Assess Your Plan Performance

Lessons From Maslow: The Hierarchy of SPM Needs

Your Career in Sales Compensation: The What, Why and How

BOOKS

"Compensating the Sales Force," (Third edition), David J. Cichelli, 2017, McGraw-Hill, ISBN: 9781260026818

"Drive," 2011, Daniel H. Pink, Riverhead Books, ISBN: 9781594484803

"Game the Plan: Every Sales Rep's Dream; Every CFO's Nightmare," Christopher Cabrera, 2014, River Grove Books, ISBN: 9781938416545

"Handbook of Compensation & Benefits Formulas, Featuring Dianne Auld's Excel Tips, 2nd Edition," 2016, WorldatWork Press, ISBN: 9781579633776

"Market Pricing: Methods to the Madness," 2002, WorldatWork Press, ISBN: 1579631134

"Sales Compensation Essentials: A Field Guide for the HR Professional, 2nd Edition," Jerry Colletti, Mary Fiss, Ted Briggs, S. Sands, 2014, WorldatWork Press, ISBN: 9781579633615

"Sales Compensation Made Simple," Joseph DiMisa, 2010, WorldatWork Press, ISBN: 9781579632144

"Sales Compensation Math," Jerry Colletti, Mary Fiss, J. Mark Davis, 2008, WorldatWork Press, ISBN: 9781579631864

"Sales Compensation Solutions," Andris Zoltners, Prabhakant Sinha, Chad Albrecht, Steve Marley, Sally Lorimer, 2017, ZS Associates, Inc., ISBN: 9780998934709

"The Complete Guide to Sales Force Incentive Compensation: How to Design and Implement Plans That Work," Andris A. Zoltners, Prabhakant Sinha, Sally E. Lorimer, 2006, AMACOM, ISBN: 9780814473245

"The Future of Sales Compensation," Chad Albrecht, Steve Marley, 2016, ZS Associates, Inc., ISBN: 9780985343651

"What Your CEO Needs to Know About Sales Compensation: Connecting the Corner Office to the Front Line," Mark Donnolo, 2013, AMACOM, ISBN: 9780814432273

CASE STUDIES

SALES COMPENSATION CASE STUDIES

Learn how other companies examine and update their sales compensation practices with case studies from the Alexander Group's client engagements. Our mid-career consultants prepare these case studies; they add to our catalog of hundreds to thousands of client engagements.

IN THIS SECTION

This year's case studies include the following industries:

- Financial Services
- Hospitality
- Manufacturing (2)
- Media (2)
- Pharmaceutical Distribution

Industry: Financial Services

FINANCIAL SERVICES PROVIDER ACQUIRES COMPANY AND ALIGNS SALES COMPENSATION PROGRAMS

By Yang Liu

Project Identification

The Company is a provider of payment solutions, which includes a suite of customer life-cycle solutions to its customers across multiple channels. It operates in three segments: small business services, financial services and direct checks. Product and service offerings consist of checks, forms, accessories and other products. The small business services segment provides printed forms to small businesses. The financial services segment provides products and services to financial institution clients and offers financial technology (fintech) solutions. Finally, the direct checks segment is a direct-to-consumer check supplier. It also offers fraud protection and security services, online and offline payroll services, and electronic checks.

The Company is in different growth phases across its business segments. The small business services segment is a slow growth segment featuring an annual growth of 3% year-over-year (YoY). The financial services segment is similar at 2% growth YoY. While the direct checks segment is a declining business featuring an annual loss of 4% YoY. The Company hired the Alexander Group (AGI) to assess, design and implement sales compensation plans. In addition, the project featured an assessment of the Company's customer coverage model. The Company wanted to reduce losses in its checks business, while increasing wallet share and brand recognition in its fintech offerings. The Company needed sellers to remain engaged with check buyers, while cultivating relationships with new buyers for its fintech offerings. Strategic, product-specific objectives were important to the client.

Industry Profile

The financial services and fintech markets are converging as more financial institutions seek fintech solutions (in-house or outsourced). More consumers are seeking fintech solutions from non-traditional financial institutions, e.g., online-only banks. The Company's financial services segment must execute a "land-and-expand" strategy with both traditional and non-traditional financial institutions.

Recently, the Company acquired a company to increase its capability in the fintech offering. This new company uses targeted data-driven campaigns to deliver marketing solutions for financial institutions. Re-targeting software allows the Company to follow potential financial services customers as they shop for offerings such as mortgages and loans. Clientele can track a consumer's search and browsing patterns in order to deliver custom, targeted ads along the way. The Company's coverage model segments by customer tier for its client management (account management) organization. The client manager role features steps from community client manager to senior client manager, and each step is responsible for covering a given customer tier. The Company segments the sales executives, who sell fintech products, by product offering. Sales executives take ownership of a primary and secondary offering by providing expertise and serving customers across all tiers based on that offering. The recently acquired company's sales directors and relationship managers sell only one product and are segmented by customer tiers.

The Company segments its customers into six tiers. Tier one customers include top banks and financial institutions. This segment is the highest priority for the Company and the top target for fintech solutions. Tiers two and three include large credit unions and larger nontraditional financial institutions, e.g., electronic-only banks and organizations. Tiers four and five include smaller regional banks and regional credit unions. Finally, tier six is comprised of small, community banks and credit unions. These customers often have only one or two locations. The final customer segment consists of the newly acquired company's customers.

Primary Jobs and Performance Metrics

Title	Job Abstract	Performance Metrics
Sales Executive (SE) (All Product Lines)	Cultivate, drive and close sales opportunities within assigned accounts and/or territories. Partner with client managers and other roles as required. Cross-sell into existing clients when CMs provide qualified leads	• Fintech product sales total contract value (80%) • In-year revenue (20%) • New logo modifier (Multiplier)
Client Manager (CM) (All Tiers)	Maintain and expand client relationships through ongoing engagement, assuring satisfaction and uncovering additional potential to create value. Generate qualified leads to hand over to the SE team	• Check retentions (80%) • Fintech product sales total contract value (20%)

Newly Acquired Company's Sales Director	Cultivate, drive and close sales opportunities within assigned accounts and/or territories. Partner with relationship managers and other roles as required	• Fintech product sales total contract value (80%) • In-year revenue (20%)
Newly Acquired Company's Relationship Manager	Maintain and expand client relationships through ongoing engagement, assuring satisfaction and uncovering additional potential to create value. Qualify leads and close up-sell opportunities in existing clients	• Gross revenue (100%)

Project Solution and Outcome

AGI assisted the Company to simplify its sales compensation plan designs to focus on corporate growth initiatives. Expanding the fintech business in new and existing customers was an important strategic focus. Retaining check customers and protecting price points was a secondary focus for the group.

The key contributions AGI made to the Company's sales compensation plan were:

- **Significantly increased upside pay for above-goal achievement in sales executives.** Previous plans featured a flat individual commission rate for fintech product sales. The existing plans also featured a one-time fixed dollar bonus for annual quota attainment. AGI determined the year-end bonus did not motivate the sellers. AGI found that the budget allocated to the year-end bonus programs, as well as other inconsistent key sales objectives, could be reallocated to increase the individual commission rate (ICR). The design team chose to double the ICR after quota attainment as a new plan design. This design element significantly increased the upside pay for above-goal achievement. The cost-impact analysis predicted similar compensation cost of sales in the new plan designs, thus new plan design remained cost neutral.
- **Improved fintech new logos focus through use of modifiers.** Previous plan design did not include a dedicated measure for conversion selling. AGI found that conversion dollars in the fintech space was an important strategic focus for the sales leadership team. The design team came to a consensus that not every dollar was equal to the company. Conversion dollars were more valuable than upsell and renewal dollars. The design team decided to use sales incentive multipliers to incent conversion selling in fintech. The new plan designs placed explicit focus on new logos acquisition for sales executives.

- **Enhanced client manager cross-sales focus.** The existing plans for client managers focused primarily on check retention revenue. Traditionally, check retention selling was a core focus, but sales leadership wanted client managers to expand their role. A key reason client managers were not embracing fintech selling was the lack of proper compensation. AGI identified the right measures and weightings for the new compensation plan. The design team incorporated a fintech sales measure in the role's sales compensation plan. This encourages more cross-selling behavior in the client manager role.

Performance Metrics

Metric	Definition of Metric, Importance and Unique Issues
Fintech Product Sales Total Contract Value	Individual commission rate that ramps (doubles) based on quota attainment and pays on fintech product sales. Each seller's ICR doubles once he/she achieves his/her annual quota. Quota credited on the sales' total contract value
New Logos Modifier (Multiplier)	Modifier (multiplier) that multiplies the fintech product sales measure by 1.5x if sold to a new logo customer
In-Year Revenue	Base commission rate of 4% paid quarterly on achieving quarterly year-to-date fintech product's sales goal
Check Retentions	Quota-based bonus that pays for check retention revenue secured. Above-goal payout paid at an additional 12% of component target incentive for every 1% over goal. No threshold
Gross Revenue	Quota-based bonus that pays for the newly acquired company's gross product revenue from existing clients, secured by the relationship manager. The threshold is 65% and the pay curve has a regressive ramp once the seller achieves beyond 100% quota attainment

Glossary

Compensation Cost of Sales: The actual cost of sales compensation payment (base salaries plus actual target incentive paid) divided by the total sales; expressed as a percentage

Individual Commission Rate (ICR): ICR plans follow bonus formula concepts by providing a unique (individual) commission rate to each seller. This method ensures relative equal payouts for dissimilar size territories by assigning a unique ICR to each seller. Calculate by dividing the (common) target incentive by the unique target sales volume of each territory. In this manner, target performance times the various ICRs will produce the same payout for all incumbents, even though the absolute size of each territory differs

Key Sales Objectives: Individual, team or job-specific sales goals that can change from one performance period to the next

Yang Liu is a manager in the Alexander Group's Chicago office.

Industry: Hospitality

TIMESHARE SALES COMPANY DRIVES LESS-PROFITABLE SALES TO NEW CUSTOMERS TO SUSTAIN LONG-TERM GROWTH

By Mason Ginsberg

Project Identification

The Company is a division of a larger hospitality organization that sells property timeshares to consumers. It struggles with balancing sales to new customers versus profitable sales to existing customers. The company can maximize profitability by devoting its best sales resources to existing customers. Although less profitable, new sales drives the Company's overall growth, the Company must decide on the right headcount allocation and compensation solution to optimize these two customer types.

The Company's sales compensation project included multiple phases. It started with a foundational analysis and assessment of the company's sales and marketing roles. Plan design for these roles followed the assessment, along with implementation. Core project deliverables included an assessment of compensation plans against guiding principles, sales cost and compensation design benchmarks, and sales and marketing compensation plan design. Design phase deliverables included full plan designs for all in-scope sales and marketing roles. Implementation deliverables included plan communication training documents and written plan documents.

Industry Profile

The Company is a vacation ownership business. The timeshare industry has long struggled with the stigma associated with timeshares and their dubious history. The industry has a more refined value proposition and offering. Sellers are responsible for both representing the product's true value and for restoring consumer confidence in the product.

The Company utilizes a direct sales model for its property sales to end-users. Commonly evaluated metrics beyond revenue are number of resorts, number of timeshare units and number of owners. These metrics are important to show not only the financial health of the business, but also the long-term viability. A company with high revenue could be in danger of a sharp decline if its number of owners is low. Businesses measure individual seller success on the amount of revenue that they bring in for vacation ownership properties. Another important metric is the amount of money that they receive from customers as a down payment. Cancellations are more common in this industry than in other industries, and a higher down payment percentage correlates to lower cancellation rates.

Products, Customers, Coverage and List of Jobs

The Company's sales representatives offer one core product, which is vacation home ownership. The Company provides this product to two main customer segments: new owners and existing owners. The Company also uses marketing representatives to generate leads for the sales force. These representatives work either on the Company's property or at other popular local vacation areas and events. The Company's telemarketing representatives work in call centers, handling customer service issues and selling timeshare packages.

Title	Job Abstract	Performance Metrics
Sales Representative (In-House and Front Line)	Sales of timeshare vacation property ownership	1. Per-deal sales volume commission (modifier for owner type and down payment percentage; primary measure) 2. Monthly sales volume commission based on goal attainment (secondary measure)
Sales Manager	First-line sales manager for timeshare vacation property ownership sales representatives	1. Per-deal team sales volume commission (modifier for owner type and down payment percentage; primary measure) 2. Monthly team sales volume commission based on goal attainment (secondary measure)
Marketing Agent	Market timeshare ownership to qualified new owners through tour generation	1. Weekly tour-tiered commission rate based on number of tours 2. Monthly transaction-tiered commission rate based on number of transactions
In-House Marketing Agent	Market timeshare ownership to qualified new owners and existing owners through tour generation	1. Weekly tour volume tiered commission rate based on number of tours and owner type 2. Monthly transaction volume tiered commission rate based on number of transactions and owner type
Telesales Representative	Inside sales of vacation packages or timeshare vacation property ownership	1. Per-deal sales volume commission (modifier for owner type and down payment percentage; primary measure) 2. Monthly sales volume commission based on goal attainment (secondary measure)

Project Solution and Outcome

The Company's sales compensation plans presented different issues depending on the job role. Sales representatives prioritized shortsighted selling behavior at the expense of future profitability. Penetration sales to existing customers are more profitable than conversion sales to new customers and easier for sellers to make. However, new customers are essential to the long-term success of the company, even though the initial return on investment (ROI) is lower. Due to the increased difficulty of such a sale, the Company assigned it a higher commission rate. Unfortunately, the commission rate difference offered was not large enough to drive the desired behavior from the sales force. Top salespeople drifted towards existing owner selling, maximizing their own earning potential and simultaneously putting the Company at risk. Because the immediate impact of this selling activity on the Company's bottom line was positive, a change in the allocation of compensation dollars was difficult to justify.

The original sales representative plan utilized three core performance measures. Those measures were a tiered commission rate per deal, a ramped commission rate paid on monthly sales volume, and an annual sales volume bonus. The new plan incorporated several important decisions made by the design team. First, the plan discarded the annual bonus in order to allocate those compensation dollars to measures that more directly drive behavior. Second, the team made significant changes to the commission rate tiers for the primary per-deal sales volume measure. The delta between the rates paid for existing customers and new customers doubled. The client deliverable also included recommended year-over-year rate changes in order to achieve the Company's stated growth goals while maintaining a fixed cost of sales percentage. Finally, the new design standardized the monthly bonus tier structure for all sellers. Previously, the plan utilized inconsistent numbers of tiers and rates for each tier, which caused earnings inequities despite similar performance. Historical performance data provided the basis for six standardized performance tiers at 50%, 75%, 100%, 125%, 150% and 180% of goal. Upon reaching each tier, the plan pays commission rates of 1%, 2%, 4%, 5%, 7% and 9% respectively. These rates closely resemble the prior version of the plan, keeping disruption and confusion to a minimum.

The Company's marketing roles posed their own set of challenges. The Company allocated the majority of its incentive pay for the marketing agents' plan to tour (visit) volume. The design team kept this measure with slight commission rate tweaks, but the key issue was much more subtle. Marketing agents would sometimes pass to the sales tour, recipients who lacked the financial means to purchase timeshares. Design meeting conversations about this issue led to improved emphasis and language within plan communication documents about lead qualification. The secondary measure was a tiered monthly commission rate paid on net sales volume generated by the tours booked. The design team replaced this measure with a similar tiered monthly commission rate based instead on whether or not a tour results in a purchase. The logic behind this change was simple: A marketer has more control over generating demand for the product than how much that person may spend.

Performance Metrics

Metric	Definition of Metric, Importance and Unique Issues
Deal Volume Commission (With Modifier)	Tiered commission rate for each individual sale based on owner type (new owner vs. existing owner) and amount of total sale price paid as a down payment
Monthly Volume Bonus	Ramped commission rate based on monthly goal attainment percentage of commissionable sales volume

Mason Ginsberg is a manager in the Alexander Group's Chicago office.

Industry: Manufacturing

INDUSTRIAL PACKAGING COMPANY SHIFTS TO COMPENSATION PLANS ALIGNED WITH STRATEGIC OBJECTIVES

By Dashon Catlett

Project Identification

The Company is a leading paper and packaging manufacturer with thousands of employees across the world. The Company manufactures several product types, including fiber packaging, which was the Alexander Group's focus for the sales compensation project.

Within the fiber packaging division, the Alexander Group (AGI) helped redesign the sales compensation plans for the North American segment. The team faced several business issues at the beginning of the project. Recently, the Company acquired a manufacturer and distributor of kraft paper and bags. The Company wanted to ensure a successful integration of the newly acquired company to drive account penetration/profitability and increase North American market share.

The Company asked AGI to develop comprehensive sales compensation plans to compensate growth and profitability to instill a more aggressive attitude among the sales force. The average tenure of the sales force was more than 20 years featuring a high salary, conservative pay mix and a retention-focused direct selling team.

The scope of the project included assessing the current compensation plans for their sales and management roles, as well as designing sales compensation plans for new roles, including key account manager and inside sales representative. This project required AGI to cost-model the plans to ensure fiscal viability. In addition, AGI would develop a transition plan to phase the sales force from the current plans to the new sales compensation plans.

Industry Profile

Market Trends

The paper and packaging industry have experienced a number of key trends. Sustainability and recyclability of products has become a virtual requirement to be a major player in the industry. Increased global environmental concerns have forced market leaders to develop products that are either recyclable or easily biodegradable.

The industry lacks stability due to the high volume of acquisitions, mergers and new product development among small, medium and conglomerate companies. High-expected growth in the Asia Pacific region during the next five years will lead to even more mergers and acquisitions by the large companies within the industry. During the next several years, maximizing share in the current market will lead to exponential growth as the industry continues to expand.

Sales Segments/Channels

One of the Company's competitive advantages is its vertical integration. The organization owns forests and production plants across the world. This allows the company to produce and sell direct to industrial customers, as well as sell through distributors.

Key Industry Performance Metrics:

- Market share
- Gross margin
- Retention
- New product sales

Title	Job Abstract	Performance Metrics
VP of Sales	Responsible for leading the U.S. commercial sales organization and developing the go-to-market strategy to drive profitable sales growth	• Total Sales Volume (Units)–50% (QBB) • Division EBITDA–30% (QBB) • MBOs–20% (QBB)
Region Sales Manager	Responsible for managing the regional P&L (Sales, GM$) across all product categories and customer segments	• Regional Sales Volume (Units)–50% (QBB) • Region Gross Margin \$–30% (QBB) • MBOs–20% (QBB)
Key Account Manager	Responsible for managing assigned key accounts to ensure retention and drive penetration	• Key Account Sales Volume–50% (QBB) • Key Account Gross Margin \$–30% (QBB) • KSOs–20% (QBB)
Sales Executive	Responsible for managing mid-sized accounts within their assigned territory to drive penetration and profitability	• Territory Sales Volume (Units)–65% (QBB) • Territory Gross Margin \$–35% (QBB)
Inside Sales Representative	Responsible for managing inbound/outbound sales calls for house accounts and low value customers	• Sales Volume (Units)–75% (QBB) • KSOs–25% (QBB)

Project Solution and Outcome

During the assessment phase, AGI discovered several key compensation issues that contributed to the misaligned behaviors of the sales force. The first issue involved incumbent target total compensation (TTC) levels and pay mixes. The second issue involved the mechanics and pay curves of the current sales compensation plans. The last sales compensation issue involved the pay and performance periods for the front-line sellers. AGI collected and analyzed data to demonstrate how each of these misalignments tied to the behaviors that the management team wanted to eliminate.

Analysis of current practices revealed that management had allowed TTC levels to inflate over the years for the long-tenured sellers. Average TTC levels were approaching the 90th percentile of AGI's benchmarks. In addition to the high pay levels, the pay mix was too conservative to drive the desired sales behaviors. AGI recommended phasing the sellers to a plan that kept the same TTC for established incumbents, but shifted the pay mix to be more aggressive. In addition, AGI recommended assessing the skills and competencies of the sales force to ensure the highly paid incumbents were equipped with the correct skillset to be successful in the roles moving forward. Finally, newly hired incumbents would see TTC pay levels in line with industry benchmarks and more aggressive pay mixes.

In the current plan, sellers faced the challenge of meeting a 90% threshold before earning incentive payout. Sellers' payouts were also capped at 200% once the incumbent reached 110% of goal. Another issue was the step bonus payout curve, which resulted in individuals being paid the same percentage of their target incentive for performances that varied up to 10%. AGI recommended relaxing the thresholds to mirror the historical performance distributions of the bottom 10% of performers. AGI also replaced the demotivating caps with decelerators. Finally, AGI recommended a shift from a step bonus pay curve to a linear quota-based bonus pay curve.

The organization's annual pay and performance periods didn't align with the sales cycle or the company's future-state objectives. While interviewing the sellers, AGI heard many comments from the sales force about not recalling the sales that drove their payouts at the end of the year. Sellers mentioned how difficult it was to stay motivated for a payday, which can occur up to 365 days after the close of a sale. Instead of receiving the rewards in a timely manner, sellers would lose sight of the rewards and disregard the particulars of their pay plans.

The outcomes mentioned were common. However, the planned implementation needed customization to fit the needs of the resource limited and overall reluctant to change sales organization. For example, AGI and the design team agreed that profitability needed added into the plan. However, instead of measuring on the most granular margin number, which accounts for capital and overhead production costs, the teams decided a more simplistic and trackable margin number only measuring cost of goods sold (COGS) would be more appropriate. Then in subsequent years, the organization would move to the more detailed profitability measure once its systems were better equipped to track the overhead and capital costs.

Performance Metrics

Metrics	Definition of Metric, Importance and Unique Issues
Sales Volume	• Individual or team metric measured in terms of units sold • Historical primary measure used; aligns with operational performance indicators
Gross Margin	• Individual or team metric measured in terms of dollars based on cost of goods sold • Aligns with key objective to drive profitable growth
MBO	• Individual or team metric that measures personal development objectives and quantifiable direct report development
KSO	• Individual metric that measures key activities that facilitate sales

Glossary

Cap: Point at which no additional incentive paid for incremental quota attainment

KSO: Key sales objectives

MBO: Management bonus objectives

Pay Mix: Base salary expressed as a percent of TTC

QBB: Quota-based bonus

Target Incentive: Incentive paid at 100% of goal

Target Total Compensation (TTC): Base salary plus target incentive at 100% of goal

Threshold: Minimum level of performance before incentive payments paid to the sales representative

Upside: Potential earnings for above-target performance

Dashon Catlett is a manager in the Alexander Group's Atlanta office.

Industry: Manufacturing

AFTERMARKET AUTOMOTIVE ACCESSORIES COMPANY INTEGRATES ACQUIRED SALES FORCE

By Devan Cortland

Project Identification

The Company is a growing manufacturer and distributor of branded aftermarket towing and cargo management solutions. It manufactures towing products specializing in custom-fit trailer hitches and custom wiring harnesses. It was quick to embrace the e-commerce sales channel within the specialty equipment automotive aftermarket (SEAA) industry. This positioned the Company to stay ahead of the competition and maintain future growth.

In addition, the Company's strategic acquisitions enabled it to offer additional product offerings. The Company acquired an aftermarket automotive parts manufacturer, as well as a trucking accessories manufacturer. The latter acquisition introduced approximately 40 new field territory sales representatives to integrate into the current go-to-market coverage model. The Alexander Group (AGI) was engaged to optimize EBITDA and avoid ineffective integration pitfalls while developing a new integrated sales organizational structure.

Industry Profile

There are many notable trends/characteristics of the SEAA industry that define the landscape and direction of the industry in the United States. Brand recognition, consumer lifestyle changes and the rise of internet research all have quantitative impacts on the industry's trajectory. According to an industry study performed by the Specialty Equipment Market Association (SEMA), 66% of consumers consider the brand to be either important or very important to their purchasing decision. This sentiment extends to the towing solutions segment, as well as the overall functional accessories aftermarket as brands associated with quality, consistency, speed of delivery and style tend to win over generic alternatives sourced from offshore, low-cost manufacturers.

Secondly, consumers are spending more time outdoors and living active lifestyles. They are choosing to purchase smaller, more fuel-efficient vehicles. According to the Outdoor Industry Association, the outdoor recreation market has grown at an average of 5% per year. In a given year, 141 million Americans participated in outdoor activities and consumers spent $121 billion on related products and services. Likewise, according to WardsAuto, U.S. light vehicle sales have grown at a double-digit pace in recent years. This is great news for the SEAA industry incumbents, as many outdoor activities require external storage and transportation capacity driving sales of towing solutions and complementary accessories.

Finally, the amount of information available via the internet heavily influences end-user buying behavior in the SEAA industry, as well as the manner in which the typical consumer lives his/her life. Historically, consumers have had their hitches installed by professionals, making the towing solutions industry predominantly a "do-it-for-me" market. In recent years, however, consumers have become more self-sufficient by installing their own hitches with detailed instructions and online demonstrations. However, the installation process for most aftermarket automotive parts is still difficult and requires expertise in several different types of tools. The Company responded to this industry trend by manufacturing easily installed hitches and offering custom installation videos for various products via YouTube. Thus, giving the end-user an avenue in which to install product by themselves and appealing to their growing DIY nature.

Distribution Channels

The Company focuses on providing its end-users with quick delivery and widespread availability of its products. With multiple warehouses across the U.S., the Company can ship product to consumers in the U.S. and population centers in Canada within 24 to 48 hours. This represents a significant competitive advantage in the industry. The Company utilizes three-step (the Company to distributor to retailer to end-user), two-step (the Company to retailer to end-user) and direct to consumer (primarily via the Company website) distribution methods.

Products, Customers, Coverage and List of Jobs

Title	Job Abstract	Measures	Mechanic
Inside Sales Support	Inside sales resource who helps with customer relationship management and fulfillment after initial sale and supports territory managers in reaching existing customers more frequently	Product Revenue (100% weight)	Step Bonus Formula
Territory Managers	Hunter/farmer field sales resource who sells product through direct, distributor and lower-tier e-commerce channels	Product Revenue (100% weight)	Step Bonus Formula
Regional Sales Managers	First-line sales managers responsible for maintaining the regional P&L	Product Revenue (100% weight)	Step Bonus Formula

Key Performance Metrics

- Product Revenue

Project Solution and Outcome

The Company engaged AGI to build an optimized sales structure subsequent to the trucking accessories integration along with a sales compensation structure that reflected the go-to-market strategy. Ensuring that the company strategy aligns to the designed compensation plans was paramount to success.

AGI began the assessment by identifying a design team with sales leadership to gain an understanding of the Company's go-to-market strategy. From the interviews, AGI determined that there may be brand quality issues to manage between the Company and its two recently acquired organizations. Leadership said they believed customers viewed the Company as a leading and high quality manufacturer while end-users viewed the acquisitions as regionally focused manufacturers, which often cut costs and provided lower quality products to the market. In addition to the brand quality differences, sales leadership believed that the trucking accessories representatives would have trouble acclimating to selling in major metropolitan territories; however, historically those sales representatives have thrived in the low populous Midwest portions of the country. The selling motions in these two types of territories were different, because the sales channels for metropolitan areas mainly consisted of a three-step distribution sale to distributor while the Midwest markets sold mostly via one-step to retailers or direct-to-consumer. As a result, the AGI team collected historical revenue data and launched a sales time survey to the entire sales force to gather the field sales team's point-of-view.

AGI held two strategy design meetings with the leadership team. Bolstered by data analytics via historical revenue data and survey responses, AGI led the design team towards one of three potential integration options. Operating as a meeting facilitator, AGI provided expertise and knowledge of the manufacturing industry; however, the sales leadership team was accountable for the eventual integration route chosen. This ensured that the team gained the "buy-in" from the entire team before agreeing on a go-forward decision. AGI generated three different analyses to lead the team down the correct path for integration.

First, the AGI team presented the survey findings analysis. AGI created survey questions around the end-user quality perceptions and sales channel acumen of the representatives. Overall, the analysis corroborated the feedback that was heard from leadership. The sales representatives echoed the brand quality customer perceptions heard in the interviews. Scoring the Company higher in terms of quality than either acquired company by approximately 4.5 points (on a scale from 1-10), leadership opted to keep the brand names separate as to not erode the Company's current brand quality perceptions.

Secondly, the AGI team performed a penetration analysis by ZIP code in the United States to visualize penetration rates by region and company. Using ZIP code level population data and mapping historical revenues of all three company to ZIP codes, AGI calculated a median dollar amount per person by ZIP code. Using this methodology, regions that are highly penetrated would be towards the 90th percentile of dollars/person meanwhile underpenetrated regions would be closer to 10th to 25th of dollars/person. AGI findings in this area also validated leadership's hypothesis. The trucking accessories company was highly penetrated in the low populated Midwestern states; meanwhile, the Company's strongest footholds were within the major metropolitan markets. This led the design team to keep the trucking sales representative territories within the Midwest intact while territories outside of the Midwest would be left untouched. This allowed for the lowest amount of disruption to current accounts in the field by allowing the three companies to keep their highest performing territories intact.

Finally, AGI performed a cross-sell opportunity analysis that showed the potential amount of revenue gained from increasing each sales representative's product bag. By leveraging the established channels within each region, AGI was able to calculate the incremental revenue from selling complementary products from the acquired companies to current customers and vice versa. AGI also added sensitivity analysis to determine the conservative, moderate and optimistic scenarios. Generally, under all scenarios the Company could expect to see a significant rise in revenue by cross-selling products. This led the design team to give each representative the full portfolio of products to aggressively cross-sell products into its current customer base. These three decisions led to a unified go-to-market strategy that would inform sales compensation decisions going forward.

The design team was inclined to keep the current pay structures from the two legacy sales teams isolated from each other. Since the sales teams were staying intact, and both companies had enjoyed success with the current sales compensation structure, leadership decided to implement an integrated compensation plan during the next phase of integration. The AGI team agreed that this decision would provide the lowest amount of disruption to the two sales forces. AGI built out a sales integration road map for the Company, which detailed steps and considerations to ensure successful integration during a three-month timeline.

Performance Metrics

Metric	Definition of Metric, Importance and Unique Issues
Product Sales	Territory revenue from assigned product bag

Devan Cortland is a consultant in the Alexander Group's Atlanta office.

Industry: Media

AD TECH COMPANY EVOLVES SALES COMP PLANS TO FIT WITH NEW ROLES AND GLOBAL STANDARDS

By Tim Meuschke

Project Identification

The Company specializes in digital performance marketing—the retargeting of advertising across consumer devices. It operates in countries around the world through a network of international offices located in Europe, the Americas and the Asia-Pacific region. The Company has more than 3,000 employees worldwide and operates across two major customer segments: large enterprise and mid-market/small and medium-sized business (SMB).

The Company has experienced several years of rapid, profitable growth about 35% per year. During this time, its customer base grew 39.9%. This rapid growth has outpaced the strategy, structure and process of the current sales compensation program. Continued growth and expansion will only add to challenge and strain of the current organizational sales compensation capabilities. Due to the rapid growth and expansion, it was determined the current sales compensation program "one size fits all" is too limiting. The Company needed to adapt the program to meet the needs of new roles across markets and segments, while at the same time adhering to a globally consistent philosophy and set of principles and guidelines.

The Company retained the Alexander Group (AGI) to assess the current pay plan and design a best-in-class sales compensation program.

Industry Profile

When a potential customer browses a website, a cookie installs in his or her browser. This cookie follows the customer as he/she browses on other sites and allows ad platforms to deliver very specific advertisements. About 2% of web traffic for most websites coverts on the first visit. Retargeting helps advertisers reach the 98% of customers who did not convert on the first try.

This way of marketing to customers allows advertisers to focus their advertising spend on people, who are already familiar with their brand and have recently proven interest. Retargeting companies, also known as remarketing companies, offer CPM (cost per thousand impressions) pricing models for advertisers to retarget these audiences by customer segmentation and the ability to follow these audiences regardless of the device they are using.

Typically, retargeting works the best in conjunction with inbound and outbound marketing or demand generation. Retargeting helps to increase conversions, but it cannot drive people to a website. Content marketing strategies are great for driving traffic to a website, but they do not help with conversion/purchase optimization.

The typical sales coverage approach for this industry follows a hunter/farmer model. The main sales role is an account executive, who is responsible for net new business acquisition. The second role is an account manager, who is responsible for nurturing the newly landed account for retention and expansion growth opportunities.

Remarketing companies measure success by lead conversion, nurture touches, view through conversions, page visits, email opens and marketing qualified leads.

Products, Customers, Coverage and List of Jobs

The Company's main product line is a dynamic retargeting product. This product re-engages shoppers throughout their path to purchase with tailored video and display ads. Thousands of different marketers use this product to deliver their ads across the world's best publishers. In recent years, the Company evaluated additional product lines to include as part of their value offering such as search and brand solution products.

To sell to the majority of the largest marketers, the Company's field sales coverage model included two main roles: the account executive and the account manager. The account executive was responsible for landing net new marketing logos and called on a list of accounts in one of three geographies of EMEA, Americas or APAC. After landing a new account, the account executive would stay engaged in the account for at least 90 days to assist with initial adoption and configuration. During this transition period, the account executive introduces the account manager, who takes over the relationship to maintain and grow the account. Lower revenue accounts were handled by the same types of roles, but engaged through an inside sales team called mid-market sales (MMS).

Title	Job Abstract	Performance Metrics
Tier 1 AE	• Prospects, onboards and launches large-sized advertisers to hit on new business individual targets	• 100% individual 90-day revenue
Tier 1 Sales Manager	• Manages a team of AEs to help each prospect, onboards and launches large-sized advertisers to hit on new business individual targets	• 100% team 90-day revenue

Tier 1 VP Sales	• Manages a sales team to help each prospect, onboards and launches large-sized advertisers to hit on new business targets	• 70% team new business live revenue • 30% team revenue
MMS Senior AE	• Prospects, onboards and launches mid-sized advertisers to hit on new business individual and team targets	• 100% individual 90-day profit
MMS AE	• Prospects, onboards and launches mid-sized advertisers to hit on new business individual and team targets	• 100% individual 90-day profit
MMS Sales Team Lead	• Leads a sales team through operational support and sales guidance to achieve individual and team new business targets	• 100% team 90-day profit
MMS VP Sales	• Builds appropriate one to two years sales strategy and strong organization to ensure constant achievement of regional new business target	• 100% team in quarter launched profit
Tier 1 AM	• Drives the client strategy to grow and retain existing business ensuring the overall customer satisfaction and maximum profitability for the business	• 85% individual profit • 15% team in quarter launched profit
Tier 1 AM Manager	• Drives the POD strategy to grow and retain existing employees ensuring high employee retention and grows and retains existing business ensuring the overall customer satisfaction and maximum profitability for the business	• 80% team profit • 20% region profit
Tier 1 AM VP	• Drives the strategy to grow and retain existing employees ensuring high employee retention and grows and retains existing business ensuring the overall customer satisfaction and maximum profitability for the business	• 100% team profit
MMS AM	• Develops and builds strategic relationships to educate, nurture and grow the Company's clients and contributes to achievement of mid-market account strategy quarterly and annual revenue growth and client retention goals	• 85% individual profit • 15% team in quarter launched profit
MMS Senior AM	• Develops and builds strategic relationships to educate, nurture and grow the Company's clients and contributes to achievement of mid-market account strategy quarterly and annual revenue growth and client retention goals	• 100% individual profit

MMS AM Manager	• Leads a high-functioning, performance-driven team towards achievement of revenue growth, client retention goals and client KPIs; motivates and retains top talent with skillsets that meet immediate business needs and keeps in mind short- and long-term value for the Company and clients	• 100% team profit
MMS AM VP	• Develops and executes a long-term growth strategy and leads a high-functioning, performance-driven team towards consistent overachievement of existing business revenue targets; hires, motivates and retains top talent with skillsets relevant in meeting immediate and long-term business needs	• 100% team profit

Project Solution and Outcome

The sales compensation design team included the CRO, HR, finance and the heads of sales for each of the four regions where the Company conducted business. Many of the design team members were new to the company and sales compensation concepts. AGI conducted interviews with each member of the design team and steering committee, and quickly realized that there was a large difference of opinions for the future design of the sales compensation plans.

AGI presented a comprehensive sales compensation assessment. The main findings of the assessment were:

- Current sales compensation plans and target setting create a "nice place to work" culture with the majority of the individuals receiving nearly 100% of annual target incentive.
- Similar plans for account executives and account managers lead to undesirable behaviors due to very different job responsibilities.
- Sales and account managers do not feel their actual incentive accurately represents their performance due to measures out of their control.
- Lack of motivation to over perform due to low target incentive payouts at excellence points.

After multiple design meetings, the team landed on initial recommendations for future sales compensation plans that they believed solved for the main assessment findings. Below are the top high-level key design team proposals:

1. Replace cap with decelerator
2. Introduce quota bands
3. Increase quota transparency

4. Standardize plans across regions and business units
5. Design plans for future job roles that could carry new products

AGI then presented the proposal to the steering committee for final approval. Each proposal was highly scrutinized, but eventually approved after some modification and further explanation of how the design team came to their recommendations. The CEO and CFO agreed these changes would help to attract, retain and reward best-in-class sales talent to profitably grow the business.

Performance Metrics

Metric	Definition of Metric, Importance and Unique Issues
Individual 90-Day Revenue	All revenue for eligible products accrued within the first 90 days after a new account launches and within the current performance period
Individual 90-Day Profit	All profit for eligible products accrued within the first 90 days after a new account launches and within the current performance period
Individual 180-Day Profit	All profit for eligible products that accrued within the first 180 days after a new account launches and within the current performance period
Launch Bonus Draw	Fixed bonus awarded when an account launches. This bonus will be a draw from target variable incentive, and determined before each performance period
Individual Profit	All profit for eligible products that accrued within the current performance period
Incremental Profit	Profit for eligible products accrued within the current performance period and exceeds the profit from the prior period
Team New Biz Revenue (or Profit)	Sum of revenue (or profit) for eligible products from members of a team, region, country, etc., which accrued within the first 90 days after a new account launches and within the current performance period
Team New Biz Live Revenue	Sum of revenue for eligible products from members of a team, region, country, etc. that is accrued for new accounts that launched within the current performance period
Team 90-Day Profit	Sum of profit for eligible products from members of a team, region, country, etc., which accrued within the first 90 days after a new account launches and within the current performance period
Team Profit (MMS, T1 AS)	Sum of profit for eligible products from members of a team, region, country, etc. equal to the following formula: Team Profit = Existing profit + Pure New Biz profit + Rolling 90-Day profit
Team Profit (T1 Sales)	Sum of profit for eligible products from members of a team, region, country, etc. equal to the following formula: Team Profit = Existing profit + Pure New Biz profit

Glossary

CPM: Cost per one thousand advertisement impressions on one webpage

Lead Conversion: Leads directly attributed to remarketing ads

Nurture Touches: Engagement from your existing contacts with your remarketing display ad campaigns with reference to late-stage offers

Page Visits: Number of visitors that arrived at your remarketing landing page from your ad

Profit: Revenue excluding traffic acquisition costs (non-US GAAP financial measure). Traffic acquisition costs primarily consist of purchases of impressions from publishers on a CPM basis

View Through Conversions: A conversion that occurs when a prospect views your remarketing display ad, but doesn't click, and returns to your website on their own

Tim Meuschke is a manager in the Alexander Group's New York City office.

Industry: Media

INTEGRATED PRINT PUBLISHING COMPANY INVESTS HEAVILY IN DIGITAL FOR ITS SALES COMPENSATION PLANS

By Tim Meuschke

Project Identification

The Company is an integrated print publishing company that operates multiple media companies across many states. Overall, revenue had been declining at an alarming rate of about 15%, with nearly 85% of revenue coming from traditional print advertisements. Growth in the industry was pointing to digital, which had a growth rate of 20% to 25%. The Company's leadership team was interested in a complete sales transformation of its largest revenue newspaper properties to increase sales focus towards digital products. Without a full sales transformation to increase digital revenue, the Company was facing the possibility of closing its underperforming properties.

The Company chose one of its markets as the seventh property to go through a complete sales transformation with the Alexander Group (AGI) due to its revenue size and potential opportunity in the market. AGI conducted an assessment, design and implementation engagement over eight months to help set up the Company for revenue growth. AGI and the Company created 15 different workstreams for the sales effectiveness design portion of the project. Sales compensation design was a major workstream of the transformation. Leadership sought to introduce more of a pay-for- performance culture, as well as focusing sellers on selling digital products. This study focuses on the sales compensation design workstream of one property of the Company.

Industry Profile

Integrated print companies typically use a direct sales model and offer their clients both print and digital advertising products. Each seller is in direct contact with the account's advertising buyer. Sales typically have a short 30-day sales cycle and require extensive support throughout the sales process, from access to renew. The integrated print industry typically captures the following performance measures:

- Print
    - Percent newspaper readership
    - Number print circulation
    - Percent revenue from printed ads

- Digital
    - Number unique visitors per page
    - Number page views
    - Number time spent online
    - Number CPM (cost per thousand impressions)

Data analytics are completely changing the advertising industry. Advertisers now expect real-time performance metrics to calculate their return on investment (ROI). Publishers need to know what keeps an audience engaged and how to write stories for each different audience type. Advertisers expect publishers to target their ads to the unique buyers with the highest potential to buy their products.

These trends are leading advertisers to move their print advertising dollars towards digital. Digital advertising can offer metrics to more accurately track the purchasing intent of the consumer. Publishers are racing to improve their digital products to capture this revenue and need a digital fluent and motivated sales force to push the product. New sales roles are emerging to help prove to advertisers that their digital ads are actually generating audience impact.

Products, Customers, Coverage and List of Jobs

The Company sells both print and digital advertising space to clients in its local market. Print advertising includes display advertising in the newspaper. Digital advertising consists of display ads on the Company's website. Additional digital products through other companies are also available for sellers to sell.

The Company divides its clients into four main categories: national, strategic, local and inside accounts. National accounts are large corporate accounts negotiated by a separate corporate team from headquarters. One national representative handles local advertising for 10 to 15 accounts. Strategic accounts consist of the top clients. These accounts require in-person contact and have the highest historical or potential value to the organization. Strategic representatives are typically the top sellers and are responsible for 35% of the revenue. Each strategic representative's account list focuses on one or two specific verticals that have the highest importance to the local market. Market leadership identified six strategic vertical groupings during the revenue segmentation design workstream:

- Medical/assisted living
- Food/agency/furniture
- Financial/home improvement
- Real estate/medical

- Education/entertainment/national
- Auto

Local accounts make up the remaining in-person accounts, but have lower revenue potential than strategic accounts. Local representatives are typically junior sellers and their account lists can be a mix of different verticals.

The digital overlay specialist role assists both strategic and local account teams on digital sales. The main responsibilities include assessing and developing plans for areas for digital growth and transferring knowledge of digital offerings, trends, strategies and results to the sales team. The design team created a new role called the customer success analyst (CSA) during this engagement. The CSA is responsible for reporting to the advertiser on the real-time progress of the digital campaign, recommending any needed course corrections and upselling the client on additional products.

The remaining accounts are inside accounts and do not require in-person visits. These accounts are handled by an inside account team, who is responsible for inbound and outbound calls. Every six months the leadership team will follow a process to determine if accounts need to be transferred between strategic, local or inside teams.

Title	Job Abstract	Performance Metrics
Strategic Accounts Representative	• Responsible for driving growth in strategic accounts, existing and new leads through all product sets (large local and regional accounts with local decision-makers)	• Total revenue • Digital revenue
Local Accounts Representative	• Drive existing and new account growth for local accounts, as defined, through all product sets within the local market	• Total revenue • Digital revenue
Auto Accounts Representative	• Responsible for driving existing and new account growth for auto accounts, including dealers, dealer associations, boats, RVs, heavy equipment, etc. as assigned	• Total revenue • Digital revenue
Strategic Auto Representative	• Drive existing and new growth for weekly auto niche publication for auto accounts	• Total revenue • Digital revenue
Digital Overlay Specialist	• Responsible for driving digital within assigned local and strategic territories	• Total team digital revenue
Inside/Outbound Representative	• Inside sales (telesales) • Responsible for driving new sales growth and retention revenue in smaller and/or transactional accounts	• Total revenue • Digital revenue

Project Solution and Outcome

The project created a new sales organization to focus the advertising department on the right opportunities for growth. With these new roles, the sales compensation design team felt fully prepared to build plans to help reinforce the right behaviors. The sales compensation assessment clearly outlined some of the major issues the design team needed to fix. The design team knew the new plans needed to focus representatives on selling digital product, create more of a pay-for-performance culture and remain simple for representatives to understand.

The first step in designing the new plans involved determining what roles should actually be eligible for sales compensation. After an extensive discussion, the design team decided not to include any role that did not have significant influence on the customer's buying decision. The design team instead put these roles on add-on bonus plans. The roles included:

- National accounts representative
- Call center representative
- Obituaries representative
- Sales assistant
- Multimedia planner
- Customer success analyst

Sellers previously had between three and four measures included in their sales compensation plans, which diluted sales focus. To fix this issue, the design team decided to include no more than two measures in each seller's plan. Management identified digital sales as the primary revenue measure. However, print revenue still accounted for 85% of ad department revenue, so a total revenue measure was included as a secondary measure to keep representatives focused on total revenue. For representatives to receive any upside on their digital measure, they must hit the threshold of their total revenue measure. These two measures and hurdle indicated to the representatives just how important the Company believed in digital growth as the future driver of its success.

Plans included a threshold of 90% and 3x leverage to increase the pay-for-performance culture. Low performers would see less variable incentive than in the original plans, while high performers had the opportunity to make two to three times as much as they had before. Strategic representatives received a 25% higher target total compensation (TTC) than local representatives to signal the significance of their revenue responsibilities and help to enhance the career lattice in the organization.

The leadership team decided to provide a guarantee to all sellers for the first month of the new sales compensation plans. The objectives of the guarantee were to protect sellers during a month of high disruption and protect finance's expense to performance ratio.

Performance Metrics

Metric	Definition of Metric, Importance and Unique Issues
Total Revenue	Revenue from selling any product (including print, direct marketing, allocated digital and digital-only revenue)
Digital Revenue	Revenue from selling digital-only solutions (includes revenue allocated to digital as part of a package). This metric was the biggest change for the client from its previous plans
Total Team Digital Revenue	Revenue from selling digital-only solutions (includes revenue allocated to digital as part of a package). This goal is a total team digital revenue goal (strategic or local), and would be used for digital overlay roles

Glossary

Audience: The people or a market segment targeted by an advertising message or campaign

CPM: Cost per thousand is a marketing term that denotes the price of one thousand advertisement impressions on one webpage

Print Circulation: The number of copies a newspaper or magazine distributes on an average day

Unique Visitor: A term used in digital web analytics to refer to a person who visits a webpage at least once within the reporting period

Tim Meuschke is a manager in the Alexander Group's New York City office.

Industry: Pharmaceutical Distribution

PHARMACEUTICAL DISTRIBUTION COMPANY SIMPLIFIES COMPLEX PLAN TO MOTIVATE SELLERS

By Mason Ginsberg

Project Identification

The Company distributes branded and generic pharmaceuticals, surgical and consumable products and other similar products to customers such as animal health clinics and physician practices. The Company's sales compensation plans featured a complex configuration of both profit and product-focused measures. This plan has fostered an independent income producer seller mentality. The plan did not effectively address supplemental commissions offered by suppliers. The plan used a commission rate table with 17 incremental sales volume tiers. It also incorporated three separate bonuses outside of the core commission rate table that totaled less than 10% of target total compensation.

The scope of this project included three phases. The project started with an assessment of the client's existing sales compensation plan for its territory managers (TMs), followed by plan design and an implementation road map for the designed plans. The core assessment deliverable was an assessment of compensation plans against guiding principles. Key design phase deliverables included both a full plan design for the territory manager role, along with a detailed cost model used to determine commission rates. Finally, AGI provided communication materials to facilitate the plan implantation process.

Industry Profile

The Company is a veterinary distribution company. It sells an array of products—supplied by pharmaceutical manufacturing companies—primarily to animal health clinics and physician practices. The Company's core business issue is margin erosion due to increased pricing pressure. Supplier dynamics and customer buying processes also are shifting, requiring different sales motions. Suppliers utilize non-company sanctioned SPIFFs that are nearly impossible for the Company to track and effectively direct the Company's territory managers.

The Company uses a direct sales model for its products, which is the norm for the industry. Territory managers make sales calls to animal health clinics and veterinarians, who buy their products to treat patients. In most cases, these territory representatives fulfill the majority of the sales process. They are responsible for accessing and persuading the customer. It is the responsibility of inside sales representatives to develop, maintain and service accounts. Key performance measures for pharmaceutical distribution companies include a combination of both sales volume and profit margin. With continuous pricing pressure, an increasingly important metric is the ability to sell generics and in-house branded products. These products typically provide superior margins while improving customer loyalty to the brand.

Products, Customers, Coverage and List of Jobs

The Company sells a wide range of products from many different pharmaceutical vendors. These products include branded and generic pharmaceuticals, surgical and consumable products, medical equipment, vaccines, diagnostic tests, infection-control products, X-ray products and vitamins. The company sells almost exclusively to animal health clinics and physician practices.

Title	Job Abstract	Performance Metrics
Territory Manager	Details and sells pharmaceuticals, biologicals, sundries, equipment, programs and services through in-person sales calls to veterinary professionals in an assigned territory	Paid a commission on gross profit dollars that increases based on total sales volume
Region Manager	Manages the performance of territory managers and territory trainees by maintaining frequent contact with and working directly with the territory manager	No data provided
Zone Manager	Devises and implements regional sales programs to achieve maximum efficiency and sales results in the field at a direct cost to sell equal or lower than the Company's goals	No data provided
Capital Equipment Specialist	Creates full solution for the customer, encompassing equipment, technology and services	No data provided; similar to region manager

Project Solution and Outcome

The Company's territory manager sales compensation plan struggled with three major issues. Two of the issues were relatively typical—the plan was overly complex, and the plan measures beyond the core measure used weights that were too insignificant to be motivational. However, the third issue was much less common—the client struggled to maintain control over its territory managers due to the full commission plan. The Company's best performing sellers often exhibited some of the least compliant behaviors. Turnover rates of sellers in smaller territories were far higher than industry norms. Additionally, the prior plan failed to compensate territory growth. As a result, sellers would spend a disproportionate amount of time catering to high spend existing accounts while ignoring lower spend accounts with high potential.

The final territory manager plan design consisted of four separate measures. These measures were in-house brand and generic products, "main products" (other vendor products), diagnostics and equipment and gross profit dollar growth. The mechanic for each measure was a commission rate, with the only difference being that the main products measure used three different rates based on the product's vendor tier. The design team agreed that a goal-based bonus was the ideal state design solution. However, due to previously negotiated contracts with some key vendors, this solution would not be feasible by the beginning of the next year. The new plan accomplished many of the client's objectives. It created greater strategic alignment and focus. The four plan measures drove attention to the prioritized product types. It provided greater emphasis on growing territories, since one of the measures paid purely on year-over-year increase in profit dollars. It simplified the plan structure by removing the under-funded measures and the 17-tier commission system.

Apart from changes to the core plan measures and mechanics, the design team made other modifications as well. One change was the addition of non-recoverable draw tiers (based on prior-year earnings) into the plan as a way to eventually transition to a base salary. A key finding from the current state assessment pay-for-performance analysis was the existence of an implied base salary. Once the client can seamlessly implement a base salary, this analysis should help to measure thresholds. One last change was the removal of a plan feature that allowed territory managers to "shop" the plan based on their individual circumstances. Previously, the Company allowed TMs to choose between two versions of the plan—one with a car allowance and lower commission rates, or one without a car allowance and higher commission rates. This option allowed TMs who did not travel long distances to select the higher rate plan and TMs who travel often to select the car allowance plan. The design team mandated that TMs must accept the car allowance and reduced the available compensation dollars accordingly.

Performance Metrics

Metric	Definition of Metric, Importance and Unique Issues
In-House Brand/ Generics	This metric pays a commission rate on sales of in-house Company branded products or generic brand products and excludes fixed rate items
Main Products	This metric pays a commission rate on sales of non-fixed rate products that do not fall into the in-house brand/generics measure or diagnostics/equipment measure. Products in this measure fall into one of three distinct vendor tiers, with different commission rates paid based on tier
Diagnostics/Equipment	This metric pays a commission rate on sales of approved diagnostic products or equipment and excludes fixed rate items
Gross Profit Dollar Growth	This metric pays a commission rate on core gross profit dollar sales in excess of prior-year core gross profit sales total and excludes fixed-rate items

Glossary

Agency Commissions: Commissions that are the fixed rate of sales paid on the business the Company sells, but does not actually ship and bill

Fixed Rate Commissions: Certain items are set up to have a "fixed commission rate," which means this rate will apply to the sales dollars for those items

Mason Ginsberg is a manager in the Alexander Group's Chicago office.

WHITEPAPERS

SALES COMPENSATION ALMANAC • 2020

WHITEPAPERS

The Alexander Group encourages our consultants to share their experiences, formulate new ideas and contribute to the profession. In this section, explore select topics authored by the Alexander Group's consultants.

IN THIS SECTION

This year's whitepapers feature the following topics:

- Key Considerations for Transitioning Between Sales Compensation Plans
- Sales Compensation: Are Corporate Measures Wrong?
- Sales Compensation Options for Sales Force Integration
- Sales Compensation Plans: Should Payouts Have A Performance Threshold?

KEY CONSIDERATIONS FOR TRANSITIONING BETWEEN SALES COMPENSATION PLANS

By Mike Burnett

Introduction

When sales organizations undergo substantial changes, strategic or structural, there are bound to be downstream effects on the sales force programs. This often includes making changes to the sales compensation plans—a needed, but risky move that can cause unrest within any sales organization.

While minor plan changes can occur year-over-year without causing significant upheaval in the sales organization, sales leadership must take extra care when planning major changes to compensation plans. Unlike minor, year-over-year changes, major changes require management to take additional precautionary steps during the design process and the transition between plans. During these instances, design teams must take into account the plans' potential impact on company results, as well as the welfare of their customers and the salespeople participating in the compensation plan. Major changes can have a lasting impact on a sales organization, potentially altering the direction of a sales force for years to come. As an example, the company can experience unwanted seller distraction and turnover. The transition between drastically different plans can go smoother if sales management is mindful of constituent concerns and open to utilizing several powerful short-term transition techniques.

1. Sellers' Degree of Influence

During the transition between incentive plans, sales management needs to know the degree of influence, impact and connectedness sellers have with their accounts. When representatives have a high degree of influence (i.e., more control over their accounts), there is a possibility sellers will leave the company and take their customers' business with them. For example, sellers tend to have higher degrees of influence in industries such as insurance or financial services. After building strong, trusted relationships with a seller/broker/agent, customers show more loyalty to the individual seller than the actual company. This is also true in other industries, such as commoditized goods, where a representative's persuasion and selling capabilities take precedence over product or brand loyalty. Sales management cannot ignore this fact. If the new compensation plan has the potential to upset a portion of the sale force, there is a good possibility sellers can leverage customer loyalty for another company and steal away business. Plan design teams may want to consider taking steps to help limit representative turnover.

2. Effects on Sellers' Income

There will be both winners and losers when companies make a change to the sales compensation plan. While some sales representatives will financially benefit from the new plan, others will likely experience a loss in income. Incentive design teams need to remain conscious of the potential negative impact, or income loss, which can result from plan changes.

This is especially true when companies make changes to any of the following plan components:

- **Target Total Compensation (TTC).** While sellers welcome nearly all increases in TTC levels, most decreases in TTC rarely go over well. In situations where pay levels will decrease, management must justify the reasoning (e.g., the job is currently paid well above market pay levels; the job's roles and responsibilities have changed; the organization has been forced to cut costs) and be prepared for some level of representative turnover. Companies use different plan techniques to help alleviate sellers' immediate decrease in income, especially for high performers.
- **Pay Mix.** Although there may not be a change to TTC levels, making changes to a plan's pay mix can impact the amount of dollars "at-risk" for a seller. If a new compensation plan involves lowering a role's target incentive value, management must be prepared to increase the role's base salary to keep the established TTC levels intact. This change can be difficult because of the related increase in fixed costs, as well as the difficulty to decrease base salary levels, once raised. In contrast, if a plan seeks to increase its target incentive levels, management faces the challenge of decreasing base salary and dealing with sellers who only view the increase in incentive pay as an increase in overall "risk." Whenever this is the case, management should emphasize the increase in upside, which often accompanies a more leveraged pay mix. This message often is very appealing to a sales force's top performers (i.e., the sellers who will benefit most from an increase in upside opportunity).
- **Performance Measures and Mechanics.** When management introduces a new measure (e.g., units or profit versus territory revenue), there is bound to be a learning curve for some portion of the sales force. Sellers may be required to change their current ways or learn new selling activities, which are critical to sales success and incentive earnings.

Depending upon the extent of changes required, it could take weeks or months until a seller has fully adopted the new selling requirements. Learning time decreases seller success, until sales personnel acquire the new selling competencies. The new sales requirements include management recognizing that the amount of time it places sellers on a learning curve has an indirect relationship to the amount of compensation sellers would earn. Consider introducing the new measures in advance of the outcomes affecting sales compensation payout.

- **Payout Mechanics.** A change in the relationship between performance and resulting payout can also impact sellers' income. For example, if leadership decides to place a threshold or hurdle on a payout curve used to pay from dollar one, leadership should expect to hear complaints regarding the workload required before earning an incentive. Another example includes leadership switching from a territory commission to a bonus plan. Representatives with larger territory opportunity may experience a decrease in income if the bonus plan intends to equalize earnings among different size territories.
- **Payout Periods.** If management implements a new payout period, there may be a significant impact on the timing of incentive payouts to representatives. This can present a cash flow issue for sellers, especially those moving to a plan with a prolonged payout period, such as moving from monthly to quarterly or semi-annual incentive payouts. In this example, plan designers should introduce a draw or a guarantee into the new plans. This helps to improve the sellers' cash flow, and potentially gains more buy-in for the proposed plan change.

Management needs to address the monetary effects that plan changes will have on their sellers' income before implementing them. To gain this understanding, sales management must perform thorough and extensive cost modeling. This includes examining the aggregate plan costs, and the range and variability of incentive pay for each individual (or sample of individuals) under the new plan. This incumbent-level analysis provides management with a better view of how much incentive the company anticipates for each individual, as well as how the organization's incentive money will be redistributed among individuals on the plan. Management should pay attention to the effects the new plan will have on the income of the sales force's highest performers. If a substantial number of high performers experience a decrease in income, sales management should prepare for a difficult transition or reconsider their proposed changes. If the analysis finds any high performing representative experiencing a significant negative impact on income, leadership should provide special treatment to ensure satisfaction with the new compensation plans.

3. Transition Plan Techniques

Management should consider implementing temporary transition plans when introducing dramatic changes to a compensation plan. This helps support the sellers as they move to the new pay program. While transition plans are most effective when there is a higher chance for income loss on a new compensation plan, companies can use this concept to prepare a sales force for a new strategy, structure or compensation plan.

Some of the most common transition plan techniques include the following:

- **Retention Bonus.** A bonus paid out on the condition the individual stays with the organization for a pre-determined period following the introduction of the new compensation plan. Management uses this technique to limit representative turnover, offering additional incentive to those salespeople willing to stay with the company through and directly after the transition period.
- **Guarantees.** A "promised" or guaranteed level of incentive payout during either the transition and/or new compensation plan. There are several types of guarantees that can serve different purposes:
    - **Flat or Fixed Guarantee.** A set bonus amount with no potential downside or upside opportunity. This is the simplest guarantee in terms of communication and implementation (e.g., guaranteeing each plan participant's income will be equal to at least the prior-year's earnings on the old compensation plans).
    - **Guarantee With Upside.** A guarantee that provides additional upside for performance for exceeding a pre-determined goal. By providing upside based upon a goal, companies motivate the sales force to work hard on sales efforts and/or focus on other management objectives during the transition. However, this technique protects the seller from any shortfall during the transition period.
    - **Declining Guarantee.** A guarantee paid out in intervals and gradually declines in value until paid out in full. The benefit of this guarantee is it slowly weans salespeople off the guaranteed payout, which they have been receiving during the transition or new compensation plan periods.
- **Grandfathering.** A technique to exempt any veteran or other highly paid members of the sales force from any reduction in base or target incentive and/or enrollment in the new compensation plan. This protects any

plan incumbents who may experience a significant decrease in income due to their current pay levels tied to their veteran-standing or strategic importance to the sales force.

- **Buybacks With Split Bonus/Commissions.** This technique provides some incentive payout for performance in accounts or territories reassigned to other representatives after the new plan rolls out. This transition plan is especially useful in companies with long sales cycles, because it allows the former representative to continue working alongside the newly assigned representative to maintain the customer relationship and aid the safe transition of the account between the two representatives.

4. New Plan Rollout Techniques

Compensation plans are only as good as the sales force perceives them to be. This is especially true when sales management is making substantial changes to the compensation plans. If the sales force is unable to understand or does not buy into the new plan, then there is a good chance the plan will not have the intended impact nor produce the expected results.

- How is the plan changing? Why is the plan changing?
- Will this new plan benefit or hurt me?
- How will the company pay me?
- What are my new goals and expectations?
- Am I ready for these changes?

These examples depict the type of questions a sales force will have when learning about the upcoming changes to their incentive plan. Although some sellers may express interest, others may feel a profound sense of unease or distrust with sales management. In order to alleviate any potential concerns, management needs to clearly articulate the new plan and answer any plan-related questions from the field. With the higher level of anxiety often associated with a new plan's implementation, sales management should also consider providing more extensive plan communication and rollout efforts than in previous years. Some of these additional efforts may include:

- **Pilot test the new plan communications.** Leadership should consider sharing the new plan communication materials with a small sample of the sales force. This can provide valuable feedback regarding the field's understanding, and the overall perspective of the plan. With advanced planning, leadership may be able to address or eliminate unexpected outcomes.

- **Ensure plan buy-in from high performers.** As with any rollout, the plan's message should cascade down from sales leadership to sales managers to the sale representatives. However, during a transition period, it is critical that leadership gains plan buy-in from their highest performers. If there is any negative noise from the sales force's highest performing representatives, there is likely to be more noise from the mid-to-low performing representatives.
- **Post-implementation communication.** Leadership should follow-up with the field for several months after implementing the new sales compensation plan to gain feedback, and to remind sellers of any critical changes made to the plan.

Conclusion

The purpose of a sales compensation plan is to guide and manage a sales force towards achieving its collective financial objectives. Over time, these objectives, along with the strategy and structure put in place to achieve them, are bound to change. Sales leadership will be forced to make significant changes to the sales incentive plans from time to time. When this occurs, leadership must be able to balance the needs of the company and its customers, as well as the needs of its sales force. This is why sales compensation design teams should use caution when designing dramatic plan changes. These changes can have lasting effects on the sales force, which can lead to negative effects on customer relationships, as well as overall company performance.

Mike Burnett is a principal in the Alexander Group's Stamford, Conn., office.

SALES COMPENSATION: ARE CORPORATE MEASURES WRONG?

By Tim Meuschke

"No one—including salespeople—should earn above their target incentive if the company underperforms to goal." —Adamant Chief Financial Officer

"The sales compensation plans must have a corporate customer service measure as part of the payout." —Insistent CEO

Do these statements sound familiar? It is not surprising that corporate leaders want sellers to participate in corporate-wide performance expectations.

Company-wide measures are appealing: They help drive teaming, a shared destiny and a "we're all in it together" collectivism. However, sales compensation plans heavily tilted toward corporate measures can result in lower overall sales performance.

This article examines why leaders want corporate measures, investigates their limitations and suggests appropriate application of corporate measures.

Typical Reason Corporate Measures Appear

Starting with finance. Why would finance leaders seek to ensure sales compensation plans carry important corporate performance measures? The answer is simple: Finance does not want to pay incentives, particularly if they are substantial, unless the company reaches its overall financial objectives. If the company as a whole does not achieve its targets, why should some of the individuals in sales still be able to overachieve on their target incentive?

Seller compensation is very different from the pay plans for other employees. Most roles outside of the sales organization have their bonuses partially tied to overall company performance. In sales, during each performance period, sellers place a portion of their target total compensation (TTC) "at risk." This portion is their target incentive (TI). Depending on the actual performance against their targets, they will receive different levels of actual incentive. Sellers typically are responsible for growing an assigned list of accounts. Sellers assume they can earn above their target incentive if they exceed their sales goal regardless of company performance. Companies want sellers to believe that growing their individual revenue would return increased incentive. If not, sellers might not expend their full effort to excel.

Corporate Measures Erode Focus on Individual Results

Each performance measure within the sales compensation plan contributes to the seller's incentive earnings. The earning potential of each measure reflects management weighting of the measures. Best practices suggest a plan should have no more than three measures and no measure less than 20% weight. If a plan were to include a corporate measure, then by default, one of the three individual measures would be sacrificed or diluted to accommodate the corporate measure. The importance of the remaining individual measures only diminishes the individual measures further as the weight on the company measure increases. Figure 1 shows this erosion.

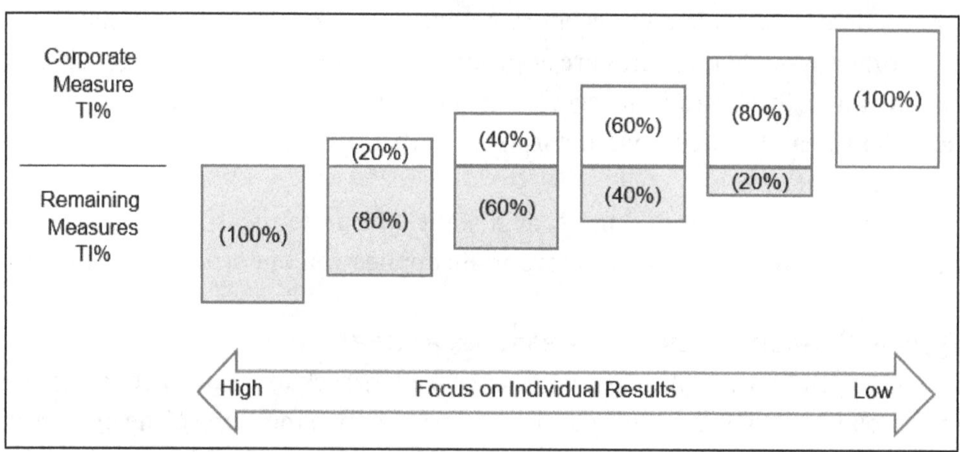

Figure 1: Example of Remaining Target Incentive Based on Corporate Measure Weighting

A balanced set of measures allows for the execution of specific tactics within the overall company strategy. Consider a company that has five strategic focus areas for the sales team for the upcoming operating period:

1. Prioritized product focus
2. Balanced performance across product targets
3. Net new business acquisition
4. Team collaboration
5. Strategic pricing

The company wants to make sure the sales team focuses on these strategic objectives.

Management has techniques other than sales compensation to drive performance. Other options include accountability/reporting, supervisor coaching, SPIFFs, recognition, contests and set-aside add-on plans. Carving out part of an individual seller's target incentive to pay on corporate performance leaves less room for sales-centric measures.

How This Hurts Revenue Growth

The typical revenue growth equation for a company consists of three strategies:

1. Sell more current products to existing customers (retention)
2. Sell new products to existing customers (penetration)
3. Sell new or current products to prospective customers (conversion)

Job roles within a sales organization can focus on one or more of these strategic sales objectives. For example, a new business hunter typically focuses on driving new opportunities with prospective customers. While an account manager typically focuses on post-sale adoption and upsell activities with existing customers.

A company's revenue growth equation is the sum of all sales strategies across all sales jobs. Decreased focus from any of these roles on their strategic responsibilities might cause the sales team to miss its sales targets. This can also affect long-term revenue growth equations. Consider a small but growing new product just released by a company. Leadership might need that piece of the business to play a bigger role in the company's growth year over year. By not focusing a significant part of sales compensation on this piece of the business, the new product may never reach its full potential.

Diffusion of Responsibility

Diffusion of responsibility is the psychological phenomenon that individuals are less likely to take action when others are assigned the same task. As the size of a group increases, it is less likely that any individual will take any accountability for action.

Company-wide measures can encourage freeloading and drive less accountability than measures within an individual's control. This can change based on an individual's level within the sales organization. The application of sales compensation works best when each seller has measures that he/she can directly influence. Most corporate measures are outside the seller's control.

How This Hurts Revenue Growth

Consider the plan where the seller has a major portion of pay tied to corporate revenue. A potential customer might want to place a new order with a seller. After some negotiations, the customer asks the seller for a 20% discount on the quoted price. In this example, the seller has the majority of his/her sales compensation tied directly to the overall company revenue. The seller discounts the price by 20% to meet the customer's request. This person believes a 20% discount on this small order will hardly affect the overall company revenue. The seller also believes that someone else in the company is probably looking out for pricing. Many other sellers might behave in this manner, driving down overall profitability of the company. The company could have tied more sales incentive to individual revenue or pricing. This may have led to a different decision by the seller, thus benefiting the company.

Diminished Motivation for High Performers

The number one reason sales compensation plans fail is a *loss of hope*. If sellers believe for any reason, perceived or real, that there is no hope to actually achieve or overachieve on their incentive, they can lose their focus and exacerbate underperformance.

High performing sellers expect above average earnings. They also are interested in the ability to control their own destiny to achieve those earnings. If high performers feel their performance does not fully drive their incentive earnings, expect them to be less motivated to over-perform. Corporate measures impose a hurdle to a high performer's ability to overachieve. Corporate measures, such as total revenue or total profit, are generally very large numbers. The ability to over- or underachieve on those measures is marginal. Unfortunately, average or low performers actually view corporate measures more positively than high performers. They feel this portion of their target incentive can protect them against poor sales results.

How This Hurts Revenue Growth

Recently, a company missed its annual revenue target for the past eight years in a row. The company was in the middle of designing new sales compensation plans for its sales teams. The CFO was adamant that the legacy plans with individual measures needed to change to one corporate revenue number. The CFO did not want sellers to be able to achieve above target earnings if the company did not reach its targets.

Qualitative analysis from interviews with top performers on this topic indicated that up to 50% would leave the company. The main reasoning was potentially no longer having the ability to overachieve on individual targets and associated target incentive. Corporate measures do not allow for this. In this example, 55 account executives (AEs) cover the nation for a collective goal of \$5B. If one AE overachieved on the individual list (approximately \$90M), the incremental growth to the company would be insignificant.

Top performing AEs would only have a few ways to achieve high upside:

1. All AEs overachieved on their individual goals
2. A few AEs closed extremely large deals to carry the rest of the company

While every company wishes these options would happen, this is not a realistic strategy. What is realistic is that top performing sellers expect their total compensation package to match the top of the market. Losing top talent in a sales organization can drastically lower a company's overall revenue growth. These individuals typically own very important customer relationships. They also are the sellers that have the ability to overachieve on aggressive sales targets. These sellers can help to keep the revenue equation on track and make up for lower performers.

The sales compensation design team wisely decided to keep individual measures in the plan for front-line sellers. They introduced corporate revenue numbers as a portion of the senior vice president's sales compensation plans. This aligned more with their strategic job responsibilities.

When Corporate Measures Can Be Correct for Sales Compensation Plans

Corporate measures do have a role in the pay plans for sales leaders. These include roles such as chief revenue officers, heads of sales and executive vice presidents. At these levels, decisions can directly affect overall company performance.

Corporate measures tend to decrease in weight as the executive level of the role decreases. Companies seldom use them for second- or first-level sales managers. Manager plans are normally a roll-up of their direct report's plans to ensure alignment within the sales organization.

Another common use of corporate measures in sales compensation plans is during a large-scale sales transformation or integration. Sales compensation transition plans are typically in place for only one or two quarters. These plans help to shift sellers into the new world. Corporate measures for sellers can make sense if there are still unclear sales or coverage strategies. Once the initial transition period ends, clearer strategies can help to design more focused sales compensation plans.

Summary

Corporate measures should be incorporated at the senior sales leadership ranks within an organization. When used in individual seller or middle-management plans, companies tend to see a lack of focus on individual results, diffusion of responsibility and diminished motivation for high performers. Each of these implications can have a negative impact on a company's overall revenue growth equation. Performance measures for these roles need to focus on factors that are within an individual's control. This way, individuals have the opportunity to earn incentive based on their own efforts. Collectively, this drives growth for the entire company's revenue equation.

Tim Meuschke is a manager in the Alexander Group's New York City office.

SALES COMPENSATION OPTIONS FOR SALES FORCE INTEGRATION

By Arshad Carim

When two sales forces converge under the same corporate umbrella due to an acquisition, sales leadership faces numerous challenges. One key challenge is how to compensate the merged sales team. This whitepaper will explore a set of considerations and plan design options when an acquired sales force integrates into an existing sales force.

Companies acquire or merge with other companies for many reasons—to gain new technology, eliminate a competitor, broaden product portfolios, gain market access, vertically integrate...the list goes on. Any merger presents immediate sales coverage questions:

- Should the two sales teams stay separate or integrate?
- What should the sales coverage model look like? Separate sales forces, overlay specialists or full integration into a unified sales force?
- What compensation solutions make sense for the new organization, whatever its deployment?

Deciding on whether or not to integrate the new sales force typically hinges on two primary factors: How different are the buyers? How different are the products? If major differences exist in these areas, then integration is typically not an immediate option given the gap in knowledge and capability for each sales force to sell the other's offerings effectively. However, if there is enough commonality in buyers/products, allowing both sales forces to effectively sell the combined offerings, then integration, combined with required enablement, training and compensation plan changes, is typically the course of action for sales leadership. Clearly, other factors play a role in the integration decision, such as channel overlap, account crossover, difficulty of sale and systems compatibility. However, the buyer and product similarities or differences usually drive the decision.

Separate Sales Forces

When existing and acquired sales forces remain separate, the compensation solution very often is quite simple—let the existing plans run for at least the next performance period (usually six months or one year). Companies will sometimes introduce lead generation or cross-sell referral bounties to begin capitalizing on the synergies between sales forces. Spiffs can also play a role in providing a "carrot" opportunity for sellers to move beyond their comfort zone of selling only familiar, legacy offerings.

Overlay Specialists

Establishing the acquired sales force as a team of overlay specialists to the existing sales force is an interim step that companies use for varying lengths of time (often one to three years). Sales leadership will deploy overlay sales coverage solutions when the acquired sales force has specific product/solution knowledge that the existing sales force cannot quickly absorb. Overlay specialists support the account/territory sellers who "own" the customers. These sellers use overlay specialists to help close deals that include the new offerings made available by the acquisition.

Sales compensation for the overlay specialist team adheres to one of two common designs—either a product/solution specific goal based on a set of accounts or geographic territory, or simply the overall total goal for a set of accounts or territory. Drivers of the measurement level include ability to set accurate quotas, deployment model for overlays and systems/reporting capabilities.

Integrated Sales Force

Turning to the scenario of integrating two sales forces, a more complex landscape and set of compensation solutions arise for sales leadership to consider. Key plan design elements and integration decisions include: eligibility. What if roles that are eligible for sales compensation plans in one sales force are not eligible in the other sales force?

- **Pay Levels.** What happens if target pay levels differ significantly between sales forces?
- **Pay Mix.** What happens if the aggressiveness profile for amount of pay at risk differs markedly between sales forces?
- **Upside.** How to handle differing philosophies on the amount of pay to offer top performers?
- **Measures and Mechanics.** How should the "machinery" of the plan work, given the importance of various factors driving the sales strategy?
- **Performance Period and Payout Frequency.** What if these plan elements differ based on sales cycle, goal-setting horizon and cash flow considerations?
- **Crediting.** How to reconcile different "trigger" events for providing credit for incentive pay purposes? (example: bookings vs. revenue)

While these topics may warrant significant attention from sales leadership, the focus is on a specific set of solutions that direct how the company pays the new integrated sales force for selling the combined portfolio of offerings.

Similarity of Products and Risk of 'Comfort Zone' Selling

The strategic importance and similarity of the acquired company's product set determines whether the merged set of product offerings can be combined into a single performance metric, such as total bookings or total revenue. If all of the integrated sales force's offerings can be combined, and sellers appropriately focus on existing and acquired products based on customer need and ability to quickly ramp up on the new product set, then the primary challenge for sales leadership is setting the right goals based on the new portfolio. Typically, companies establish an overall quota and use a "dollar is a dollar" approach for sales compensation purposes. In other words, all sales are of equal value—traditional products and the new, acquired products.

'Dollar Is Not a Dollar'

When cross-selling is required, but there is an inherent risk of "comfort zone selling" from the existing or acquired sales force, sales leadership must consider compensation levers that ensure the appropriate seller behavior to achieve balanced results. After all, if the seller sees a more lucrative return from continuing to sell what is known and comfortable vs. what is new and uncomfortable, he/she has no compelling reason to take the more difficult path. The following considerations describe conditions and options for addressing situations where the risks are too great to combine all offerings into one bucket for compensation purposes.

Quota Setting/Allocation Capability

After identifying the strategic relationship between existing and acquired product sets, sales leadership must determine if accurate quotas/goals can be set for the acquired products. If goal setting is viable, then a number of solutions are available, including:

- **Separate Weighted Metrics.** Two separate performance metrics, each with a weighting out of 100% of target incentive that reflects the desired attention from sellers
- **Balanced Performance Metric.** Rewards sellers for achieving goals in multiple defined product buckets. For example, if five product buckets

exist, the maximum payout is for achieving/exceeding goal in all five product buckets

- **Hurdle/Payline Accelerators.** Requires achievement of a goal on a secondary metric (often a product bucket) to receive any upside pay or accelerated pay on the primary metric (usually the primary product bucket)
- **Matrix Design.** Used for "competing" metrics such as revenue and profitability to drive behavior that maximizes achievement on both metrics for highest payouts

If goal setting is not viable, then a shorter list of options is available:

- **Multiplier/Modifier on Incentive Payout.** Adjusts the incentive payout by a factor based on the type of product sold
- **Value Adjustment to Quota Credit.** Multiplies or reduces the quota crediting value based on the type of product sold (e.g., 0.8x credit for low-margin products, 1.2x credit for high-margin products)

'Carrot vs. Stick' Approach

In situations that require a greater emphasis on the acquired products, sales leadership can employ both sales compensation "carrots" or "sticks" in the plan.

Carrot-based approaches reward sellers for driving the desired amount of results on specific product(s), but do not create downside risk if the product-specific goals are missed. Stick-based approaches remove incentive pay for not meeting product-specific goals, thereby penalizing the seller for missing such goals. Often, companies use combinations of carrot and stick approaches to provide a balanced incentive design. Examples of "pure carrot" approaches include payout multipliers and value adjustments that only increase the quota credit value of specific products or categories. Examples of "pure stick" approaches include linkages between weighted metrics (which require minimum performance on one measure to receive payout or acceleration on the other measure), downside modifiers and performance hurdles.

Emphasis Level and Intensity

The amount of emphasis placed on acquired products directly relates to the strategic importance of the products and the expected behavior of the sales force. Increase incentive intensity if the acquired products represent the company's ticket to growth. Keep the intensity mild if core existing products are the main drivers of sales, with the acquired products representing a smaller piece of the pie. Calibrate emphasis/intensity using different types of compensation solutions—weighting of metrics (e.g., 50/50 or 80/20), magnitude of multipliers/ modifiers (e.g., 5x or 2x), amount of value adjustment to quota credit (e.g., 1.2x or 0.8x).

Linkage Needs

Is there a need to link sales performance on existing and acquired product sets in the compensation plan? This depends on the importance of balancing performance across portfolios and the risk of seller complacency in selling only one portfolio and "shopping the plan" based on what is easiest to sell. Linkages provide a powerful motivator that directs seller behavior to ensure a desired management condition is met before certain levels of payout are available. A common implementation of this is requiring that x% of goal is achieved on the acquired/emphasis product before any accelerator pay above 100% is earned on the legacy product. Without linkages, and particularly in situations where the metric weightings are quite different (e.g., 80%/20% or 90%/10%), the risk of a seller shopping the plan is higher. This is because he/she can more easily make up for any lost target incentive in the lower weighted metric by selling more of the highly weighted metric, which is typically easier to sell or more familiar to the seller (in the "comfort zone").

Other Important Considerations

When contemplating how to compensate a newly integrated sales force, other key considerations always play a role in the final solution:

- **Simplicity.** Is the plan simple enough that sellers can quickly understand desired behaviors and execute with transparency to the rewards for such behavior?
- **Timing and Transition.** Is it feasible to make the plan design changes for the next performance period, or do some changes require a phased approach?
- **Balancing Objectives.** Are we balancing the positive and negative changes that sellers perceive in the plan?
- **Top Performer Impact.** Is there a thorough understanding of how changes impact the top performing sellers? Is management comfortable with these impacts or do other measures need to be taken to protect/ retain top performers?
- **Communication Plan.** Do we have a comprehensive communication plan in place to ensure the appropriate leadership messaging behind the new plan?

- **Ability to Administer, Track, Report.** Can we put in place the required tools, resources and/or processes to properly track, report and pay sellers based on the new plan design?

Conclusion

Sales force integration resulting from acquisition raises numerous challenges for sales leadership—when attention turns to how to pay a newly integrated sales force, many design considerations and options exist. Thinking through the selling risks, quota-setting capabilities, desired emphasis level and intensity, carrot vs. stick tradeoffs and linkage requirements will guide sales leadership to the appropriate integrated plan design. Only then can the "heavy lifting" of execution and communication begin.

Arshad Carim is a principal in the Alexander Group's San Francisco office.

SALES COMPENSATION PLANS: SHOULD PAYOUTS HAVE A PERFORMANCE THRESHOLD?

By Mick Cannon

When designing a sales compensation plan, should management consider a performance threshold? Should sales management expect a minimum level of sales performance before sales personnel can earn sales incentives?

For many sales compensation plans, a threshold is an integral and versatile component of the pay program. At the most basic level, threshold can reduce a company's incentive payouts by reducing incentive dollars paid to low performers. Management can use these dollars to reward high performers or save these dollars to lower selling costs.

Threshold performance level directly contributes to the overall performance message of the sales compensation plan. A particularly high threshold reduces the percent of sellers who earn incentive payouts. However, a high threshold might appear unattainable to sellers, leading to potential disengagement by the sales force. Meanwhile, a plan without a threshold, or a threshold set particularly low, makes earning an incentive payout much more likely. The motivational impact of early participation in incentive earnings may help drive additional performance. However, a low threshold can be irrelevant, because all sellers surpass it.

Setting the threshold is a major decision with important implications. This paper examines five different options for setting threshold: minimum performance expectation, product renewal rate, assured contracts, pay mix ratio and past performance. It will highlight the pros and cons of each approach.

Option 1: Set Threshold at Minimum Performance Expectation

The most common method to set the performance threshold is at minimum performance expectation. Among a population of sellers in the same job, management could consider the lowest 10% of performance as the minimum performance level.

Calculating the 10th percentile performer

To use this strategy, sales compensation administrators need to analyze historical sales performance to determine the performance-to-goal of the 10th percentile performer.

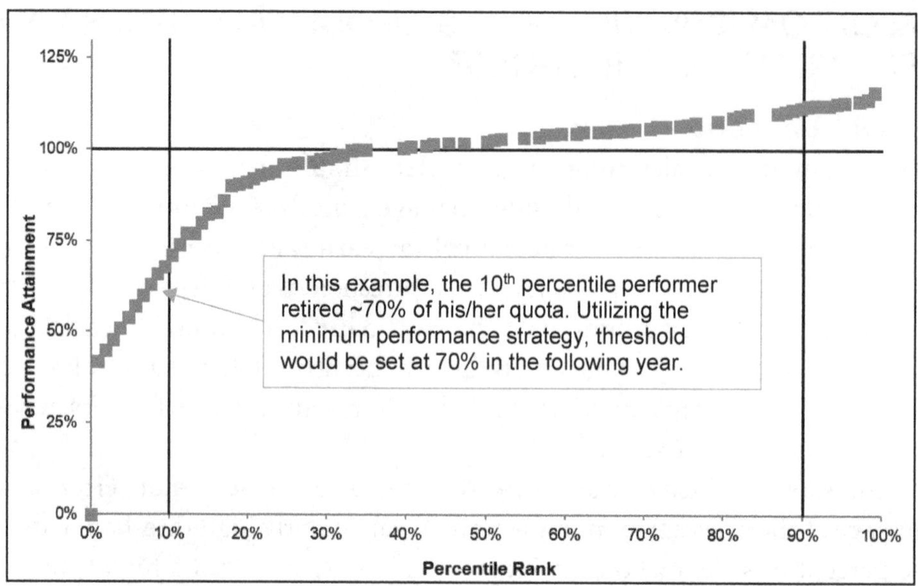

Figure 1: Calculating the 10th Percentile Performer

When calculating the 10th percentile of performance, sales compensation designers should consider only full-year incumbent sales representatives. The inclusion of partial-year incumbents may skew the calculation and provide an inaccurate result.

Designers need to account for factors that are likely to affect average performance-to-goal in the coming year. For example, if the company is 130%-to-goal in the current year and the 10th percentile of performance appears to be 95%, sales compensation plan designers need to account for the inevitable adjustment that sales leaders make in quota setting. To solve this issue, plan designers should shift the 50th percentile performance level to 100%, and recalculate the 10th percentile performer.

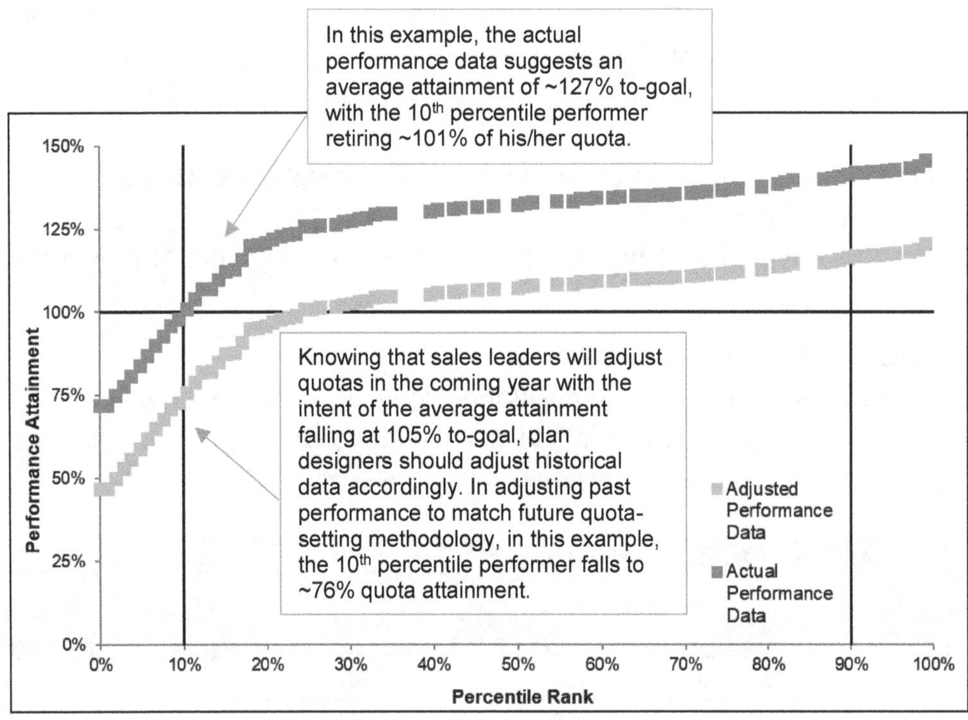

Figure 2: Shifting Performance Results and Re-Calculating the 10th Percentile Performer

Pros and cons of setting threshold at minimum performance expectation

There are two benefits to the minimum performance method to set the threshold. First, this option is simple: simple to calculate for plan administrators, simple for sales leaders to communicate and simple for sales representatives to understand. The notion of 10% of sales representatives falling below threshold is clear-cut and objective, leaving little room for confusion.

Second, threshold set at the 10th percentile performer is reasonable from a sales representative's perspective. While other threshold strategies may appear to pose a threat or even demotivate the sales force, communicating that the vast majority of sellers will exceed threshold is generally received as a fair standard. After all, the type of sales representatives a company should aim to employ will be confident in their ability to at least surpass the mark of the 10th percentile performer.

The downside to using the minimum performance strategy is that it necessitates fair and accurate quota setting. With threshold set on prior performance of an entire team, a seller is negatively impacted if he/she faces a quota that is less attainable than his/her peers. For this strategy to be effective, sales leaders need to set fair quotas for all members of the sales team, with each seller having a relatively equal opportunity to achieve his/her quota.

Option 2: Set Threshold at the Average Renewal Rate of the Company's Products

A second strategy for setting threshold is at the average renewal rate of the company's products.

Calculating the average renewal rate

To employ this strategy, sales compensation designers need to analyze historical sales performance. Designers should calculate the percentage of sales of each product bought by the same customer year-over-year.

Customer	Year 1 Sales of Product A	Year 2 Sales of Product A	Value of Renewals (Year 2 less Year 1, cannot exceed Year 1)	Calculation Notes
Customer A	$1,000	$800	$800	
Customer B	$500	$500	$500	
Customer C	$400	$200	$200	
Customer D	$350	$0	$0	
Customer E	$1,000	$1,100	$1,000	Value of renewal is limited to the total sales in Year 1
Total	$3,250	$2,600	$2,500	
		Renewal Rate:	76.9%	Renewal rate is calculated as total value of renewals divided by Year 1 sales

Table 1: Calculating a Product's Average Renewal Rate

Upon determining the renewal rate for each product, designers should calculate the weighted average for the company. This requires an analysis of the company's overall revenue, and multiplying a product's renewal rate by its relative prevalence in the company's revenue mix.

Product	Product's Renewal Rate	Product's Share of Total Company Revenue	Weighted Average Renewal Rate
Product A	73.8%	50%	36.9%
Product B	60%	25%	15%
Product C	40%	25%	10%
		Weighted Average Renewal Rate:	61.9%

Table 2: Calculating Weighted Average Renewal Rate

Pros and cons of setting threshold at product renewal rate

The primary benefit of this strategy confirms the very purpose of sales compensation: paying sellers for persuasion. By setting threshold at the average product renewal rate, companies isolate the contribution of sales representatives. The underlying principle behind the strategy is that the average product renewal rate can function as a proxy for the value brought by the product itself, independent of the work of a salesperson. In turn, rather than rewarding sellers for the value of the products they are selling, the company pays only for revenue above what the product would have brought in on its own.

Obviously, only companies with renewable products can employ this strategy. An additional challenge is to accommodate for factors that may cause fluctuations in product renewal rates. Historical renewal rates may not accurately predict future renewal rate. Internally, product changes or alterations in marketing strategy may influence product renewal rates, too. Externally, macroeconomic factors, industry trends or the actions of competitors could all play a role in influencing product renewals. Plan designers must incorporate these influences when setting threshold. Without considering such factors, the sales compensation plan may reward or punish sellers for events completely out of their control, effectively negating the purpose of the threshold.

Option 3: Set Threshold at the Value of Assured Contracts

A third strategy for setting threshold is to do so at a sales representative's value of assured contracts.

Calculating the value of assured contracts

Employing this strategy requires that a company issues a unique threshold for each individual sales representative. Sales compensation administrators calculate the total value of a seller's guaranteed contracts for the upcoming performance period. Administrators arrive at an individual's threshold by dividing that total value by the individual seller's goal.

Product	Contract's Assured Revenue
Contract A	$200,000
Contract B	$50,000
Contract C	$350,000
Total Value of Assured Contracts	$600,000
Seller's Quota (pre-determined)	$1,000,000
Seller's Threshold	60%

Table 3: Calculating Threshold at Value of Assured Contracts

Successfully executing this option requires companies to have explicit adjustment policies. Sales representatives would need to receive relief for mid-year changes to the value of assured contracts, especially if the change in value was out of their control. Mergers, acquisitions, customer bankruptcy and product delivery issues are only a small sample of the factors that could influence assured contract value. To ensure success, sales compensation plans setting threshold at assured contract value must have a detailed framework for modifying threshold when needed.

Pros and cons of setting threshold at the value of assured contracts

The benefit of setting threshold at the value of assured contracts is that it positions companies to pay only once for persuasion. Given that assured contracts have been booked as revenue, sellers should be turning their focus to new opportunities. In turn, their sale compensation should align with the opportunities they should pursue, rather than past efforts. Setting threshold at the value of assured contracts sends this message loud and clear to the sales force.

An added benefit of this strategy is its ability to level-set sellers at the beginning of the fiscal year. Sales representatives cannot get ahead via multi-year contracts. Instead, all members of the sales team begin the year with a fresh start and equal footing.

On the downside, the prerequisites to install this strategy can be limiting. Most evidently, the strategy only applies to companies whose product portfolio lends itself to multiyear contracts. Similarly, the lack of existing contracts for new hires and new territories causes a need to employ a different threshold setting methodology for certain sales representatives.

The individual nature of the option could also prove a deterrent. The need to set a unique threshold for each sales representative, and possibly unique thresholds for each *measure* on an individual sales representative's compensation plan could be prohibitive for large sales organizations.

Option 4: Set Threshold Based on Pay Mix Ratio

A fourth strategy for setting threshold is to align it with pay mix. The rationale behind this option is that base salary pays for all performance below threshold; therefore, base pay as a percentage of target total compensation should align to threshold.

Calculating threshold based pay mix

Using this strategy requires minimal calculation. An individual's threshold is set in-line with his/her pay mix. For example, a seller with a 70/30 pay mix (i.e., 70% of target total compensation is base pay, 30% is target incentive) receives a threshold of 70%. Alternatively, a seller with a 50/50 pay mix receives a threshold of 50%.

Pros and cons of setting threshold based on pay mix ratio

The benefits of setting threshold based on pay mix ratio are two-fold. First, this method directly aligns the messaging behind target incentive percentage with performance expectations. From a seller's perspective, the company is communicating that his/her base pay is compensation for all performance below threshold level. Understandably, the seller only earns incentive pay if/when he/she exceeds that minimum performance level. Second, this method is extremely easy to calculate and communicate. The sales operations teams requires no additional effort to set thresholds, and communication to the sales force is simple.

This approach presents two notable drawbacks. First is the possibility of strategic incongruence presented by aligning pay mix with threshold. Pay mix is typically set based on a role's involvement in persuading buyers (i.e., the role's ability to influence sales outcomes). In turn, by aligning threshold to pay mix, plan designers are decreasing the likelihood of earning incentive pay for sellers who have relatively little influence on outcomes. For example, a seller with a 90/10 pay mix, a 90% threshold, is punished for being in a role that involves little persuasion. On the contrary, sellers with a 50/50 pay mix, a threshold of 50%, seem rewarded for being in a role heavily involved in persuasion. In both cases, the message sent by the seller's threshold may fail to align with the strategic messaging behind the seller's pay mix. Second is difficultly in operationalizing the strategy. Depending on the company's consistency in setting pay mixes, each seller may have a unique threshold, even within the same job. In this case, communicating the plan and calculating payouts quickly becomes complicated.

Option 5: Set Threshold Based on Individual Past Performance

A fifth strategy for setting threshold is to do so based on an individual's past performance. This option allows companies several possibilities on how to modify past performance ahead of setting it as a threshold. In any case, setting threshold based on individual past performance requires unique thresholds for each seller.

Calculating threshold based on individual past performance

On one end of the spectrum, a company could choose to set threshold at the most recent year's performance, effectively communicating that it will pay sellers only for outperforming themselves year-over year.

Sales Representative	Year 1 Total Sales	Year 2 Quota (pre-determined)	Year 2 Threshold (set by dividing Year 2 quota by Year 1 performance)
John Doe	$1,000,000	$1,300,000	76.9%
Jane Doe	$1,400,000	$1,500,000	93.3%
John Smith	$300,000	$500,000	60.0%

Table 4: Calculating Threshold at Individual Past Performance

On the other hand, a company could choose to modify past performance and set threshold accordingly. An example would be setting threshold at 50% of a sales representative's revenue in the prior year.

Sales Representative	Year 1 Total Sales	50% of Year 1 Sales	Year 2 Quota (pre-determined)	Year 2 Threshold (set by dividing Year 2 quota by Year 1 performance)
John Doe	$1,000,000	$500,000	$1,300,000	38.4%
Jane Doe	$1,400,000	$700,000	$1,500,000	46.6%
John Smith	$300,000	$150,000	$500,000	30.0%

Table 5: Calculating Threshold at 50% of Individual's Performance Last Year

Of course, a multitude of variations exists beyond these two versions.

This option assumes year-over-year similarity in the revenue opportunity available to a seller. With threshold set on prior results, management needs to account for a change in opportunity from one year to the next. Of course, not all shifts in available opportunity are foreseeable. When available opportunity fluctuates beyond expectation, the need for mid-year changes to threshold may arise. Subsequently, similar to setting threshold at value of assured contracts, using this option requires companies to have explicit adjustment policies in place.

Pros and cons of setting threshold based on individual past performance

The benefit of setting threshold based on past performance is the opportunity to drive growth. By putting sellers in a position in which they earn only if/when they exceed past year's performance, the company is effectively forcing revenue growth, or at least applying maximum pressure on the sales team to do so.

> *Real-world example: threshold based on individual past performance*
>
> Leading research & advisory firms employ Net Contract Value Increase (NCVI) compensation plans. This strategy entails setting threshold at last year's performance. It sends the message that sellers will earn incentive pay only if/when they exceed in growing total sales above prior year's performance.
>
> As a result, management incents sellers to focus almost exclusively on syndicated, repeatable revenue. From a seller's perspective, one-off sales prove harmful in future years due to their inclusion in expected future performance.

Many of the downsides to setting threshold based on past performance mirror the downsides of setting threshold at the value of assured contracts. To use this option, a company's product portfolio would likely need some component of renewability, or at least re-buy-ability for consumable goods. Additionally, the lack of past performance for new hires and/or new territories causes a need to employ a different threshold setting methodology for certain sales representatives. Further, the strategy requires a unique threshold for each sales representative, which could be unreasonable for organizations with a large sales force.

An added deterrent to setting threshold based on past performance is the possibility of discouraging sales representatives to maximize potential sales. Knowing that their employer will set future threshold based on their current performance could lead to sellers withholding orders in order to lower their threshold in the coming year. Comparably, sellers may focus exclusively on deals they believe they can renew in the coming year, ensuring they can exceed the future-state threshold.

Importance of Threshold

Regardless of where and how threshold is set, plan designers cannot overlook its importance in the sales compensation plan. Threshold plays a significant role beyond saving money and reducing compensation cost of sales. Sales compensation designers have a variety of threshold-setting strategies available, and should carefully weigh those options and their impact on the broader sales compensation program.

Mick Cannon is a manager in the Alexander Group's New York City office.

ARTICLES LISTING

RECENT ARTICLES OF INTEREST

This section provides a listing of the latest published sales compensation articles.

IN THIS SECTION

- 2018 Articles Listing
- 2019 Articles Listing

2018 ARTICLES

“5 Steps to an Effective Sales Compensation Plan,” Quotable

“7 Essential Elements to a Sales Compensation System,” Contracting Business

“9 Commission Structures That Will Keep Your Sales Team Motivated,” Forbes

“9 Steps for Rolling Out a Sales Compensation Plan,” Workspan Daily

“9 Tips for Building a Competitive Sales Compensation Plan,” HubSpot Blog

“10 Ways to Thank Sales on National Salesperson Day (and Every Day),” Xactly

“2018 Med Rep Job Satisfaction Report,” MedReps.com

“2018 Sales Compensation ‘Hot Topics’ Survey Results Are In,” The Alexander Group Blog

“2018 Sales Compensation Pay Levels: No Wage Inflation…Yet,” The Alexander Group Blog

“Banks Took Wide-Ranging Actions to Head Off More Sales Abuses,” American Banker

“Controller Charged in Revenue Recognition Scheme,” CFO.com

“David Aboody’s Research Gives Corporate Boards Pause When Changing Compensation Models,” UCLA Anderson Review

“Digital Health Sales Compensation Trends Report,” Bowdoin Group

“Don’t Tell Your Salespeople to ‘Put on Their Company Hats,’” Modern Distribution Management

“Drug Firm Ended Link between Opioid Sales & Employee Pay in 2012, Report Says,” Charleston Gazette-Mail

“Effective Quota Setting in Manufacturing Sales,” MFR Tech

“Embattled Wells Fargo to Face Protests and More Calls for Change at Annual Meeting,” Los Angeles Times

“Exclusive: Morgan Stanley to Squeeze Mutual Fund Sales Compensation,” AdvisorHub

“Experience Counts for CSCP and CECP,” Workspan

“Fourth Annual XaaS Sales Compensation & Coverage Symposium—Highlights,” The Alexander Group Blog

“Future Commissions Can’t Be Trebled Under Wage Act,” New England In-House

"How OT Affects Sales Comp for Hourly Workers," Workspan
"How Sales Compensation Must Change With the Introduction of Automation," Forbes
"How to Build Sales Compensation Plans for Recurring Revenue," Xactly
"How to Compensate Your Sales Team for Cloud," Channel Partners
"How to Make 2018 a Year of Sales Success (2017 Roundup)," Xactly
"HPE Global Channel Chief Hunter: Next Initiative is Driving 'Significant' Increase in Partner Sales Velocity," CRN
"Key Considerations for Designing a Sales Comp Plan That Attracts, Retains and Motivates," Workspan Daily
"Map Out a Partnership," Workspan
"Massachusetts Seeks Sales-Practice Information From Discount Brokers," Wall Street Journal
"Median Base Pay Increases for Sales Comp Will Be Moderate in 2018," Workspan Daily
"Nevada's First Report on Compensation & Samples Distributed by Pharmaceutical Sales Representatives—Significant Number of Samples for Diabetes Drugs," Policy & Medicine Blog
"New Federal Anti-Kickback Law May Alter How Clinical Laboratories Compensate Sales Personnel: Sales and Marketing Compliance," The National Law Review
"Pay Problem for Sales Teams: Korn Ferry Survey Shows Compensation is the Biggest Turnover Issue, Yet Nearly One-Quarter of Companies Not Offering Increases," Business Wire
"Pharmaceutical Sales Reps Gave Monetary Compensation to Two in Five Nevada Doctors They Lobbied," The Nevada Independent
"Riches to Rags: How to Reach Your Sales Goals But Blow Your Budget," The Alexander Group Blog
"Running Hot? Time to Check Your Sales Comp Temperature," Workspan
"Sales Compensation Challenge and Points of View," Deloitte
"Sales Compensation Considerations for Key Manufacturing Roles," The Alexander Group Blog
"Sales Compensation Solutions for Merging Companies: 3 Action Steps," Workspan Daily
"Sales Compensation: Who Gets Credit for the Sale?" Workspan Daily

“Sales in Motion—Recurring Revenue Streams Call for New Pricing Models,” Workspan

“Salespeople and Total Rewards,” Workspan

“SEC Chairman Jay Clayton Calls for End to Broker Sales Contests,” Investment News

“Tesla Settles $1 Million Lawsuit With Its Salespeople Over Compensation, Says Advisors Can Make Over $150K,” Electrek

“The Law Offices of Daniel Feder Files Lawsuit: Wells Fargo Sued by Former Head of Foreign-Exchange Currency Trading Who Blew Whistle on Sales Practices at Wells,” Business Wire

“The Line of IBM Salespeople Suing the Company Over Their Pay Just Got Longer,” The News & Observer

“Thriving Without Incentive Compensation,” Barron’s

“Tips for Rallying Your Team Behind Cloud Sales,” Channel Partners

“Today’s Manufacturing Sales Teams: How to ‘Lean’ the Sales Compensation Program,” The Alexander Group Blog

“Top Medical Technology Trends to Accelerate Revenue Growth in 2019,” The Alexander Group Blog

“United States: SEC Regulation Best Interest—Charting a Course for Securities and Annuity Sales, Avoiding Collision and Potential Regulatory and Litigation Issues Q&A 5,” Mondaq

“Want Cloud Growth? Focus on Sales Team Incentives, Education,” Channel Partners

“Wells Fargo Again Forces Sales Scrutiny, This Time in Its Wealth Advice Division, WSJ Says,” CNBC

“Wells Fargo Not Alone: OCC Finds Sales Abuses at Other Banks,” American Banker

“Wells Fargo Sales Push Extended to Wealth Unit, Ex-Workers Say,” American Banker

“When Your Sales Mobility Program Is Stuck in a Compensation Rut,” Workspan Daily

“Why Tesla’s Sales Staff Say They’re Being Shortchanged in the Electric Car Revolution,” Jalopnik

“Xactly Study Finds Incentive Compensation Errors Costing Enterprise Companies Millions,” Business Wire

“Your Sales Compensation Plan Needs This to Be Competitive,” Xactly

2019 ARTICLES

"AmEx Executive Suspended Over Probe," Wall Street Journal

"Banking Royal Commission Report Takes Axe to Sales Culture in Finance," Australian Broadcasting Association

"Broker-Dealers Selling Annuities: Preparing for the Best Interest Standard Under New York's Amended Insurance Regulation 187," Lexology

"Commissions May be Due a Former Employee," The Telegraph

"Dealers' Perspective: The Issue With Manufacturers Compensating Their Sales Reps," Farm Equipment

"District Court: Privacy Claims Can Proceed Related to Incentive Compensation Sales Program," Lexology

"Firing an Employee Over a Compensation Dispute May be Costly," The Telegraph

"HP and Hewlett Packard Enterprise Will Pay a $25 Million Settlement to Salespeople Who Sued Over Messed Up Pay," Business Insider

"Measures for Success," Workspan

"Media: Communication Is Key When Launching New Sales Comp Plans," The Alexander Group Blog

"New Alexander Group Survey Examines Sales Comp Trends in the UK," Business Wire

"Pharma's Incentive Compensation Plan Landscape," PharmExec

"Regulators Want Brokers, Advisors to Disclose They 'Will' Sell Pricier Products," Financial Advisor

"Regulatory, Investor Expectations Elevate Compensation Committee Role," ABA Banking Journal

"Seven Trends in Sales Comp for 2019," Workspan

"Sloan on the Defensive (Again) About Wells Fargo's Sales Tactics," American Banker

"Tesla's Online-Only Sales Strategy Disguises Massive Pay Cuts," Electrek

"Thousands of Wells Fargo Consultants Win Cert. in Wage Suit," Law 260

"Wells Fargo CEO Heads to Congress Amid Claims That Reforms Are Slipping," Los Angeles Times

"Wells Fargo Faces Class-Action Suit Over LO Pay," Mortgage Professional America

"Wells Fargo Loan Officers Granted Class Action in California Pay Dispute," National Mortgage News

About Alexander Group—Revenue Growth Consultants

The Alexander Group (www.alexandergroup.com) provides go-to-customer consulting services to the world's leading revenue acquisition resources, serving Global 2000 companies from across all industries. Founded in 1985, Alexander Group combines deep experience, a proven methodology and data-driven insights to help revenue acquisition leaders anticipate change, align their go-to-customer resources—sales, marketing and service—with company goals and make better informed decisions with one goal in mind—to grow revenue. The Alexander Group has offices in Atlanta, Chicago, San Francisco, Scottsdale, Stamford and London.

Our Consulting Services

The Alexander Group provides the world's leading revenue acquisition organizations with management consulting services for the full spectrum of sales, marketing and service needs, as well as performance benchmarking based on the industry's richest repository of revenue program performance data. We apply years of experience and our Revenue Growth Model™, a proven methodology for evaluating go-to-customer organizations, to provide insights that are rooted in facts. We not only deliver insights—we understand sales, marketing and service business challenges. We roll-up our sleeves to work alongside our clients, whether they are realigning revenue acquisition programs or radically overhauling their go-to-customer resources. Our keen focus on measurement ensures that we deliver value and results to our clients.

About Alexander Group Events

The Alexander Group produces and facilitates a specialized portfolio of events that help the world's leading revenue teams to drive growth. From the Chief Sales Executive Forums to Executive Roundtable conference calls, all events cover topics that range from big-picture strategy to hands-on execution. Participants benefit from connecting with other top sales, marketing and service leaders, and gain exclusive access to the latest ideas and deeper insights needed to create high-performance revenue-growth organizations.

CPSIA information can be obtained
at www.ICGtesting.com
Printed in the USA
BVHW050735150122
626151BV00001B/12

9 780989 948081